"Bland....drew on 20 years of research to scout out communities with amenities important to baby boomer retirees."

Dana Bartholomew, Los Angeles Daily News

"Bland's new book...takes a serious look at communities that fit the demands of baby boomer retirees."

Carmon Ramos Chandler, Public Relations,
California State University Northridge

"Bland...rates 50 US communities based upon criteria such as climate, cost of living, transportation, health care, cultural and recreational offerings, crime rates, and volunteer opportunities."

Book News, Inc.

". . . the book is a great resource to use to start the screening process because it makes it easy to quickly evaluate each location."

E. Thomas Wetzel, Retirement Living News

"It is refreshing to read such a clear and focused book that can be a great guide for those considering retirement. Dr. Bland demonstrates that good scholarship and readability are not mutually exclusive outcomes."

Lay James Gibson, Professor, Geography and Regional Development,
Director, Economic Development Research Program,
The University of Arizona, Office of Arid Land Studies

"Clear and focused guide that will appeal particularly to moderately affluent, active and sophisticated retirees."

Ronald Davis,
Assistant Provost,
Western Michigan University

"Retirees faced with the dilemma of where to relocate may well find the answer in Dr. Bland's comprehensive, informative and well-researched book, 'Retire in Style'."

Norma A. Ackerman, Retiree, Brevard, NC

"A book for those planning retirement and those only dreaming of it."

Jean Burnet, Professor Emeritus,
York University, Toronto, Canada

"If you want to find just the right place to make your retirement years an adventure in stylish but affordable living, buy this wonderfully readable and highly informative book."

Ronald L.F. Davis,
Professor of History,
California State University, Northridge

"Warren has taken on a daunting challenge to describe retirement towns. He explores our town quickly and effectively, and reported its ambiance well."

Hervey W. Ackerman,
Retiree

Retire in Style

50 Affordable Places Across America

Retire in Style

50 Affordable Places Across America

By Warren R. Bland, Ph.D.

Published by:
Next Decade, Inc.
39 Old Farmstead Road
Chester, New Jersey 07930-2732 USA
www.nextdecade.com

Published by:
Next Decade, Inc.
39 Old Farmstead Road
Chester, New Jersey 07930-2732 USA
www.nextdecade.com

Library of Congress Cataloging-in-Publication Data

Bland, Warren R., 1941-
    Retire in style: 50 affordable places across America/ by Warren R. Bland.
        p.cm.
    Includes bibliographical references and index.
    ISBN 0-9700908-0-3 (alk. paper)
     1. Retirement, Places of –United States. I. Title.

HQ1063 .B53 2001
646.7′9′0973—dc21   2001030396

To my wife Sarah, whose talent, hard work, and
loving support made this book possible.

Table of Contents

About the Author

Dr. Warren Bland has spent the last thirty-two years teaching college-level geography. Educated in Canada and the United States, Dr. Bland earned a BA at Wilfrid Laurier University in Waterloo, Ontario and MA and Ph.D. degrees at Indiana University, Bloomington. He is currently a Full Professor in the Department of Geography at California State University, Northridge. His department is rated as one of the best academic geography departments in the United States.

During his long career, Dr. Bland has served as a Visiting Professor at the University of Winnipeg, organized major conferences in the United States and China, and delivered lectures at academic conferences in Canada, the United States, China and India. For twenty years he has specialized in the regional geography of the United States and Canada. Throughout this period he has traveled extensively and done geographical research all over North America, meanwhile developing a strong interest in and knowledge of the towns and cities most suitable for retirement.

Dr. Bland is a member of the Association of American Geographers, the National Council for Geographic Education, and several other professional organizations. He is the author of numerous academic articles and has served as primary reviewer for several major textbooks in economic and regional geography.

Dr. Bland has lived in Los Angeles with his wife Sarah for over thirty years. They look forward to eventually relocating to one of the splendid retirement towns discussed in his book.

Disclaimer

The purpose of this book is to provide interested individuals with an overview of upscale and affordable retirement towns. The author has spent many years researching this topic. It is presented with the understanding that the publisher and author are not engaged in rendering legal, financial, travel, real estate or other professional services in this book. When expert assistance is required, the services of a competent professional should be sought.

This book was not written to provide all the information that is available to the author/and or publisher, but to complement, amplify and supplement other texts and available information. While every effort has been made to ensure that this book is as complete and accurate as possible, there may be mistakes, either typographical or in content. Therefore, this text should be used as a general guide only, and not as the ultimate source of retirement town information. Furthermore, this book contains current information only up to the printing date.

Information herein was obtained from various sources whose accuracy is not guaranteed. Opinions expressed and information are subject to change without notice.

The author and Next Decade, Inc. shall not be held liable, nor be responsible to any person or entity with respect to any loss or damage caused, or alleged to be caused, directly or indirectly by the information contained in this book.
If you do not wish to be bound by the above, you may return this book to the publisher for a full refund.

Acknowledgments

Viewed in retrospect, this project began about 15 years ago when I started reading popular books on American retirement towns. Because I am a geographer with, some might argue, an obsessive concern with good writing style and factual accuracy and relevance, I was never entirely satisfied with what I read. I naturally shared my reservations about the retirement place literature with all who would listen. Two of my best friends, Ralph Vicero, then Dean of the College of Social and Behavioral Sciences at California State University, Northridge (CSUN), where I have taught geography for over 30 years, and Becky Jiang, a graduate student at CSUN, challenged me to write and publish something better. My bluff had been rightly called; I had to write this book.

In addition to Ralph and Becky, I want to express my appreciation to a large number of people without whose help I could not have completed this project. Several reference librarians at CSUN, most notably my friend Jack Kranz, assisted my literature search. The staff of local chambers of commerce and visitors bureaus in over 60 retirement places visited during our many months of travel across America were very helpful in providing useful information and in conveying a sense of what it is like to live in their towns. Likewise, college and university faculty and staff in countless cities contributed greatly to our appreciation of their institutions and communities. Friendly people that we had the good fortune to meet and chat with while walking streets and checking out amenities provided additional valuable insights.

Special thanks are due CSUN, its College of Social and Behavioral Sciences, and the Department of Geography. A sabbatical leave granted by the university and several research grants from the college and department greatly assisted my work. My colleague and friend I-Shou Wang, chair of the Geography Department, was unflagging in his support. Departmental cartographer David Fuller designed the book's beautiful cover and his colleague Robert Provin produced the 50 Best Retirement Places map. My friends and colleagues in the History Department, Shiva Bajpai and Ron Davis read parts of the manuscript and on many occasions helped me to clarify my thoughts and writing. My geography colleague, Darrick Danta, himself an editor, was helpful on matters of style.

I am especially indebted to my friend Rebecca A. Nadybal, who designed and produced the 40 illustrations featured in the write-ups of the top 40 retirement places. The book would not be the same without them.

I owe most to Sarah, my wife, best friend and frequent traveling companion. Her assistance with field research, her editorial skills, and most of all, her encouragement in difficult moments, were invaluable.

Finally, I would like to thank my publisher, Barbara Brooks Kimmel, whose vision, skills, good sense, and unwavering support enabled the transformation of my manuscript into a book.

Introduction

There is good news for people contemplating retirement in the first decade of the new millennium. Americans are living longer, healthier and more affluent lives than their grandparents and parents could have imagined. A growing number of today's retirees can look forward to spending 20 or 30 years in active, fulfilling retirement. The problem, though a pleasant one, is deciding how and where to enjoy your "golden years." This book will make your task a little easier.

Making the Decision to Relocate

There is much to be said for staying put. You already know the community where you live and probably feel connected to it. You may be reluctant to leave the neighborhood where you raised your children, even though they may now be living half a continent away. Familiarity doesn't always breed contempt. It is convenient to know your local doctor, bank manager and retail stores and comfortable to be in your old neighborhood.

But there are also compelling reasons to consider relocating. At retirement you are entering a new and different chapter of your life. For many, staying in familiar surroundings and not working is vaguely discomforting. On the other hand, settling into a different community that is safe, friendly, and rich in opportunities for shopping, recreation and culture provides an exciting new beginning in an atmosphere free of the stresses of the workaday world. Even if you are psychologically comfortable in familiar surroundings, you may wish to relocate to places with sunnier and warmer weather. Research indicates that mild temperatures (around 66 degrees F), moderate relative humidity (around 55 percent), and fairly constant barometric pressure are ideal for human health. In contrast, extreme heat and cold, and to a lesser extent, very high and very low relative humidity and drastic changes in barometric pressure can adversely stress the body. Not surprisingly, migration to the Sunbelt and Pacific Coast has been a long-term demographic trend in the United States. Finally and perhaps most importantly for those of moderate means, many retirement places offer lower costs of living, especially for housing, than do most major metropolitan areas. The ability to recoup and profitably invest some of your home equity by relocating to comparable but less expensive housing in a more affordable area increases your disposable income. For many retirees, such additional income could mean the difference between living modestly and retiring in style.

Retire in Style is not just a catchy title, it is the central concept of this book. It does not connote a cloistered existence in a gated retirement or resort community. The retirement places described here are real towns and cities that are very special and highly livable. They are the kinds of places where one can enjoy an active or relaxed retirement in a safe, clean, friendly and uncrowded community rich in services and amenities. In brief, they offer a stimulating lifestyle and a high quality of life.

How this Book is Organized

This book is organized as follows:

- **Introduction** (Chapter 1) describes the criteria used to evaluate the towns and cities described in this book. Also included in the introduction are a map of the U.S. pinpointing the locations of the 50 retirement places, a Ratings at a Glance chart that summarizes the individual ratings for each of the categories evaluated for the top 40 retirement places, and Lookup Tables for quick reference to place descriptions by climate and by state.

- **Place descriptions** (Chapters 2 through 11) provide detailed descriptions of 40 selected retirement locations in 10 geographically diverse regions throughout the United States; each location is evaluated using the criteria described in the Introduction. Ten additional retirement locations are briefly described throughout the chapters as other places to consider for retirement in style.

- **Sources** are provided at the back of the book for more information, including names and addresses of the Chambers of Commerce and Visitors Bureaus for the places described in this book and additional references for climate, cost of living, crime rates, and health care.

Evaluating the Towns and Cities

I used the following criteria for selecting and evaluating the top 40 retirement places described in this book: landscape, climate, quality of life, cost of living, transportation, retail services, health care, community services, cultural activities, recreational activities, work and volunteer activities, and crime rates and public safety. I assigned a rating between 1 and 5 for each of the 12 criteria: 5 is excellent, 4 is very good, 3 is good, 2 is fair, and 1 is poor.

A hypothetical city that received a rating of 5 on each of the 12 criteria would earn a total of 60 points. Not surprisingly, no such perfect place exists. In reality, the highest score attained was 52 by Boulder, Colorado.

The total points scores are not intended as a means of ranking the retirement towns from best to worst; they are meant to help you assess a community's overall resources for retirement. Indeed, because individual wants and needs vary, the ratings for particular criteria may be more important in your evaluation of a place than its cumulative score. Boulder, Colorado provides a useful example. With an overall score of 52 and excellent individual ratings for landscape, quality of life, transportation, community services, cultural activities, recreational activities, and work and volunteer activities, Boulder provides a wealth of resources for retirement. But is it clearly the best place in America in which to retire in style? That probably depends on whether you can afford Boulder's high cost of living and whether you would enjoy its fairly rigorous winter weather.

It is also worth noting that statistics and numeric ratings cannot tell the whole story about a place. Statistics are not always available or uniformly reliable. For example, costs of living data utilized here were drawn largely from the excellent *ACCRA Cost of Living Index,* published quarterly for over 300 American urban areas. But for several smaller communities, data had to be obtained from city and county agencies and local chambers of commerce and are somewhat uneven in quality. Moreover, many aspects of a place that give it character and make it worth considering for retirement, cannot be statistically measured or described. For these reasons, the detailed written descriptions of each of the retirement places, based on literary and statistical sources and several days of field research in each place, should be read with care. They will help you narrow your choices to a few outstanding locations worthy of further consideration. A brief introduction to the 12 criteria considered in each place description follows.

Landscape

 An aesthetically appealing and interesting landscape can add to one's sense of well-being and give character to a place; therefore, I evaluate the natural and modified environment of each community. I consider site characteristics, such as elevation and terrain, and background features, such as views of coastal waters, desert plains or snow-capped mountains. I also briefly describe the natural vegetation of the area, and the typical planted landscape of residential areas.

Climate

Although there is no general agreement as to which climate is best, Americans seem to prefer sunny skies, moderate temperatures, moderate humidity and precipitation, and gradual rather than drastic seasonal changes in weather. Unfortunately, except for coastal central and southern California, few areas of the United States have climates with all of these preferred characteristics. On the other hand, areas without these preferred characteristics are often less populated and offer a high quality of life at lower cost.

Each of the retirement locations rated in this book fall into one of the following climate categories. Where appropriate, I identify any variants (subtypes) of the climatic conditions that are typical for the region. For example, the hot-summer variant of the Mediterranean climate found in some inland valleys of California is distinctly warmer in summer than the cool-summer variant found along the central California coast.

The **humid continental climate,** with four distinct seasons, is characteristic in the Northeast and Midwest Retirement Regions. Summers here are typically pleasantly sunny and warm, whereas winters are cloudy, cold and damp. Rapid weather changes are routine, especially in spring and fall when warm, humid episodes alternate with cold, dry periods. Precipitation is ample in all seasons with winter's falling mostly as snow.

The **humid subtropical climate** is found throughout the Upper South, Interior South, Heart of Texas and Southeast Coast Retirement Regions, except for southernmost Florida where the climate is tropical. Upper South and Interior South locations experience a temperate, four-season variant of the climate, with more dramatic seasonal changes than are felt farther south in Florida, along the Gulf Coast, and in south central Texas. Throughout the entire humid subtropics, though, summer afternoons are hot and tend to be uncomfortable because of high humidity; summer nights are warm. Winters are cool to warm, depending on latitude and elevation. Precipitation is ample and well distributed throughout the year. Snow is infrequent in the Upper South and Interior South and almost unheard of in Florida and along the Gulf Coast. The entire region is fairly sunny with maximum sunshine being received in peninsular Florida and central Texas.

A **tropical savanna climate** is found near the tip of the Florida peninsula. Essentially a two-season climate with hot, humid and rainy summers and warm and comparatively dry winters, this sunny and virtually frost-free climate has helped lure many permanent residents and winter visitors to Naples and other South Florida cities.

A *semi-arid (steppe) climate* is characteristic in the Southern Rockies Retirement Region, at elevations between 4,500 and 8,000 feet in the Desert Southwest, and at locations east of the Cascade Range in the Pacific Northwest. A sunny, moderately dry, four-season climate with low relative humidity, this crisp, invigorating climate has great appeal to the outdoors oriented. Although each winter sees several snow storms, most snow melts within a few days as average daily high temperatures are above freezing even in mid-winter.

A true *desert climate* is found at elevations below 4,500 feet in the Desert Southwest Retirement Region and in interior southern California. Walled off from the moisture and moderating influence of the Pacific Ocean by California's Sierra Nevada and Coast Ranges, the entire region is very sunny and dry although not uniformly so. Average daily high temperatures exceed 95 degrees Fahrenheit in summer but are generally bearable thanks to low relative humidity. Spring and fall weather is nearly ideal with warm days and cool nights; winters are mild to warm, sunny and pleasant. Although frosts are common on winter nights, little snow falls at lower elevations.

The *Mediterranean (dry-summer subtropical) climate* is found in coastal areas of central and southern California, in the state's Central Valley, and in the Medford/Ashland area of southern Oregon. There are really only two seasons here. A mild, fairly wet winter is balanced by a warm to hot, dry summer. Coastal locations like San Luis Obispo are sunnier and warmer in winter and cooler and somewhat cloudier in summer than Central Valley locations like Chico. Many people regard the sunny, mild, virtually frost-free coastal variant of the Mediterranean climate as the best in the world, a true paradise climate.

The *marine climate* is characteristic west of the Cascade Range in the Pacific Northwest Retirement Region. Winters here are mild, cloudy and wet; summers are warm, sunny and relatively dry. Spring and fall weather is variable with cool to warm days and cool nights. Upwards of 70 percent of annual precipitation occurs between October and March. Cloudy to partly cloudy skies are more typical than clear skies except in summer. There is very little snow at lower elevations and it seldom persists on the ground for more than a few days.

Quality of Life

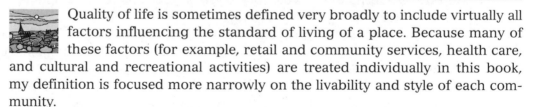 Quality of life is sometimes defined very broadly to include virtually all factors influencing the standard of living of a place. Because many of these factors (for example, retail and community services, health care, and cultural and recreational activities) are treated individually in this book, my definition is focused more narrowly on the livability and style of each community.

Livability and style are enhanced by the absence of some things and the presence of others. Freedom from aircraft, highway, railroad and industrial noise; from traffic congestion and tight parking; from noxious industries and tacky neighborhoods cluttered with boat trailers and recreational vehicles parked on streets and in yards translates into a superior quality of life. Conversely, the presence of clean air and attractive parks, neighborhoods and downtown shopping districts are essential to one's well-being. Clean air is especially important to older people as lung capacity diminishes with advancing age. Aesthetically appealing and well-equipped parks, attractive—well-landscaped and maintained—residential neighborhoods, and charming and viable downtown shopping districts are also vital. The city should be well planned and managed efficiently, and the community should manifest a peaceful and friendly ambiance.

Local living costs measure the relative affordability of places. Based on cost-of-living estimates from ACCRA and local sources, I describe the overall (composite) cost of living and costs of housing, transportation, health care, groceries, utilities, and miscellaneous goods and services according to their percentage deviation from national norms. Because ACCRA does not report on state and local tax burdens and excludes them from its indices, it was necessary to turn to state and local sources for tax information. I provide estimates of the overall state and local tax burden and rates for sales, income and property taxes, with reference to national averages for each, and consider them along with ACCRA data in determining the cost of living rating for each place.

Local and Regional Services

This is a broad category that includes transportation, retail services, health care and community services. These four criteria are rated individually in the place descriptions throughout this book.

Transportation

Although the private automobile dominates travel within and between American cities, there is much to be said for places offering a range of transportation alternatives. Not everyone wants or will be able to continue driving into their seventies, yet in a community where good roads are supplemented by excellent public transit, sidewalks and trails for walking and biking, and good intercity transportation, one could remain mobile for years after giving up driving. For that reason, I evaluate local public transit in terms of frequency and quality of service, adequacy of route network and cost. Likewise, I describe and evaluate intercity transportation options including air, bus and rail passenger service.

Retail Services

Shopping is one of America's favorite pastimes; therefore, convenient access to a good variety of retail services is an important consideration. Even the smallest places discussed in this book can provide for the basic wants and needs of their residents and many offer much more. At minimum, I describe the major regional shopping centers in terms of their anchor (department) stores, specialty stores and services, movie theaters and restaurants or food courts. Additionally, I evaluate downtown shopping districts for their retailing opportunities and general ambiance. Most of our towns and cities have renovated and revitalized their historic downtowns in recent years and now offer unique and distinctly upscale shopping and dining experiences.

Health Care

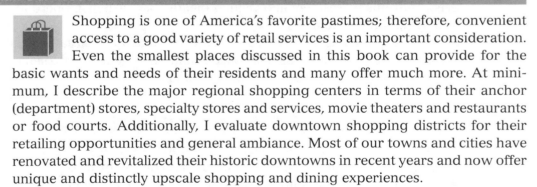

This criterion appraises the availability and quality of medical services locally and in nearby metropolitan areas. Although medical specialists and major medical centers tend to cluster in larger and more affluent cities, even our smallest towns offer adequate routine medical care. College towns like Gainesville, Florida, with top-rated medical school teaching hospitals, and larger cities in low-cost areas like San Antonio, Texas, provide among the best medical care in the country at prices below the national average.

Community Services

 Services of special interest to seniors are typically available from city, county and state agencies and from various nonprofit and community organizations. Overall ratings of this criterion take into account the quality and quantity of activities provided by senior centers, parks and recreation departments, state or local Councils on Aging, American Association for Retired Persons (AARP) and other social and civic organizations.

Leisure Activities

This is a broad category encompassing culture and education, recreation, and work and volunteer activities. These three criteria are rated individually in the place descriptions throughout this book.

Cultural and Educational Activities

 Although large metropolitan areas like New York, Los Angeles and Chicago boast the greatest repertoire of cultural events and some of the best universities in the country, you need not forgo quality culture and education when moving to a smaller town. College towns, particularly those home to a state's flagship university, and upscale resort and retirement communities have much to offer in the performing and visual arts and in educational programs of interest to seniors. Many colleges and universities host Elderhostel programs that provide lifelong learning experiences for those 55 and older. Each program has a coordinator who arranges accommodations, meals, classes and field trips. Instructors are often faculty members at participating institutions and courses taught range from music appreciation to archeology to film-making. Programs typically run for five or six days and are free of assignments and tests. Ratings for culture and education consider the frequency and quality of performing arts programs by resident and visiting theater, dance, ballet, operatic, orchestral and symphonic ensembles.

Also considered in this category are the quality of area art galleries and museums, how welcoming local colleges and universities are to seniors, and the costs of attending cultural performances and college classes.

Recreational Activities

 Opportunities for outdoor recreation are many and varied in our 10 geographically diverse retirement regions. In most of the retirement towns, community recreation centers, movie theaters and restaurants provide indoor diversions. University towns also boast intercollegiate basketball and football while major metropolitan areas and places near them have access to one or more major league sports.

The recreation criterion measures the variety and quality of popular recreation available locally. I evaluate city parks and recreation assets for golf, tennis, fitness training, swimming, bicycling and nature study. Similarly, I consider picnicking, hiking, boating, swimming, fishing and sightseeing opportunities in nearby county, state and national parks and forests, as well as indoor assets in town such as heated swimming pools and gymnasiums.

Work and Volunteer Activities

For many people, retirement means a change from full-time work to a more varied lifestyle that includes part-time paid or volunteer work. Now that those continuing to work between age 65 and 70 are no longer penalized by the loss of part of their Social Security benefits, the incentive to continue working for pay after retirement has increased. Others seek satisfaction by giving back to their communities through meaningful volunteer work.

Wanting paid work does not necessarily result in finding it. The local job market for seniors reflects the general state of the economy in the particular place, whether it is service-based or industrial, and the level of competition from younger people, especially college students, entering the labor force. In many college towns, competition with college students is acute, particularly for part-time service jobs on campus and in retailing in the wider community. Towns with more balanced economies and demographic profiles less skewed toward young college-age adults generally offer superior employment prospects for seniors.

Opportunities for volunteer work also vary somewhat from place to place but most communities need more volunteers than they can recruit. The Retired Senior Volunteer Program (RSVP) and the Service Corps of Retired Executives (SCORE) are nationwide organizations that assist seniors in finding fulfilling volunteer work. Opportunities for paid and volunteer work are weighted equally in my evaluation of this criterion for the various retirement places.

Crime Rates and Public Safety

This factor evaluates public safety in terms of rates of overall crime, violent crime and property crime per 100,000 population. Although crime rates have declined significantly across the United States during the last decade, crime remains a serious problem in many cities. However, those relocating at retirement can minimize their future potential exposure to crime by choosing among safer retirement places and by selecting a home in a relatively crime-free neighborhood.

FBI Uniform Crime Reports for cities and counties provide the data base for calculating rates of overall crime; property crime, which includes burglary, larceny-theft and auto theft; and violent crime, which includes murder, rape, robbery and aggravated assault. When FBI data were unavailable, I obtained comparable data from municipal police departments and county sheriffs. I rated public safety in each retirement place in terms of the extent to which overall crime, property crime and violent crime rates deviate from national norms. In large cities where crime rates vary considerably from one part of town to another, I recommended ways to help you select safer neighborhoods.

Overall Ratings

Following are the overall ratings of our *50 Affordable Places Across America*. For ratings of the 12 individual criteria and the accompanying detailed written descriptions of each community, please turn to chapters 2–11. Happy reading!

Top 40 Retirement Towns

Points	City and State	Page	Points	City and State	Page
52	Boulder, Colorado	151	46	Oxford, Mississippi	113
50	Portland, Oregon	241	46	Santa Fe, New Mexico	162
49	Asheville, North Carolina	65	45	Bellingham, Washington	253
49	Austin, Texas	131	45	Ithaca, New York	21
49	San Antonio, Texas	137	45	San Luis Obispo, California	209
48	Chapel Hill, North Carolina	54	44	Bloomington, Indiana	35
48	Colorado Springs, Colorado	156	43	St. George, Utah	203
48	Eugene, Oregon	229	42	Burlington, Vermont	15
48	Fayetteville, Arkansas	124	42	Carson City, Nevada	198
48	Fort Collins, Colorado	145	42	Covington, Louisiana	106
48	Gainesville, Florida	95	42	Lexington, Virginia	49
48	Medford/Ashland, Oregon	224	42	Naples, Florida	84
47	Boulder City, Nevada	187	42	Olympia, Washington	247
47	Charlottesville, Virginia	44	42	Pinehurst/Southern Pines, North Carolina	60
47	Hendersonville, North Carolina	71	41	Hot Springs, Arkansas	119
47	Madison, Wisconsin	29	41	Thomasville, Georgia	101
47	Sarasota, Florida	89	39	Chico, California	215
47	Tucson, Arizona	176	39	Las Cruces, New Mexico	170
46	Brevard, North Carolina	76	39	Salem, Oregon	235
46	Las Vegas, Nevada	192	38	Prescott, Arizona	182

Next 10 Retirement Places

(unranked; listed alphabetically)

City and State	Page	City and State	Page
Annapolis, Maryland	81	Kerrville, Texas	143
Bend, Oregon	258	New Bern, North Carolina	81
Fairhope, Alabama	112	Palm Springs/Palm Desert, California	221
Fredericksburg, Texas	143	Reno, Nevada	208
Hanover/Lebanon, New Hampshire	27	Savannah, Georgia	111

Ratings at a Glance

Legend:
5 = Excellent
4 = Very good
3 = Good
2 = Fair
1 = Poor

	Landscape	Climate	Quality of Life	Cost of Living	Transportation	Retail Services	Health Care	Community Services	Cultural/Educational Activities	Recreational Activities	Work/Volunteer Activities	Crime Rate and Public Safety	Total
Northeast													
Burlington, Vermont	5	2	4	2	4	3	4	4	4	5	2	3	42
Ithaca, New York	5	2	5	3	3	3	3	5	4	4	4	4	45
Midwest													
Madison, Wisconsin	5	2	5	2	4	4	5	5	4	4	3	4	47
Bloomington, Indiana	4	3	4	4	2	4	3	3	5	5	3	4	44
Upper South													
Charlottesville, Virginia	5	3	5	3	3	4	5	4	4	5	3	3	47
Lexington, Virginia	5	3	5	4	2	2	2	3	3	5	3	5	42
Chapel Hill, North Carolina	4	3	5	2	5	3	5	5	5	5	3	3	48
Pinehurst/Southern Pines, North Carolina	4	3	5	3	2	3	4	4	2	4	4	4	42
Asheville, North Carolina	5	4	4	3	3	5	5	4	4	5	4	3	49
Hendersonville, North Carolina	5	4	5	3	2	3	4	4	5	5	3	5	47
Brevard, North Carolina	5	4	5	3	2	3	3	3	5	5	3	5	46
Southeast Coast													
Naples, Florida	4	3	4	2	2	5	4	3	3	5	4	3	42
Sarasota, Florida	4	3	3	3	3	5	5	4	5	5	5	2	47
Gainesville, Florida	4	3	5	4	5	3	5	4	4	5	4	2	48
Thomasville, Georgia	4	3	5	5	2	2	4	3	3	4	3	3	41
Covington, Louisiana	4	3	5	4	2	3	3	3	3	5	3	4	42
Interior South													
Oxford, Mississippi	4	3	5	4	3	4	3	4	4	4	4	4	46
Hot Springs, Arkansas	4	3	4	5	3	3	3	3	3	4	4	2	41
Fayetteville, Arkansas	5	4	5	5	3	4	4	3	4	4	4	3	48
Heart of Texas													
Austin, Texas	4	3	4	3	5	5	4	4	5	5	5	2	49
San Antonio, Texas	4	3	4	5	5	5	5	4	5	4	3	2	49
Southern Rockies													
Fort Collins, Colorado	4	3	5	3	4	4	4	4	5	5	4	3	48
Boulder, Colorado	5	4	5	2	5	4	4	5	5	5	5	3	52
Colorado Springs, Colorado	5	3	4	3	4	4	4	4	5	5	4	3	48
Santa Fe, New Mexico	4	4	5	2	4	4	4	4	5	5	2	3	46
Desert Southwest													
Las Cruces, New Mexico	4	4	3	3	3	4	3	4	4	3	2	2	39
Tucson, Arizona	5	3	3	3	4	4	5	4	5	5	4	2	47
Prescott, Arizona	4	4	5	3	2	2	3	3	2	4	3	3	38
Boulder City, Nevada	4	3	5	2	4	4	4	4	4	5	3	5	47
Las Vegas, Nevada	3	3	3	3	4	5	5	4	5	5	4	2	46
Carson City, Nevada	5	4	5	3	2	3	3	3	2	4	3	5	42
St. George, Utah	5	4	5	3	2	3	3	5	2	4	4	3	43
California													
San Luis Obispo, California	5	5	5	2	3	3	3	4	4	4	3	4	45
Chico, California	4	4	5	3	3	3	3	3	3	3	2	3	39
Pacific Northwest													
Medford/Ashland, Oregon	5	4	5	3	3	3	4	4	5	5	4	3	48
Eugene, Oregon	4	3	4	3	5	4	4	5	5	5	3	3	48
Salem, Oregon	3	3	4	3	3	3	3	4	2	4	4	3	39
Portland, Oregon	5	3	5	2	5	5	4	5	5	5	4	2	50
Olympia, Washington	4	3	4	3	4	3	4	4	3	4	3	3	42
Bellingham, Washington	5	3	5	3	4	3	3	4	4	5	3	3	45

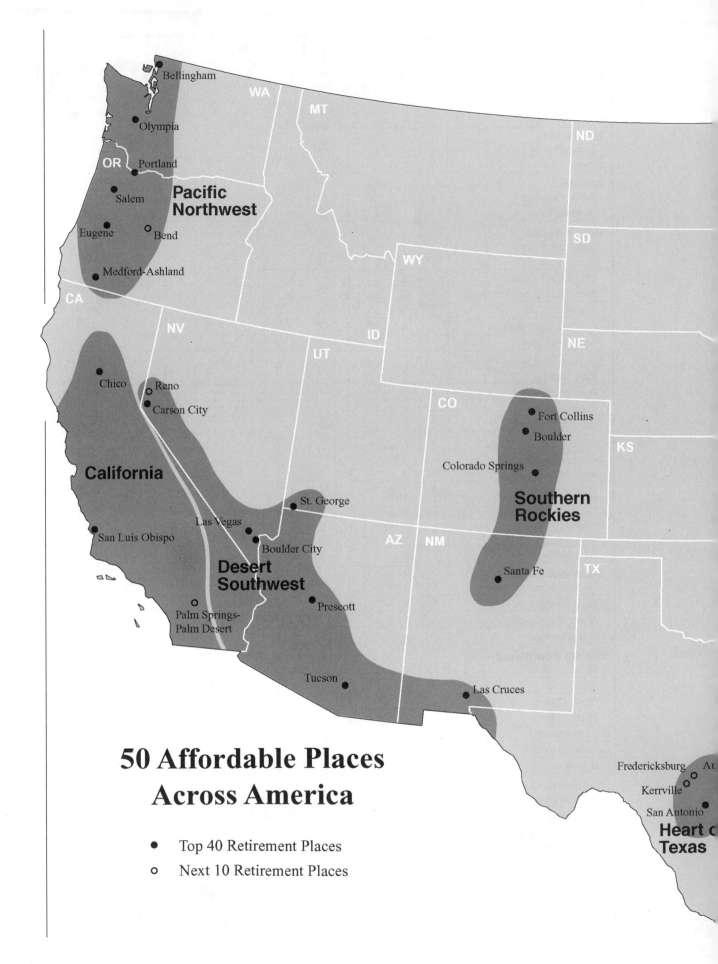

Bellingham

WA

MT

ND

Olympia

OR Portland

SD

**Pacific
Northwest**

Salem

WY

Eugene Bend

Medford-Ashland

CA

NV

ID

NE

UT

Chico Reno

Carson City

CO

Fort Collins

Boulder

California

Colorado Springs

KS

St. George

**Southern
Rockies**

San Luis Obispo

Las Vegas

Boulder City

AZ NM

TX

**Desert
Southwest**

Santa Fe

Palm Springs-
Palm Desert

Prescott

Tucson

Las Cruces

Fredericksburg

Au

Kerrville

50 Affordable Places
Across America

San Antonio

**Heart o
Texas**

- ● Top 40 Retirement Places
- ○ Next 10 Retirement Places

50 Best Retirement Places

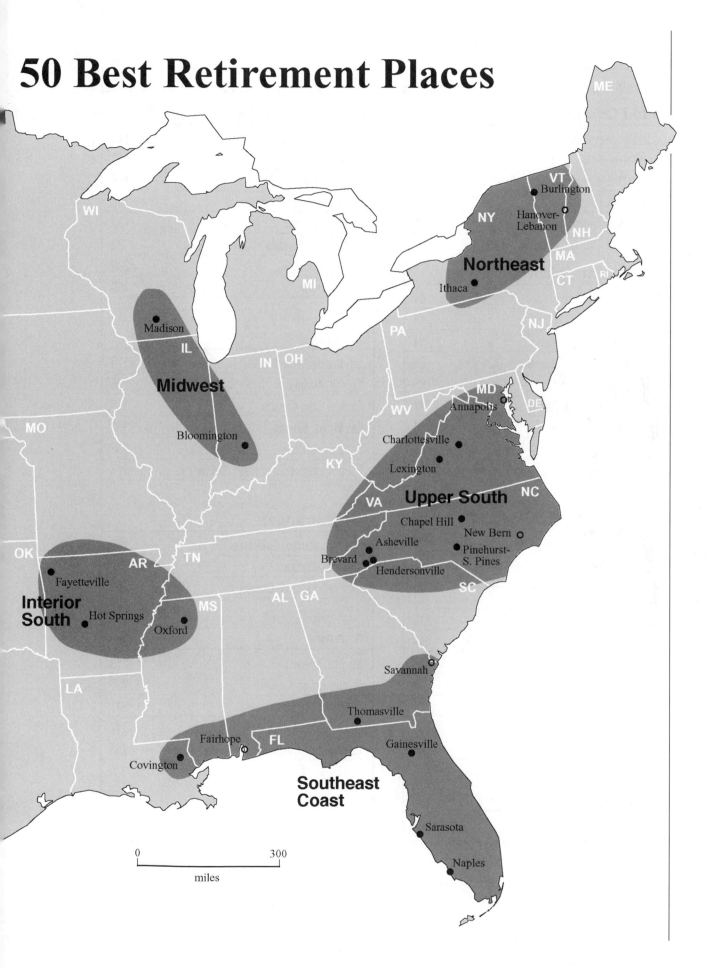

ME

WI

VT
Burlington

NY
Hanover-
Lebanon

NH

MA

CT

RI

Northeast

MI

Ithaca

Madison

IL

IN
OH

PA

NJ

Midwest

MD
Annapolis

WV

Bloomington

Charlottesville

KY

Lexington

VA
Upper South
NC

MO

Chapel Hill

New Bern

OK

AR

TN

Asheville

Pinehurst-
S. Pines

Brevard

Fayetteville

Hendersonville

SC

**Interior
South**

Hot Springs

MS

Oxford

AL
GA

LA

Savannah

Thomasville

Fairhope

FL

Gainesville

Covington

**Southeast
Coast**

Sarasota

Naples

0   300

miles

Lookup Table: by Climate

Lookup Table: by State

State/City	Page
Alabama	
Fairhope	112
Arizona	
Prescott	182
Tucson	176
Arkansas	
Fayetteville	124
Hot Springs	119
California	
Chico	215
Palm Springs/Palm Desert	221
San Luis Obispo	209
Colorado	
Boulder	151
Colorado Springs	156
Fort Collins	145
Florida	
Gainesville	95
Naples	84
Sarasota	89
Georgia	
Thomasville	101
Savannah	111
Indiana	
Bloomington	35
Louisiana	
Covington	106
Maryland	
Annapolis	81
Mississippi	
Oxford	113
Nevada	
Boulder City	187
Carson City	198
Las Vegas	192
Reno	208

State/City	Page
New Hampshire	
Hanover/Lebanon	27
New Mexico	
Las Cruces	170
Santa Fe	162
New York	
Ithaca	21
North Carolina	
Asheville	65
Brevard	76
Chapel Hill	54
Hendersonville	71
New Bern	81
Pinehurst/Southern Pines	60
Oregon	
Bend	258
Eugene	229
Medford/Ashland	224
Portland	241
Salem	235
Texas	
Austin	131
Fredericksburg	143
Kerrville	143
San Antonio	137
Utah	
St. George	203
Vermont	
Burlington	15
Virginia	
Charlottesville	44
Lexington	49
Washington	
Bellingham	253
Olympia	247
Wisconsin	
Madison	29

The Northeast Retirement Region

Climate: Humid continental

Place Description	Overall Rating	Page
Burlington, Vermont	**42**	**15**
Burlington is an amenity-rich college town that will appeal to hardy souls who enjoy winter weather and winter sports. Although its cost of living is moderately high, it is a beautiful, civilized and uncrowded place.		
Ithaca, New York	**45**	**21**
Ithaca will appeal to those who prefer a four-season climate, enjoy summer and winter outdoor recreation, and appreciate the combination of small town virtues and big city amenities that the best college towns provide.		
Hanover/Lebanon, New Hampshire	**not rated**	**27**
Hanover and Lebanon are lovely, small villages that offer outdoor recreation and the many cultural and educational amenities provided by Dartmouth College.		

The Northeast Retirement Region occupies a relatively small part of the northeastern quadrant of the United States just south of the Canadian Border. Nonetheless, this small region, which stretches 350 miles from the White Mountains of New Hampshire and the Champlain Valley of Vermont to the rolling hills of the Finger Lakes Region of upstate New York, includes some of the most pleasant rural landscapes and three of the most appealing small cities to be found in America. Admittedly not for the climatically faint-of-heart, Burlington, Vermont, Ithaca, New York and Hanover/Lebanon, New Hampshire will appeal primarily to those who prefer a fairly rigorous four-season climate, enjoy summer and winter outdoor recreation, and appreciate the combination of small town virtues and big city amenities that the best college towns provide.

Burlington, Vermont

Explored by Samuel de Champlain in 1609 and fought over by British, French and American forces during several wars through the 1770s, the strategic and fertile Champlain Valley was first settled by Europeans in 1775. Originally an agricultural and timber processing community (Revolutionist Ethan Allen had a farm north of town), Burlington gradually emerged as a fresh-water port and commercial center for Vermont and northern New England. Founded in 1791 on a hill overlooking the town, Lake Champlain and the Adirondack Mountains, the University of Vermont now has over 9,000 students and 1,800 employees. The university and several other colleges give Burlington the unmistakable stamp of a college town and add immeasurably to its cultural and recreational amenities. Although Burlington itself has a population of only 40,000, nearby communities such as South Burlington, Winooski and Shelburne help bring the Chittenden County total to 140,000 making Burlington the largest metropolitan center of

Burlington, Vermont

CLIMATE				
Month	Average Daily Temperature High Low		Daily Rel. Humidity Low	Average Monthly Precipitation
	°F		%	Inches
January	25	8	64	1.8
February	28	9	61	1.6
March	39	22	58	2.2
April	54	34	53	2.8
May	67	45	51	3.1
June	76	55	52	3.5
July	81	60	53	3.7
August	78	58	57	4.1
September	69	49	61	3.3
October	57	39	61	2.9
November	44	30	66	3.1
December	30	16	68	2.4

Annual Average

Total Days		Total Inches	
Clear	58	Precipitation	34.5
Partly Cloudy	101	Snowfall	78.0
Cloudy	206		

RATINGS

Rating Scale: 5 = excellent; 4 = very good;
3 = good; 2 = fair; 1 = poor

Rating:	1	2	3	4	5
Landscape					●
Climate		●			
Quality of Life				●	
Cost of Living		●			
Transportation				●	
Retail Services			●		
Health Care				●	
Community Services				●	
Cultural Activities				●	
Recreational Activities					●
Work/Volunteer Activities		●			
Crime			●		

Total Points: 42

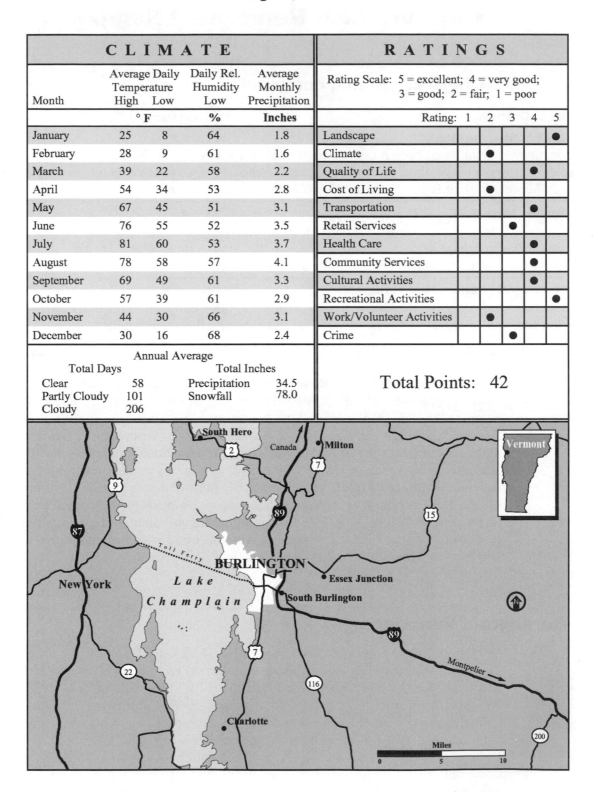

northern New England and the region's cultural and commercial focus. A lively town in a region of great natural beauty, Burlington and vicinity offer a plethora of winter and summer recreation. Montreal, Canada, one of the world's most sophisticated cities, is only 90 miles north.

Landscape   Rating: 5

 Burlington occupies a lovely site on several natural terraces overlooking beautiful Lake Champlain and New York's Adirondack Mountains. The heavily wooded Green Mountains, cresting at over 4,000 feet elevation 20 miles east of Burlington, and the pastoral countryside between the city and the mountains with its small farms, woodlots and streams, are highly picturesque. At lower elevations deciduous trees including sugar maple and beech are conspicuous while at higher elevations pine is more common. The town and the college campuses are pleasantly landscaped with lawns, shade trees and shrubs and an abundance of flowers in summer. The surrounding countryside, lush and green in summer, snow white in winter, and a riot of reds and yellows in autumn, is among the most beautiful anywhere.

Climate   Rating: 2

 Burlington has a fairly severe humid continental climate with four distinct seasons of approximately equal length. Summers are typically pleasantly sunny and warm whereas winters are cloudy, cold and damp. Rapid weather changes are routine, especially in spring and fall when warm, humid episodes alternate with cold, dry periods. Precipitation is ample in all seasons with winter's falling mostly as snow. On average, Burlington is sunny approximately 50 percent of the time, varying from about 40 percent in winter to 60 percent in summer. The frost-free period averages 140 days, adequate for growing crops of apples, potatoes and vegetables in summer gardens.

Quality of Life   Rating: 4

 Burlington offers a very good quality of life. The most serious problem is excessive jet noise from Burlington International Airport, three miles east. One flight path passes low over neighboring Winooski with deafening effect. Locals, though, seem to take little notice, claiming "we are used to it." Despite the air traffic, air quality is excellent, the absence of billboards (throughout Vermont) is visually pleasing, and there is little traffic congestion except at rush hour along Highway-7 (Shelburne Road) south of downtown. There is little noise from motor vehicles except in built-up areas adjacent to Interstate-89, which skirts central Burlington. Parking is plentiful and generally free except on the university campus, downtown and at the waterfront. The city seems well planned; even modest neighborhoods are in good shape and many parks and recreation areas grace the city, especially the Lake Champlain shoreline. People exhibit small-town friendliness and drivers are unusually courteous and law abiding.

Cost of Living   Rating: 2

 The cost of living in Burlington is evaluated as follows:

- *Composite.* ACCRA data show that the overall cost of living in Burlington is about 16 percent above the national average.

- *Housing.* According to ACCRA, housing costs are about 28 percent above the national average. Local sources and exploration of the area reveal that the Burlington area offers a good variety of housing from antique farmhouses in nearby villages to contemporary ranches and town homes elsewhere. In

Burlington itself, modest two-bedroom condominiums are available in the $50,000 to $100,000 price range while large upscale townhomes are typically priced between $100,000 and $200,000. Many attractive single-family homes are priced between $120,000 and $200,000; larger contemporary homes in prime locations, some with lake and/or mountain views, cost upwards of $200,000. Prices are somewhat lower in neighboring South Burlington and Winooski and in outlying towns and villages.

- *Goods and Services.* Goods and services are priced above national norms in Burlington. Utility costs have increased recently to levels about 40 percent above the national average, whereas health care costs have declined slightly to 14 percent above average. Groceries, miscellaneous goods and services, and transportation costs are between two and nine percent above national norms.

- *Taxes.* Vermont residents demand high quality services from government and are evidently willing to pay for them. The overall tax burden in Burlington is modestly above the national average. State income taxes are 10 to 30 percent below average depending on the taxpayer's bracket, whereas the state sales tax of 5 percent is at the national average. Property taxes average perhaps 30 percent above the national norm, about $4,000 annually on a typical $200,000 house.

Local and Regional Services

Burlington is the regional capital of the Champlain Valley and northwestern New England. It provides an extensive range of services to its market area.

Transportation	Rating: 4

Interstate-89 runs between Burlington and South Burlington so most travel in both cities is on local streets. Except for a few four-lane thoroughfares, most streets in Burlington are only two lanes yet seem adequate for current demand. Chittenden County Transportation Authority (CCTA) provides adequate bus service throughout Burlington and to Burlington International Airport and outlying communities including South Burlington, Winooski and Essex Junction. Typical intervals between buses are half hourly on weekdays, hourly on weekends. Fares are reasonable. The base fare is $1.00, 50 cents for seniors. A monthly pass costs $33, discounted to $15 for seniors. A free shuttle on College Street connects the waterfront, downtown, university and Fletcher Allen Hospital.

Intercity travel is possible by air, rail, bus and ferryboat. Burlington International Airport is a small hub providing nonstop jet service to major hub airports at New York, Boston, Chicago, Philadelphia and Washington. Amtrak offers daily service from Essex Junction, five miles east, south to New York and Washington and north to St. Albans, Vermont and (via connecting bus) to Montreal. Vermont Transit provides intercity bus service from Burlington and several car and passenger ferries link Burlington with New York State locations across Lake Champlain.

Retail Services	Rating: 3

University Mall, located just east of I-89 in south Burlington, is Vermont's largest enclosed shopping center. Anchored by Ames, JCPenney, Sears and Steinbach department stores, University Mall also features over 75 national and local retailers. A Wal-Mart is also located in South Burlington next to I-89. More interesting are Burlington's Church Street

Marketplace, a four-block pedestrian promenade downtown with specialty shops and services including Ben and Jerry's Ice Cream, restaurants and sidewalk cafes, and Winooski's Champlain Mill, a tastefully renovated 19th century woolen mill full of upscale shops and restaurants.

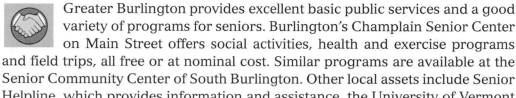

Health Care   Rating: 4

Fletcher Allen Health Care provides diverse medical services at three sites in the Burlington area. Its largest facility, Medical Center Hospital Campus at the University of Vermont, is a regional referral center offering 24-hour emergency service, cardiac care, dialysis and kidney transplants, cancer care and orthopedics, among other services. With over 600 beds at its three hospitals and over 250 physicians in the county, Burlington has unusually comprehensive medical care for a small city.

Community Services   Rating: 4

Greater Burlington provides excellent basic public services and a good variety of programs for seniors. Burlington's Champlain Senior Center on Main Street offers social activities, health and exercise programs and field trips, all free or at nominal cost. Similar programs are available at the Senior Community Center of South Burlington. Other local assets include Senior Helpline, which provides information and assistance, the University of Vermont Center for the Study of Aging, and the Chittenden County Senior Citizen's Alliance.

Leisure Activities

The University of Vermont and other Burlington colleges, Lake Champlain, and the city's mountain and valley areas provide plenty of leisure activities choices in all seasons.

Cultural and Educational Activities   Rating: 4

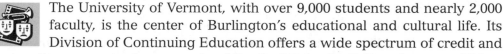

The University of Vermont, with over 9,000 students and nearly 2,000 faculty, is the center of Burlington's educational and cultural life. Its Division of Continuing Education offers a wide spectrum of credit and noncredit courses to the general public. St. Michael's College hosts an Elderhostel and runs a continuing education program with some classes and programs designed specifically for seniors. Several other colleges in and around Burlington, including business and professionally oriented Champlain College, provide additional educational options. The university's Lane Series is an academic yearlong guest artist series. Recital Hall at the University of Vermont is a principal venue for baroque, cello, piano and string quartet recitals and jazz concerts. Main Street's Flynn Theatre for the Performing Arts, a restored Art Deco landmark, hosts the Vermont Symphony as well as visiting national and international musical, opera and theater companies. St. Michael's Playhouse on the campus of St. Michael's College produces four professional summer theater productions annually. Other special summer events include the Jazz Festival in June at 50 venues such as City Hall Park, the Church Street Marketplace, Flynn Theatre, and numerous clubs and beaches, and the Mozart Festival of chamber music in July and August. The Vermont Symphony performs outdoor concerts in summer; in July and August, the Champlain Shakespeare Festival is held in the university's Royall Tyler Theatre. In October, the Vermont International Film Festival kicks off the winter cultural season.

The Fleming Museum on the university campus and the Shelburne Museum in nearby Shelburne are the area's principal visual arts venues. The Fleming displays ancient Egyptian and Middle Eastern, African, American and European art in its permanent collections and visiting exhibitions. The Shelburne Museum consists of 37 restored early New England buildings housing art and artifacts typical of the 18th and 19th centuries. The museum's Webb Galleries feature a fine collection of works by European artists including Corot, Courbet, Degas, Goya, Edouard and Claude Monet, and Rembrandt, as well as paintings by leading American artists of the past three centuries.

Recreational Activities   Rating: 5

Burlington and its surrounding areas are a paradise for winter and summer recreation. Within 50 miles there are 8 downhill ski areas, including Smuggler's Notch, Stowe and Sugarbush, and upwards of 20 cross-country ski areas. Ice boating, ice fishing, ice-skating and snow-shoeing are also popular in winter. Golf is played in summer at six courses in and around Burlington. Hiking and biking are popular in town and countryside. Seven miles of bike paths wind from park to park along the Lake Champlain shoreline. Quiet country roads between the city and the Green Mountains also provide a gorgeous billboard-free environment for biking. Seasoned hikers will enjoy the Long Trail, a segment of the famous Appalachian Trail, which extends from Maine to Georgia. It runs along the crest of the Green Mountains 20 miles east of Burlington. Burlington has 27 parks ranging from small neighborhood parks with several amenities, such as playgrounds, ball fields, and basketball or tennis courts, to large multi-purpose community parks like Leddy and Oakledge. The former boasts a beach, indoor ice rink, soccer field, and playground, four tennis courts, five ball fields, and trails and natural areas. The latter has a beach, picnic shelters, tennis courts, three ball fields and surfaced roads and trails. Battery Park, on a bluff overlooking downtown's Waterfront Park and promenade, offers spectacular views of Lake Champlain and the Adirondacks and summer evening concerts at its band shell.

For those who enjoy hunting for treasures from times past, Burlington and surrounding areas are brimming with antique shops and markets.

Like many top college towns, Burlington offers competitive intercollegiate sports and an exceptional number of movie theaters and good restaurants for its size. The University of Vermont basketball and hockey teams enjoy strong support from students and town folk and more than 30 movie screens provide additional entertainment options. Several good restaurants downtown and at the waterfront specialize in moderately priced seafood and ethnic and American cuisine. Other restaurants are found in South Burlington and in suburban locations.

Work and Volunteer Activities   Rating: 2

High-tech industry and the University of Vermont, neither of which generate much part-time work, dominate the local economy. Service jobs are mostly in retailing; competition with students is severe, resulting in low wages. Volunteer opportunities, though, are plentiful. Chapters of the Retired Senior Volunteer Program (RSVP) and the Service Corps of Retired Executives (SCORE) help place seniors where they are most needed. The Senior Resource Directory, published by Vermont Maturity Magazine, also provides useful leads.

Burlington's crime situation is mixed. The violent crime rate is among the lowest in the country yet overall property crime occurs at nearly twice the national rate in the city, although at a lower rate countywide. Burglary and larceny-theft are the principal threats in both city and county.

Conclusion

Overall Rating 42

Burlington is a beautiful, amenity-rich college town overlooking Lake Champlain and backed by the Green Mountains. It will appeal for retirement especially to hardy souls who enjoy winter weather and winter sports. Others should perhaps visit Vermont in summer and fall and reside in the subtropics.

Burlington's greatest assets are its gorgeous physical landscape and matching outdoor recreation. The Green Mountains offer some of the best skiing in the eastern United States in winter and excellent hiking and biking in summer, while Lake Champlain and rivers draining into it provide endless opportunities for canoeing, sailing, fishing and swimming. Burlington also ranks very highly in quality of life, transportation, health care, community services and culture. Downtown's Church Street Marketplace and Waterfront Park are delightful pedestrian-oriented refuges from suburbia, and the city's residential areas and parklands are very pleasant. Retail services are quite good for a small town and violent crime is rare. Burlington's greatest weaknesses are its long cold winters, severe competition for part-time work, and a moderately high cost of living. Not surprisingly, Burlington residents agree that these are a small price to pay for the privilege of living in such a beautiful, civilized and uncrowded place.

Ithaca, New York

The home of Cornell University since 1865 and Ithaca College since 1931, Ithaca gradually evolved from a diversified commercial and industrial center to a classic college town during the twentieth century. Today, Cornell University with 19,000 students and Ithaca College with 6,000 students physically, economically and culturally dominate the community. Cornell covers 740 acres on East Hill and counts among its assets 200 major buildings, including 16 libraries. Relocated in the 1960s from its downtown campus to a new one on South Hill, Ithaca College maintains strong community ties through its outstanding cultural programs. Together, the university and college employ twice as many people as the next eight employers in the city. With a population of 29,000 (excluding students) in the city and 97,000 in Tompkins County, Ithaca is a very small place. But thanks to its institutions of higher learning and its lovely Finger Lakes Region surroundings, it boasts more culture, recreation and services than many major metropolitan centers. It is arguably New York's best small town.

Landscape   **Rating: 5**

Ithaca is located in the Finger Lakes Region of New York State's glaciated Allegheny Plateau. The downtown is situated on a valley floor, which opens out onto the south shore of Cayuga Lake. Residential areas climb the slopes that ring the city except on its northern (lake) side. The surrounding countryside is a rolling surface with farms, forested hillsides, and spectacular waterfalls that drop into deep gorges. The region's natural vegetation is broad-leafed deciduous forest, with beech and maple predominating. The town

Ithaca, New York

CLIMATE				
Month	Average Daily Temperature High Low		Daily Rel. Humidity Low	Average Monthly Precipitation
	°F		%	Inches
January	28	14	71	2.4
February	30	15	67	2.3
March	40	25	62	2.8
April	53	35	56	3.1
May	65	46	56	3.3
June	74	54	58	3.6
July	79	59	58	3.5
August	76	58	60	3.4
September	68	50	63	3.3
October	57	40	62	2.9
November	45	31	69	3.3
December	33	20	73	3.0

Annual Average

Total Days		Total Inches	
Clear	52	Precipitation	37.0
Partly Cloudy	102	Snowfall	72.0
Cloudy	212		

RATINGS

Rating Scale: 5 = excellent; 4 = very good; 3 = good; 2 = fair; 1 = poor

	Rating: 1	2	3	4	5
Landscape					●
Climate		●			
Quality of Life					●
Cost of Living			●		
Transportation			●		
Retail Services			●		
Health Care			●		
Community Services					●
Cultural Activities				●	
Recreational Activities				●	
Work/Volunteer Activities				●	
Crime				●	

Total Points: 45

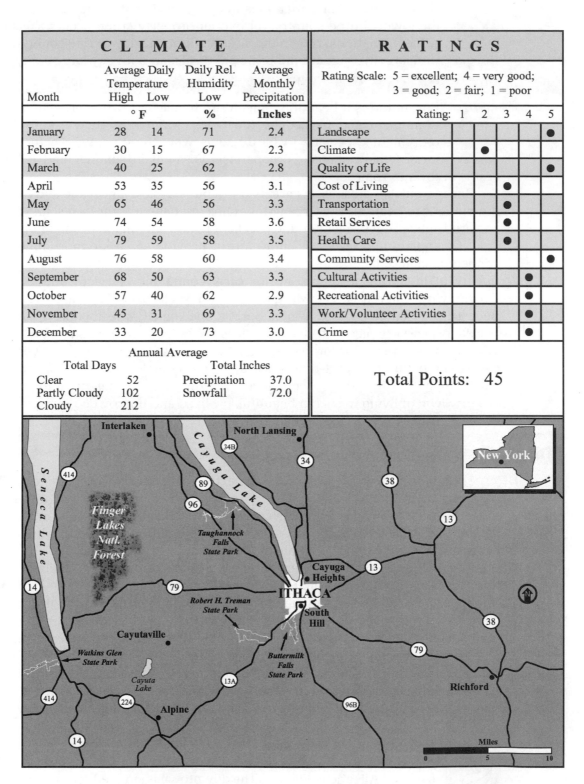

and campuses are well landscaped with a variety of broad-leafed and coniferous trees and shrubs. The wooded, rolling terrain embracing the southern end of Cayuga Lake is extraordinarily beautiful in all seasons, especially during the fall show of color. Distant views of the lake from the uplands are best in winter when the trees are bare of leaves.

Climate Rating: 2

Ithaca has a fairly severe humid continental climate with four distinct seasons of about equal length. Summers are typically pleasantly sunny and warm; winters are cloudy, cold and damp. Rapid changes in weather are routine, especially in spring and fall when warm, humid episodes alternate with cold, dry periods. Precipitation is ample in all seasons with most of winter's falling as snow. On average, Ithaca is sunny approximately 50 percent of the time, varying from about 30 percent in winter to 60 percent in summer. The frost-free period averages 160 days, long enough to grow grapes and other soft fruits.

Quality of Life Rating: 5

Ithaca offers an excellent quality of life. Although a county airport is close by, little jet noise intrudes because flights are few. There are no freeways and automobile traffic moves fairly slowly and quietly on the narrow streets. Even so, one can drive across town in a few minutes and generally find parking at destinations. Public transit is excellent around town and on the Cornell campus and is well patronized, thereby reducing the pressure of vehicles on the limited road network. Ithaca has a good mix of modest and upscale neighborhoods and is dotted with beautiful parks, including Stewart Park on the lakefront. The refurbished historic downtown (Ithaca Commons) is a delightful automobile-free area as are several natural areas like Cornell Plantations and Sapsucker Woods bird sanctuary on the otherwise busy Cornell campus. Ithaca residents are typically friendly, notoriously liberal and progressive, and apparently determined to preserve the integrity and charm of their delightful little city.

Cost of Living Rating: 3

The cost of living in Ithaca is evaluated as follows:

- *Composite.* ACCRA data are lacking for Ithaca so those of Binghamton, a college town 53 miles southeast, are used here. On that basis, the composite cost of living in Ithaca is estimated to approximate the national average.

- *Housing.* Housing costs have risen in recent months but remain perhaps 10 percent below the national average. Local real estate guides reveal excellent, inexpensive housing stock in Ithaca and nearby villages. Attractive older homes in the city tend to be priced between $90,000 and $130,000; even prestigious Cayuga Heights has elegant residences on large wooded lots priced between $150,000 and $200,000.

- *Goods and Services.* With the exception of utilities, which are priced perhaps 30 percent above the national average, goods and services costs are within a few percentage points of national norms.

- *Taxes.* The overall tax burden in Ithaca is well above average for most residents. The state/local sales tax rate of eight percent is very high and property taxes are well above the national average. The state income tax situation is more complex. Although working residents and retirees with large incomes from private pensions or investments pay high taxes, those depending largely on public pensions are more fortunate. Public pensions, social security income, and the first $20,000 from private pensions are fully exempt from New York State income tax.

Local and Regional Services

The small population of the Ithaca trade area somewhat limits the scope of its retail and medical services. However, transportation and community services are unusually good for a city of its size.

Transportation — Rating: 3

Tompkins Consolidated Area Transit (TCAT) provides good bus service to Ithaca, its suburbs and to population centers throughout the county. Routes connect downtown with Cornell University, Pyramid Mall and other outlying locations. TCAT also provides daytime local service around the Cornell campus. Base fare is 60 cents, senior citizen discount tickets are 30 cents, and a monthly pass costs $19 for all passengers. Parallel services for the elderly and disabled are furnished by Gadabout, Inc. Tompkins County Airport, four miles northeast, provides limited commuter and jet service including flights to New York/La Guardia, Boston, Philadelphia, Pittsburgh and Syracuse. Syracuse/Hancock International Airport, 60 miles north, offers nonstop jet service to over 15 locations including major hubs at Chicago, Detroit and Pittsburgh. Syracuse also boasts frequent east-west Amtrak service within New York State and daily service to Toronto and Chicago. Greyhound and several smaller bus companies offer intercity service to many points from Ithaca.

Retail Services — Rating: 3

Pyramid Mall, located on the eastern outskirts of town, is Ithaca's largest indoor mall. Anchored by The Bon Ton, JCPenney and Sears, the mall has over 70 specialty stores and eating places and a 10-screen cinema complex. Historic downtown Ithaca, now dubbed Ithaca Commons, is an award-winning pedestrian promenade and marketplace with a European flair. Unique specialty shops feature apparel, arts and crafts, books, music, sporting goods and home furnishings. Center Ithaca, an attractive small shopping complex on the Commons, boasts 20 specialty shops, 2 movie theaters, and several cafes in a central sky lit area. Just southwest of downtown is the Ithaca branch of Wegman's Food Markets, perhaps the biggest and best upscale supermarket anywhere. More down to earth is the Ithaca Farmers Market at Steamboat Landing on Saturdays and Sundays in summer and fall.

Health Care — Rating: 3

Cayuga Medical Center, a 204-bed acute care facility, is Tompkins County's sole provider of emergency care. Its 180-member medical staff offers a full range of medical and surgical specialties as well as primary care. Excellent additional medical facilities are less than 100 miles away in Rochester and Syracuse.

Community Services — Rating: 5

Ithaca and Tompkins County provide excellent community services. Since Ithaca's population is predominantly young, most services are not specifically targeted toward seniors. Nonetheless, Cornell University's Cornell–Ithaca Volunteers in Training and Service (CIVITAS) program assists the elderly in a variety of ways. The local Senior Citizens' Council publishes directories, serves as a referral agency, and coordinates social programs. Ithaca College's recently established Gerontology Institute is a valuable community resource through its outreach efforts.

Leisure Activities

Cornell University, Ithaca College, the City of Ithaca, and the surrounding Finger Lakes Region provide limitless leisure activities.

Cultural and Educational Activities	Rating: 4

 Internationally known as an elite research-oriented university, Cornell also contributes to the performing and visual arts. The Cornell Center for the Theatre Arts stages six to twelve plays, offers the Cornell Dance Series, and hosts numerous guest artists from September through May. The university's Herbert F. Johnson Museum of Art, designed by I. M. Pei, houses a collection spanning 40 centuries and six continents with particular strengths in prints, Asian and contemporary art. An outgrowth of the Ithaca Conservatory of Music founded in 1892, Ithaca College is ranked today among the nation's best small colleges for the quality and value of its educational offerings. Its Dillingham Center is home to the Hoerner and Clark Theatres where the college Department of Theatre Arts presents comedy, drama, music, opera and dance productions. So busy is the cultural calendar at Ithaca College that a concert, theatrical production, art show or public lecture, many of them free of charge, is scheduled nearly every day of the academic year.

The performing arts are also strong off campus. Professional ensembles include the 35-member Cayuga Chamber Orchestra, the Cayuga Vocal Ensemble, and the Ithaca Ballet, upstate New York's only repertory company. The Ithaca Opera Association and the New York State Baroque are also based locally. The Hanger Theatre, a professional theater since 1975, presents five mainstage productions during its summer season in Cass Park along Cayuga Lake, and reaches out to schools during the winter season. The Ithaca Performing Arts Center, located in downtown's majestic State Theater, is a principal venue for ballet, concerts, film and dance.

International, national and regional arts and crafts are exhibited at several commercial galleries. The Handwerker Gallery at Ithaca College and the John Hartell and Olive Tjaden Galleries at Cornell display primarily contemporary art by students and faculty.

Recreational Activities	Rating: 4

 The varied landscape of the Ithaca area offers many recreational options. One can walk all or part of Circle Greenway, a 10-mile walking path linking the Cornell campus, scenic gorges and waterfalls, the waterfront and Ithaca Commons. Accessible by road or by bike or foot along a waterside path, Cass Park features ice-skating in winter and pool swimming in summer. Its other assets include picnic and fishing areas, a fitness trail, lighted softball and soccer fields and tennis courts. Stewart Park, beautifully sited on the shore of Cayuga Lake, provides panoramic views of the lake and surrounding hills and facilities for picnicking, swimming, tennis and ball games. A children's playground and a restored carousel are notable attractions.

Sapsucker Woods Sanctuary and Cayuga Nature Center provide easy access to natural wonders. Sapsucker Woods, home of the Cornell Laboratory of Ornithology, has 4.2 miles of trails winding through the woods and over swamps and ponds. Waterfowl and other wildlife abound here. Cayuga Nature Center has five miles of trails for hiking, nature study, cross-country skiing and snow-shoeing, a farm exhibit and nature programs. Four beautiful state parks with fine facilities are found within 10 miles of Ithaca. Alan H. Treman State Marine Park on the shores of Cayuga Lake is notable for picnicking, boating and fishing whereas Buttermilk Falls, Robert H. Treman and Taughannock Falls state parks boast some of the most scenic gorges and waterfalls in the eastern states. The latter three parks also have sites for camping, picnicking, hiking, swimming and fishing, among other activities. In summer one can golf at four 18-hole and two 9-hole courses in and around Ithaca; in winter, downhill skiing is available at Greek Peak, 20 miles east of town, or at three other resorts only slightly farther afield. Cross-country skiing venues, including those at nearby state parks, are even more abundant locally.

In all seasons, wine connoisseurs can sample excellent wines at a number of family-owned wineries along the scenic Cayuga Wine Trail. Among the best of these is Cayuga Ridge Estate Winery, about 20 miles north along Highway-89. As befits a college town, Ithaca has several very good restaurants featuring mostly American but also Italian and ethnic cuisine at very reasonable prices. Movie theaters are found at the Commons and at Pyramid Mall.

Work and Volunteer Activities   Rating: 4

With nearly as many students as permanent residents in Ithaca, competition for part-time service employment is severe. Nonetheless, Ithaca has little unemployment at present and many seniors find work of some kind. Volunteerism is highly valued in the enlightened atmosphere of Ithaca. Each year thousands of student and faculty volunteers, mobilized by CIVITAS, join seniors and other residents in assisting more than 100 community agencies in the city and county.

Crime Rates and Public Safety   Rating: 4

Ithaca is one of America's safest small college towns and distinctly safer than large metropolitan areas. Although the city's property crime rate is only slightly below the national average, the rate of violent crime is extremely low. Indeed, except for larceny-theft, all subcategories of violent and property crime now exhibit below average rates. More impressionistically, the community feels safe as one walks the sidewalks, streets and paths of downtown, residential suburbs, and the university and college campuses.

Conclusion

Overall Rating 45
If you are attracted to the excitement of a big city and you dislike small towns and winter, you would not likely choose Ithaca for retirement. Ithaca is, indeed, a very small city in a region of cold, cloudy and snowy winters. As such, it will appeal primarily to those who prefer a four-season climate, enjoy summer and winter outdoor recreation, and appreciate the combination of small town virtues and big city amenities that the best college towns provide.

Located on Cayuga Lake in the scenic hill and valley landscape of New York's Finger Lakes Region, Ithaca has a beautiful setting and offers an excellent quality of life unspoiled by congestion, pollution or unplanned growth. Downtown Ithaca Commons is a delightful pedestrian marketplace and community center, and the city's residential areas and parklands are exceptional. Community services are excellent, and, as a result of the presence of Cornell University and Ithaca College, cultural and educational offerings are outstanding. The city and surrounding area provide abundant outdoor recreation in lovely surroundings, there are many work/volunteer options, and the area is relatively free of serious crime. Transportation, retail and health care services are good, and the cost of living is at about the national average. Luckily, Ithaca is growing rather slowly so it should remain an uncrowded, civilized and environmentally attractive refuge for discerning retirees for a long time to come. It is one of America's most attractive small cities.

Hanover/Lebanon, New Hampshire

Hanover/Lebanon, New Hampshire is also worth considering for retirement. Hanover is a beautiful little college town located on the eastern bank of the Connecticut River. Lebanon, just five miles south of Hanover, also offers an excellent quality of life but at a lower cost. The Green Mountains of Vermont lie a few miles to the west; the White Mountains of New Hampshire are a few miles to the east.

Hanover/Lebanon's strongest assets are its lovely physical landscape, outdoor recreation and the many cultural and educational amenities provided by Dartmouth College. The Green and White Mountains offer some of the best skiing in the eastern United States. Ten ski resorts lie within an hour's drive. In summer, one can canoe or kayak on the Connecticut River or hike the Appalachian Trail, which runs through Hanover. Classes at Dartmouth's Institute for Lifelong Education are inexpensive and the campus hosts several hundred concerts, films and plays each year. Other pluses include first-rate medical care at Dartmouth-Hitchcock Medical Center, excellent air quality, good public transit and very low crime rates. The overall tax burden is low. New Hampshire does not tax sales or most income.

Hanover/Lebanon's principal weaknesses are its long, cold, cloudy winters, limited employment opportunities and, at least in Hanover, high housing costs. Some may be put off by the towns' small size—they are little more than villages. But don't be deceived; they have a lot to offer.

The Midwest Retirement Region

Climate: Humid continental

The Midwest Retirement Region occupies only a small part of the central states area sometimes described as America's Heartland or Middle West. Stretching roughly 400 miles from southeastern Wisconsin to southern Indiana, this small region belies the popular image of the Middle West as an uninteresting landscape of industrial cities and uniform farmland. Though farming and industry are important here (northern Illinois and Indiana are part of the rich Corn Belt agricultural region and Chicago is one of America's largest manufacturing centers) the choicest retirement spots are neither heavily industrial nor located in monotonous landscapes.

Madison, Wisconsin, capital of the state and home of the University of Wisconsin, and Bloomington, Indiana, site of the main campus of Indiana University, are the twin jewels of the Midwest Retirement Region. Occupying a rolling glaciated surface and embraced by four beautiful lakes, Madison experiences a fairly rigorous four-season climate and will appeal especially to those who enjoy both winter and summer recreation. Bloomington is located on a gently rolling plain surrounded by southern Indiana's scenic hill country. Warmer in all seasons than Madison, Bloomington is a little too mild for winter sports on natural snow and ice. Both cities offer the cultural and recreational amenities, services, and high quality of life characteristic of the best Big Ten college towns.

Madison, Wisconsin

Little more than a place on a map when it was selected as territorial capital in 1838, Madison struggled along as a remote frontier village until Wisconsin attained statehood and established the University of Wisconsin in 1848. State government and higher education have been the twin pillars of the city's economy ever since. Even today the public sector is preeminent in Madison's economy. About one-third of Greater Madison's labor force, or more than 68,000 residents, are employed in local, state or federal government jobs. The University of Wisconsin, ranked consistently as one of the nation's best public universities, has 40,000 students and over 30,000 employees counting student workers at the university and its hospitals and clinics. Wisconsin's 1,000-acre campus,

Madison, Wisconsin

CLIMATE				
Month	Average Daily Temperature High Low		Daily Rel. Humidity Low	Average Monthly Precipitation
	°F		%	Inches
January	25	7	69	1.1
February	30	11	66	1.1
March	42	23	62	2.2
April	57	34	55	2.9
May	69	44	54	3.1
June	78	54	56	3.7
July	82	60	58	3.4
August	80	57	60	4.0
September	72	48	62	3.4
October	60	38	60	2.2
November	44	27	68	2.1
December	30	14	72	1.8

Annual Average

Total Days		Total Inches	
Clear	89	Precipitation	30.9
Partly Cloudy	96	Snowfall	44.0
Cloudy	180		

RATINGS

Rating Scale: 5 = excellent; 4 = very good; 3 = good; 2 = fair; 1 = poor

Rating:	1	2	3	4	5
Landscape					●
Climate		●			●
Quality of Life					●
Cost of Living		●			
Transportation				●	
Retail Services				●	
Health Care					●
Community Services					●
Cultural Activities				●	
Recreational Activities				●	
Work/Volunteer Activities			●		
Crime				●	

Total Points: 47

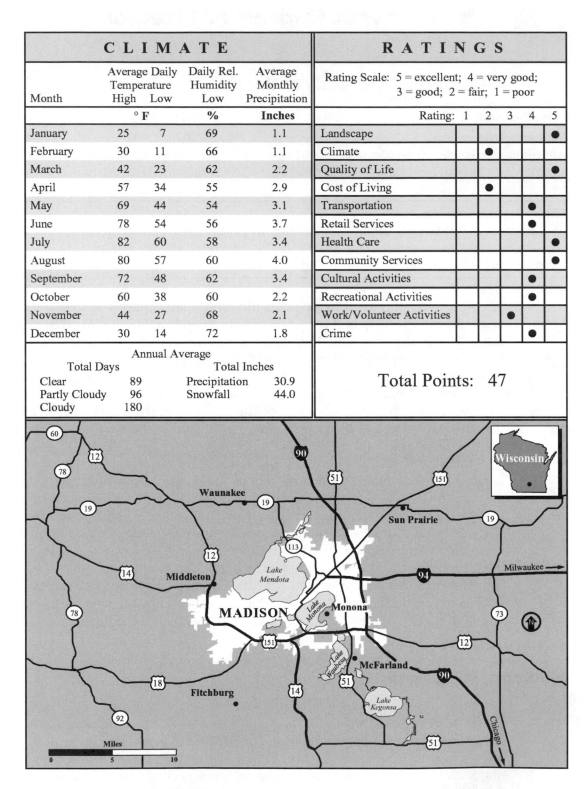

overlooking Lake Mendota, is one of the most beautiful in the country and nicely complements the impressive state capitol, one mile away. With a population of 200,000 in the city and 400,000 in the metropolitan area (Dane County), Madison is a lively and progressive town offering outstanding cultural and recreational amenities in an unspoiled environment.

Landscape   Rating: 5

 Centered on a natural isthmus between Lake Mendota and Lake Monona and extending around these and other smaller lakes, Madison occupies a magnificent site. The land, part of America's glaciated interior plains region, is gently rolling and well wooded with a mixture of broadleafed deciduous trees—oak, maple and hickory predominating. The lakes, with much of their shorelines occupied by upscale residences and parks, offer a scenic backdrop to the urban area. Proximity to Lake Mendota is one of the many charms of the University of Wisconsin. The lake is visible from most places on the campus, the union terrace overlooks it, and the lovely lakeshore path traversed by students on their way to class parallels it. With its eclectic blend of neoclassical and modern architecture and its carefully landscaped grounds and plazas, the campus is a delight to eye and mind.

Climate   Rating: 2

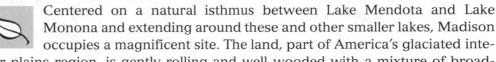 Madison's climate is a fairly severe variant of the humid continental climate found in the Middle West. Winters are long and cold, summers relatively short but delightfully warm and sunny. Lying west of the Great Lakes, Madison is not as cloudy or snowy in winter as snowbelt cities like Cleveland and Buffalo but it is somewhat colder. Average annual snowfall is upwards of 40 inches and the ground is snow covered 60 percent of the time from mid-December through March. Rapid changes in weather are routine in all seasons, and precipitation is adequate with maximum amounts occurring in summer when it is most needed. On average, Madison is sunny 55 percent of the time, varying from 45 percent in winter to 66 percent in summer. The frost-free period averages 170 days, extending from late April through mid-October.

Quality of Life   Rating: 5

 Madison offers an excellent quality of life. Although there is some noise pollution from freeways and highways, the city's many trees buffer residential neighborhoods from much of it. Rush hour traffic is moderately heavy in the city center where governmental and educational facilities are concentrated, and parking is tight downtown and on the university campus. Generally though, Madison's excellent road system and fine public transit allow easy access to area attractions. Air quality is excellent and the city is a model of good planning and progressive government. Most neighborhoods are architecturally interesting, well landscaped and maintained, and downtown's tree-lined State Street Mall, with its shops, restaurants, galleries and theaters, is a gem. An abundance of city parks and miles of bikeways and walking paths add to the city's peaceful ambiance.

Cost of Living   Rating: 2

 The cost of living in Madison is evaluated as follows:

- *Composite.* ACCRA data show that the overall cost of living in Madison is about nine percent above the national average.

- *Housing.* According to ACCRA, housing costs are about 30 percent above the national average. Local sources and exploration of the area suggest that Madison offers a good variety of resale housing at moderate prices. In Madison itself, many attractive single-family residences with three bedrooms and two baths are priced between $125,000 and $225,000; prices are only slightly higher countywide. Condominiums and smaller homes are available at lower prices in the city and Dane County. In general, Madison's higher than average housing costs appear to reflect the area's better than average housing stock rather than a shortage of housing or any undue inflation of prices.

- *Goods and Services.* Goods and services are priced near national norms. Groceries and miscellaneous goods and services are priced within 3 percent of their national averages whereas transportation, utilities and health care are 6 to 10 percent above.

- *Taxes.* In a state known for the excellence of its public services, it is not surprising that the overall tax burden is well above the national average. State income taxes are perhaps 30 percent above the national average while property taxes are 70 percent above. The state income tax of five percent approximates the national norm. The City of Madison does not add a local supplement to the state levy but Dane County adds 0.5 percent.

Local and Regional Services

By virtue of its dual status as state capital and regional economic capital of south central Wisconsin, Madison provides an excellent range of services to residents.

Transportation	Rating: 4

Interstates-90 and 94 skirt Madison on the east so most trips within the city are on two-lane and multi-lane streets. The excellent street and highway network is seldom overburdened. Although more auto trips than bicycle trips are made per day, the approximately 100,000 daily bicycle trips in summer significantly reduce traffic congestion and air pollution. Madison Metro Transit, with 140 buses, provides excellent local bus service focused on downtown and the University of Wisconsin and Metro Plus offers dial-a-ride service for the elderly and handicapped. Discounts are available to students and seniors. Dane County Airport, five miles northeast, is served by Northwest Airlines and six commuter carriers. Nonstop destinations include Chicago, Cincinnati, Detroit, Milwaukee and Minneapolis-St. Paul. Intercity bus service to many points is offered by Badger Coaches, Greyhound Bus Lines and Val Galder/Alco Bus Company. Daily Amtrak service east to Chicago and west to Seattle and Portland is available from Columbus, 25 miles east.

Retail Services	Rating: 4

Downtown Madison is in excellent shape with many very attractive shops and restaurants, including a Land's End outlet store near the capitol. State Street Mall, a revitalized, pedestrian-friendly shopping street stretching from Capitol Square to the university campus, is a favorite of residents and visitors. Typical suburban shopping is available at Madison's twin malls, East Towne Mall, just west of I-40, and West Towne Mall, off Belt Line Highway near the western fringe of Madison. Each is anchored by Boston, JCPenney, Sears and Younkers department stores and includes over 100 specialty stores and services and a food court. Several Wal-Mart and Target discount stores are also found in outlying parts of the city.

Madison offers unusually excellent medical care, particularly for a relatively small city. The University of Wisconsin Hospital and Clinics, a research and teaching hospital of the University of Wisconsin Medical School, is a state-of-the-art facility providing the widest range of specialties and services. With 482 beds, it is the largest general hospital in Madison. Meriter Capital Hospital and St. Mary's Hospital Medical Center are only slightly smaller. Both also have a wide variety of specialties and services. William S. Middleton Memorial Hospital, a 200-bed facility, provides medical care for veterans.

Community Services   Rating: 5

 Taxes are high in Madison but they do pay for excellent basic public services as well as those oriented toward seniors. The Madison Senior Center, located downtown, provides an unusual variety of services and activities free or at nominal cost. Classes in arts and crafts, computers, and dancing are scheduled regularly, lectures are presented on topics such as travel and nutrition, a tai chi program occurs twice weekly and movies are shown twice monthly. The Senior Center cooperates with RSVP to recruit seniors for volunteer service and with AARP to provide tax assistance. Health screenings are provided periodically and noontime meals are hosted weekdays. Similar programs are offered at the Northside and Westside Senior Centers in suburban Madison.

Leisure Activities

An all-season playground for outdoor recreation, Madison is also notable for its flourishing arts scene. Boredom is not an option here.

Cultural and Educational Activities   Rating: 4

 The University of Wisconsin, with over 40,000 students from all over the world, is a vital center of education and culture. Its comprehensive continuing education program offers an enormous variety of credit and noncredit courses to the general public. Edgewood College, a small liberal arts institution, and Madison Area Technical College provide additional educational choices. All three institutions host a variety of theatrical performances, music and lectures.

The performing and visual arts are flourishing in Madison. The Civic Center with its Madison Art Center, the elegant 2,200 seat Oscar Mayer Theatre and the more intimate Isthmus Playhouse, home of Madison Repertory Theatre, are principal venues. Ten other local live theater production companies are currently active including Broom Street Theater, one of the country's oldest and best experimental theaters. Additionally, several dance companies produce musical theater ranging from classical dance to jazz and tap dancing. Only 35 miles west in the village of Spring Green, site of Frank Lloyd Wright's home, Taliesin and his school of architecture, the American Players Theatre Company performs Shakespeare and other classics outdoors in summer.

Madison is alive with the sound of music in countless informal and formal settings. You can stroll down State Street and listen to street musicians, walk up Bascom Hill to hear the ringing of the Carillon Tower bells, and enjoy a summer evening on the capital lawn listening to the Wisconsin Chamber Orchestra's Concerts on the Square. At the Civic Center you can attend performances by the Madison Civic Opera, the Madison Symphony Orchestra, the Wisconsin

Chamber Orchestra and Ballet Colbert. Various nightspots provide popular music and dancing nearly every night of the week.

The visual arts are showcased at several galleries and museums. The Madison Art Center contains three floors of changing exhibits of modern and contemporary art. The Elvehjem Museum of Art at the University of Wisconsin houses over 15,000 works of art including American and European drawings, paintings, prints and sculpture, as well as ancient and Asian art.

Recreational Activities   Rating: 4

 Madison's changing seasons allow for all kinds of outdoor recreation. Over 21,000 acres of lakes and 150 parks and recreation areas in Greater Madison provide water recreation and dry-land activities. Boating, canoeing, sailing, water-skiing, fishing and swimming are popular in summer. Golf, which is played on more than 20 courses in Dane County, including 5 that are municipally operated, and biking, racquetball, roller-skating and tennis have longer spring through fall seasons. Biking is a major mode of transportation as well as a recreational activity in Madison. More than 150 miles of bike trails and routes encircle Lake Monona and crisscross the city. Winter activities are also understandably popular in this land of snow and ice. The lakes are normally frozen over from late December through late March with ice fishing occurring in January and February. Ice-skaters have 40 outdoor rinks to choose from plus the Hartmeyer Ice Arena. There are more than 100 miles of cross-country ski trails in Greater Madison, while several modest downhill ski areas are located within 50 miles of the city.

The University of Wisconsin, a member of the Big Ten Conference, competes energetically in a variety of varsity sports. Madison's fans are typically enthusiastic and loyal, especially when supporting their football and hockey "Badgers." Like other top college towns, Madison boasts an unusually good selection of movie theaters and restaurants for its size. More than 20 kinds of ethnic restaurants are scattered throughout this increasingly diverse city. Those who prefer to do their own cooking throng to Saturday's massive but orderly farmers market, May through October. One of the biggest and best farmers markets in the country, Madison's sells everything from fresh produce to bratwurst, smoked trout and local cheese.

Work and Volunteer Activities   Rating: 3

 Madison's moderate economic and population growth in the 1990s, its preponderance of service sector jobs, and an unemployment rate hovering around two percent annually, all imply a favorable job market for seniors. However, the presence of 80,000 students, many of whom need to work while pursuing their education in a county of 400,000 people, does not. Competition for part-time jobs on campus and in retailing is especially acute. Plenty of opportunities, though, are available for volunteers in area schools, hospitals, libraries, museums and social service organizations. The local chapter of the Retired Senior Volunteer Program is helpful in securing placements.

Crime Rates and Public Safety   Rating: 4

 Madison is one of the safest cities of its size. Overall crime and property crime rates are declining and both are now about 10 percent below their national averages. The violent crime rate is about 30 percent below the national rate and homicides are rare indeed.

Overall Rating 47 In 1996 *Money* magazine rated Greater Madison (Dane County) as the best place to live in America. Like every other place, though, Madison is not perfect for everyone. Some would find its winters too harsh, its taxes too high and its housing too expensive. But others would argue that these faults, if they are faults, are a small price to pay to live in such a wonderful place.

Madison's strongest assets are probably its gorgeous physical landscape, excellent quality of life, and superb health care and community services. Embraced by four beautiful lakes and dotted with municipal parks, the city's residential areas are among the most attractive in the country. Attractive too are Capitol Square, the historic State Street pedestrian mall, and the University of Wisconsin campus. Madison also offers very good intercity and intracity transportation, good shopping, and a plethora of cultural and recreational choices commonly found only in much larger cities. Perhaps best of all, Madison is a safe, friendly and progressive community with a healthy mix of people and diversions. You will not be bored here.

Bloomington, Indiana

The home of Indiana University since 1820, Bloomington remains a classic Big Ten college town despite significant diversification of its economy over the years. The university physically and culturally dominates the community. Even though enrollment has grown to 35,000 students, much of the beautiful 1,850-acre campus retains the charm of an earlier age with historic and modern buildings secluded amidst gardens and woods. With a population of 65,000 (excluding students) in the city and 120,000 in Monroe Country, Bloomington is a small place. But thanks to the university, it has more culture and recreation than most metropolitan areas and at bargain prices. Additional big city assets are readily available in nearby Indianapolis, 50 miles north, and Cincinnati, 120 miles east.

Landscape   Rating: 4

Bloomington is situated at an elevation of 800 feet on the gently rolling Mitchell Plain, a porous limestone formation notable for its architectural-grade building stone, in south central Indiana. The rugged and forested hills and valleys of Brown County, with their several state and federal parks and forests, are a few miles east. A number of small lakes, including Lake Monroe and Lake Lemon, are within 10 miles of town. The area's natural vegetation is broad-leafed deciduous forest, with beech, maple, oak and ash predominating. The town and campus are attractively planted with these and other ornamental trees and shrubs.

Climate   Rating: 3

Bloomington has a humid continental climate with four distinct seasons including a long, warm to hot summer and a short, relatively mild winter. Although marked day-to-day weather changes are routine, Bloomington weather is, on average, a little sunnier and much less snowy in winter than that experienced in cities 200 miles north near the Great Lakes. Summers are typically sunny and warm, with episodes of hot, sultry weather being

Bloomington, Indiana

CLIMATE				
Month	Average Daily Temperature High Low		Daily Rel. Humidity Low	Average Monthly Precipitation
	°F		%	Inches
January	37	17	67	2.8
February	41	20	65	2.5
March	51	29	61	3.8
April	65	40	55	3.9
May	75	50	55	4.4
June	84	59	55	4.7
July	87	63	59	4.6
August	86	61	60	3.9
September	80	53	57	3.0
October	69	40	56	2.7
November	53	31	64	3.5
December	42	23	69	3.2

Annual Average

Total Days		Total Inches	
Clear	90	Precipitation	43.0
Partly Cloudy	100	Snowfall	18.2
Cloudy	175		

RATINGS					
Rating Scale: 5 = excellent; 4 = very good; 3 = good; 2 = fair; 1 = poor					
Rating:	1	2	3	4	5
Landscape				●	
Climate			●		
Quality of Life				●	
Cost of Living				●	
Transportation		●			
Retail Services				●	
Health Care			●		
Community Services			●		
Cultural Activities					●
Recreational Activities					●
Work/Volunteer Activities			●		
Crime				●	

Total Points: 44

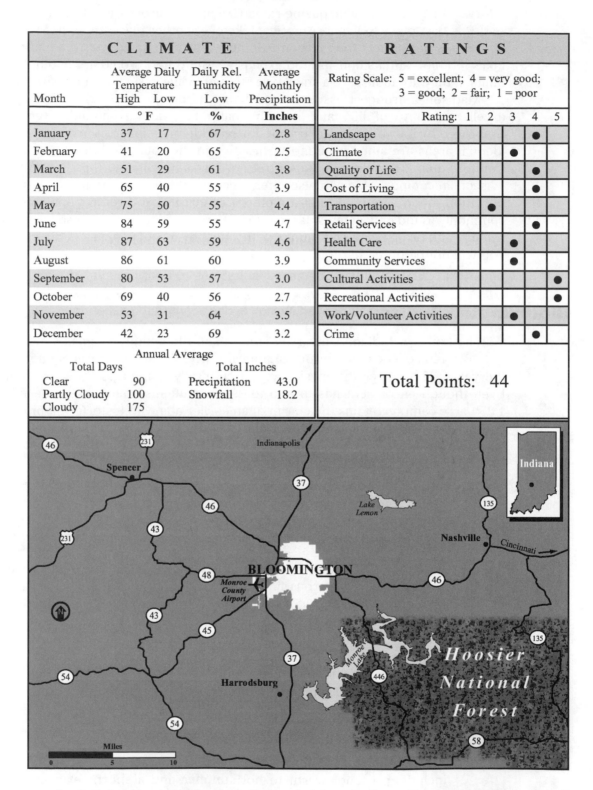

broken by the arrival of cooler and drier air from Canada. Spring and fall weather is perhaps the most pleasant of the year with warm days balanced by cool nights. On average, Bloomington is sunny 55 percent of the time, varying from about 40 percent in winter to 70 percent in summer. The frost-free season lasts about 170 days and precipitation is well distributed throughout the year.

The quality of life is very good in Bloomington. There is no major airport nearby and no freeway so noise pollution is minimal except adjacent to the Highway-46 bypass. Air quality is excellent even though high humidity reduces visibility in summer. Parking is adequate in most places but heavily restricted and very tight on the central campus; here public transit and walking are recommended. Local manufacturing is dominated by relatively clean electrical goods and elevator production, and noxious industries are absent. Although Bloomington is not uniformly affluent, most neighborhoods are wooded, show pride of ownership, and are served by an excellent network of city parks. Downtown's revitalized Courthouse Square and Kirkwood Avenue, which links it to the university, provide lively venues for walking, shopping and dining. The campus, ranked recently as one of the most beautiful in the nation, is a delight to the senses as one walks its meandering paths along the Jordan River, up and down hills and through the woods. Unfortunately, the university also generates heavy traffic at rush hour and during major sports events. This overwhelms the city's marginal road system creating transient but nightmarish knots of congestion.

 The cost of living in Bloomington is evaluated as follows:

- *Composite*. ACCRA data for Bloomington show a composite cost of living just below the national average.

- *Housing*. According to ACCRA, housing costs are about seven percent below the national average. Housing costs are kept down by low wage levels prevailing in Bloomington rather than by an abundance of new housing. Even Indiana University professors' salaries are lower than at many comparable flagship state universities. Service sector and industrial wages are also relatively low. Only a small proportion of housing in Bloomington itself is new although new subdivisions are being built beyond the city limits in Monroe and Brown counties. Resale homes of varied size, type and price are available but the market seems tight. Smaller houses are typically priced between $100,000 and $150,000 while luxury homes are priced upwards of $200,000. Condominiums are considerably cheaper.

- *Goods and Services*. Goods and services are generally priced near national norms. Groceries run about eight percent above average but utilities, transportation, health care and miscellaneous goods and services all approximate their national averages.

- *Taxes*. The overall tax burden in Bloomington is modestly below the national average. The combined state/county income tax rate of 4.4 percent and the state sales tax rate of 5 percent are close to national norms. Property taxes are low; on a $200,000 home, they would be about $2100.

Local and Regional Services

Bloomington is the largest city of south central Indiana and the regional market center. It provides a good variety of services to residents.

Transportation   Rating: 2

Transportation is perhaps Bloomington's weakest attribute. As yet no freeway connects it to Indianapolis and the local street network is marginal in the context of increasing traffic. I U Transit provides good bus service to the campus community via its five routes and Bloomington Transit's six lines access most local destinations. Nonetheless, most people drive everywhere except on the central campus where walking and public transit work better. Bloomington has a small commuter airport but Indianapolis International Airport, 50 miles north, is a better choice. It offers nonstop jet service to over 30 destinations including major hubs at Atlanta, Chicago and St. Louis. Indianapolis also provides Amtrak service six times a week to Chicago and three times a week to Washington, D.C. Greyhound intercity bus service is available from Bloomington and Indianapolis.

Retail Services   Rating: 4

College Mall, located east of the university on 3rd Street, is the major regional mall. Anchored by JCPenney, Lazarus, L.S. Ayres, Sears and Target stores, College Mall also boasts over 80 specialty shops including a health foods-oriented market. A farmers market is held Saturday mornings in the mall parking lot. Adjacent to College Mall are several additional shopping centers featuring grocery stores, specialty shops and restaurants. Scattered about the city are several smaller shopping centers typically anchored by supermarkets. A Wal-Mart is located in the southwest corner of town at the junction of highways 37 and 45. Most interesting of all are the beautifully restored specialty stores and restaurants of the four blocks facing Courthouse Square downtown. Less than half a mile from the Sample Gates entrance to the Indiana University campus, this area has become very popular with students and Bloomington residents in recent years.

Health Care   Rating: 3

Bloomington Hospital serves nine counties and is the largest health care facility in south central Indiana. With 297 beds in the general hospital, an additional 362 in a nursing home unit, and over 200 physicians on staff, Bloomington Hospital provides good medical care in a wide range of specialties. Cancer care, heart care including angioplasty, open-heart surgery and cardiac rehabilitation, and diabetes are particular emphases. Southern Indiana Surgery Center is a state-accredited ambulatory-surgery center complementary to Bloomington Hospital. Its surgical specialties include gynecology, ophthalmology, podiatry and orthopedics, and urology. An even greater variety of medical services is only an hour away in Indianapolis. Its 19 accredited medical centers include seven teaching hospitals, among which the Indiana University Medical Center is perhaps most renowned.

Community Services   Rating: 3

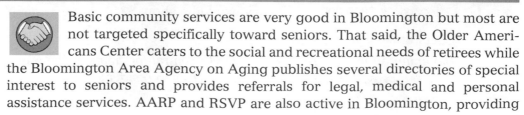

Basic community services are very good in Bloomington but most are not targeted specifically toward seniors. That said, the Older Americans Center caters to the social and recreational needs of retirees while the Bloomington Area Agency on Aging publishes several directories of special interest to seniors and provides referrals for legal, medical and personal assistance services. AARP and RSVP are also active in Bloomington, providing information and volunteer employment leads to seniors. A dozen or so social and fraternal organizations host socials, dances and other entertainment.

Leisure Activities

Indiana University, the City of Bloomington, and the surrounding southern Indiana hill country provide a multitude of leisure choices to local residents.

Cultural and Educational Activities	Rating: 5

 Indiana University, with over 35,000 students and 1,500 faculty on the Bloomington campus, is the state's top liberal arts institution of higher learning. With 337 degree programs organized in 13 schools and colleges, the university is an enormous educational, cultural and recreational asset. Noncredit courses offered by the School of Continuing Education are open to Indiana residents at nominal cost and do not require formal admission to I U. Classes in arts and sciences, business, computer science, horticulture and other fields are typically offered. The university's internationally acclaimed School of Music fields a year-round program of ballet, opera and music at the Musical Art Center, a state-of-the-art concert hall completed in 1971. Additionally, concerts or recitals are presented nearly every day by various student and faculty ensembles of the School of Music. The I U Auditorium, which seats up to 3,760 patrons, hosts a variety of touring Broadway shows, ballet and dance companies, international celebrities and other entertainment. Productions ranging from the classics to original plays are presented by I U students each year in two campus theaters by the Department of Theater and Drama. Fortunately, all this culture is priced so reasonably that one can afford to partake of it several times a week all year long.

The visual arts are not neglected at I U. Just across Fine Arts Plaza from the Auditorium is the university's stunning glass and concrete art museum, designed by I. M. Pei. Its permanent collection includes works by Matisse, Monet, Picasso, Rodin and Warhol; an ancient and Asian gallery, and collections from Africa, the Americas and Oceania. Also located on Fine Arts Plaza is the Lilly Library, home of some of the world's rarest books and manuscripts. The collection includes a Gutenberg Bible and George Washington's letter accepting the Presidency. Nearby is I U's Main Library, one of the finest university libraries in the United States.

Culture is not confined to the campus. The Waldron Art Center in downtown Bloomington is a focus of the visual arts. The Bloomington Playwright's Project produces new plays by playwrights from all over the country, Windfall Dancers perform a repertoire of modern and jazz dance, and the Bloomington Symphony presents classical concerts. Several arts and crafts fairs are held annually including the Fourth Street Festival on Labor Day weekend. Also in summer, plays are performed by the I U Department of Theater and Drama to full houses at the historic Brown County Playhouse in the charming village and art colony of Nashville, 20 miles east of Bloomington.

Recreational Activities	Rating: 5

 Bloomington and surrounding area offer an excellent variety of recreational opportunities. The Bloomington Parks and Recreation Department operates 21 parks, 8 recreational facilities, a golf course, and the Lake Griffy Natural Area. Parks and recreation facilities include baseball, basketball and tennis courts, sports fields, an indoor ice-skating rink and two swimming pools. Upwards of 3,000 acres of woodland provide hiking and nature observation. Golfers can choose among three additional golf courses including I U's championship course. The university also provides high-caliber sports events for fans of Big Ten competitions. Hoosiers basketball and football teams draw huge, enthusiastic crowds to their games at Assembly Hall and Memorial Stadium. Interest in soccer, swimming and diving, cross country and tennis competitions runs high, and the whole campus turns out for the Little 500, a 200-lap bicycle race made famous in the movie Breaking Away. Bloomington is also notable for its 5 movie theater chains with 20 screens and for several good restaurants serving inexpensive conventional and nouvelle American cuisine.

Within 20 miles of Bloomington, two lakes, two state parks, two state forests, and Hoosier National Forest provide lovely scenery and many activities. Lake Lemon, a 1,650-acre lake nestled in the hills northeast of Bloomington and owned by the city, provides boat launching, canoeing, fishing, swimming and camping, as does the much larger Lake Monroe, just southeast of town. Brown County State Park, 15 miles east of Bloomington, and McCormick's Creek State Park, 14 miles northwest, are good places for picnicking, camping, swimming and hiking, as are Morgan-Monroe and Yellowwood State Forests and Hoosier National Forest. Sightseeing by car or bike along the country roads of Monroe and Brown counties is delightful in all seasons but especially when the hillsides explode in fall's colors.

Work and Volunteer Activities   Rating: 3

 Competition for jobs in Bloomington's service-based economy is severe owing to the large student population. Even though unemployment has been at historic lows in recent years, wages remain stubbornly low. Fortunately, low wages are balanced by a relatively low cost of living, so even low paying part-time openings in retailing and service industries are snapped up. Volunteers serve in schools, in museums on and off campus, at Bloomington Hospital and Monroe County Library, and in other public service areas. RSVP is helpful in finding the right niche.

Crime Rates and Public Safety   Rating: 4

 Bloomington is one of America's safest mid-sized college towns and much safer than large metropolitan areas. Although the city's property crime rate is only slightly below the national average, the rate of violent crime is extremely low. In a recent year there were no homicides in Bloomington, a remarkable record for a city of 65,000. Residents perceive the community to be safe and it certainly feels that way as one walks downtown sidewalks or campus paths, daytime or evening.

Conclusion

 Overall Rating 44 Often overlooked as a retirement town, perhaps because of its Midwest location and continental climate, Bloomington deserves better. In reality this small southern Indiana college town is one of America's best places for an active retirement. Indiana University, the scenic hill country surrounding Bloomington, and the city itself offer an unbeatable combination of culture and recreation to suit every taste from grand opera and ballet to basketball and fishing. The I U campus is among the most beautiful in the land, while the town, with its mature, wooded residential areas and historic Courthouse Square, retains its small town charm despite recent growth and downtown renovation.

Shopping is very good and health care, community services and work/volunteer opportunities are more than adequate.

Bloomington's modest transportation infrastructure results in considerable traffic congestion at rush hour and during special events at the university, but distances are short in town so the inconvenience is not too great. The bus system now provides adequate service, crime is under control and the weather, although less than ideal in summer and winter, is rarely extremely hot or cold. All in all, Bloomington is a safe and friendly place offering a plethora of cultural and recreational amenities at low cost. For many it would be an ideal place for retirement.

4   The Upper South Retirement Region

Climate: Humid subtropical

The Upper South Retirement Region extends 400 miles inland from the Tidewater cities of Annapolis, Maryland and New Bern, North Carolina to the Blue Ridge Mountains. The heavily wooded mountains, fertile valleys, and swift-flowing streams of the Blue Ridge provide lovely settings for the college town of Lexington, Virginia and the resort and retirement communities of Asheville, Hendersonville and Brevard, North Carolina. Between the Tidewater and Blue Ridge regions lies the gently rolling surface of the Piedmont Plateau where Charlottesville, Virginia and Chapel Hill and Pinehurst/Southern Pines, North Carolina are sheltered from urban sprawl by surrounding farms and forests. Charlottesville and Chapel Hill are defined and dominated by the University of

Virginia and the University of North Carolina, each the premier public university of their states. Both towns offer natural beauty, a high quality of life, excellent health care, and plentiful service and leisure options. Pinehurst/Southern Pines is an ideal retirement spot for golfers.

Charlottesville, Virginia

Founded in 1762 by an Act of the Virginia General Assembly and named for Queen Charlotte, wife of King George III, Charlottesville has been steeped in history from colonial times. Its most famous son, Thomas Jefferson, founded and designed the University of Virginia, which remains to this day among the most beautiful of American college campuses and the center of life in Charlottesville. History also lives on at Jefferson's home, Monticello, just south of town, and at Court Square and the historic downtown area, which still constitute the legal and retail center for the city and Albemarle County. With a population of about 40,000 in the city and 80,000 in the county, the urban area is relatively small. But thanks to the university and its many resources, Charlottesville is able to offer residents an upscale and cosmopolitan way of life. Additional amenities typical of larger cities can be found in Richmond, 70 miles southeast, and Washington D. C., 120 miles northeast.

Landscape	Rating: 5

Charlottesville is located in central Virginia where the Piedmont Plateau meets the foothills of the Blue Ridge Mountains. Spread across a gently rolling surface with an average elevation of 600 feet, the city's landscape is very attractive with higher vantage points like Monticello providing gorgeous vistas of the Blue Ridge off to the west. A lush southern deciduous forest featuring oak, maple, elm and hickory trees envelops the city and its picturesque agricultural surroundings, which now include hundreds of acres of grape vines and several wineries. Residential areas in town exhibit many large magnolias as well as flowering shrubs such as azalea, camellia and rhododendron.

Climate	Rating: 3

Charlottesville has a temperate version of the Southeast's humid subtropical climate. Winters are mild for the latitude but summers are hot and humid. Precipitation averages 46 inches annually and is well distributed seasonally. About 24 inches of snow accumulates in the city in a normal winter, but much more falls in the Blue Ridge. Snow typically persists on the ground in town for only a few days at a time as cold waves are soon followed by warm spells. Average high temperatures vary from 46 degrees in winter to 86 degrees in summer; overnight lows are about 20 degrees lower. On average, Charlottesville is sunny about 60 percent of the time and enjoys a frost-free period of 210 days. Its principal climatic negative is summer's combination of heat and humidity. This results in discomfort and a hazy atmosphere that can hide the Blue Ridge from view. Weather conditions are much more pleasant in spring and fall when temperature and relative humidity readings are lower.

Charlottesville, Virginia

CLIMATE				
Month	Average Daily Temperature High Low		Daily Rel. Humidity Low	Average Monthly Precipitation
	°F		%	Inches
January	44	26	53	3.3
February	46	28	50	3.2
March	56	36	48	4.2
April	68	46	45	3.3
May	76	55	51	4.2
June	83	62	53	3.9
July	87	67	53	4.5
August	86	66	56	4.5
September	80	60	57	3.9
October	69	49	52	4.2
November	58	39	52	3.3
December	47	30	54	3.4

Annual Average

Total Days		Total Inches	
Clear	112	Precipitation	45.7
Partly Cloudy	107	Snowfall	24.2
Cloudy	147		

RATINGS

Rating Scale: 5 = excellent; 4 = very good; 3 = good; 2 = fair; 1 = poor

Rating:	1	2	3	4	5
Landscape					●
Climate			●		●
Quality of Life					●
Cost of Living			●		
Transportation			●		
Retail Services				●	
Health Care					●
Community Services				●	
Cultural Activities				●	
Recreational Activities					●
Work/Volunteer Activities		●			
Crime			●		

Total Points: 47

Quality of Life   **Rating: 5**

Charlottesville provides an excellent quality of life. There is little noise from automobile traffic or airplanes and air quality is excellent. The city is uncrowded and there is little traffic congestion. Parking is adequate downtown and at other major destinations, and public transit use, especially by students, reduces pressure on the transportation infrastructure. The city seems well planned. Heavy industry is absent and the city is generally free of unsightly industrial areas. Most neighborhoods are well maintained, attractively landscaped, and feature a good variety of contemporary and historic homes. Commercial development is largely confined to downtown and the Highway-29 strip with its several malls. Downtown's historic Main Street business district, now a charming and vibrant pedestrian mall, is a triumph of good human-scale planning over three decades by the Charlottesville Downtown Foundation. It is a wonderful center for community life and along with the University of Virginia lends a unique character to the city.

Cost of Living	Rating: 3

 The cost of living in Charlottesville is evaluated as follows:

- *Composite.* ACCRA data are currently unavailable for Charlottesville so statistics for Richmond, a nearby city with a similar per capita income, are used here. On that basis, the composite cost of living in Charlottesville is estimated to be five percent above the national average.

- *Housing.* Housing costs are about 10 percent above the national average but housing is not expensive considering its quality. The city has a good stock of houses of various styles in attractively landscaped neighborhoods. A charming three-bedroom, two-bath Cape Cod in the Greenleaf Terrace area near the university, advertised recently for $149,000, provides a good example.

- *Goods and Services.* ACCRA data suggest that the costs of goods and services are moderate. Groceries, health care, transportation and miscellaneous goods and services are all priced a few percentage points above or below national norms.

- *Taxes.* The overall tax burden is significantly below the national average. State income tax rates peak at 5.75 percent of taxable income exceeding $17,000. This results in an average income tax bill. The sales tax of 4.5 percent and the property tax rate of $1.11 per $100 of assessed valuation, based on 100 percent of fair market value, are below national norms.

Local and Regional Services

For a small city, Charlottesville provides an exceptional array of services. These are easily supplemented by the vast resources of nearby Richmond and Washington.

Transportation	Rating: 3

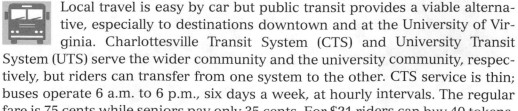 Local travel is easy by car but public transit provides a viable alternative, especially to destinations downtown and at the University of Virginia. Charlottesville Transit System (CTS) and University Transit System (UTS) serve the wider community and the university community, respectively, but riders can transfer from one system to the other. CTS service is thin; buses operate 6 a.m. to 6 p.m., six days a week, at hourly intervals. The regular fare is 75 cents while seniors pay only 35 cents. For $21 riders can buy 40 tokens. UTS operates seven days a week during the academic year but only on weekdays during summer and student holiday periods. Intercity rail service is exceptional,

as Charlottesville is located on north-south and east-west lines. About 40 trains per week connect the city to destinations like Washington, New York, New Orleans and Chicago. Charlottesville/Albemarle Regional Airport offers commuter service to Charlotte, Cincinnati, New York/La Guardia, and Washington/Dulles, among other locations.

Retail Services   Rating: 4

Charlottesville's historic downtown pedestrian mall, with its red brick promenade and post Civil War Georgian buildings, is a wonderful place to shop. There you will find over 150 stores, restaurants and galleries—mostly independently owned—and 2 movie theater complexes. Charlottesville Fashion Square, an indoor mall on Highway-29, is the city's largest mall. Anchored by Belk, JCPenney, Sears, and Stone and Thomas department stores, the mall also features about 70 specialty shops including many national chain stores, services and casual eateries. Also on Highway-29 are the upscale Barracks Road Shopping Center and freestanding Wal-Mart and Kmart discount stores.

Health Care   Rating: 5

Charlottesville is notable for the excellence of its medical care. The University of Virginia Health Sciences Center is one of the best academic medical centers in the nation. Its Health System, closely associated with the University of Virginia School of Medicine, is an integrated network of primary and secondary care offering services from wellness programs and routine checkups to the most technologically advanced care. Health System's 591-bed hospital and clinics throughout Charlottesville and neighboring counties attract patients from the local area, Virginia, and the Southeast. Services provided include primary and emergency care, comprehensive cancer and cardiac care, women's health concerns, and gastrointestinal care and neurology, among others. Also in Charlottesville is Martha Jefferson Hospital, a not-for-profit community facility furnishing state-of-the-art health care services to central Virginia. Martha Jefferson's more than 200 physicians represent more than 30 specialties. Key services include cancer and cardiac care, critical care, diagnostics, endoscopy and rehabilitation.

Community Services   Rating: 4

Charlottesville and Albemarle County provide a good selection of community services to all age groups from children to seniors. Facilities and services of the Senior Center are available to anyone 55 or older. The center offers recreational and educational programs such as games, book reviews, music, travelogues, arts and crafts classes, and parties, picnics and out-of-town trips.

Leisure Activities

Leisure activities to suit every taste are available in Charlottesville and nearby in the upper Piedmont and Blue Ridge Mountains. Big city attractions are only two hours away in Washington.

Cultural and Educational Activities   Rating: 4

The University of Virginia is the primary center of culture and recreation. Its Cabell Hall Auditorium is the home of the Charlottesville and University Symphony Orchestra while Old Cabell Hall hosts a Tuesday

Evening Concert Series. Plays produced by the university's Drama Department are performed on campus at the Culbreth Theatre. Other principal performing arts venues in and around Charlottesville include Lane Auditorium in the County Office Building, the Downtown Mall Amphitheater, and the Ashlawn–Highland Summer Festival. The Charlottesville Municipal Band presents free winter and spring concerts in Lane Auditorium before moving to the Downtown Mall Amphitheater for its summer evening concert series. The Amphitheater is also home to summer's Fridays After Five free concerts by various ensembles. Nearby Ashlawn–Highland, home of President James Monroe, hosts a Summer Festival of Opera and Musical Theatre in June, July and August, as well as other musical, dance and drama programs.

The University of Virginia and Piedmont Virginia Community College (PVCC) both offer comprehensive adult education programs. The university's School of Continuing Education fields a wide variety of credit and noncredit courses on topics ranging from computers to foreign languages and literature. PVCC also offers a wide range of courses from art to technology. Seniors are allowed to audit PVCC courses at no charge or take them for credit for nominal fees.

Recreational Activities	Rating: 5

 Diverse recreational options exist in and near Charlottesville. Spectator sports and participatory activities are popular here. The Virginia Cavaliers regularly host nationally ranked intercollegiate teams in football and basketball. Both city and county have excellent park systems and recreational programs. Charlottesville's 25 parks cover 890 acres and boast 6 recreation centers. Amenities include playgrounds, picnic shelters, sports fields, gymnasiums, golf courses and pools. Albemarle County's seven parks and three recreation centers cover approximately 2,000 acres. Their amenities include picnic shelters, swimming and boating facilities, and nature trails. Golf can be played at Charlottesville's public Birdwood Golf Course and at several other public, semi-private and private golf courses within a 30-mile radius of the city.

For a small city, Charlottesville has an excellent selection of movie theaters and restaurants. Quite a variety of cuisines, ranging from Brazilian and Indian to Colonial American, are available in settings as varied as the Historic Mitchie Tavern, the Downtown Mall, and suburban shopping centers.

Within an hour's drive of town are several farm wineries, Shenandoah National Park, and the Blue Ridge Parkway. The Monticello viticulture area, centered on Charlottesville, is now producing fine wines from European grape varieties formerly thought ill suited to the central Virginia environment. Many area wineries welcome visitors and offer facility tours and wine tasting. The Blue Ridge Parkway, which passes within 25 miles of Charlottesville, is a 469-mile scenic road connecting Shenandoah National Park in Virginia with Great Smoky Mountains National Park in North Carolina.

Following the crest of the Blue Ridge, the parkway provides ready access to George Washington National Forest and Shenandoah National Park. Sightseeing from numerous overlooks along the parkway and the national park's Skyline Drive, camping, hiking and picnicking are popular activities.

Work and Volunteer Activities	Rating: 3

 Although local unemployment rates have fallen to less than three percent in recent years, seniors continue to face tough competition from college students for paid work. Volunteer work, though, is plentiful.

Hospitals, libraries, schools, colleges, and historic sites such as Monticello and Ashlawn-Highland depend heavily on volunteers.

Crime Rates and Public Safety   Rating: 3

Charlottesville's crime statistics are somewhat mixed. Although the metropolitan area has lower than average rates for violent and property crime, the situation in the city itself is less satisfactory. Charlottesville's rate of violent crime is just below the national average but property crime is roughly 35 percent above average. A high rate of larceny-theft largely accounts for the high property crime rate; burglary and auto theft rates are below national norms. Upscale neighborhoods in the city and its surrounding areas appear quite safe.

Conclusion

Overall Rating 47

Charlottesville is a beautiful college town offering many advantages for retirement. Its greatest strengths are its lovely landscape, high quality of life, excellent health care and plentiful recreational choices. Its temperate subtropical climate will appeal to those who appreciate experiencing four distinct seasons but wish to avoid winter's worst rigors. There is little traffic congestion, residential neighborhoods and the downtown are very appealing, and air quality is excellent. The threat of earthquakes and hurricanes is very low, and tornadoes are infrequent in central Virginia. The city provides good community and retail services and many cultural and educational opportunities. Its principal weaknesses are middling crime rates, limited work and air transportation choices, and a cost of living slightly above the national average. Charlottesville rates as one of America's best small towns for a physically and mentally stimulating retirement.

Lexington, Virginia

The historic town of Lexington, with its beautifully restored and revitalized 19th century downtown, lovely residential neighborhoods, and picturesque campuses, is an exquisite southern college town and an excellent site for retirement. Founded in 1777 as the county seat of Rockbridge County, the town owes much of its character and success to heroic figures like George Washington, Stonewall Jackson, Robert E. Lee, and George Marshall, who once walked its streets. George Washington rescued Liberty Hall Academy (later to become Washington College) from financial oblivion in 1796 with a bequest of $50,000 and Robert E. Lee, as president of Washington College, revitalized the college during his 1865–1870 tenure. After his death in 1870, the institution was renamed Washington and Lee University. It has subsequently developed into one of America's outstanding small liberal arts colleges and is a vital center of cultural life in Lexington. Virginia Military Institute (VMI) is also significant in the history and intellectual life of Lexington. Thomas J. (Stonewall) Jackson was a professor at VMI prior to the Civil War, and that institution has educated thousands of citizen-soldiers over the years, including George C. Marshall and George S. Patton.

With a population of just 7,000 (excluding students) in town and 35,000 in Rockbridge County, Lexington is a very small town. But thanks to its colleges, it is able to offer residents an upscale and interesting lifestyle. Additional amenities are available in Charlottesville, 75 miles northeast, and in Washington, 190 miles away.

Lexington, Virginia

CLIMATE				
Month	Average Daily Temperature High Low	Daily Rel. Humidity Low	Average Monthly Precipitation	
	°F	%	Inches	
January	44 25	53	3.2	
February	47 27	50	2.7	
March	57 35	48	3.5	
April	67 43	45	3.0	
May	75 52	50	3.2	
June	83 60	52	4.6	
July	86 64	53	3.8	
August	85 63	56	4.1	
September	78 56	57	2.8	
October	68 44	52	3.0	
November	58 37	52	2.3	
December	47 28	54	3.1	

Annual Average

Total Days		Total Inches	
Clear	105	Precipitation	38.8
Partly Cloudy	112	Snowfall	22.0
Cloudy	148		

RATINGS

Rating Scale: 5 = excellent; 4 = very good; 3 = good; 2 = fair; 1 = poor

Rating:	1	2	3	4	5
Landscape					●
Climate			●		●
Quality of Life					●
Cost of Living				●	
Transportation		●			
Retail Services		●			
Health Care		●			
Community Services			●		
Cultural Activities			●		
Recreational Activities					●
Work/Volunteer Activities			●		
Crime					●

Total Points: 42

Landscape — Rating: 5

Lexington is located in west central Virginia on the gently rolling surface of the Shenandoah Valley. Bracketed by the Blue Ridge Mountains to the southeast and the Allegheny Mountains to the northwest, the

Shenandoah Valley is a lovely, largely rural region offering easy access to some of the most scenic terrain in the eastern states. Lexington's site at an elevation of 1,100 feet is extraordinarily beautiful. The town is skirted by the Maury River and enveloped by woodlands and small farms. Its residential areas and the college campuses are very nicely landscaped in a collage of lawns, flowers, and seasonally flowering dogwood and redbud under a canopy of large trees such as oak, maple, magnolia and pine.

Climate   Rating: 3

 Lexington experiences an upland version of the Southeast's humid subtropical climate. Weather changes are frequent and sometimes dramatic in fall, winter and spring, with steadier weather characterized by hot and humid conditions prevailing in summer. Spring and fall are delightful with milder temperatures and somewhat lower humidity. On average, winter days are cool rather than severely cold. The annual precipitation of 39 inches is well distributed throughout the year. About 22 inches of snow falls in a typical winter but it seldom lasts more than a few days at a time on the ground. Lexington enjoys an average frost-free season of 180 days and is sunny about 60 percent of the time.

Quality of Life   Rating: 5

 Lexington is a delightful community noted for its excellent quality of life. There is little noise from aircraft or motor vehicles. Interstate-64 and Interstate-81 come within three miles of town and provide convenient access to points east, west, north and south, yet are far enough away so as not to disturb the tranquility. The town and Rockbridge County comply fully with all national air quality standards. Lexington is clean and uncrowded, there are no noxious industries, and parking appears adequate downtown and on the college campuses. The community is very well planned and maintained. In the mid-1970s, the downtown streets were completely rebuilt, utility wires were put underground and brick sidewalks were installed in place of concrete. Meanwhile the Lexington Downtown Development Association restored and revitalized the retailing core. Currently, the entire downtown, Washington and Lee University, and VMI are listed in the National Register of Historic Places. And, thanks to the patronage of visitors and local residents, the charming downtown is economically thriving. Residents are particularly friendly and helpful even by the standards of other small college towns, and the uniformly polite greeting from VMI cadets is refreshing indeed.

Cost of Living   Rating: 4

 The cost of living in Lexington is evaluated as follows:

- *Composite.* ACCRA data are unavailable for Lexington so statistics for Roanoke, the nearest city for which ACCRA data are available, are used here. On that basis the cost of living in Lexington is estimated to be slightly below the national average.

- *Housing.* Housing costs approximate the national average. Many attractive homes with three or four bedrooms and two baths were priced between $100,000 and $200,000 in 1999. Prices are somewhat lower in nearby Buena Vista and in the surrounding countryside.

- *Goods and Services.* ACCRA data suggest that in Lexington the various categories of goods and services are priced at or below national norms. Costs of miscellaneous goods and services approximate the national average, whereas groceries, health care, transportation and utilities are priced five to ten percent below their national averages.

- *Taxes.* The overall tax burden in Lexington is well below the national average. State income tax rates peak at 5.75 percent of taxable income over $17,000 resulting in an average income tax liability. The sales tax rate of 4.5 percent and the property tax rate of 69 cents per $100 of assessed value, based on 100 percent of fair market value, are both below national norms.

Local and Regional Services

For a small town, Lexington provides an adequate array of services. These may be supplemented in Roanoke, 55 miles south, and Charlottesville, 75 miles northeast. Each is easily reached in an hour or so by freeway.

Transportation	Rating: 2

Although the private automobile dominates local transportation, the town is small enough that walking or bicycling are viable alternatives for many trips. There is no local bus service. Interstate-64 and Interstate-81 intersect about three miles east of town, providing convenient access to Roanoke, Charlottesville, and Washington, among other locations. Daily Greyhound intercity bus service is available in Lexington, and Amtrak trains stop in Clifton Forge, 30 miles west, and in Staunton, 40 miles north. Three trains per week travel west to Chicago and three east to Charlottesville and Washington. Additional north and southbound trains serve Charlottesville. Roanoke/ Woodrum Regional Airport, 50 miles south, provides nonstop jet service to four destinations including major hubs in Atlanta, Charlotte and Pittsburgh. Nonstop commuter destinations include Detroit and Washington.

Retail Services	Rating: 2

Lexington's charming downtown features a wide variety of unique shops, restaurants and service establishments, many housed in magnificently restored historic buildings. Several bookstores, antique shops and specialty food stores grace the downtown. Other shops stock gifts, original art, prints and posters, college merchandise, sporting goods, and men and women's clothing. Typical mass merchandise is available at the local Kmart on Highway-60 East and at a Wal-Mart on Highway-11, two miles north of town.

Health Care	Rating: 2

Stonewall Jackson Hospital, a community nonprofit facility with 50 beds and about 30 physicians on staff, provides primary health care services. An additional 50 beds are available in the hospital's extended care facility. Specialties provided include emergency services, family medicine, internal medicine, general surgery, ophthalmology, orthopedics, radiology, and gynecology. Stonewall Jackson Hospital recently became a partner in VaLiance Health, an association of independent health providers including Charlottesville's excellent University of Virginia Health System. The partners share resources and coordinate health care delivery to avoid duplication.

Basic public services are more than adequate. The Rockbridge Regional Library, headquartered in Lexington, is complemented by the college libraries, which are also open to the public. The colleges and various clubs and social organizations including the Jaycees, Lions Club, Rotary, Kiwanis, art and history clubs, and garden and social clubs offer members and guests a good mix of services.

Leisure Activities

For a small town, Lexington offers a very good assortment of leisure activities.

 Life in Lexington is significantly enhanced by the presence of two excellent colleges. Washington and Lee University is the ninth oldest institution of higher learning in the country and one of the strongest liberal arts colleges. Adjacent to its picturesque white colonnaded, red brick buildings and grounds is the expansive campus and parade ground of the Virginia Military Institute, the nation's oldest state-supported military college and fourth oldest technical college. Senior residents of Lexington may audit classes at Washington and Lee and attend summer session at VMI. Concerts and plays are performed regularly by students, faculty, and local and visiting artists at Washington and Lee's splendid Lenfest Center. Both colleges also sponsor numerous lectures free to the public. All summer long much of Lexington's culture moves outdoors. On the northern edge of town, the professional Theater at Lime Kiln hosts regional theater and music. Downtown's Davidson Park is the scene of Friday evening "Lexington Alive" concerts, while every two or three weeks in summer "Fridays in the Park" concerts are held in Glen Maury Park in nearby Buena Vista.

 Recreational opportunities of great variety are found in Lexington and nearby areas. Spirited intercollegiate athletic competition including nationally ranked teams in lacrosse and horseback riding may be seen at local colleges. On 10 Saturdays each fall the town goes wild as the Cadets of VMI or the Generals of Washington and Lee take on football rivals. Outdoors enthusiasts, especially, will appreciate the abundance of participatory activities in the beautiful Shenandoah Valley and Blue Ridge Mountains. One can hike, run, bird watch, picnic, and occasionally ski cross country along the Woods Creek Park and Chessie Nature Trails, which extend across Lexington and along the Maury River to Buena Vista. In Buena Vista's 315-acre Glen Maury Park, there are several picnic shelters, tennis courts, an outdoor roller-skating rink, and ball fields, an Olympic-size pool, nature trails and river fishing. Countywide there are 29 parks and playgrounds, 7 tennis courts, 11 swimming pools, 12 campgrounds and 18 picnicking sites. Golf can be played at the Lexington Golf and Country Club, and the Virginia Horse Center, a nationally renowned equestrian facility, lies just north of town. You can canoe on the Maury River and, 10 miles east, drive to the scenic Blue Ridge Parkway which offers spectacular vistas of the Shenandoah Valley and the Piedmont Plateau and easy access to the hiking, swimming, camping and other recreational resources of George Washington and Jefferson National Forests.

Historically significant attractions are also plentiful in Lexington and

Rockbridge County. Within a 20-mile radius are Natural Bridge, once owned by Thomas Jefferson, and the Cyrus McCormick Farm, with its restored blacksmith shop, gristmill and museum.

The best known sites in Lexington itself include Lee Chapel and Museum on the Washington and Lee University campus, the VMI and George Marshall museums at VMI, and the Rockbridge Historical Society and Stonewall Jackson House, downtown. Indeed, the college campuses and downtown Lexington are themselves historically and architecturally notable. Downtown also features a variety of dining experiences from informal sandwich and pub fare to full-course restaurant meals in gracious pre-Civil War buildings.

Work and Volunteer Activities	Rating: 3

Unemployment rates have been below three percent in Lexington and five percent in Rockbridge County in recent years. Even so, paid employment opportunities are limited by the small size of the local economy. Retailers, especially Kmart and Wal-Mart, employ some seniors. Many others find satisfaction in volunteer activities. Stonewall Jackson Hospital depends heavily on its 200 volunteers, as do the community's several educational institutions, cultural organizations, museums and libraries. Lexington's excellent visitor center is also staffed largely by energetic and helpful retirees.

Crime Rates and Public Safety	Rating: 5

Lexington and Rockbridge County are too small to be listed in the FBI's annual report Crime in the United States. Crime data from the local police department confirm that the incidence of property and violent crime in the town and the county are well below national norms. Lexington, particularly, has a very safe and secure feel to it, night or day.

Conclusion

Overall Rating 42 Lexington is a perfect little college town. Its physical and human environment is nearly ideal. Its site in Virginia's beautiful Shenandoah Valley, within view of the Blue Ridge Mountains, is beautiful and its historic colleges and downtown are idyllic. The valley's upland variant of the humid subtropical climate, with four distinct seasons and few severely hot or cold days, will appeal to many. Lexington's quality of life is excellent; it is clean, uncrowded, peaceful, and its residents are unusually friendly and well educated. For a small town, the availability of community services, culture, recreation, work and volunteer activities is very good. The community is relatively free of crime, and living costs are low. Only the town's modest endowment of retail and health care services and the absence of public transit and a commercial airport detract from its otherwise high rating. If you are open to retirement in a very special college town amidst the natural beauty and recreational assets of the Shenandoah Valley and Blue Ridge Mountains, give Lexington a careful look.

Chapel Hill, North Carolina

Described as the "Southern Side of Heaven" in Thomas Wolfe's classic autobiographical novel Look Homeward Angel, Chapel Hill remains one of America's exquisite smaller cities and an excellent place for an active retirement. Founded in 1795 as the home of the University of North Carolina (UNC), the

Chapel Hill, North Carolina

CLIMATE

Month	Average Daily Temperature High (°F)	Average Daily Temperature Low (°F)	Daily Rel. Humidity Low (%)	Average Monthly Precipitation (Inches)
January	50	27	55	3.7
February	53	29	52	3.8
March	61	37	49	4.3
April	72	46	45	3.6
May	79	54	54	3.9
June	85	62	56	4.0
July	89	66	58	4.3
August	87	65	60	4.5
September	82	58	59	3.7
October	72	46	53	3.1
November	62	37	52	3.2
December	53	29	55	3.3

Annual Average

Total Days		Total Inches	
Clear	111	Precipitation	45.5
Partly Cloudy	106	Snowfall	7.9
Cloudy	148		

RATINGS

Rating Scale: 5 = excellent; 4 = very good; 3 = good; 2 = fair; 1 = poor

Rating:	1	2	3	4	5
Landscape				●	
Climate			●		
Quality of Life					●
Cost of Living		●			
Transportation					●
Retail Services			●		
Health Care					●
Community Services					●
Cultural Activities					●
Recreational Activities					●
Work/Volunteer Activities			●		
Crime			●		

Total Points: 48

nation's first state university, Chapel Hill's civic life is very much intertwined with that of the academic community. The square-mile campus, with its Georgian-style red brick buildings, linked by brick paths and surrounded by wooded and grassy landscapes, dominates the town. The university provides educational, cultural and recreational opportunities galore and some of the best medical facilities in the United States. Downtown Chapel Hill, which stretches along Franklin Street where it parallels the campus, is one of the most vibrant downtowns in America and a delightful place to shop, dine or be entertained. With a population of about 45,000 in Chapel Hill itself, about 15,000 in adjacent Carrboro, and 120,000 in Orange County, the city and its surrounding areas are much busier than they were 30 years ago. Even so, Chapel Hill residents would argue that their community continues to offer the best of small town life in a highly cosmopolitan environment.

Landscape   Rating: 4

 Chapel Hill is located toward the eastern edge of the Piedmont Plateau in the central part of North Carolina. Spread across a gently to steeply rolling surface with an average elevation of 500 feet, the city is so heavily wooded that in some neighborhoods little sunlight reaches the ground when the trees are in leaf. Much of the city is sheltered by a canopy of large deciduous trees including oak, maple and hickory, while suburban areas are enveloped in a pine forest. Flowering shrubs such as dogwood and azalea are characteristic understory plantings.

Climate   Rating: 3

 Chapel Hill experiences a fairly mild variant of the Southeast's humid subtropical climate. Winter weather is cool and quite variable from day to day, whereas summer weather is relatively steady with average highs in the upper 80s and average lows in the mid-60s. Spring and fall are the most pleasant seasons, with mild to warm days and cool nights. Annual precipitation averages 45 inches and is well distributed throughout the year. Only eight inches of snow accumulates in a normal winter and it seldom persists on the ground for more than a few days. On average, Chapel Hill is sunny approximately 60 percent of the time and enjoys a frost-free period of about 200 days. The city's principal climatic negative is summer's fatiguing combination of heat and humidity. In contrast, weather conditions are nearly ideal in spring and fall when temperature and relative humidity readings are lower.

Quality of Life   Rating: 5

 Chapel Hill is notable for its excellent quality of life. Air quality is excellent and although there is some aircraft noise from the local airport and automotive noise from the traffic along the U.S.-15 bypass, noise levels are not excessive. Traffic congestion is increasing downtown and on the Carolina campus, and parking is tight. Fortunately, Chapel Hill's excellent public transit allows bus riders to escape driving and parking hassles. The city and campus are well planned and maintained and no heavy industry blights the landscape. Local shopping malls are wisely located on the periphery of town so as not to disrupt the village atmosphere of the traditional downtown, yet are easily accessed by car or public transportation. Residential neighborhoods are distinctly upscale and feature a good variety of housing from historic brick or frame dwellings near the city center to sprawling, brick ranch-style houses on the edge of town, all on wooded or carefully landscaped lots. Although Chapel Hill is not as quiet or peaceful as it was 20 or 30 years ago, its residents seem as friendly and well educated as ever, and very content with their lifestyle.

The cost of living in Chapel Hill is evaluated as follows:

- **Composite.** ACCRA data show that the overall cost of living in Chapel Hill is about 15 percent above the national average and nearly 10 percent above that of nearby Raleigh and Durham.

- **Housing.** Housing costs have risen sharply in Chapel Hill in recent years and are now fully 40 percent above the national average. Most middle-class housing is priced between $150,000 and $300,000. Such high prices reflect the high quality of Chapel Hill houses and the prestige value of the community. Comparable housing is available in the Raleigh–Durham area for perhaps 25 percent less.

- **Goods and Services.** ACCRA data indicate that goods and services are moderately priced in Chapel Hill. Utilities and transportation are priced at or slightly below national norms, whereas groceries and miscellaneous goods and services are priced seven or eight percentage points above. Health care costs are about 12 percent above the national average.

- **Taxes.** The overall tax burden significantly exceeds the national average. State income taxes are high. The first $12,750 of taxable income is taxed at the rather high rate of 6 percent, with rates topping out at 7.75 percent on income over $60,000. The combined state and local sales tax rate of six percent (five percent on groceries) is also above the national average. Although property tax rates are not unusually high, the high assessed value of properties translates into high property tax bills. At the current rate of $1.80 per $100 valuation, one would pay $3,600 per year on a $200,000 home, $5,400 on one worth $300,000.

Local and Regional Services

Chapel Hill's endowment of services is exceptional in quality and quantity. Additional resources are available in nearby Raleigh and Durham.

 Despite increasing traffic congestion downtown and on campus, the automobile remains the mode of choice for local travel. For many, though, Chapel Hill Transit bus service is a convenient and inexpensive alternative. Buses are clean and service is courteous and frequent along 15 fixed-route lines during daytime hours on weekdays. Fixed-route service is much thinner evenings and weekends but is nicely supplemented evenings and Sundays by Shared Ride, a door-to-door, dial-a-ride service. Shared Ride also links outlying suburban areas, which do not receive regular bus service, to the fixed-route system. The regular fare is 75 cents but seniors pay only 35 cents. Books of discounted tickets and bus passes offer substantial savings, and seniors can purchase passes at half price. Additional service is provided by Triangle Transit, which serves the Raleigh/Durham/Chapel Hill metropolitan area, and Greyhound, which provides service to more distant cities. Daily rail service is available north to New York and south to Tampa from the Durham Amtrak station, 10 miles north. Raleigh/Durham International Airport, 20 miles east of Chapel Hill, provides over 200 departures daily on 16 carriers. All major U.S. cities are accessible from the airport, 48 via nonstop flights.

The downtown areas of Chapel Hill and neighboring Carrboro are busy and exciting places despite competition from suburban malls and shopping centers. At all hours Franklin Street is alive with people strolling, shopping, dining and enjoying popular entertainment. Carr Mill Mall City Center, notable for its specialty shops and large upscale grocery, is also very popular. University Mall, a rather undistinguished enclosed mall on South Estes Drive, is Chapel Hill's largest shopping center. Anchored by Hudson/Belk and Dillard's department stores, the complex includes a number of national chain and specialty stores. Farmers markets operate on Tuesdays, April through October, at Cedar Falls Park in Chapel Hill and on Saturdays, March through December, in downtown Carrboro.

Health Care   Rating: 5

Chapel Hill is justifiably renowned for the excellence of its medical care. The University of North Carolina (UNC) medical complex includes the associated UNC Hospitals, Dental School, School of Medicine, School of Nursing, School of Public Health, and the Jaycee's Burn Center. With 665 beds and 470 resident and 750 attending physicians, UNC Hospitals compose an outstanding teaching facility offering complete health care services. Only 10 miles away in Durham is the outstanding Duke University Medical Center, noted especially for cardiac care and surgery. A large VA hospital is also located in Durham.

Community Services   Rating: 5

Chapel Hill, Carrboro and Orange County provide an excellent array of community services. Organizations such as the Retired Senior Volunteer Program (RSVP), Welcome Wagon and Newcomers Club help new residents feel at home. Senior centers operate in Chapel Hill, Carrboro and Hillsborough in Orange County and at numerous locations in the Raleigh/Durham area. Their programs include athletic and recreational activities, arts and crafts classes and workshops, and travel.

Leisure Activities

Leisure activities are rich and varied in Chapel Hill and additional attractions in Durham, Raleigh and the Piedmont countryside are within an hour's drive.

Cultural and Educational Activities   Rating: 5

The University of North Carolina, with 24,000 students and 2,400 faculty members, is the focus of culture and education in Chapel Hill. Its 1,600-seat Memorial Hall is home to the Carolina Union Performing Arts Series, which features musical concerts, musical theater and dance. The Carolina Union also hosts concerts, lectures and art exhibits in smaller performance venues at its campus facility. The UNC Departments of Music and Dramatic Art contribute much to community cultural life. The Music Department, one of the best in the country, sponsors a series of concerts showcasing classical music at Hill Hall and Person Hall. PlayMakers Repertory Company, a nationally recognized program of the Dramatic Art Department, presents six productions each academic year at the Paul Green Theatre on campus. Additional theatrical and musical events are offered in the intimate setting of the 300-seat Arts Center Theater in Carrboro, and the North Carolina Symphony pays frequent visits to Chapel Hill. Nearby venues in Raleigh and Durham, most notably those at Duke University, also schedule major performing arts series.

The visual arts are not neglected. The University's Ackland Art Museum's permanent collection exhibits Western art from the classical to contemporary eras, and the art of Africa and Asia. The Morehead Planetarium offers indoor astronomy, scientific exhibits and lectures, and an art gallery. Art exhibits may also be seen at the historic Horace Williams House downtown and at many privately owned galleries in Chapel Hill and Carrboro.

The university has much to offer educationally whether or not attendees enroll in a course or program. Its exceptional 4.3 million-volume library system is open to retirees, as are public lectures and symposia. In addition to regular academic programs, which are not expensive for state residents, seniors have access to classes on a wide variety of subjects at bargain prices through the Carolina College for Learning in Retirement.

Recreational Activities   Rating: 5

 Whether your sports and recreational interests are passive or active, Chapel Hill and vicinity has opportunities for everyone. UNC is a member of the NCAA's Atlantic Coast Conference, fielding 27 varsity teams in women and men's intercollegiate sports. The Carolina Tar Heels football and basketball teams regularly pack the house at Kenan Stadium and Dean E. Smith Center. Chapel Hill and Carrboro have excellent parks and recreation facilities, and neighboring communities provide additional resources. Chapel Hill's 10 parks contain picnic areas, play equipment, nature trails, athletic fields, lighted tennis courts, recreation centers, indoor and outdoor pools, and volleyball courts. The Parks and Recreation Department sponsors a summer Concert in the Park series and two big street fairs, Apple Chill in April and Festifall in October. Carrboro's five parks and recreation facilities provide picnic shelters and playgrounds, athletic fields, and basketball and tennis courts. The Chapel Hill/Carrboro YMCA boasts an Olympic-size indoor pool and numerous other athletic facilities. Just outside of town you can boat and fish at beautiful University Lake or enjoy a wider range of water sports at B. Everett Jordan Reservoir. Golf is played at the university's Finley Golf Course or at several other public courses within a 20-mile radius of Chapel Hill. Ice-skating is available all year at the Triangle SportsPlex in Hillsborough.

Chapel Hill is remarkable for its fine selection of excellent restaurants and movie houses. Several are clustered downtown on or just off Franklin Street; others are located at several of the city's smaller shopping centers. A variety of cuisines, from regional American to Northern Italian and Chinese, is available.

Work and Volunteer Activities   Rating: 3

 Although the local economy is booming and unemployment is at record low levels, retirees face severe competition from thousands of college students for paid work. Consequently, many older adults join local senior centers or get involved by volunteering. The YMCA, Service Corps of Retired Executives, local libraries, North Carolina Botanical Gardens, UNC Hospitals, and RSVP, are among the many organizations dependent on volunteers.

Crime Rates and Public Safety   Rating: 3

 Crime rates are moderate in Chapel Hill and vicinity, with Chapel Hill itself being somewhat safer than the rest of Orange County. The city's overall rate of violent crime is 30 percent below the national average while the property crime rate exceeds the national average by 15 percent. A high rate of larceny-theft largely accounts for the high property crime rate; rates for burglary and auto theft are below national norms.

Conclusion

Overall Rating 48 Chapel Hill may not be the idyllic small college town that it was 30 years ago but it remains an exquisite city offering many advantages for retirement. Its wooded landscape is pleasing to the eye and the community earns excellent ratings in quality of life, transportation, health care, community services and leisure activities. Residential neighborhoods, the downtown commercial core, and the UNC campus are very attractive and air quality is excellent. Although some may find summer's heat and humidity oppressive, most appreciate the mildness of the other seasons. The city's principal weaknesses are its moderate crime rates, modest endowments of retail services and part-time work opportunities for seniors, and rather high cost of living. Assuming you can afford to live here, though, Chapel Hill is one of America's best choices for an active and rewarding environment.

Pinehurst/Southern Pines, North Carolina

Referred to as the Pine Barrens by Scottish settlers who managed to eke out a meager living farming its poor, sandy soils during the 18th century, the Sandhills region centered on Pinehurst and Southern Pines has developed into a major resort and retirement center during the last 100 years. Attracted by the mild winter weather and good rail service, John Patrick founded Southern Pines as a health resort in 1887. Pinehurst was established as a winter resort in 1895 by Boston philanthropist James Tufts, who hired famed landscape architect Frederick Law Olmsted to design the village's New England-style layout, and a young Scot, Donald Ross, to design Pinehurst's first golf course. Their inspired designs helped define Pinehurst particularly, and the Sandhills area generally, as one of America's classic resort and retirement communities. With a population of about 8,000 in Pinehurst, 10,500 in Southern Pines, and 70,000 in Moore County, Pinehurst/Southern Pines today boasts over 40 golf courses, many of championship caliber, and a plethora of other recreational attractions including tennis, horseback riding, polo, bicycling, walking and swimming. Shopping in the villages' charming downtowns and at the local mall is adequate for day-to-day needs, and the amenities of the Raleigh/Durham/Chapel Hill metropolitan area are only 70 miles away.

Landscape   Rating: 4

Pinehurst/Southern Pines is located in the Sandhills toward the western edge of North Carolina's Coastal Plain. Named for their deep sandy soils and rolling hills, the Sandhills region is higher and better drained than most parts of the Coastal Plain. Rain disappears quickly into the sands so the environment seems relatively dry even though annual precipitation totals nearly 50 inches. Much of the landscape is mantled in a longleaf pine forest that also includes seasonally colorful magnolia, azalea, camellia, dogwood, holly, and other flowering trees and shrubs.

Pinehurst-Southern Pines, North Carolina

CLIMATE

Month	Average Daily Temperature High	Average Daily Temperature Low	Daily Rel. Humidity Low	Average Monthly Precipitation
	°F		%	Inches
January	55	33	51	3.5
February	57	34	50	3.7
March	66	40	48	3.7
April	74	47	45	3.5
May	82	56	50	3.5
June	89	64	48	4.6
July	91	68	56	5.8
August	89	67	58	5.4
September	84	63	55	3.9
October	75	50	51	2.9
November	64	40	52	2.1
December	55	34	51	3.6

Annual Average

Total Days		Total Inches	
Clear	112	Precipitation	46.2
Partly Cloudy	106	Snowfall	5.6
Cloudy	147		

RATINGS

Rating Scale: 5 = excellent; 4 = very good; 3 = good; 2 = fair; 1 = poor

Rating:	1	2	3	4	5
Landscape				●	
Climate			●		
Quality of Life					●
Cost of Living			●		
Transportation		●			
Retail Services			●		
Health Care				●	
Community Services				●	
Cultural Activities		●			
Recreational Activities				●	
Work/Volunteer Activities				●	
Crime				●	

Total Points: 42

Map showing Pinehurst-Southern Pines, North Carolina area, including Uwharrie National Forest, Whispering Pines, Aberdeen, Fort Bragg Military Reservation, Camp Mackall, and highways 15, 24, 1, 211, 220.

Climate **Rating: 3**

Good air and water drainage modify the humid subtropical climate, making it somewhat milder and drier than in surrounding areas. Winter weather is quite variable from day to day but is usually mild enough for golf. Summer's combination of heat and humidity, though, discourages afternoon play. Spring and fall are nearly perfect, with warm days followed by cool nights. Annual precipitation averages 46 inches, and is heaviest in summer and lightest in fall. Less than six inches of snow accumulates in a typical winter and generally melts within a day or so. On average, the Sandhills area is sunny about 60 percent of the time and has a frost-free period of about 215 days. The region's principal climatic negative is summer's fatiguing, hot humid weather. On the other hand, weather conditions are very pleasant in spring and fall when moderate temperatures and humidity prevail.

Quality of Life   Rating: 5

 The quality of life in the Sandhills region is excellent. Pinehurst and Southern Pines are both very quiet with little noise from road or air traffic. Air quality is excellent and the low population density, good urban design, and absence of heavy industry contribute to uncrowded streets except during major golf tournaments. The park-like atmosphere of the towns is pronounced, especially in the uniformly affluent Pinehurst, which reminds one of much more expensive Carmel, California. In both communities, a good variety of historic and contemporary housing lines well-wooded streets surrounding the village centers. Pinehurst's central core, with Olmsted's complex of looping tree-lined streets converging on the village shopping district, is uniquely charming, but the traditional downtown and grid pattern residential area of Southern Pines are also attractive. Residents and visitors tend to be affluent, well mannered and friendly. Both communities are enviably peaceful and free of the stresses commonly associated with urban areas.

Cost of Living   Rating: 3

 The cost of living in Pinehurst/Southern Pines is evaluated as follows:

- *Composite.* No ACCRA data are available for the Sandhills region but inferences can be drawn from ACCRA data for nearby cities such as Raleigh and Durham. Additional data were gathered from field observations and local sources. On these bases, the composite cost of living in Pinehurst/Southern Pines approximates the national average.

- *Housing.* Exploration of the area reveals a moderate supply of housing of varied age and style for sale at bargain prices. Many single-family residences, with three bedrooms and two baths, located alongside or near golf courses, sell for between $100,000 and $200,000. Condominiums are even less expensive—some adjacent to fairways are priced in the $60,000 to $70,000 bracket. A good selection of senior housing from apartments to long-term care facilities is also available.

- *Goods and Services.* Groceries, transportation, health care, and miscellaneous goods and services are priced near national norms. Utility costs are perhaps 10 percent above the national average as a result of summer air conditioning and winter heating requirements.

- *Taxes.* The overall tax burden in Pinehurst/Southern Pines modestly exceeds the national average. Relatively high state income tax and sales tax rates are nearly balanced by lower-than-average property taxes.

Local and Regional Services

The Sandhills region offers a good array of services considering the small size of its towns. Substantial additional resources are an hour's drive away in the Raleigh/Durham/Chapel Hill metropolitan area.

Transportation   Rating: 2

Local travel is primarily by private automobile; there is no fixed-route public transit in Moore County. Sandhills Place to Place provides local limousine, van and minivan service, while Kirk Tours furnishes bus service to Raleigh, Durham, Chapel Hill and Fayetteville. Additional intercity bus service is provided by Greyhound-Trailways. Daily rail service north to Washington and New York, and south to Tampa and Miami, is available from the Southern Pines Amtrak station. Commuter air service connects Moore County Airport in Pinehurst with USAir's hub in Charlotte, while Raleigh/Durham International Airport, 65 miles north, provides comprehensive air service to all major American cities.

Retail Services   Rating: 3

Although the historic downtown areas of Southern Pines and nearby Aberdeen, with their antique and specialty shops, galleries and restaurants, are pleasant enough, the Pinehurst Village shopping district, laid out by Frederick Law Olmsted, is nothing short of idyllic. Essentially a replica of a late 19th century New England town center, Pinehurst Village is a perfect place to stroll from boutiques to galleries to restaurants. Goods and services sold here are typically of excellent quality.

Standard shopping is available at Pinecrest Plaza on Highway 15-501 and along the Highway 15-501 retail strip between Pinehurst and Southern Pines. Pinecrest Plaza is a modern shopping center anchored by Belk and JCPenney department stores. It also features numerous clothing stores, specialty shops and restaurants. The retail strip along the highway includes a variety of large and small stores including a Kmart. A daily farmers market operates year-round at 450 Pennsylvania Avenue in Southern Pines.

Health Care   Rating: 4

Pinehurst /Southern Pines is notable among smaller places for the high quality of its medical care. Firsthealth Moore Regional Hospital in Pinehurst is an up-to-date 397-bed facility serving as regional referral center for a 14-county area. Its medical staff of more than 135 physicians represents every major medical specialty and its respiratory care department is considered among the best in the Southeast.

Community Services   Rating: 4

Pinehurst, Southern Pines and Moore County collectively provide an excellent array of community services. Moore County Transportation Services transports older adults to shopping, work and medical facilities. The County Department of Aging provides arts and crafts, educational, exercise, and social and recreational programs. It also operates four nutritional sites that provide hot lunches, runs a Meals-on-Wheels program, and hosts popular annual special events such as Senior Games in the Pines and the Senior Citizen Handicraft and Hobby Fair.

Leisure Activities

Golf epitomizes leisure activities in the Sandhills region but the golf-impaired also find plenty to do here. Additional cultural and recreational attractions are only an hour or two away in Raleigh, Durham, Chapel Hill, and Charlotte.

Cultural and Educational Activities	Rating: 2

 Sandhills Community College in Southern Pines is a focus for education and culture. The college's continuing education division provides a variety of academic and practical courses of general interest and its Owens Auditorium is the site of the Sandhills Little Theater, which offers five community theater productions each year. Owens Auditorium also hosts band, orchestral, choral, jazz, and visiting artists concerts. The Arts Council of Moore County provides a variety of programs for its 2,500 members. It owns the Performing Arts Center in downtown Southern Pines, which hosts Jazz in January concerts, visits by the North Carolina Symphony Orchestra, plays, and a travelogue series.

Recreational Activities	Rating: 4

 Golf is played year-round on courses suited to all skill levels. Pinehurst # 2, the jewel of the golfing crown and one of eight courses at the Pinehurst Resort and Country Club, was the site of the 1999 U.S. Open Golf Tournament. Forty additional courses, most of which operate on a daily fee basis, are found within a 25-mile radius of Pinehurst # 2. The whole area—Pinehurst, Southern Pines, and neighboring communities—is truly a golfer's heaven.

As befits a major year-round resort area, many recreational choices tempt golfers and non-golfers alike. Horseback riding, tennis, archery, trap and skeet shooting, and hunting are popular sports. Area streams and small lakes offer many attractive sites for sailing, canoeing, swimming and fishing, while over 10 fitness trails circling lakes and reservoirs and traversing scenic woodlands provide countless opportunities for hiking, jogging and bicycling. Municipal parks in Aberdeen, Pinehurst, Southern Pines and neighboring communities boast a good variety of facilities including tennis and volleyball courts, ball fields, playgrounds, and picnic areas and shelters. Indoor fitness facilities are open to the public on a daily fee basis at Moore Regional Health and Fitness Center. Its assets include an eight-lane lap pool, sauna and steam room, indoor track, racquetball, weight and workout equipment, and aerobics classes. Alternately, you can bowl or play pool at the large Sandhills Bowling Center in Aberdeen, enjoy croquet and lawn bowling at the Pinehurst Resort and Country Club, take in a movie at a local movie house, or dine at one of the excellent restaurants in Pinehurst or Southern Pines. American cuisine is the norm here, with several dining rooms offering a health-conscious menu in addition to their regular fare.

For spectator sports, you must travel 100 miles to Charlotte or 70 miles to the Raleigh/Durham/Chapel Hill area. Charlotte boasts NBA basketball and NFL football whereas the latter cities offer outstanding NCAA basketball and football at North Carolina State, Duke, and the University of North Carolina.

Work and Volunteer Activities	Rating: 4

 The Sandhills economy, based mainly on tourism and retailing, has generated a number of jobs in recent years. Owing to minimal competition from college students, seniors can compete effectively for many of these positions. Volunteer work is also abundant. Moore Regional Hospital in Pinehurst, the Southern Pines Library, the County Department of Transportation Services, the County Department of Aging and area schools provide many openings.

Crime Rates and Public Safety   Rating: 4

 Although Moore County as a whole has crime rates lower than the national average, great variations occur from place to place. Pinehurst and most rural and golf course communities have among the lowest crime rates in the nation. On the other hand, a very high incidence of violent and property crime in one minority neighborhood in the western part of Southern Pines skews that city's overall crime rate to levels not experienced in most parts of town. As elsewhere, if you pick your neighborhood carefully, there is little to fear from crime in Pinehurst or Southern Pines.

Conclusion

 Overall Rating 42 The Sandhills region centered on Pinehurst and Southern Pines is an ideal retirement place for golfers and a very good one for devotees of outdoor recreation wishing to live in a fairly cosmopolitan small town. The heavily wooded, gently rolling Sandhills landscape is beautiful, and the region's climate is mild enough for outdoor activities in all four seasons. The quality of life is excellent throughout the region and especially so in the charming Village of Pinehurst and the historic center of Southern Pines. Residential areas, parks, and village retail centers are delightful places to walk about in an environment unspoiled by pollution, traffic congestion, architectural ugliness or crime. Local availability of health care, community services, recreation, and work and volunteer opportunities is exceptional for such small towns. Even the area's lesser assets in retail services, transportation and culture meet most peoples' day-to-day needs, and much greater resources are only an hour or two away in Raleigh/Durham/Chapel Hill and Charlotte. Finally, all the advantages of living in Pinehurst/Southern Pines are available at a cost of living near the national average. On that basis, the Sandhills region is surely a best buy among America's upscale retirement places.

Asheville, North Carolina

Founded in 1793 as a small crossroads village in the wilderness of western North Carolina, Asheville has blossomed in the 20th century into one of the major mountain resorts in the eastern United States. With a population nearing 70,000 in the city and 195,000 in Buncombe County, Asheville is the regional center for manufacturing, transportation, health care, retailing, and banking and professional services. Virtually surrounded by the unspoiled grandeur of the Blue Ridge Mountains, Asheville is small enough to retain much of the intimacy and gentle pace of a small city while offering urban services and amenities usually found only in much larger places. Although the majority of recent residential development has occurred in nearby retirement oriented communities like Hendersonville and Brevard, Asheville remains a choice retirement locale for those desiring a busy, productive lifestyle in an environment of great natural beauty.

Landscape   Rating: 5

 Asheville is located at an elevation of 2,200 feet on the rolling surface of the Asheville Plateau. The French Broad River flows across the western part of the city, adding interest to the landscape and posing an

Asheville, North Carolina

CLIMATE				
Month	Average Daily Temperature High Low	Daily Rel. Humidity Low	Average Monthly Precipitation	
	°F	%	Inches	
January	48 26	59	3.5	
February	51 28	56	3.6	
March	58 34	53	5.1	
April	69 43	50	3.8	
May	76 51	57	4.2	
June	81 58	59	4.2	
July	84 62	63	4.4	
August	84 62	63	4.8	
September	78 56	64	4.0	
October	69 43	57	3.3	
November	59 34	56	3.3	
December	50 28	59	3.5	

Annual Average

Total Days		Total Inches	
Clear	101	Precipitation	47.7
Partly Cloudy	113	Snowfall	15.8
Cloudy	151		

RATINGS

Rating Scale: 5 = excellent; 4 = very good; 3 = good; 2 = fair; 1 = poor

	Rating:	1	2	3	4	5
Landscape						●
Climate					●	
Quality of Life					●	
Cost of Living				●		
Transportation				●		
Retail Services						●
Health Care						●
Community Services					●	
Cultural Activities					●	
Recreational Activities						●
Work/Volunteer Activities					●	
Crime				●		

Total Points: 49

occasional threat of flooding to low-lying areas. The older part of town is built on the fairly gentle plateau surface but newer neighborhoods extend into the densely wooded foothills of the Blue Ridge. From almost any vantage point, Asheville's site is spectacular. The Blue Ridge Mountains, traversed by the scenic

Blue Ridge Parkway, arc around the city from northeast to southwest, and extend off to the west where they meld with the peaks of the Great Smokies. Several peaks visible from town, including Mount Pisgah, are more than a mile high. They provide a lush green backdrop to Asheville in summer and a snowy white one in winter.

The lower slopes of the mountains and much of the city are clothed in a luxuriant southern forest of deciduous and coniferous trees grading into hardy northern conifers such as spruce at higher elevations.

Climate   Rating: 4

 Asheville enjoys an upland variant of the humid subtropical climate; the city's moderate elevation causes temperatures to be a little cooler in all seasons than those recorded nearer sea level at the same latitude. Precipitation averages 48 inches annually and is well distributed throughout the year. About 16 inches of snow falls in the city in a normal winter, but considerably more accumulates in the mountains. Snow seldom persists on the ground for more than a few days at a time in Asheville because winter days are fairly mild, with temperatures rising well above freezing most afternoons. Spring and fall weather is variable from day to day, but is generally pleasant. Summer has the steadiest weather of the year, with warm to hot days and cool nights. On average, the city is sunny 61 percent of the time and has an average frost-free season of 190 days. All in all, Asheville's climate is quite pleasant. It offers four distinct seasons, the stimulation of frequent weather changes during much of the year, and ample precipitation. Its principal negative is high relative humidity, especially in summer. This results in discomfort and a hazy atmosphere that impedes views of the Blue Ridge. Conditions are more pleasant in spring and fall when relative humidity reaches its annual minimum.

Quality of Life   Rating: 4

 The quality of life in Asheville varies from good to excellent depending on proximity to annoyances like the airport and freeways. Some jet noise is encountered on the southern edge of town near the airport, and the Interstate-40 and 240 loop around central Asheville impacts nearby areas with traffic noise, although not severely. The city meets all federal air quality standards and most parts of town are free of unsightly industrial areas. There is little evidence of crowding or traffic congestion. Plenty of parking is available at the malls and downtown. Unfortunately, the large downtown parking ramps are among the ugliest seen anywhere and quite out of character with the central business district's many delightful art deco buildings that date from the 1920s and 1930s. The downtown is undergoing something of a revival with an eclectic mix of antique and specialty shops, apparel stores, arts and crafts galleries, bookstores and restaurants. Nonetheless, some storefronts downtown remain empty, and the area's New Age flavor may not appeal to all. Most residential neighborhoods—whether in the older core of the city, in the hills overlooking downtown, or in the suburban fringe—are very pleasant and show considerable pride of ownership.

The cost of living in Asheville is evaluated as follows:

- *Composite.* ACCRA data for Asheville reveal a composite cost of living about four percent above the national average.

- *Housing.* Housing costs are about 18 percent above the national average but the housing stock is excellent. Many attractive older homes with three bedrooms and two baths located in leafy settings in the city were recently priced between $110,000 and $160,000. The lower slopes of the mountains just north and east of downtown are dotted with lovely homes on heavily wooded lots, many offering spectacular views of the Asheville Plateau and the Blue Ridge Mountains.

- *Goods and Services.* ACCRA data show transportation costs to be about four percent above the national average. Groceries, utilities, and miscellaneous goods and services are priced near their national averages, whereas health care is a bargain at a cost approximately nine percent below average.

- *Taxes.* Unlike many southern states, North Carolina does not have low taxes. In fact, the overall tax burden in Asheville is slightly above the national average. State income taxes and the combined state/local sales tax rate of six percent both exceed national norms, whereas local property taxes approximate the national average.

Local and Regional Services

As regional capital of western North Carolina, Asheville offers a wide range of services to residents and visitors. Additional resources are available in Greenville, South Carolina, 65 miles south.

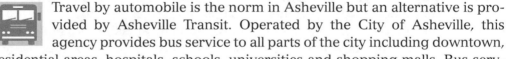 Travel by automobile is the norm in Asheville but an alternative is provided by Asheville Transit. Operated by the City of Asheville, this agency provides bus service to all parts of the city including downtown, residential areas, hospitals, schools, universities and shopping malls. Bus service is free downtown; elsewhere fares are a nominal 75 cents a ride or $30 for a monthly pass. Seniors and the handicapped pay half these rates. Unfortunately, most routes do not operate on weekends and weekday service is infrequent, with hourly or half-hourly service being typical. Greyhound provides intercity bus travel, and air travel is possible from Asheville Regional Airport, 12 miles south. Nonstop jet service connects Asheville Airport to major hubs at Atlanta and Charlotte. A greater variety of flights is provided at Greenville/Spartanburg Airport, 68 miles south. Daily Amtrak service north to New York and south to New Orleans is also available in Greenville.

Most shopping occurs at two major malls and several smaller shopping centers. The downtown business district, although somewhat revitalized in recent years in a rather funky New Age style, is not yet a competitive threat to the rather antiseptic mainstream retailers at the malls. Asheville Mall, in the eastern part of town, is by far the largest retailing complex. Anchored by Belk, Dillard's, Sears, and JCPenney department stores, the mall also includes 100 specialty stores and restaurants and a multiscreen cinema complex. Biltmore Square, on the southwestern fringe of the city, has Belk, Dillard's, Goody's and Proffitt's stores as anchors, plus 50 specialty shops and a six-screen theater. Two Wal-Mart and four Kmart discount stores are located in smaller shopping centers around the city. Considerably upscale from these is historic Biltmore Village, located near the entrance to the Biltmore Estate in south Asheville. It markets a variety of arts and crafts, gifts, antiques, and apparel in charming turn-of-the-century buildings.

Health Care   Rating: 5

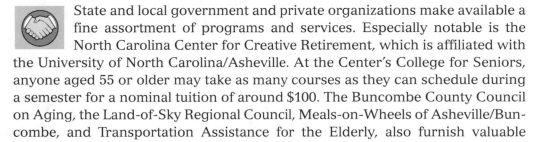

Asheville is justifiably renowned for the quality and sophistication of its medical care. The area's two main not-for-profit hospitals, Memorial Mission Hospital and St. Joseph's Hospital, are now partnered as the Mission St. Joseph Health Care System, which offers almost every medical specialty from neonatology to gerontology. Its centers of excellence include: Owen Heart Center, Ruth and Billy Graham Children's Health Center, Helen Powers Women's Health Center, oncology, orthopedics, urology, and emergency and trauma services. With about 700 beds, the unified system is by far the largest hospital complex and the medical referral center for western North Carolina. Veterans can use the facilities of the Asheville VA Medical Center; this 535-bed hospital offers a wide range of medical services and functions as a major VA system referral center for heart surgery.

Community Services   Rating: 4

State and local government and private organizations make available a fine assortment of programs and services. Especially notable is the North Carolina Center for Creative Retirement, which is affiliated with the University of North Carolina/Asheville. At the Center's College for Seniors, anyone aged 55 or older may take as many courses as they can schedule during a semester for a nominal tuition of around $100. The Buncombe County Council on Aging, the Land-of-Sky Regional Council, Meals-on-Wheels of Asheville/Buncombe, and Transportation Assistance for the Elderly, also furnish valuable resources and opportunities to seniors.

Leisure Activities

Asheville, its neighboring communities, and the mountains surrounding the city provide a great variety of leisure activities.

Cultural and Educational Activities   Rating: 4

Cultural and educational opportunities are abundant and varied in Asheville. The Asheville Symphony and visiting ballet and operatic companies perform at the Thomas Wolfe Auditorium downtown. Asheville Community Theater provides a series of professional theatrical productions annually, and a foreign film series offers feature films not generally shown in mainstream movie houses. Music and dance are featured at the annual Mountain Dance and Folk Festival, and the nearby Brevard Music Festival hosts a staggering list of classical and popular music events during a six-week summer season.

The visual arts are also prominent locally. The Asheville Art Museum, the Folk Art Center, the Asheville Art League, the Arts Alliance, and Pack Place showcase native American and contemporary artistic works and handicrafts. Biltmore Estate is the pride of Asheville. This 255-room French Renaissance chateau, built by George Vanderbilt in 1895, is America's largest private residence. The house, which is surrounded by magnificent gardens, contains Mr. Vanderbilt's collection of 50,000 art objects, antiques and furnishings. It merits repeated visits. Finally, the University of North Carolina/Asheville (UNCA) deserves favorable mention. Rated as one of the country's six best public arts universities in 1993, UNCA offers undergraduate and graduate degrees in the liberal arts. And, in affiliation with the North Carolina Center for Creative Retirement, it offers a great variety of low-cost short courses of interest to seniors.

Recreational Activities	Rating: 5

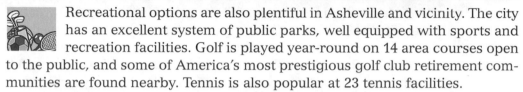 Recreational options are also plentiful in Asheville and vicinity. The city has an excellent system of public parks, well equipped with sports and recreation facilities. Golf is played year-round on 14 area courses open to the public, and some of America's most prestigious golf club retirement communities are found nearby. Tennis is also popular at 23 tennis facilities.

Outdoor enthusiasts appreciate Asheville for its proximity to national parks and forests. The Blue Ridge Parkway, best thought of as a long, narrow national park, skirts Asheville and provides access to some of the highest and most scenic mountain regions of the eastern United States. Great Smokey Mountains National Park, only 60 miles west of town, may be reached via the parkway or alternate routes. The national park features gorgeous vistas of heavily wooded mountains and valleys from roadside overlooks or from points along the park's more than 850 miles of trails. Picnicking, sightseeing, camping, hiking, swimming and fishing are popular activities. Outside the park, numerous lakes and rivers provide opportunities for boating, sailing, rafting, canoeing and fishing. The mountains are also valued for hunting, and in winter skiing is possible at several resorts within 100 miles of the city. The Asheville area is also known for the variety and excellence of its restaurants, some of which are clustered downtown while others are widely scattered throughout the urban area. Movie theaters, bowling centers, and the excellent Asheville/Buncombe Library System offer additional diversions.

Work and Volunteer Activities	Rating: 4

Asheville's strong retailing sector generates many part-time jobs, some of which may appeal to seniors. The North Carolina Center for Creative Retirement and the Senior Opportunity Center place seniors in enriching volunteer assignments. Many retirees tutor students through the former organization's Seniors in the Schools program. Others contribute to the community by volunteering in hospitals, senior centers, the public library, and at the visitor center.

Crime Rates and Public Safety	Rating: 3

Asheville's crime statistics are somewhat mixed. Although the metropolitan area has lower than average rates of violent and property crime, the situation in Asheville itself is less satisfactory. Asheville's violent crime rate is about 15 percent above the national average and its property crime rate is perhaps 40 percent above average. These data largely reflect fairly high rates of aggravated assault, burglary, and larceny-theft in the city, and especially in its economically poorer neighborhoods. Much of Asheville, especially its afflu-ent suburban areas, is quite safe.

Conclusion

Overall Rating 49 Asheville ranks highly on most indicators of suitability for retirement; its principal weaknesses are moderate crime rates and a rather weak down-town. The city's greatest strengths are its lovely natural setting, high-quality and relatively inexpensive health care, strong retail sector, and plentiful recreation. Its subtropical climate, moderated by elevation, appeals to those who desire four seasons but do not want to be snowbound for days at a time. Although suburban areas and nearby towns like Hendersonville and Brevard have attracted an increasing percentage of the Asheville region's retirees in recent years, Asheville still rates highly in quality of life factors. There is little traffic congestion and air quality is excellent. The city provides very good community services and ample opportunities in culture, education, part-time work and volunteerism. Hap-pily, all these positives are available at a cost of living only slightly above the national average. What more could you ask of a retirement town?

Hendersonville, North Carolina

Once a hunting ground for the Cherokee, Hendersonville received its first town charter in the 1840s when it had a population of several hundred res-idents living a basic rural farming existence. As transportation improved, Hen-dersonville became a popular summer resort for lowland Carolinians who came to the mountains to escape that season's intense heat. In the 20th century its long-standing reputation as a health and summer resort has contributed to its becom-ing the leading retirement center of North Carolina's mountainous west. Although only 25 miles south of Asheville and 22 miles east of Brevard, Hen-dersonville is separated by open space from these neighboring centers and retains its own unique identity. Yet it is close enough to them for its residents to easily access their many attractions. With a population approximating 10,000 in the city and 80,000 in Henderson County, the urban area is small enough to pos-sess small-town charm while large enough to offer the many amenities crucial to upscale retirement. Notable for abundant cultural opportunities, an attrac-tively refurbished pedestrian-friendly downtown and lovely residential areas, Hendersonville also offers convenient access to the Blue Ridge and Great Smokey Mountains. Not surprisingly, local residents tend to congratulate them-selves on their good fortune to live here.

Landscape   Rating: 5

Hendersonville rests at an elevation of 2,200 feet on the gently rolling surface of the valley of the French Broad River. Virtually surrounded by the foothills of the Blue Ridge, with major peaks along the Blue Ridge Parkway only 20 or 30 miles to the north and northwest, Hendersonville has a beautiful setting. Much of the county is forested with oaks and pines pre-dominating on the lower hillsides while hardier coniferous trees are found at higher elevations. Gentle slopes in the valley typically offer a visually appealing mixture of land uses featuring farmland, golf courses, and suburban housing interspersed with wooded areas.

Hendersonville, North Carolina

CLIMATE				
Month	Average Daily Temperature High Low	Daily Rel. Humidity Low	Average Monthly Precipitation	
	°F	%	Inches	
January	48 26	59	4.2	
February	51 27	56	4.3	
March	59 34	53	6.1	
April	70 42	50	4.5	
May	76 50	57	4.7	
June	82 57	59	5.0	
July	85 61	63	4.7	
August	84 60	63	5.8	
September	78 54	64	4.5	
October	69 42	57	4.2	
November	58 33	56	3.9	
December	51 27	59	4.4	

Annual Average

Total Days		Total Inches	
Clear	110	Precipitation	56.1
Partly Cloudy	103	Snowfall	9.2
Cloudy	152		

RATINGS

Rating Scale: 5 = excellent; 4 = very good; 3 = good; 2 = fair; 1 = poor

Rating:	1	2	3	4	5
Landscape					●
Climate				●	
Quality of Life					●
Cost of Living			●		
Transportation		●			
Retail Services			●		
Health Care				●	
Community Services				●	
Cultural Activities				●	
Recreational Activities					●
Work/Volunteer Activities			●		
Crime					●

Total Points: 47

Climate   Rating: 4

 The local climate is broadly similar to that of Asheville and Brevard, although somewhat rainier than Asheville and less rainy than Brevard. The upland variant of the humid subtropical climate is pleasantly mild

compared to that experienced at lower elevations in the Carolinas. The annual average of 56 inches of precipitation is evenly distributed seasonally. About nine inches of snow falls in the city in a typical winter but considerably more accumulates in the mountains. Snow tends to persist on the ground in town for only a few days at a time because winters are fairly mild, with average highs near 50 degrees. Spring and fall weather varies considerably from day to day but most days are warm and nights cool. Summer weather is steadier with average highs in the low 80s and lows near 60 degrees. The frost-free period averages 168 days, allowing outdoor gardening from late April through early October. In summary, Hendersonville's climate is mild yet variable enough to be stimulating. It features four clearly defined seasons, frequent changes in weather, and moderate levels of sunshine. Its major negatives are high relative humidity and moderately heavy precipitation throughout the year.

| Quality of Life | Rating: 5 |

 Hendersonville offers residents an excellent quality of life. It is quiet, although not quite so quiet as Brevard, and its air quality is excellent. The city is peaceful, clean and uncrowded, and parking is adequate downtown and at the mall. There are no noxious industries, population densities are low, and traffic is fairly light though major streets can be moderately busy at rush hour. The city itself seems well planned; its nicely landscaped, revitalized downtown is delightful, and its residential areas are attractive. These days, though, most new homes are found outside the corporate limits in county territory where attractive single-family residences are rather widely scattered across the landscape. Residents are friendly and helpful and seem anxious to welcome visitors and potential residents alike to their delightful city and region.

| Cost of Living | Rating: 3 |

 The cost of living in Hendersonville is evaluated as follows:

- *Composite.* ACCRA data are unavailable for Hendersonville but costs there do not likely differ greatly from those of nearby Asheville. The overall cost of living is about five percent above the national average.

- *Housing.* Data from local sources suggest that the median price of a home with three bedrooms and two baths is about $150,000. A great variety of housing is available, ranging from factory-built houses on their own land for $70,000 through condominiums in the $60,000 to $100,000 category, to suburban estate homes on huge lots for prices exceeding $250,000. A drive through the many desirable neighborhoods reveals attractive homes in wooded settings or perched on hillsides offering breathtaking views.

- *Goods and Services.* ACCRA data for Asheville and local sources of information suggest that in Hendersonville transportation costs are slightly above national norms, whereas groceries, miscellaneous goods and services, utilities and health care are priced near or slightly below their national averages.

- *Taxes.* As in Asheville, the overall tax burden is slightly above the national average. State income taxes and the combined state/local sales tax rate of six percent both exceed national norms. Property taxes, though, are somewhat below the national average. Within Hendersonville city limits, the annual property tax on an average $150,000 home would be $1,700. Property taxes are lower in unincorporated county territory.

Local and Regional Services

For a small town, Hendersonville provides an unusually fine assortment of services. Exceptional additional resources are available in Asheville, only 25 miles away.

Transportation   Rating: 2

 As in Brevard, travel in Hendersonville is overwhelmingly by private automobile. There is no local area public transit; Greyhound/Trailways, though, does provide intercity bus service to Asheville and, from there, to all parts of the country. Volunteers, especially from local churches, shuttle from place to place elderly residents who are unable to drive. Commercial air transportation is available from Asheville Regional Airport, 11 miles north, but Greenville/Spartanburg Airport, 50 miles southeast, provides a greater variety of flights. Daily Amtrak service north to New York and south to New Orleans is also available in Greenville.

Retail Services   Rating: 3

Historic downtown Hendersonville—centered on the distinctively serpentine Main Street, lined with trees, shrubbery, and flower planters, and featuring bright green benches placed strategically along wide sidewalks—is the heart and soul of the city. Added to the National Register of Historic Places in 1988, downtown is home to 150 businesses comprising an ideal mix of specialty shops, antiques stores, and service and eating establishments. Unlike many older downtowns, Historic Hendersonville is thriving, being extremely popular with residents and visitors alike. In contrast, Blue Ridge Mall, located two miles east of the city center near Interstate-26, is less successful. Although anchored by JCPenney, Belk Simpson, and Kmart stores, at least 17 empty stores were counted there during a recent visit.

Health Care   Rating: 4

Margaret R. Pardee Memorial Hospital, with 222 beds and more than 200 physicians and dentists on staff representing 31 specialties, provides good routine medical care. Standard services include 24-hour emergency care, medical, surgical, orthopedic, intensive and coronary care, radiation therapy, and mental health services. Nearby Asheville offers excellent additional medical resources.

Community Services   Rating: 4

 The city and county provide high-quality services. Opportunity House, a nonprofit organization located at 1411 Asheville Highway, Hendersonville houses classrooms, woodworking and woodcarving rooms, facilities for lapidaries and potters, two auditoriums, and a large kitchen. Opportunity House is the area's largest organizer of activities for newcomers, hobbyists and seniors. It provides lectures, arts and crafts courses, exercise classes, bridge, sports, trips, dinners and dances. College courses are fielded in cooperation with Blue Ridge Community College. Also notable is the Henderson County Public Library, located in downtown Hendersonville. With over 188,000 books, extensive reference and audio and videotape collections, and varied program offerings, the library is a valuable resource for people of all ages.

Leisure Activities

Hendersonville, like neighboring Asheville and Brevard, offers many leisure options to residents and visitors.

Cultural and Educational Activities   Rating: 4

 The performing arts are well represented in Hendersonville and the surrounding area. Flat Rock Playhouse, designated as the State Theater of North Carolina and recognized as one of the top summer-stock theaters in America, is only three miles south of town. From late May through mid-October it produces comedies, musicals, and dramas having wide audience appeal. Theatrical entertainment is also offered by the Hendersonville Little Theater, Absolute Theater Company, and the Belfry Players, while musical performances suiting all tastes are provided by the Hendersonville Community Concert Band, the Carolina Chamber Singers, and the 70-piece Hendersonville Symphony Orchestra. Additionally, the Hendersonville Friends of Chamber Music annually host five concerts featuring outstanding guest artists from around the country. Top-quality musical talent is also featured in summer at the nearby Brevard Music Center, and Asheville hosts a multitude of cultural and artistic offerings throughout the year. Both Brevard and Asheville are within a 30-minute drive of Hendersonville.

The visual arts and education are also significant in Hendersonville. The Arts Center, located in the historic Skyland Hotel on Main Street, includes classrooms, studio space, and a gallery for local and visiting art shows. The Singleton Center in Flat Rock features bimonthly exhibitions of the works of local, regional, and national artists in its main gallery. Also in Flat Rock is state-supported Blue Ridge Community College, which offers academic and applied courses of interest to students of all ages, as well as lectures and concerts for the general public.

Recreational Activities   Rating: 5

 Hendersonville is justifiably renowned for its recreational advantages. Golf is played year-round on most of the area's five public courses and five private/semi-private courses. City and county parks are well staffed and equipped. Nine parks provide athletic fields, miniature golf, tennis, racquetball, basketball and shuffleboard courts, as well as picnicking facilities, nature trails, and an outdoor Olympic-sized pool. The city's recently expanded YMCA is strongly fitness oriented. Its excellent facilities include an indoor 25-meter pool, a whirlpool, sauna, gymnasium, four lighted indoor tennis courts, and a weight-training/wellness center complete with free weights, Nautilus and aerobic equipment. Just two miles north of downtown is a 32-lane bowling center, the largest in western North Carolina.

Movie buffs can choose among three unique venues. The most conventional of these is the five-screen 4-Seasons Cinema located near Blue Ridge Mall. Skyland Arts Cinema is located downtown in the former ballroom of the Skyland Hotel. This theater seats 70 in comfortable chairs at small tables. Catering to mature audiences, this unique theater serves food, coffee, wine and beer. Devotees of high quality foreign and alternative films are welcome to join the Henderson Film Society, which has a screening room at Blue Ridge Mall.

Outdoors enthusiasts benefit from Hendersonville's proximity to national parks and forests. The Blue Ridge Parkway, which passes within 12 miles of the city, provides convenient access to Pisgah National Forest and the most scenic route to Great Smokey Mountains National Park, 70 miles west of town.

Work and Volunteer Activities   Rating: 3

A limited number of part-time jobs of interest to seniors are typically available in local retail and service industries. Larger numbers of Hendersonville's very active senior population do important volunteer work at the local hospital, library, visitors bureau, and at various cultural and educational venues. Opportunity House makes extensive use of volunteers from its membership of 2,000 in carrying out its many senior and community programs.

Crime Rates and Public Safety   Rating: 5

Hendersonville and Henderson County are among America's most crime-free places. In fact, in one recent year Hendersonville had the lowest overall crime rate in a sample of 60 retirement towns. In all categories of crime, the local area ranks far below national norms year after year. Such an excellent public safety record doubtless derives in part from the favorable demographics of the county population but it also reflects a highly visible and effective police presence in the community.

Conclusion

Overall Rating 47 Like its neighbor Brevard, Hendersonville is a highly desirable place for retirement for those wishing to live in a safe and friendly small city offering many amenities typical of much larger places. Its gently rolling landscape in the foothills of the Blue Ridge Mountains is beautiful, and its mild, upland variant of the humid subtropical climate will appeal to many. The local quality of life is excellent. The delightfully refurbished yet traditional downtown is a joy whether you are shopping, seeking entertainment, food or drink, or simply walking about. Air quality is excellent and there is little noise, visual pollution or traffic congestion. Most services and amenities essential for upscale retirement are well represented in Hendersonville and are easily augmented in nearby Asheville. Health care, community services, and culture and recreation are strong pluses here, while retail services and work and volunteer opportunities are good for a small city. Finally, all these blessings are available at a moderate cost of living in a virtually crime-free environment. This makes Hendersonville very appealing indeed.

Brevard, North Carolina

Although only 35 miles southwest of Asheville and 22 miles west of Hendersonville, Brevard is a world apart from these larger western North Carolina cities. It is a picture-postcard perfect place reminiscent of the mythical town of Mayberry in the classic Andy Griffith television show. But Brevard is no Disneyesque movie set; it is a real community of lovely but unpretentious frame and brick homes on sloping tree-lined streets surrounding a thriving, traditional downtown business district. With a population approaching 7,200 within the corporate limits, 16,000 in the urban area and 28,000 in Transylvania County, Brevard preserves the look and feel of a small town while offering many amenities not generally available in places of its size. Thanks to Brevard College and the Brevard Music Festival, higher culture is as abundant in town as outdoor recreation is in the nearby Blue Ridge Mountains. The town's friendly residents congratulate themselves on their good fortune to live in Brevard and agree that it is an ideal place in which to retire.

CLIMATE				
Month	Average Daily Temperature High Low		Daily Rel. Humidity Low	Average Monthly Precipitation
	°F		%	Inches
January	50	25	59	5.4
February	53	27	56	5.5
March	61	33	53	7.2
April	70	41	50	5.4
May	77	49	57	5.8
June	82	57	59	5.8
July	85	61	63	5.9
August	84	60	63	6.5
September	78	55	64	5.4
October	70	42	57	4.9
November	60	32	56	4.7
December	52	27	59	5.5

Annual Average

Total Days		Total Inches	
Clear	110	Precipitation	67.9
Partly Cloudy	103	Snowfall	11.2
Cloudy	152		

RATINGS

Rating Scale: 5 = excellent; 4 = very good; 3 = good; 2 = fair; 1 = poor

Rating:	1	2	3	4	5
Landscape					●
Climate				●	
Quality of Life					●
Cost of Living			●		
Transportation		●			
Retail Services			●		
Health Care			●		
Community Services			●		
Cultural Activities					●
Recreational Activities					●
Work/Volunteer Activities			●		
Crime					●

Total Points: 46

Landscape   **Rating: 5**

Brevard lies in a fertile southwest to northeast-trending valley drained by the French Broad River. With rolling hills to the southeast of town and Pisgah National Forest and the Blue Ridge Mountains forming its northwestern boundary, Brevard's setting is unusually beautiful. Fully 85 percent of the county is wooded and 35 percent is included in national forest, known locally as the Land of Waterfalls. Although Brevard itself is located at an elevation of 2,230 feet, elevations as high as 6,000 feet above sea level are found only 10 or 12 miles to the northwest in the Blue Ridge Mountains. Except for patches of farmland on the rolling valley floor, much of the valley, the town and the lower slopes of the mountains are wooded with oaks and pines, grading into hardier conifers like spruce at the highest elevations.

Climate   Rating: 4

 Brevard's climate is similar to that of Asheville but considerably rainier. The upland humid subtropical climate, moderated by elevation, is a little cooler and wetter all year than the climate at places at the same latitude but nearer sea level. The town's annual average of 68 inches of precipitation is evenly distributed seasonally. About 11 inches of snow falls in the valley in a normal winter but much more accumulates in the higher mountains. Snow seldom persists for very long in Brevard because winter days are typically mild. Spring and fall weather is generally pleasant, with warm days and cool nights. Summer weather is relatively steady with average highs in the low 80s, average lows around 60 degrees, and abundant rainfall. The frost-free period averages 160 days. In summary, Brevard's climate is mild yet stimulating. It features four clearly defined seasons, frequent changes in weather, and moderate levels of sunshine. Its principal negatives are high relative humidity and rather heavy precipitation.

Quality of Life   Rating: 5

 Brevard provides an excellent quality of life. There is very little noise from automobiles or aircraft, and air quality is excellent. The town is peaceful, clean and uncrowded. Parking is adequate downtown, at local shopping centers, and on the grounds of the Brevard Music Festival. There are no heavy industries, population densities are low, and traffic is light, except on festival evenings in summer. The town is well planned and its nicely landscaped neighborhoods reflect a pleasing combination of moderate affluence, good taste, and a desire to preserve the community's unique character.

Brevard is growing more slowly than Asheville or Hendersonville and thus has been spared the rough edges of these and other Sunbelt cities. Historic downtown Brevard is charming and economically healthy, thanks to the hard work of members of the Heart of Brevard Downtown District and the patronage of local shoppers and visitors. Residents are extremely friendly and welcoming, and evidently dearly love their little town and seek to keep it the perfect place it is.

Cost of Living   Rating: 3

The cost of living in Brevard is evaluated as follows:

- *Composite*. ACCRA data are unavailable for Brevard but costs there probably do not differ greatly from those of nearby Asheville. The overall cost of living is about five percent above the national average.

- *Housing*. Data from local real estate sources indicate that the median price of a single-family residence with three bedrooms and two baths in the City of Brevard is between $130,000 and $160,000 with condominiums being perhaps half as expensive. Just outside the city limits, many new homes in the $100,000 to $200,000 price range are on the market.

- **Goods and Services.** ACCRA data for Asheville and local sources suggest that in Brevard transportation costs are slightly above the national average, whereas groceries, miscellaneous goods and services, and health care are priced near or slightly below national norms. Utilities are somewhat cheaper in Brevard than in Asheville. Day-to-day purchases are available locally at reasonable prices. Competition between local Wal-Mart and Kmart stores and a popular seasonal farmers market helps keep costs down.

- **Taxes.** As in Asheville, the overall tax burden is slightly above the national average. State income taxes and the combined state/local sales tax rate of six percent both exceed national norms. Property taxes, though, are somewhat below the national average. Within Brevard city limits, the annual property tax on an average $130,000 house would be $1,400. Property taxes are considerably lower in county territory.

Local and Regional Services

Although a very small town, Brevard provides an array of services quite adequate for day-to-day needs. Exceptional additional resources are found only 35 miles away in Asheville.

Transportation	Rating: 2

 Travel in the Brevard area is largely by private automobile; no public transportation except taxi service is available. Fortunately, most destinations are so close that walking or bicycling are reasonable alternatives to driving. Commercial air travel is possible from Asheville Regional Airport, 22 miles north, but Greenville/Spartanburg Airport, 70 miles southeast, provides a greater variety of flights. Daily Amtrak service north to New York and south to New Orleans is also available in Greenville.

Retail Services	Rating: 3

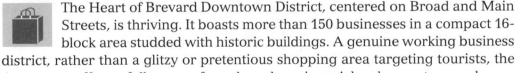 The Heart of Brevard Downtown District, centered on Broad and Main Streets, is thriving. It boasts more than 150 businesses in a compact 16-block area studded with historic buildings. A genuine working business district, rather than a glitzy or pretentious shopping area targeting tourists, the downtown offers a full range of goods and services. A hardware store, a charming toy store, an excellent bakery, several jewelry and music stores, and numerous restaurants are among the highlights here. Three days a week, June through October, a farmers market sets up downtown. On the outskirts of the city, discount shopping is available at Kmart and Wal-Mart.

Health Care	Rating: 3

 Transylvania Community Hospital, with 94 beds and more than 35 physicians and surgeons on staff, provides good, routine medical care including coronary and cancer care and 24-hour emergency service. Nearby Asheville offers excellent and comprehensive medical resources.

Brevard, Transylvania County, Brevard College, and several fraternal organizations furnish high-quality services to residents. Especially notable is the Transylvania County Library. With over 60,000 books, this facility is exceptionally well funded and stocked for a small-town library. Its resources are easily supplemented by those at Brevard College, just north of downtown. Local branches of social and fraternal organizations such as AARP, Elks, Eastern Star, Jaycees, Kiwanis, Lions, Masons, Rotary and Shrine provide many services to members and the community. Transylvania Community Hospital operates the local Meals-on-Wheels program.

Leisure Activities

Brevard, nearby communities, and the Blue Ridge Mountains provide a good variety of leisure activities.

Cultural and Educational Activities   Rating: 5

 Although strong cultural and educational programs are ongoing throughout the year, summer is a special time in Brevard. From late June through early August, the Brevard Music Festival hosts a seemingly endless series of over 40 consecutive band, choral, chamber music, and symphonic concerts, as well as musical theater and opera at its covered open-air auditorium. Indefatigable music lovers can take in the entire summer program for a season ticket price of only $275. The Brevard Festival of the Arts, held annually in the week beginning July 4th, features orchestral and choral music, craft and museum exhibitions, art and flower shows, and a forest tour. Most festival events are free. The Brevard Chamber Orchestra and Brevard Little Theatre present four concerts and four popular plays in spring, summer, fall and winter, while Brevard College hosts faculty and student musical recitals and the Brevard Concert Series in its outstanding new Porter Center for the Performing Arts. The college's continuing education program is of particular interest to seniors. Each year more than 250 noncredit courses in academic subjects, health and fitness activities, cultural experiences, local interest topics and field courses, hobbies, and self-improvement courses are offered. Courses are also available for audit by seniors at the Brevard campus of Blue Ridge Community College, which also hosts a series of lectures, plays and concerts. Additional cultural and educational resources are found in Asheville and Hendersonville. The May through October program of plays and musicals at the Flat Rock Playhouse, home of the State Theatre of North Carolina, is especially noteworthy.

Recreational Activities   Rating: 5

 Brevard and nearby areas offer many and varied recreational choices. Golf is played year-round on 4 local courses with over 20 additional golf courses being found within an hour's drive in the Asheville/Hendersonville area. Eighteen tennis courts, ten public and eight at the Racquet Club, are available locally. Swimming is popular at the municipal swimming pool and in the lakes and rivers of Pisgah National Forest. Main Street, downtown, is the site of the newly renovated one-screen Falls Theatre. Several excellent restaurants and a wonderful 1950s-atmosphere soda shop offer additional diversions downtown, and an 18-lane bowling facility is located on U.S.-64 West.

Pisgah National Forest, which borders Brevard on the northwest, provides residents and visitors unlimited outdoor recreation. Popular pursuits there include sightseeing by car, picnicking, camping, and hiking; canoeing, swimming and fishing in countless lakes and streams; and hunting for deer, turkey, waterfowl and small game. In winter, cross-country skiing is possible on numerous trails at higher elevations. The Blue Ridge Parkway is only 20 miles away at its closest approach to Brevard. It provides a wonderfully scenic route to Great Smokey Mountains National Park through some of the eastern United States' most dramatic valley and mountain landscapes.

Work and Volunteer Activities   Rating: 3

 Brevard's strength as a center for culture, education, recreation and retailing generates a number of part-time jobs of interest to seniors. Many retirees find fulfilling volunteer work at the Music Center, county library, Transylvania Community Hospital, and at the local chamber of commerce and visitor center.

Crime Rates and Public Safety   Rating: 5

 Brevard consistently rates as one of America's safest towns. According to FBI statistics, the city and county rank far below national norms in all crime categories. Local lore has it that "crime is almost nonexistent" and that many people feel so secure that they don't bother locking their doors at night. Such personal security doubtless derives in part from Brevard's small size and from the favorable demographics of its population. But it probably also is a result of the good work of the city's excellent police force, which is much in evidence and clearly in touch with the community and its needs.

Conclusion

Overall Rating 46

Brevard is a near-perfect place for retirement for those wishing to live in a charming, friendly and safe small town offering an abundance of amenities typically found only in much larger cities. Its physical site in a gently rolling valley at the foot of the Blue Ridge Mountains is lovely, and its mild, upland humid subtropical climate is seldom severely hot or cold. It offers residents an excellent quality of life. Environmental pollution, traffic congestion, and urban ugliness are entirely lacking. The strong downtown shopping district is the center of the community and, like the city's lovely residential neighborhoods, is a delightful place to enjoy on foot. Local availability of retail and community services, health care, and part-time and volunteer work is good, and the cultural and educational assets of Brevard and vicinity are remarkable for a small town and easily augmented in nearby Asheville.

Brevard's major weakness is the absence of a public transit system, so access to a car is almost essential. On the other hand, its many benefits are available at a cost of living only marginally above the national average. All things considered, Brevard ranks as one of the best places in America for sophisticated small-town retirement in an exceptionally beautiful and unspoiled setting.

Annapolis, Maryland and New Bern, North Carolina

Annapolis, Maryland and New Bern, North Carolina are also worth considering for retirement. Both occupy Tidewater sites and offer convenient access to sheltered coastal waters ideal for boating, sailing and fishing. Mariners and history buffs will feel at home here. Both cities are among the oldest in the United States and contain several charming historic districts.

Annapolis, Maryland

Annapolis proper is a small city of 35,000 people that exudes small-town charm in its older sections. Add in the suburbs, though, and the Annapolis area population exceeds 180,000. Just over the horizon are Washington and Baltimore, two major metropolitan areas easily accessed by car or public transportation. Annapolis is Maryland's state capital, site of the U.S. Naval academy and self-styled Sailing Capital of the World. Chesapeake Bay lies just east of Annapolis harbor and is reached via the Severn River.

The city's principal weaknesses are environmental, economic and social. Normally pleasant weather is occasionally interrupted by polar outbreaks in winter and by hot, humid periods and smog episodes in summer. Housing costs and the state sales tax burden are well above national norms. Crime rates, especially violent crime rates, are high in Annapolis even though they are below average countywide.

The greatest strengths of Annapolis are recreation, culture and transportation. Water sports are king in and around Annapolis but golf, spectator sports at the Naval Academy and several state and county parks provide recreational alternatives. The city has its own ballet, opera and symphony and the outstanding performing arts assets of Washington are only 35 miles away. Good local and intercity transit makes it easy to get around Annapolis and to travel to Baltimore and Washington. Baltimore/Washington International Airport provides excellent air service and Amtrak furnishes exceptional rail transportation from Baltimore and Washington. Easy to escape but hard to leave, Annapolis is a good place for an active retirement.

New Bern, North Carolina

New Bern, located on the Neuse Estuary at the juncture of the Neuse and Trent Rivers, is a thriving seaport of some 20,000 people with an additional 30,000 residents within a 10-mile radius. Colonial capital of North Carolina between 1766 and 1776 and state capital from 1776 to 1794, the city today boasts scores of restored historic homes, a charming old downtown and the Tryon Palace, home to the last colonial governor. Halfway between New York and Florida, New Bern is becoming increasingly popular for retirement among residents of the Northeast.

Like most small towns, New Bern has only modest shopping, cultural and public service assets. Public transit is indequate. The community's many strengths as a retirement place include its moderate subtropical climate (although summer's combination of heat and humidity can be fatiguing), high quality of life and abundant outdoor recreation. The Trent and Neuse Rivers and Pamlico Sound provide sheltered waters ideal for swimming, fishing, sailing, boating and water-skiing. Nearby Croatan National Forest offers sites for hiking, picnicking and water sports. Six 18-hole golf courses and numerous tennis courts are open throughout the year in and around New Bern. The overall cost of living is slightly below the national average, housing is a bargain and taxes are moderate. Medical care is good and crime rates are low. For many, New Bern would be an excellent place for retirement.

The Southeast Coast Retirement Region

Climate:
Humid subtropical–Sarasota, Gainesville, Thomasville, Covington, Savannah, Fairhope

Tropical savanna–Naples

Place Description	Overall Rating	Page
Naples, Florida	42	84
Perhaps unique amid the urban sprawl of south Florida, Naples offers a very high quality of life in a tropical setting.		
Sarasota, Florida	47	89
Sarasota is unique in Florida for the enormous variety and high quality of services, culture and recreation offered residents and visitors at a cost of living only slightly above the national average.		
Gainesville, Florida	48	95
Gainesville provides college town amenities at low prices in an inland subtropical environment.		
Thomasville, Georgia	41	101
Tranquil Thomasville offers gracious living at modest cost in a landscape of gently rolling hills clad with oak and pine.		
Covington, Louisiana	42	106
A blend of small town, suburban and rural elements, Covington offers retirement in a lovely subtropical setting within easy reach of the bright lights and metropolitan amenities of New Orleans.		
Savannah, Georgia	not rated	111
Attractive and affordable, Savannah has many places to explore, including more than 2,400 architecturally and historically significant buildings.		
Fairhope, Alabama	not rated	112
Fairhope, with its outstanding residential neighborhoods and architecturally interesting and commercially viable downtown, offers an excellent quality of life at low cost.		

The Southeast Coast Retirement Region stretches 700 miles from Naples, deep in southwestern Florida, to Covington, just across Lake Pontchartrain from New Orleans. Long the favorite state for retiree relocation, Florida has experienced runaway growth over several decades that has destroyed the natural beauty of large areas, pushed public services to the limit, and overwhelmed the state's infrastructure. As a result, few Florida cities are now able to provide the high quality of life and the amenities crucial to retire in style. Nonetheless, Naples and Sarasota, two affluent resort and retirement towns on the Gulf Coast, and Gainesville, in north central Florida, although not entirely free of growing pains

83

caused by rapid urban expansion, remain among the most livable places in Florida. Also highly desirable are Thomasville, Georgia and Covington, Louisiana. Both offer gracious living at modest cost in a tranquil subtropical environment. Savannah, Georgia and Fairhope, Alabama are also worth considering for retirement.

Naples, Florida

First settled in the 1880s when it was accessible only by water, Naples remained a remote outpost in coastal southwest Florida until its isolation was broken by the arrival of the railroad in 1927. Although the Great Depression and World War II slowed growth, improvements in road and air transportation beginning in the 1950s led to accelerating population growth and economic development in Naples and Collier County over the next four decades. After Hurricane Donna devastated much of Naples in 1960, the city was rebuilt according to a master plan that has produced a townscape with distinctive architecture and a manicured look in residential areas and public spaces. Like Palm Beach on Florida's east coast, Naples is a relatively small, affluent city rapidly becoming engulfed in countywide urban sprawl beyond its city limits. With a population of only 20,000, the City of Naples now constitutes only ten percent of the Naples metropolitan area (Collier County) and its percentage of the county total will doubtless continue to decline in coming years. Nonetheless, with its lovely white sand beaches, cultural and recreational amenities, excellent shopping, and uniquely attractive historic neighborhoods, Naples can be expected to remain the premier community of Collier County and one of Florida's top locales for a truly upscale retirement.

Landscape	Rating: 4

Naples is the southernmost city on Florida's west (Gulf) coast. With an average elevation of six feet above sea level, Naples is flat and unusually susceptible to flooding from hurricane storm surges, yet it continues to attract new residents drawn by its tropical ambiance. Although the natural vegetation of coastal southwest Florida consists largely of grasses, pines and bald cypress, these have been replaced in the urban area by exotic tropical ornamentals such as royal and coconut palms, which thrive only in tropical or near tropical conditions. Naples' beautiful landscape also includes a plethora of flowering plants including several varieties of bougainvillea and magnificent stands of magnolia, laurel, oak, and Australian pines which provide shade that is badly needed especially during the long, hot summer.

Climate	Rating: 3

Although most retirement guidebooks describe the climate as subtropical, the correct term is tropical savanna. In the mainland United States this virtually frost-free climate is found only in southernmost Florida; the rest of the state has a humid subtropical climate with somewhat cooler winters and occasional frosts. Naples' climate features two seasons. The winter half of the year—November through April—is warm, sunny and relatively dry, while the summer half—May through October—is hot and humid with frequent afternoon thundershowers. Annual precipitation averages 53 inches and peaks in the July through September period, which receives nearly half the annual total.

Naples, Florida

CLIMATE				
	Average Daily Temperature		Daily Rel. Humidity	Average Monthly Precipitation
Month	High	Low	Low	
	°F		%	Inches
January	76	53	59	1.9
February	77	54	57	2.0
March	81	58	56	2.3
April	84	62	54	1.7
May	87	70	57	4.6
June	90	71	63	7.8
July	91	73	65	8.1
August	91	73	67	8.5
September	90	73	67	9.2
October	86	67	63	4.0
November	82	60	61	1.2
December	77	55	61	1.4

Annual Average

Total Days		Total Inches	
Clear	98	Precipitation	52.7
Partly Cloudy	168	Snowfall	0.0
Cloudy	99		

RATINGS

Rating Scale: 5 = excellent; 4 = very good; 3 = good; 2 = fair; 1 = poor

Rating:	1	2	3	4	5
Landscape				●	
Climate			●		
Quality of Life				●	
Cost of Living		●			
Transportation		●			
Retail Services					●
Health Care				●	
Community Services			●		
Cultural Activities			●		
Recreational Activities					●
Work/Volunteer Activities				●	
Crime			●		

Total Points: 42

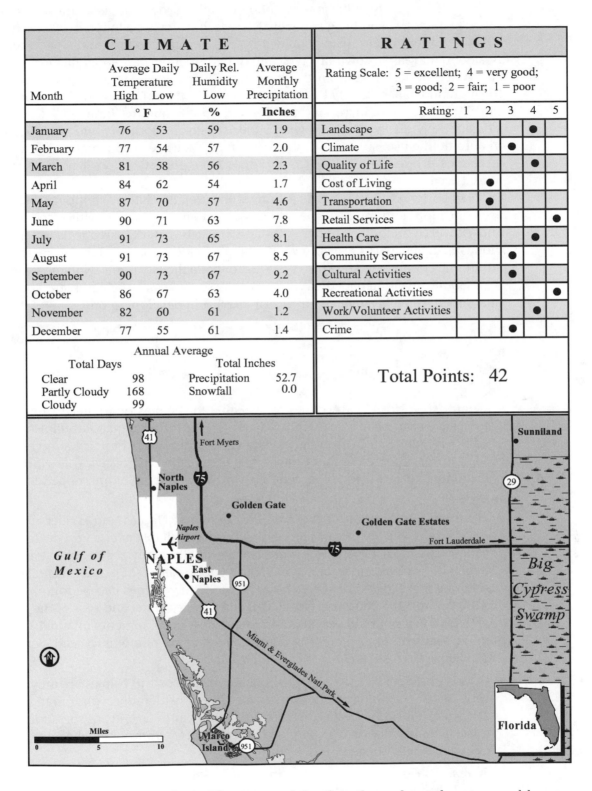

Naples is sunny about 70 percent of the time throughout the year, and has an average frost-free season of 365 days. The area's principal climatic negative is the very long, hot humid summer. On the other hand, weather conditions are generally very pleasant from November through April.

The quality of life is very good in Naples proper but is a little less satisfactory in outlying suburbs. There is little noise pollution in Naples itself except along major boulevards and adjacent to the municipal airport. Residential areas in town are typically quiet but suburban areas farther inland suffer additional noise from the Interstate-75 freeway. Air quality is excellent throughout Collier County but the rapid urbanization of areas north and east of the city is leading to increasing traffic congestion along the Tamiami Trail (U.S.-41) especially during the busy winter tourist season. Both city and county cater to automobile use, so parking is satisfactory. There are no poor neighborhoods in Naples proper, but Collier County does have pockets of poverty in its rural inland area.

Naples' long public beach is a wonderful asset, its historic shopping districts are charming, and much of the city has a park-like ambiance with nicely treed and flowered neighborhoods. Although the city's park acreage is relatively modest, Naples' parks are very well equipped, landscaped and maintained, and additional county and state parks are just outside the city limits. Naples is a well-planned and well-managed city whose notable flaws are the complete absence of a public transit system and a lack of interest in developing one.

 The cost of living in Naples is evaluated as follows:

- *Composite.* No ACCRA data are available for Naples or Collier County but inferences can be drawn from ACCRA data for the affluent south Florida city of West Palm Beach. Additional data were gathered from local sources and field observations. On these bases, the composite cost of living in Naples is estimated to be 10 to 30 percent above the national average, depending on location.

- *Housing.* Exploration of the area indicates that Naples and Collier County have a good variety of new and resale housing available over a very wide price range. The most expensive properties are single-family residences along the beach in Naples proper; prices of $500,000 to $1,000,000 are not unusual here. Inland a few blocks, attractive older single-family homes can be found in the $200,000 to $400,000 price range. Outside the city limits and east of the Tamiami Trail prices are lower still, and the newest developments inland 10 or 15 miles feature single family residences and condominiums priced between $100,000 and $200,000.

- *Goods and Services.* Aside from housing, living costs in Naples are only modestly above the national average but they are considerably higher than in less attractive Florida cities. Groceries, utilities, health care, transportation, and miscellaneous goods and services are all priced approximately 10 percent above national norms.

- *Taxes.* The overall tax burden in Naples is less than the national average largely because Florida does not tax personal income. However, the state sales tax of six percent exceeds the national norm of five percent. Property taxes, reflecting high property values, also exceed the national average in the City of Naples, but are lower on less expensive properties in inland areas of the county.

Local and Regional Services

Naples' role as the regional hub for Collier County allows it to offer a generally excellent mix of services to residents and visitors. The principal exception is the rather weak transportation infrastructure.

Transportation   Rating: 2

Naples has no public transit, a serious omission in a resort and retirement town. A privately operated trolley serves major tourist destinations, but at a cost of $12 a day is too expensive for routine use. Not surprisingly, residents are almost entirely dependent on the automobile for local travel and traffic congestion is gradually worsening. Intercity travel is mostly by car or air. Limited commuter and jet service is available at Naples Municipal Airport, just east of downtown, but better service is offered at Southwest Florida Regional Airport, 37 miles north via I-75. It provides nonstop jet service to over 30 destinations.

Retail Services   Rating: 5

You can really shop till you drop at any number of upscale retailing sites in Naples. Especially charming are the older downtown shopping districts along Fifth Avenue and Third Street. Fifth Avenue South, with its flower boxes, pocket parks and quaint storefronts, provides an ambiance conducive to strolling, shopping and dining. Third Street South and the Avenues, in historic Old Naples, has over 100 distinctive galleries, boutiques and restaurants. Westside Shops in Pelican Bay, just north of the Naples city limits, is a unique assemblage of distinguished shops and restaurants nestled within an oasis of waterfalls, lagoons and luxuriant tropical vegetation. More ordinary is Coastland Center, the major regional mall. Anchored by Burdines, Dillard's, JCPenney and Sears department stores, this large enclosed mall features a plethora of specialty shops and national chain stores. Smaller shopping centers are widely scattered about the metropolitan area. Larger stores found in these centers include Beall's, Kmart, Target and Wal-Mart.

Health Care   Rating: 4

For a small city, Naples provides unusually good medical care. Naples Community Hospital, a branch of NCH Healthcare System, is the primary medical provider for the county. A 400-bed acute care facility, it provides a wide range of services including medical, surgical, and emergency care, cancer care, and cardiac surgery and rehabilitation. North Collier Hospital, also a unit of NCH Healthcare, is a 50-bed medical, surgical and acute care facility serving the north county area beyond the city limits. In addition, the metropolitan area boasts a large number of community-oriented clinics providing routine care and referrals.

Community Services   Rating: 3

Various municipal, county and private organizations provide a good array of community services. The Collier Council on Aging for Active Seniors publishes a free directory listing services available to seniors. The Naples Senior Citizens Club meets weekly at Norris Community Center in Cambier Park, downtown. In East Naples, the Senior Citizens Club meets regularly at the East Naples Community Center.

Outdoor leisure pursuits including golf, tennis and water sports are prominent in Naples but plenty of other recreational and cultural attractions are also available.

Cultural and Educational Activities   Rating: 3

 Formerly a rather sleepy place, Naples has emerged as a lively cultural center in recent years. The Philharmonic Center for the Arts is the home of the Naples Symphony Orchestra and Chorus and the Miami City Ballet. It also hosts concerts, chamber music and Broadway plays. Plays are also produced by the Naples Players at the strikingly attractive Sugden Community Theatre on Fifth Avenue South. During the winter season, residents and visitors gather on Sunday afternoons in Cambier Park for free concerts by the Naples Concert Band. In summer, attention shifts to the free Friday evening popular music series at Waterside Shops in Pelican Bay.

Growth in southwest Florida prompted the state to establish Florida Gulf Coast University at a site just north of the Collier County line in 1997. Over time it should become a major educational asset for Fort Myers and Naples. Meanwhile, the Naples campus of Edison Community College offers lifelong learning courses on a wide variety of practical subjects for nominal fees, as do the Naples and Collier County public schools.

Recreational Activities   Rating: 5

 A unique combination of recreational assets in a tropical environment provides year-round opportunities for outdoor recreation. Miles of sugary, white sand beaches, with warm, shallow water are among America's best. Even in winter the Gulf water temperature is around 66 degrees, just warm enough for swimming, while in summer it is over 80 degrees. Fishing is popular from the beach, Naples Pier, and boats.

Much of the open space in Naples and Collier County is devoted to golf courses but land is also allocated to parks, biking and jogging paths, nature preserves and wildlife sanctuaries. With over 50 golf courses, 70 percent of which are private, Collier County is a haven for golfers and spectators. Ladies PGA and Senior PGA tournaments are held in Naples each January and February. Among Collier County communities, Naples has especially well-equipped and maintained parks. Cambier Park, downtown, is notable for its lighted tennis courts, horseshoe, shuffleboard and basketball courts, playground, community theater and auditorium. Fleishmann Park, located next to Coastland Center Mall, features lighted racquetball, volleyball and basketball courts, lighted football/soccer and softball/baseball fields and a community game room. Bicycling, jogging, in-line skating, and walking are popular along several biking and jogging paths. Biking is also popular on lightly traveled residential streets west of U.S.-41. Nature lovers appreciate Naples and nearby areas for their state, federal, and privately protected wild areas. Especially notable are the Audubon Society's Corkscrew Swamp Sanctuary, 30 miles north of town, Collier-Seminole State Park, 15 miles southeast, and Everglades National Park, whose northern (Shark Valley) entrance is off U.S.-41, 75 miles east of Naples.

Reflecting its status as a prime winter resort, the Naples area boasts an exceptional list of restaurants offering menus of excellent quality and great variety. Seafood, continental, Italian and American cuisines are especially favored locally. Three large multiplex theater complexes provide good choices for moviegoers.

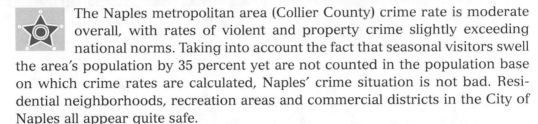

Work and Volunteer Activities   Rating: 4

The booming Collier County economy, based heavily on tourism, retailing, financial and real estate services, and construction, continues to generate large numbers of jobs. Minimal competition from college students allows seniors to compete effectively for part-time work, especially in the service sector. Openings for volunteers are also abundant. Hospitals, schools, libraries, museums, nature preserves and visitor centers are particularly dependent on volunteer staff. The Volunteer Center of Collier County is helpful in placing people where they are most needed.

Crime Rates and Public Safety   Rating: 3

The Naples metropolitan area (Collier County) crime rate is moderate overall, with rates of violent and property crime slightly exceeding national norms. Taking into account the fact that seasonal visitors swell the area's population by 35 percent yet are not counted in the population base on which crime rates are calculated, Naples' crime situation is not bad. Residential neighborhoods, recreation areas and commercial districts in the City of Naples all appear quite safe.

Conclusion

Overall Rating 42 Despite rampant growth of golf course communities and tract housing on its periphery, Naples has so far managed to retain its essential character as a charming resort and retirement town dedicated to leisure pursuits and gracious living. Beautifully landscaped with royal and coconut palms, magnolia, flowering vines and shrubs, and other exotic species, the town exudes affluence and good taste in a tropical setting. Perhaps unique amid the urban sprawl of south Florida, Naples offers a very high quality of life. Fifth Avenue downtown and Old Naples are delightful places to shop, and outdoor recreation from all-year swimming at Naples Beach, to golf at countless area courses, to walking the elevated boardwalks through local wildlife sanctuaries, is unparalleled elsewhere. The community offers very good health care and opportunities for work and volunteer activities, a good range of community services and cultural activities, and moderate crime rates. Other than the long, hot humid summer, which many find fatiguing, the principal obstacles to the good life in Naples are the complete absence of public transportation and the rather high cost of living. For those who can afford it, though, Naples may well be the mainland USA's best example of a tropical paradise.

Sarasota, Florida

Although a few Europeans settled the shores of Sarasota Bay as early as the 1700s, the area first became popular as a winter resort early in the twentieth century when the railroad connected the formerly isolated community with the northern states. Much credit for subsequent growth and cultural development of Sarasota and its offshore island beach communities of Longboat Key, Lido Key, St. Armands Key and Siesta Key belongs to John Ringling, who selected the town as the home base for his Ringling Brothers and Barnum and Bailey Circus in 1927. Ringling effectively promoted Sarasota and his circus and heavily invested in local real estate and the arts. His Italian Renaissance-style art museum and terra-cotta mansion on the shores of Sarasota Bay are legacies of

Sarasota, Florida

CLIMATE				
Month	Average Daily Temperature High Low	Daily Rel. Humidity Low	Average Monthly Precipitation	
	°F	%	Inches	
January	71 51	59	2.3	
February	73 52	55	3.1	
March	77 57	55	3.2	
April	82 62	51	2.6	
May	87 67	52	2.3	
June	89 72	60	5.8	
July	90 73	63	6.7	
August	91 73	64	8.2	
September	89 72	62	5.8	
October	85 65	58	3.8	
November	78 58	56	1.9	
December	73 53	58	1.9	

Annual Average

Total Days		Total Inches	
Clear	103	Precipitation	47.6
Partly Cloudy	142	Snowfall	0.0
Cloudy	120		

RATINGS					
Rating Scale: 5 = excellent; 4 = very good; 3 = good; 2 = fair; 1 = poor					
Rating:	1	2	3	4	5
Landscape				●	
Climate			●		
Quality of Life			●		
Cost of Living			●		
Transportation			●		
Retail Services					●
Health Care					●
Community Services				●	
Cultural Activities					●
Recreational Activities					●
Work/Volunteer Activities					●
Crime		●			

Total Points: 47

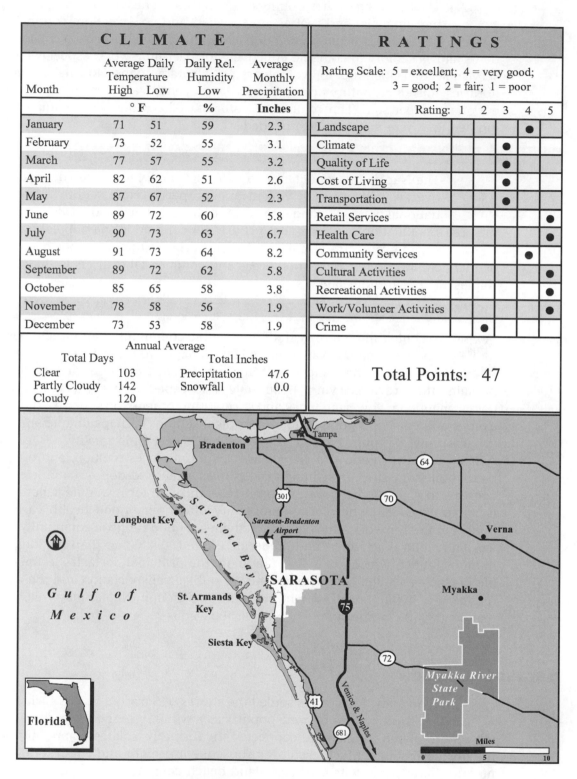

his 1920s investments. Today appropriately nicknamed the Cultural Coast, Sarasota is unique among Florida retirement towns in the diversity and quality of its cultural offerings. In addition, it has much to offer in outdoor recreation, excellent shopping, and varied and attractive residential neighborhoods in a beautiful, subtropical environment. With a population exceeding 50,000 in the city and

300,000 in Sarasota County, the metropolitan area is a busy and exciting place. Although not without problems, Sarasota should persist as one of America's best retirement places for some time to come.

Landscape — Rating: 4

 Sarasota occupies a virtually flat plain half way down Florida's west (Gulf) coast. Somewhat sheltered by barrier islands with miles of white sand beaches, the city proper is nonetheless susceptible to sea-water flooding from hurricanes as elevations range from sea level along the bay to only 20 feet above sea level inland. Natural vegetation varies from marsh grass to pine and oak but much has been replaced by exotic species including flowering plants and palms which thrive in the near tropical climate.

Climate — Rating: 3

 Like most of Florida, Sarasota has a humid subtropical climate featuring hot, humid summers and warm, relatively dry winters. Over half of annual precipitation falls during the rainy season (June through September), mostly in the form of afternoon thundershowers, and the combination of heat and humidity can be fatiguing. In contrast, the dry season (November through April) is delightful with warm days, cool nights and abundant sunshine. On average, Sarasota is sunny 66 percent of the time and experiences only one or two frosts per winter.

Quality of Life — Rating: 3

 The quality of life is generally good in Sarasota. Air quality is excellent but noise pollution is annoying alongside major highways, especially U.S.-41 (the Tamiami Trail) and I-75 and adjacent to Sarasota/ Bradenton International Airport. Although the city is uncrowded, rush hour traffic congestion is worsening on the Tamiami Trail during the winter tourist season. Sarasota city and county are relatively young and automobile oriented so parking is widely available and free. The urban area includes a wide variety of neighborhoods, with less desirable tracts being confined to inland areas north of downtown. Mainland developments near the bay and on the offshore keys are especially attractive. The Sarasota County Parks and Recreation Department operates 14 public beaches and a fine array of parks and playgrounds throughout the county. For the most part, city and county appear well planned and tastefully landscaped. In particular, the revived historic downtown shopping district, St. Armands Circle and its unique shops and restaurants, and several bayside parks offer a pedestrian-friendly ambiance not often found in Florida's bustling cities.

Cost of Living — Rating: 3

 The cost of living in Sarasota is evaluated as follows:

- *Composite*. ACCRA data for Sarasota show a composite cost of living approximately five percent above the national average.

- *Housing*. According to ACCRA, housing costs are about 15 percent above the national average. Exploration of the area indicates that an enormous variety of housing is available ranging from luxury single-family residences and condominiums in beachfront locations to modest homes inland. Generally, properties on barrier islands like Siesta Key and St. Armands Key are expensive, with some residences fetching upwards of $500,000. In contrast, plenty of two- and three-bedroom, two-bath homes are available on large, well-treed lots in attractive neighborhoods a few miles inland for $80,000 to $150,000.

- **Goods and Services.** Aside from housing, living costs in Sarasota approximate the national average. Groceries, utilities, transportation, health care, and miscellaneous goods and services are all priced within five percent of national norms.

- **Taxes.** The overall tax burden in Sarasota is well below the national average. Although Sarasota County's combined state/local sales tax of seven percent is high, modest property taxes and the absence of a state income tax more than compensate.

Local and Regional Services

Sarasota is the regional center for Sarasota County's population of 300,000 and therefore is able to provide an excellent range of services to residents and visitors.

Transportation	Rating: 3

 Sarasota is strongly automobile oriented and has adequate roads for current demand. Sarasota County Area Transit (SCAT) provides fixed route bus service throughout the county's urbanized area six days a week. Buses serve downtown, major malls, beaches, the airport, residential areas and neighboring communities. Service levels are marginal at best; service on most lines is hourly and confined to daytime hours, so you need to plan your travel carefully. Fares, though, are reasonable. The base fare is 50 cents, 25 cents for seniors. A monthly pass costs $30, discounted to $15 for seniors. Sarasota/Bradenton International Airport, five miles north, provides adequate commercial air service. Nonstop jet service is available to 15 destinations including major hubs at Atlanta, Charlotte, Detroit and St. Louis, among others. Greyhound Lines provides inter-city bus service from Sarasota but no rail passenger service is available.

Retail Services	Rating: 5

Sarasota has the usual large enclosed malls plus numerous quaint downtown and village shopping areas. Sarasota Square Mall, located alongside the Tamiami Trail on the southern periphery of town, is Sarasota's largest mall. Anchored by Burdines, Dillard's, JCPenney and Sears, it has over 140 specialty shops, mostly branches of national and regional chains, a large food court, 12 AMC theaters, and a Morrison's cafeteria. Closer to downtown along the Tamiami Trail is Southgate Plaza, an upscale mall with an atypical and rather interesting layout. Anchored by Burdines, Dillard's and Saks Fifth Avenue, Southgate Plaza has the usual chain stores plus some upscale stores, for example, Talbots and Williams-Sonoma, not commonly found in malls. Even more interesting are: St. Armands Circle and streets spoking off it, which boast over 100 distinctly upscale shops and restaurants in a charming and beautifully landscaped setting; downtown Venice with its quaintly restored shops and restaurants; and the nicely revitalized Main Street in downtown Sarasota.

Health Care Rating: 5

 Sarasota provides excellent health care. Six fully accredited hospitals with a total of 1,600 beds offer over 25 medical specialties. Sarasota Memorial Hospital, Doctors Hospital of Sarasota, and Bon Secours Venice Hospital are the largest regional facilities with the widest array of services. Fifty miles north in the Tampa Bay Region an additional 50 general surgical hospitals providing an enormous range of medical services are found.

Community Services Rating: 4

 A very good supply of community services of interest to seniors is available in Sarasota. Nonprofit Senior Friendship Centers exist in Sarasota and Venice; they also host activities at several other sites. No membership dues are charged but nominal donations are suggested for meals at special events. Center activities include: dancing and dancing lessons, jazz concerts, cards, bingo, arts and crafts classes and activities, and health and exercise programs. Sarasota City and County parks and recreation facilities, social clubs, and public libraries provide additional services.

Leisure Activities

Sarasota's repertoire of cultural and recreational activities is unmatched among American cities of comparable size. Whatever your tastes in the visual or performing arts or in outdoor recreation, they are likely to be satisfied.

Cultural and Educational Activities Rating: 5

 Ever since John and Mabel Ringling settled here in the 1920s, Sarasota has been a haven for visual and performing artists and for patrons of the arts. Today the Ringling Museum houses more than 1,000 paintings largely from the Renaissance and Baroque periods. Highlights of the collection include five large oil paintings by Peter Paul Rubens. Regular and rotating exhibitions may also be seen at the Sarasota Visual Art Center, the Selby Gallery at the Ringling School of Art and Design, and the Venice Art Center. More than 30 commercial art galleries are clustered near downtown's theater district or at St. Armands Circle.

Sarasota's performing arts calendar is so full that its richness can only be hinted at here. The Van Wezel Performing Arts Hall, designed by Frank Lloyd Wright and renowned for its outstanding acoustics, presents performances by distinguished touring musical, dance and theatrical companies each season. It is home to the Sarasota Ballet of Florida, the Florida West Coast Symphony Orchestra, and Gloria Musicae, a professional chorale ensemble. The beautifully restored downtown Sarasota Opera House hosts four operas by the critically acclaimed Sarasota Opera Company each February and March. The FSU Center for the Arts, located on the Ringling property, is home to the Asolo Theater Company, one of the state of Florida's four official theatrical troupes, and to the outstanding Asolo Theatre Festival, which runs from November through May. Performances are staged at the 500-seat Mertz Theatre and the more intimate 161-seat Cook Theatre.

Sarasota is also home to several institutions of higher learning. The University of Florida at Sarasota/New College, part of the University of Florida system, offers junior-, senior- and graduate-level courses in business administration, education, social and behavioral sciences, and engineering programs. For casual students, though, Manatee Community College, with campuses in Bradenton and

Venice, might be a better choice. Its continuing education program provides a great variety of non-degree courses of interest to seniors for nominal fees. The winter lecture series presented by Sarasota's Institute of Lifelong Learning on topics like the arts, foreign affairs and cultural and social issues, is also of interest.

Recreational Activities   Rating: 5

 With wide, white sand beaches stretching for 35 miles along warm Gulf waters, it is no wonder that Sarasota is famous for beach-going activities. Even so, sunning and swimming are only the beginning of the area's outdoor recreational possibilities. Bays, bayous and the Gulf of Mexico boast some of the best fishing in the state, while the Intracoastal Waterway, bays and inshore waters provide opportunities for all kinds of boating. Local waters also provide ideal conditions for snorkeling and scuba diving.

Although many retirees live in luxurious golf course communities or are members of private country clubs, competing public and semi-private courses offer a variety of challenges where one can play on a pay-for-play basis. About two-thirds of Sarasota County golf courses, including several of championship caliber, are open to the general public. The county is also notable for its excellent network of public parks and recreational facilities operated by city, county and state authorities. Sarasota County alone operates 117 parks and recreation facilities. These range from beach access trails and small neighborhood parks, playgrounds, and picnic areas to community and metropolitan parks that typically include sports fields, lighted tennis courts, swimming facilities, gymnasium and recreation buildings, trails and nature centers. Oscar Scherer State Recreation Area, just north of Venice, and Myakka River State Park, 20 miles southeast of Sarasota, offer camping, picnicking, hiking, boating, fishing and nature appreciation, among other activities.

Consistent with its role as a major resort area, Sarasota has a good assortment of high quality restaurants downtown, at St. Armands Circle, and at various shopping centers. Seafood, continental, ethnic, Italian and American cuisines are widely available. Mainstream movies may be seen at several large multiplex theater complexes while international and American films by independent filmmakers are exhibited by the Sarasota Film Society at its Burns Court Cinema.

Work and Volunteer Activities   Rating: 5

 The Sarasota County economy has grown moderately in recent years and steadily generates jobs in tourist related services, retailing, and financial and real estate services. Seniors are quite competitive for part-time work owing to the absence of severe competition from college students. Many seniors are able to find volunteer work in schools, hospitals, libraries, museums and parks.

Crime Rates and Public Safety   Rating: 2

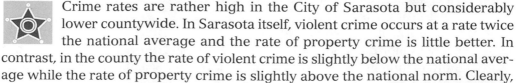 Crime rates are rather high in the City of Sarasota but considerably lower countywide. In Sarasota itself, violent crime occurs at a rate twice the national average and the rate of property crime is little better. In contrast, in the county the rate of violent crime is slightly below the national average while the rate of property crime is slightly above the national norm. Clearly, where you live in the Sarasota area has much to do with your potential exposure

to crime. Suburban areas in general, and upscale neighborhoods in particular, are much safer than areas adjacent to poor neighborhoods just northeast of the downtown area.

Conclusion

Overall Rating 47 Sarasota city and county are unique in Florida for the enormous variety and high quality of services, culture and recreation offered residents and visitors. Renowned as Florida's Cultural Coast for its repertoire of first-rate ballet, chorale, dance, opera, symphony, theater and visual arts programs and venues, Sarasota is also notable for remarkable outdoor recreational assets. An abundance of golf courses and over 120 parks and recreational areas strategically located in town, astride bays, bayous and inshore waters, and along the county's 35 miles of white sandy beaches, offer recreational options to suit every taste. Shopping and health care are excellent, work and volunteer opportunities are outstanding, and community services are better than in most Florida cities. Although Sarasota and its offshore keys are only a few feet above sea level, the local landscape with its luxurious subtropical vegetation, waterside vistas, and charming residential and retailing areas, is most attractive. Sarasota is not quite perfect. Its summers may be too hot and humid for some, a few neighborhoods are blighted and provide a less than ideal quality of life, public transit is marginal and crime rates are sobering. All in all, though, Sarasota offers a combination of amenities seldom found in medium-sized retirement towns and at a cost of living scarcely above the national average. It merits a serious look by those seeking a coastal Florida lifestyle with culture.

Gainesville, Florida

Although founded in 1854 and named for Revolutionary War General Edmund Gaines, Gainesville remained a quiet agricultural community until the twentieth century. Two events, the great freeze of February 1895, which killed over 90 percent of the orange trees of northern Florida, and the establishment in Gainesville of the University of Florida in 1906, pointed the town and surrounding Alachua County in new directions. Area agriculture diversified with cattle raising replacing citrus growing and Gainesville gradually evolved into a leafy college town offering a rare combination of small town charm, natural beauty, and bountiful cultural and educational amenities. With a population of 95,000 in the city and 210,000 in the metropolitan area (Alachua County), Gainesville remains a small town that has avoided being swept up in the frenzied growth typical of central and south Florida. Nonetheless, assets typical of major metropolitan areas are nearby. Jacksonville is 70 miles northeast, Orlando 115 miles southeast, and Tampa 125 miles south of Gainesville.

Landscape   Rating: 4

Gainesville occupies a gently rolling plain about midway across the northern extremity of the Florida peninsula. Elevations in town vary between 100 and 200 feet and numerous sinkholes, some filled with water forming small lakes and ponds, give variety to the landscape. The prevailing natural vegetation is pine forest in drier areas and prairie grasses in wetlands. Residential neighborhoods and the huge University of Florida campus are planted with a variety of ornamental species including pine, live oak, magnolia and palmetto, which lend a distinctly subtropical ambiance to the community.

Gainesville, Florida

CLIMATE				
Month	Average Daily Temperature High Low		Daily Rel. Humidity Low	Average Monthly Precipitation
	°F		%	Inches
January	66	43	62	3.4
February	68	44	57	4.2
March	75	51	55	3.7
April	81	56	52	2.6
May	86	63	51	3.8
June	90	68	55	6.8
July	91	71	58	6.8
August	90	71	60	8.0
September	87	69	64	5.3
October	81	60	63	1.8
November	74	51	62	2.3
December	68	45	63	3.3

Annual Average

Total Days		Total Inches	
Clear	94	Precipitation	51.8
Partly Cloudy	145	Snowfall	0.0
Cloudy	126		

RATINGS

Rating Scale: 5 = excellent; 4 = very good; 3 = good; 2 = fair; 1 = poor

Rating:	1	2	3	4	5
Landscape				●	
Climate			●		
Quality of Life					●
Cost of Living				●	
Transportation					●
Retail Services			●		
Health Care					●
Community Services				●	
Cultural Activities				●	
Recreational Activities					●
Work/Volunteer Activities				●	
Crime		●			

Total Points: 48

Climate

Rating: 3

Gainesville has a humid subtropical climate characterized by long, hot, humid and rainy summers, and mild and somewhat drier winters. Over half of annual precipitation falls during the rainy season (June through

September), largely in the form of afternoon thundershowers that provide temporary relief from the wilting summer heat. Winter weather is quite variable with cold fronts bringing occasional frosts and limiting the frost-free period to 290 days. Spring and fall are pleasant with warm days, cool nights, and the seasonal maxima of sunshine. Gainesville is sunny about 70 percent of the time in spring and fall, 66 percent in summer, and 60 percent in winter.

Quality of Life · Rating: 5

 The quality of life is typically excellent in Gainesville. Air quality is excellent and noise pollution is an annoyance only along Interstate-75 on the western fringe of town and alongside a few major boulevards such as Archer and Williston Roads. The city's small size and low population density give it an uncrowded feeling with little traffic congestion, even at rush hour. Adequate parking is available in most areas and the University of Florida encourages public transit use by providing free bus privileges to students. Gainesville's service-based economy lacks noxious industries and the city appears well planned, especially when compared with the sprawling urban complexes of South Florida. Most residential neighborhoods are very attractive with housing of various styles sited on large wooded lots. The revitalized historic downtown area, with its unique combination of shops, restaurants, nightclubs, theaters and housing, offers a lively pedestrian-friendly alternative to suburban malls and shopping centers. Excellent park systems in the city and county also contribute to Gainesville's high quality of life.

Cost of Living · Rating: 4

 The cost of living in Gainesville is evaluated as follows:

- *Composite.* ACCRA data for Gainesville show a composite cost of living approximately at the national average.

- *Housing.* According to ACCRA, housing costs are about three percent below the national average. However, local sources and exploration of the area indicate that Gainesville housing offers even greater value when you take into account the low cost of land and the high quality of the housing stock. You will pay less, on average, for the lot on which your house sits in Gainesville than in many American cities; therefore, more of the housing dollar is available to pay for the house itself. Many three-bedroom, two-bath houses on large wooded lots in beautiful neighborhoods are available for prices between $80,000 and $150,000.

- *Goods and Services.* Goods and services are typically priced near national norms in Gainesville. Groceries, utilities, health care, and miscellaneous goods and services are all priced within two percent of their national averages, while transportation exceeds the national norm by five percent.

- *Taxes.* The overall tax burden in Gainesville is far below the national average. The state sales tax of six percent exceeds the average state rate by one percent, but low property taxes, around $2,000 on a $100,000 home, and the absence of a state income tax more than compensate.

Local and Regional Services

Gainesville is the regional capital of north central Florida and therefore is able to provide an extensive range of services to Gainesville residents and visitors.

I-75 skirts the western side of Gainesville so most travel in town is on local streets. The road infrastructure seems adequate for current demand. Gainesville Regional Transit System (RTS) provides very good bus service on a network of routes focused on the Downtown Plaza and the University of Florida campus. Santa Fe Community College, Oaks Mall, area hospitals, and most other destinations can be reached by bus. On weekdays most buses run at 20–30 minute intervals from early morning until 9 p.m. Less frequent service is provided on weekends. Fares are very reasonable. The base fare is $1.00, 50 cents for seniors. A monthly pass costs $30, discounted to $15 for seniors. University of Florida students ride free while other students pay $35 per semester.

Intercity travel is possible by air, bus and rail. Gainesville Regional Airport provides limited nonstop jet service to hub airports at Atlanta, Charlotte and Miami. Jacksonville International Airport, 60 miles away, offers nonstop flights to more than 20 destinations. Greyhound Lines provides intercity bus service to points north and south, while Amtrak furnishes twice daily bus/rail connections to major points north and south including New York and Miami.

Retail Services   Rating: 3

The Oaks Mall, located on Newberry Road (State Road 26) just east of I-75, is Gainesville's major mall. Anchored by Belk, Burdines, Dillard's, JCPenney and Sears, this large enclosed shopping center has over 140 specialty shops (many run by national chains), restaurants and services. Also in suburban locations are a Target store near the junction of Archer Road and I-75, and a Wal-Mart and Sam's Club adjacent to Gainesville Mall, in the northern part of town. Perhaps most interesting is the revitalized historic downtown core of Gainesville, where you can stroll along brick sidewalks lined with unique shops, lively restaurants and nightclubs, a beautifully restored theater, and bed and breakfast inns.

Health Care   Rating: 5

Gainesville offers outstanding medical care by virtue of the presence of the University of Florida Health Science Center. The university medical system includes three units of Shands Hospital. Shands Hospital at the University of Florida is a 576-bed facility with centers specializing in cardiovascular, neurological, cancer and transplantation services. Shands at AGH (formerly Alachua General Hospital) is a full-service hospital with 423 beds and over 200 physicians on staff. It specializes in cardiac and cancer care, neuroscience, women's health and emergency care. Shands at Vista includes an 83-bed psychiatric hospital and a 40-bed rehabilitation facility. Columbia North Florida Medical Center, with 278 beds, and a large Veterans Administration hospital with 478 beds, are the city's other major medical facilities. Both provide diverse inpatient and outpatient services.

Community Services   Rating: 4

A good variety of services of interest to seniors is available from the City of Gainesville and various nonprofit and community organizations. The T. A. Boltin Senior Activity Center is a popular gathering place for arts and crafts activities, bingo, cards, dancing and exercise. The center also organizes day and overnight field trips to, among other places, the casinos of Biloxi, Mississippi. The Gainesville Department of Recreation and Parks operates a Wellness Center at its Martin Luther King, Jr. Multipurpose Center. Seniors can use fitness equipment there for a $25 annual fee. AARP and the Retired Senior Volunteer Program (RSVP) are also active in Gainesville, providing access to paid and volunteer employment and information useful to seniors. Social clubs and organizations and the public library offer additional services.

Leisure Activities

The University of Florida and the relatively unspoiled natural environment surrounding Gainesville provide plenty of cultural, educational and recreational choices. Whatever your tastes, you should find much to do locally.

Cultural and Educational Activities	Rating: 4

 The University of Florida, with over 40,000 students and 4,000 faculty, is the state's flagship institution of higher learning. With more than 100 undergraduate majors, 200 graduate programs, and 5 major professional schools, the university is a wonderful educational and cultural asset. Senior Florida residents may audit courses on a "space available" basis. The university's state-of-the-art 1,800-seat Center for the Performing Arts regularly hosts quality theater, dance, and symphonic and orchestral concerts. Adjacent to the Center are the Samuel P. Harn Museum of Art and the Florida Museum of Natural History. The Harn Museum displays a wide selection of art from around the world; the Florida Museum is the largest natural history museum in the southeastern United States.

Housed in a beautiful, neoclassical building in the heart of historic downtown Gainesville is the Hippodrome State Theatre, one of four state-supported theaters in Florida. The Hippodrome produces eight shows annually, each cast with actors from throughout the country and from the Hippodrome's own professional company. The Hippodrome's theatrical events are presented in a uniquely intimate space, no seat is more than seven rows from the stage, so there is not a bad seat in the house. Even so, prices are remarkably low. Season tickets are priced between $70 and $150, depending on day and seat location. In addition to the theater, the building houses an 80-seat cinema featuring avant-garde, limited release, and foreign films, and an art gallery displaying the works of North Florida artists.

Recreational Activities	Rating: 5

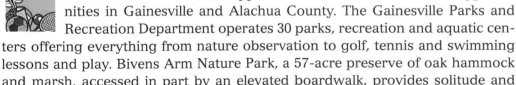 Outdoors enthusiasts will appreciate the diverse recreational opportunities in Gainesville and Alachua County. The Gainesville Parks and Recreation Department operates 30 parks, recreation and aquatic centers offering everything from nature observation to golf, tennis and swimming lessons and play. Bivens Arm Nature Park, a 57-acre preserve of oak hammock and marsh, accessed in part by an elevated boardwalk, provides solitude and excellent bird watching only two miles from downtown. Golf is a bargain at the city's Ironwood Golf Course. Green fees are $10 for 18 holes on weekdays, $14 on weekends. Golf is also played on six other local private and public courses including the University of Florida Golf Club.

Gainesville is virtually surrounded by natural beauty that can be easily reached by car or bicycle. With 60 miles of on-street bike lanes and a 15-mile paved State Trail connecting Gainesville with Hawthorne along an old railroad right-of-way, the city is distinctly friendly to bicyclists. You can ride north to visit Devil's Millhopper State Geologic Site, a spectacular sinkhole 120 feet deep and 500 feet wide, or go southwest to Kanahapa Botanical Gardens with its 62 acres of gardens, meadows and woodlands. Just south of town is Paynes Prairie Preserve, a wildlife sanctuary encompassing 20,000 acres of marsh and swamp, sinkhole lakes and pine woods. The northern part of the Preserve is traversed by the Gainesville/Hawthorne State Trail, with overlooks providing good vantage points for viewing wildlife. And just east of town is Newnans Lake, a 10-square mile freshwater lake popular for boating and fishing.

Consistent with its college town role, Gainesville boasts first-rate intercollegiate sports and a good selection of movie theaters and restaurants. The town really comes alive when fans of the Florida Gators turn out for NCAA basketball and football games at the university's Stephen C. O'Connell Center and Ben Griffin Stadium. Several fine restaurants clustered in the historic downtown area provide American, Continental and Italian specialties at very reasonable prices. Also downtown is the Hippodrome Theatre art movie house. Six cinema chains show mainstream movies on 27 screens at other locations around town.

Work and Volunteer Activities   Rating: 4

Gainesville's booming service-based economy continues to generate jobs, especially at the university, in health care and in retailing. Competition with college students is acute, though, particularly for part-time jobs on campus and in retailing. RSVP offers an excellent free guide to retirement living in Alachua County and assists seniors in finding volunteer work. Volunteers serve in local schools, hospitals, parks, museums and libraries, or serve as advocates for the aging and other groups. In a recent year over 500 Alachua County RSVP volunteers provided more than 100,000 hours of service at over 75 volunteer sites in the community. Those seeking paid work may obtain assistance through the AARP Senior Community Employment Program.

Crime Rates and Public Safety   Rating: 2

The overall incidence of crime is rather high in Gainesville and only slightly less so countywide. Overall violent crime occurs at a rate nearly twice the national average. Rape and aggravated assault rates are especially high yet the murder rate is well below the national norm. The overall incidence of property crime is also nearly twice the national average, with burglary and larceny-theft rates being especially high. Even taking into account the fact that the University of Florida's 40,000 students are not included in the population base on which crime rates are calculated, Gainesville crime rates are soberingly high.

Conclusion

Overall Rating 48

Rated the best place to live among 300 U.S. metropolitan areas by *Money* magazine in 1995, Gainesville is undeniably one of America's choice locations for retirement. Not too big, not too small, this north central Florida college town provides everything essential for upscale retirement at reasonable prices. The University of Florida, around which Gainesville is built, is the key element in the town's prosperity and a major supplier of its amenities. The community's fine quality of life, health care, cultural and recreational amenities, and intracity and intercity transportation all reflect facilities and services provided by the university and the needs of its faculty, staff and students. Gainesville also provides above-average community services and work and volunteer opportunities. As a regional capital, Gainesville is also able to provide a range of retail services unusual for a city of its size.

Thanks to its inland location and moderate elevation, Gainesville is spared the worst danger from hurricanes, storm surge flooding of low-lying areas. The natural landscape, a gently rolling surface mantled in forest and dotted with marshes and lakes, is beautiful and unspoiled and the town's wooded residential neighborhoods and historic downtown are unusually attractive. Only Gainesville's long, hot and humid summers and high crime rates detract significantly from the community's overall high rating. If you are seeking college town amenities at low prices in an inland subtropical environment, give Gainesville a careful look.

Thomasville, Georgia

Benefiting from its status as the southern terminus of a railroad connecting with the north, Thomasville blossomed into a major winter resort in the 1880s and 1890s. Northerners first came for their health, believing that the warm pine-scented air was a remedy for pulmonary ailments. Others soon joined them to escape winter's rigors and to enjoy the area's hunting, fishing and genteel social life.

Although Thomasville's "grand hotel era" came to a close when improved transportation opened Florida to tourism after 1900, a substantial legacy of landmark mansions and plantation homes has survived to the present. Together with Thomasville's colorful and vital Victorian downtown, natural beauty, and cultural advantages, these lovingly restored homes make Thomasville a special place. With its population essentially stable at about 18,000, Thomasville is peaceful and friendly and has avoided the unfortunate side effects of rampant growth. Nonetheless, metropolitan amenities including a regional airport and a wider choice of retail services are only 35 miles away in Tallahassee, Florida.

Landscape	Rating: 4

Thomasville is located on a gently rolling plain in scenic southwest Georgia approximately 17 miles north of the Florida state line. Elevations in town vary from about 200 to 300 feet. The town's adjacent area is agricultural with much of the land forested with pine and live oak. In town, streets and gardens are planted with oak, magnolia and pine, along with dogwood, camellia, azalea and roses. Several small lakes and rivers are found nearby.

Climate	Rating: 3

Like adjacent northern Florida, Thomasville has a humid subtropical climate with hot, humid summers and mild winters. Annual precipitation is ample and well distributed in all seasons; every month except October and November receives four inches or more of rain. Snow is almost unknown and the weather is typically sunny. It is sunny more than half the time every month, with maximum values of 70 percent being recorded in spring and early summer. Although relative humidity is moderate overall, the combination of 90-degree temperatures and over 60 percent relative humidity on summer

Thomasville, Georgia

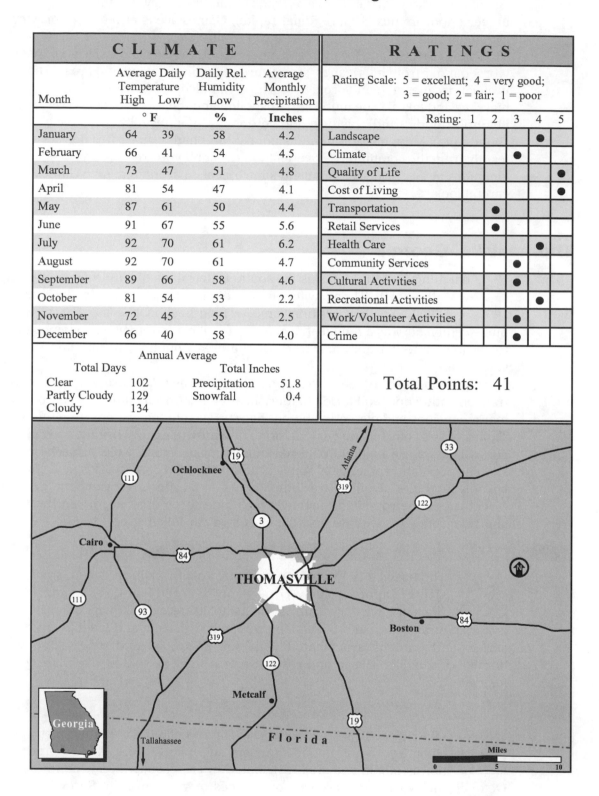

CLIMATE			
Month	Average Daily Temperature High / Low (°F)	Daily Rel. Humidity Low (%)	Average Monthly Precipitation (Inches)
January	64 / 39	58	4.2
February	66 / 41	54	4.5
March	73 / 47	51	4.8
April	81 / 54	47	4.1
May	87 / 61	50	4.4
June	91 / 67	55	5.6
July	92 / 70	61	6.2
August	92 / 70	61	4.7
September	89 / 66	58	4.6
October	81 / 54	53	2.2
November	72 / 45	55	2.5
December	66 / 40	58	4.0

Annual Average

Total Days		Total Inches	
Clear	102	Precipitation	51.8
Partly Cloudy	129	Snowfall	0.4
Cloudy	134		

RATINGS

Rating Scale: 5 = excellent; 4 = very good; 3 = good; 2 = fair; 1 = poor

Rating:	1	2	3	4	5
Landscape				●	
Climate			●		
Quality of Life					●
Cost of Living					●
Transportation		●			
Retail Services		●			
Health Care				●	
Community Services			●		
Cultural Activities			●		
Recreational Activities				●	
Work/Volunteer Activities			●		
Crime			●		

Total Points: 41

afternoons can be stifling. On the other hand, most days between October and April are very pleasant. Occasional winter frosts result in a frost-free period of about 260 days.

The quality of life in Thomasville is excellent. Lacking noxious industries, busy streets and freeways, the town is spared noise, traffic congestion and air pollution. Free parking is abundant. Most residential neighborhoods, old and new, are very attractive with houses characteristically sited on large lots graced with lawns, trees and ornamental shrubs. The city is well endowed with parkland and seems intelligently planned and zoned. Fortunately, no large mall potentially destructive to Thomasville's beautifully restored historic downtown retailing district, with its brick-paved streets, wide sidewalks and one-of-a-kind businesses, exists in the county. People are welcoming, justifiably proud of their community, and determined to preserve its unique character.

Cost of Living   Rating: 5

 The cost of living in Thomasville is evaluated as follows:

- **Composite.** ACCRA data are unavailable for Thomasville so statistics for Valdosta, a nearby small Georgia town, are used. On that basis the composite cost of living in Thomasville is estimated to be about five percent below the national average.

- **Housing.** Housing costs are perhaps 15 percent below the national average, even though the quality of the local housing stock is unusually high. Many attractive houses with three bedrooms and two bathrooms in very good neighborhoods are available in the $60,000 to $100,000 price range. Luxurious, large brick homes on wooded lots in gorgeous neighborhoods are priced between $150,000 and $200,000. Elegantly restored Victorian mansions are occasionally available at higher prices, and several condominium complexes typically have units selling for less than $80,000.

- **Goods and Services.** Goods and services, except for utilities, are priced slightly below national norms. Summer air conditioning and winter heating cause utility bills to be about five percent above the national average.

- **Taxes.** The overall tax burden in Thomasville approximates the national average even though property taxes are quite low, for example, around $1,100 on a $100,000 home. The state/local sales tax of six percent exceeds the average state/local rate by one percent, and Georgia state income tax rates rise rapidly to six percent on taxable income in excess of $10,000 for a couple. In effect, most middle and upper income Georgia residents are paying an essentially flat tax of six percent on their taxable income, a high rate by national standards.

Local and Regional Services

Protected by distance from competitors, Thomasville serves a large trade area and is able to provide a good range of services to residents and visitors.

Transportation   Rating: 2

 The private automobile dominates local transportation; there is no public transit system. Taxi service, though, is available for travel in the city and to nearby communities. Thomasville's road infrastructure is more than adequate to handle the limited demands put upon it. Tallahassee

Regional Airport, about 40 miles southwest, is served by 5 airlines with 125 daily flights. Nonstop jet destinations include Atlanta, Charlotte and Miami, among others. Greyhound bus service to many points is also available from Tallahassee, as is Amtrak service westbound to Los Angeles and eastbound to Jacksonville and Miami, three times a week.

Retail Services   Rating: 2

 Thomasville's award winning "Main Street" program has, over the past 20 years, spurred the rehabilitation of hundreds of buildings and businesses along brick-paved Broad Street and neighboring streets in the city center. The charming Victorian downtown is a wonderful place to walk and shop and attracts thousands of visitors as well as Thomasville residents. With its art galleries, service establishments, antique and specialty shops, restaurants, and two small department stores, downtown is far and away the best place to shop in Thomas County. Plenty of free parking is available in two municipal lots located on Crawford Street behind the stores facing Broad, so there is no need to go to the mall. In fact, there is no major mall to go to except for Governor's Square Mall, 35 miles away in Tallahassee. Ordinary shopping is possible, though, at the local Wal-Mart on the edge of town.

Health Care   Rating: 4

 For a small town, Thomasville offers exceptional medical care. John D. Archbold Memorial Hospital, with 328 beds including 64 in a nursing home unit, is the leading medical center of southwest Georgia. With over 100 physicians on staff representing over 30 specialties, Archbold anchors a regional not-for-profit health care system. It is especially noted for its cancer treatment, cardiac care, neurosurgery and rehabilitation services. Additional comprehensive medical services are only 35 miles away in Tallahassee.

Community Services   Rating: 3

The city provides excellent basic public services, including police, fire protection/emergency service and utilities. The Thomas County Public Library, headquartered in downtown Thomasville, the Thomasville Parks and Recreation Department, and numerous civic and service clubs provide a variety of informational, fitness, recreational and social services to seniors.

Leisure Activities

Thomasville offers a surprising diversity of leisure activities. Nearby Tallahassee provides additional choices including exciting NCAA sports at Florida State and Florida A & M Universities.

Cultural and Educational Activities   Rating: 3

Among small cities, Thomasville is a cultural standout. The Thomasville Cultural Center Auditorium, located in a former public school, is the primary venue for top-flight musical and theatrical productions hosted by the Thomasville Entertainment Foundation. Recent guest artist appearances include Denyce Graves, mezzo-soprano; the Boston Symphony Chamber Players; the Lincoln Center Jazz Orchestra, featuring Wynton Marsalis; and the Acting Company production of Shakespeare's Twelfth Night. Exhibits and classes are also offered through the Center, and On Stage and Company, a community theater group, produces four plays each year.

Thomas College, a fully accredited private four-year institution, enrolls 1,000 students on its historic and picturesque campus. Its sports, musical and theatrical events are of interest to the community. Continuing education is offered by Thomas Technical Institute, a unit of the Georgia Department of Technical and Adult Education. Courses of special interest to seniors include micro computing, Spanish, auto repair, defensive driving and floral design. Flower and nature lovers can also enjoy the community's eight active garden clubs and several nature preserves, including the Birdsong Nature Center.

Recreational Activities   Rating: 4

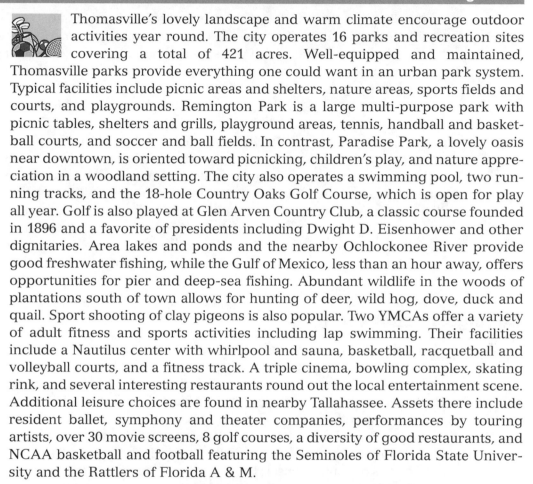

Thomasville's lovely landscape and warm climate encourage outdoor activities year round. The city operates 16 parks and recreation sites covering a total of 421 acres. Well-equipped and maintained, Thomasville parks provide everything one could want in an urban park system. Typical facilities include picnic areas and shelters, nature areas, sports fields and courts, and playgrounds. Remington Park is a large multi-purpose park with picnic tables, shelters and grills, playground areas, tennis, handball and basketball courts, and soccer and ball fields. In contrast, Paradise Park, a lovely oasis near downtown, is oriented toward picnicking, children's play, and nature appreciation in a woodland setting. The city also operates a swimming pool, two running tracks, and the 18-hole Country Oaks Golf Course, which is open for play all year. Golf is also played at Glen Arven Country Club, a classic course founded in 1896 and a favorite of presidents including Dwight D. Eisenhower and other dignitaries. Area lakes and ponds and the nearby Ochlockonee River provide good freshwater fishing, while the Gulf of Mexico, less than an hour away, offers opportunities for pier and deep-sea fishing. Abundant wildlife in the woods of plantations south of town allows for hunting of deer, wild hog, dove, duck and quail. Sport shooting of clay pigeons is also popular. Two YMCAs offer a variety of adult fitness and sports activities including lap swimming. Their facilities include a Nautilus center with whirlpool and sauna, basketball, racquetball and volleyball courts, and a fitness track. A triple cinema, bowling complex, skating rink, and several interesting restaurants round out the local entertainment scene. Additional leisure choices are found in nearby Tallahassee. Assets there include resident ballet, symphony and theater companies, performances by touring artists, over 30 movie screens, 8 golf courses, a diversity of good restaurants, and NCAA basketball and football featuring the Seminoles of Florida State University and the Rattlers of Florida A & M.

Work and Volunteer Activities   Rating: 3

Employment opportunities are limited by the small size of the city. Nonetheless, some retirees find jobs in Thomasville's many small factories, at hospitals and in retailing, although at low wages. Volunteers serve in local places of worship, schools, social organizations, and in the very active Chamber of Commerce and Visitor Bureau. Various events, including the April Thomasville Rose Festival, depend heavily on volunteers, as does the Thomas County Library.

Crime Rates and Public Safety   Rating: 3

The overall incidence of crime in Thomasville is rather high for such a small and attractive city. Middle-class residents seem not to notice or hint that most of the crime occurs in the poor (minority) parts of town and does not affect them. Be that as it may, the overall rate of property crime is nearly twice the national average, with burglary and larceny-theft rates being especially high. On the other hand, the city's violent crime rate is 30 percent below the national average. Within this broad category, murder, rape and aggravated assault rates are low and robbery rates high. Summing up, Thomasville has a high incidence of relatively minor crimes against property but is not a particularly dangerous place to live. The historic downtown, public areas and parks, and neighborhoods where retirees are likely to live all appear pleasant and safe.

Conclusion

Overall Rating 41 Rated as "one of the best retirement towns in the South" by Consumer Guide in 1988, Thomasville persists as one of America's best small towns for retirement. It will appeal especially to those seeking gracious living at modest cost in a tranquil subtropical environment. It would not satisfy those requiring good public transportation or the excitement and diversity of activities found in larger cities. The community's quality of life is near perfect, nearly 20 years ago it was labeled "a storybook town near the Florida border," and that description is still apt. The natural landscape of gently rolling hills clad with oak and pine, and the town's exquisite residential neighborhoods and colorful, historic downtown are very appealing. Health care and recreational opportunities are exceptional for a small town, and even better if the assets of nearby Tallahassee are considered. Community services, culture, and work and volunteer activities are all quite good and the city's crime rate is not particularly threatening. If you are seeking a laid-back retirement in a lovely little town offering better than average amenities, Thomasville merits serious examination.

Covington, Louisiana

Founded in 1813 as the seat of government for St. Tammany Parish, Covington and neighboring communities on the north shore of Lake Pontchartrain soon gained fame as health resorts offering fresh air and "healing" artesian waters in pleasant surroundings. Visitors from New Orleans first came by excursion boat across the lake and later by circuitous rail and road routes. Completion of the Lake Pontchartrain Causeway in 1956 improved accessibility by directly connecting New Orleans with the north shore via a 24-mile, 30-minute commute. As a result, thousands of New Orleanians have relocated to the western half of St. Tammany, making it the fastest growing parish in Louisiana.

Covington, Mandeville, Abita Springs and other western St. Tammany towns have a combined population exceeding 80,000 and rank highly for retirement. Covington and Mandeville, especially, have many attractive tree-shaded residential areas and clearly defined historic downtown areas. They offer a delightful, laid-back lifestyle in an area of great natural beauty close, but not too close, to the bright lights and unique cultural amenities of New Orleans.

Landscape   Rating: 4

Covington is located on the banks of the Bogue Falaya River about seven miles north of Lake Pontchartrain. Like other places in western St. Tammany, Covington lies on a nearly flat plain but unlike New Orleans, just across the lake, it is not below sea level. Typical elevations in the Covington area are 20 to 40 feet above sea level, probably high enough to escape

Covington, Louisiana

CLIMATE				
Month	Average Daily Temperature High Low		Daily Rel. Humidity Low	Average Monthly Precipitation
	°F		%	Inches
January	63	40	66	4.9
February	66	41	63	5.3
March	72	48	60	5.7
April	79	55	59	5.3
May	86	62	59	5.2
June	91	68	62	4.6
July	92	71	65	6.7
August	92	70	65	5.2
September	88	67	64	5.4
October	81	55	58	3.0
November	71	46	60	4.1
December	65	41	65	5.9

Annual Average

Total Days		Total Inches	
Clear	101	Precipitation	61.3
Partly Cloudy	118	Snowfall	0.5
Cloudy	146		

RATINGS

Rating Scale: 5 = excellent; 4 = very good; 3 = good; 2 = fair; 1 = poor

Rating:	1	2	3	4	5
Landscape				●	
Climate			●		
Quality of Life					●
Cost of Living				●	
Transportation		●			
Retail Services			●		
Health Care			●		
Community Services			●		
Cultural Activities			●		
Recreational Activities					●
Work/Volunteer Activities			●		
Crime				●	

Total Points: 42

the worst flooding should a hurricane strike the community head on. The parish is fertile, with farmed areas alternating with lush green forest. Residential areas are heavily planted with live oak, magnolia, pine and azalea.

Climate   Rating: 3

 Like the nearby Gulf Coast, Covington has a humid subtropical climate with long, hot humid summers and short, mild winters. Winter's typical mildness is interrupted by occasional cold waves that can drop temperatures below 20 degrees for short periods. Even so, daytime highs are nearly always above freezing, even during polar outbreaks. Annual precipitation is ample and well distributed throughout the year. Snowfall is insignificant. Sunshine levels vary from about 50 percent in winter to about 60 percent in other seasons. Summer days are generally unpleasantly muggy owing to the combination of 90-degree temperatures and over 60 percent relative humidity. In contrast, spring and fall weather is often delightful with warm days, cool nights, and slightly lower humidity. Occasional frosts in winter limit the frost-free period to about 250 days.

Quality of Life   Rating: 5

 The quality of life in Covington is excellent. The air is clean and most locations away from Interstate-12 and several major boulevards are free of serious noise pollution. As a result of the area's small town character, crowding and traffic congestion are minimal except perhaps on the approaches to the Lake Pontchartrain Causeway at rush hour. Plenty of free parking is available but there is no public transit. Taxis are the only alternative to the private car. Covington itself is a lovely, heavily treed community of older homes on large lots. Parts of Mandeville are similar but newer residential developments between the two towns, while attractive enough, manifest a more suburban character with large houses on somewhat smaller lots. Several large city and state parks add to the area's livability and Covington's restored downtown is a gem among historic districts. People seem content with their community and determined to keep it a safe and secure place sheltered by distance from crime-ridden New Orleans.

Cost of Living   Rating: 4

 The cost of living in Covington is evaluated as follows:

- *Composite.* ACCRA data for metropolitan New Orleans, of which St. Tammany Parish is a part, are used in the absence of separate data for Covington. On that basis the composite cost of living in Covington is just below the national average.

- *Housing.* Housing costs are slightly above average in Covington and considerably higher than in the City of New Orleans. Local sources suggest an average home price above $170,000 in western St. Tammany, but this reflects an abundance of upscale housing rather than high prices per se. Your housing dollar goes far in Covington.

- *Goods and Services.* ACCRA data suggest that groceries are priced at the national average. Summer air conditioning and winter heating cause utility bills to be about 25 percent above the national average, whereas transportation costs are only five or ten percent above average. Health care and miscellaneous goods and services are priced well below national norms.

- *Taxes.* The overall tax burden in Covington and neighboring communities is unusually low. Louisiana income tax rates are well below average, especially for retired public employees. Income from public pensions and social security is entirely exempt. Property taxes are also extremely low, averaging less than 50 percent of the national average. The tax bill on a $170,000 home in Covington would be about $1,600. State/local sales taxes, currently 8.25 percent in Covington and 8.75 percent in Mandeville, are very high by national norms.

Local and Regional Services

Very much in the economic shadow of New Orleans, Covington provides a limited range of services. These are easily supplemented by a 30-minute drive to Slidell or New Orleans.

Transportation   Rating: 2

Local transportation is almost entirely by car; the western St. Tammany area lacks a fixed route public transit system. This situation appears unlikely to change as many residents oppose public transit out of fear that "outsiders" would come in and pose a threat to the community. Limited dial-a-ride service is available to the elderly and disabled and van service connects Covington with New Orleans. New Orleans International Airport, 40 miles south, is a medium hub with 50 nonstop jet destinations including Atlanta, Dallas and Los Angeles. Amtrak provides daily service from New Orleans north to Chicago and New York, and thrice weekly service west to Los Angeles and east to Miami. Greyhound bus service to many points is also available in New Orleans.

Retail Services   Rating: 3

Downtown Covington is charming with many boutiques, specialty shops, galleries and restaurants located in historic buildings. Western St. Tammany still lacks a large enclosed mall although there are a number of small strip malls in the area. A Wal-Mart beside Highway 190 on the edge of Covington provides for basic shopping needs. In Slidell, 20 miles east via I-12, there is a major mall anchored by Dillard's, JCPenney, Mervyn's and Sears. A local favorite for major shopping is Esplanade Mall in Kenner, a New Orleans suburb 45 minutes from Covington via the causeway.

Health Care   Rating: 3

With two full-service hospitals and several physical therapy and rehabilitation centers, Covington provides good medical care that is easily supplemented by the outstanding medical centers of nearby New Orleans. Columbia Lakeview Regional Medical Center, with 163 beds, and St. Tammany Parish Hospital, a 131-bed nonprofit facility, are currently being expanded. Both hospitals offer nearly 40 specialties including wellness programs and classes in stress reduction and relaxation. New Orleans boasts 26 fully accredited hospitals including six American Medical Association certified teaching facilities.

Community Services   Rating: 3

St. Tammany Parish and numerous community service organizations provide an assortment of services for all age groups. The St. Tammany Parish Library operates branches in all major communities including

Covington, Mandeville, Abita Springs and Madisonville. The New Image Seniors Club, AARP, the Service Corps of Retired Executives (SCORE), the Council on Aging, and the YMCA are very active locally.

Leisure Activities

Long a playground of residents of New Orleans, the north shore of Lake Pontchartrain remains a focus of outdoor recreation and small town culture. Nearby New Orleans offers an array of sophisticated cultural and recreational attractions the envy of many larger cities.

Cultural and Educational Activities	Rating: 3

 The visual and performing arts are well represented in Covington and vicinity. The St. Tammany Art Association coordinates artistic events and area galleries display a surprising variety of art. An annual highlight is November's Three Rivers Art Festival, a juried arts show accompanied by food, music and entertainment in the galleries and streets of downtown Covington. Music and theater are also well represented locally. Choral concerts are presented by the Northshore Performing Arts Society, bluegrass music by the Piney Woods Opry, and band music by several West St. Tammany groups. Playmaker's Inc., one of America's oldest little theaters, presents several productions per year as does the new North Star Theater in Mandeville.

The performing arts calendar of New Orleans is filled with symphonic and chamber music concerts, recitals, ballet, opera and theater from September through May. Resident ensembles including the Louisiana Philharmonic Orchestra, the New Orleans Ballet, and the New Orleans Opera present a seemingly endless series of first-rate events often featuring internationally known guest artists. Jazz at Preservation Hall in the French Quarter is a New Orleans institution and an annual jazz festival is held in early spring. The Saenger Performing Arts Center, on Canal Street, presents Broadway musicals and concerts, and several other very good theatrical companies provide additional entertainment choices.

Recreational Activities	Rating: 5

 Covington's beautiful subtropical landscape, laced with rivers and bayous and fronting on Lake Pontchartrain, is highly conducive to outdoor recreation. Water sports are big here. Lake Pontchartrain sports flotillas of sailboats and other pleasure craft, the Tchefuncte and Bogue Falaya Rivers provide ideal spots for power boating and water-skiing, and scenic bayous offer quiet havens for fishing, canoeing and kayaking. Mandeville's North Shore Nature Center features elevated boardwalks through pristine cypress swamps for close-up bird watching and wildlife observation. Walkers, joggers, cyclists and skaters enjoy the 31-mile long Tammany Trace linear park, a rails-to-trails conversion with miles of paved trail crossing some of the most scenic areas of St. Tammany Parish. Western St. Tammany also claims four country clubs and two public golf courses, six athletic clubs, a skating rink, bowling complex, eleven municipal parks and playgrounds, Fontainebleau State Park on Lake Pontchartrain, and Fairview Riverside State Park on the Tchefuncte River. Elements of the movie "Eve's Bayou" were filmed in the latter park a few years ago. Both parks are notable for camping, picnicking, hiking, boating and fishing; Fontainebleau also has lake swimming and bicycle trails. Western St. Tammany also boasts four multiplex cinema complexes and several good restaurants.

A plethora of additional recreational options are available just across the lake. New Orleans assets include NFL football, NCAA basketball and football at Tulane University, basketball at the University of New Orleans, the multiple attractions of City Park, which covers 1,500 acres and is the fifth largest park in the United States, and the Audubon Zoo. Last but not least, the architectural and historic sites, antique shops, night spots and fine restaurants of the French Quarter engender frequent visits to the Crescent City.

Work and Volunteer Activities   Rating: 3

Although the Covington area is growing rapidly in population, job growth is mostly confined to the service sector, especially retailing and real estate, and wages are low. Many seniors find fulfillment in volunteer work for local hospitals, schools, libraries, the Chamber of Commerce, and various other volunteer-based nonprofit organizations. AARP and the Service Corps of Retired Executives are helpful in securing placements.

Crime Rates and Public Safety   Rating: 4

Crime rates have declined in recent years in the Covington area and St. Tammany Parish now ranks as one of America's safest retirement locales. Rates of overall crime, violent crime and property crime are all less than half of national norms. Residents need to be wary, though, when visiting New Orleans. Violent crime rates there are among the highest in the nation.

Conclusion

Overall Rating 42 Part of the New Orleans Metropolitan Area, yet physically and psychologically separated from the Crescent City by 24 miles of Lake Pontchartrain, Covington and neighboring north shore communities are in many ways a world apart from New Orleans. A blend of small town, suburban and rural elements, the Covington area offers a high quality of life and outstanding outdoor recreation in a beautiful, quiet and safe environment. Viewed in isolation from New Orleans, as it is in the ratings, it has only modest transportation, retail, health care and cultural resources. However, the enormous assets of the metropolitan center are routinely used by north shore residents, who value their separate identity yet enjoy the city's resources. Although some might find Covington's long, hot humid summers disagreeable, few would object to the weather in winter, spring or fall. A more serious concern is the absence of public transit; a car is a virtual necessity here. That said, Covington might well suit those seeking retirement in a lovely, subtropical, small town setting yet within easy reach of the bright lights and metropolitan amenities of one of America's most interesting cities.

Savannah, Georgia and Fairhope, Alabama

Savannah, Georgia and Fairhope, Alabama are also worth considering for retirement.

Savannah, Georgia

Although Savannah is a busy port and industrial center located a few miles upstream from the mouth of the Savannah River, its chief claim to fame is its lovely historic district. With more than 2,400 architecturally and historically significant buildings in a 2.5-square mile area, the Savannah Historic District is a national treasure. Just to the east, the Intracoastal Waterway separates the city and its mainland suburbs from Tybee, Little Tybee, Wilmington and Skidaway Islands, which form the northern echelon of Georgia's famous Golden Isles.

With a population of 140,000 in the city and 250,000 in Chatham County, Savannah suffers from some typical urban ills including high crime rates in inner city areas. Although the city meets federal air quality standards, sulfurous emissions from a riverfront pulp and paper mill occasionally taint the air. Savannah's long, hot humid summer may also be disagreeable to some people. On balance, though, Savannah has much to offer. It is big enough to provide the services and amenities needed to retire well. Local bus service is satisfactory and Amtrak runs 14 trains weekly northbound to New York and 14 southbound to Florida. Nonstop jet service to major hub airports is available from Savannah International Airport. The city provides very good health care and services for seniors, shopping is good at two regional malls and at trendy shops in the historic district, and the cultural scene is lively. The Savannah Civic Center Theater and Arena host the Savannah Symphony Orchestra and nationally-known touring artists and the City Lights Theater Company offers its playbill in the newly renovated Avon Theater. Coastal waters, island beaches and warm, subtropical weather provide endless opportunities for boating, sailing, fishing and swimming. Living costs are slightly below the national average and the state/local tax burden is moderate so Savannah is not only attractive but also affordable.

Fairhope, Alabama

Perched atop a high bluff overlooking Mobile Bay, the lovely little city of Fairhope is the most attractive of several towns along the bay's subtropical Eastern Shore. Canopied with large live oaks, magnolias and pines, this well-planned community boasts outstanding residential neighborhoods and a charming, architecturally interesting and commercially viable downtown. Below the bluff is a city park with picnicking and playground facilities, a sandy beach and a municipal fishing pier extending far into the bay.

Fairhope's population of 10,000 makes for modest transportation and retail assets and limited part-time work opportunities. Baldwin County Transit provides service throughout the county but buses run infrequently. Intercity bus, rail and air transportation is available from Mobile, 25 miles west. Over 100 clubs and service organizations offer many opportunities to contribute to the community.

Fairhope provides an excellent quality of life at low cost. The town was founded in 1894 by followers of Henry George, who advocated taxing only land. Much of the city is still owned by the Single Tax Corporation, which rents land to homeowners on renewable 99-year leases. This keeps housing prices low by curtailing land speculation. Other advantages of Fairhope include low taxes (Alabama does not tax most retirement income), low crime rates, very good community services and health care, and surprisingly strong cultural and recreational assets. The town has long attracted creative people, the number of writers and artists living here is remarkable. The Eastern Shore Art Center is the focus of the visual arts and plays are produced by the professional Jubilee Fish Theater and several little theater associations. Faulkner Junior College and a branch campus of the University of South Alabama offer courses of interest to seniors and local resources for golf, tennis, horseback riding, boating, sailing and fishing are almost endless. Few small towns offer as much.

6 The Interior South Retirement Region

Climate: Humid subtropical

The Interior South Retirement Region, stretching from the rolling hills of northern Mississippi to the Ouachita Mountains and Ozark Plateaus of Arkansas, has long evoked an image of subsistence farming, moon shining, poverty and isolation. For decades the region lost population as jobs and better living conditions in cities such as St. Louis, Kansas City, Dallas and Tulsa lured young people away. During the last 30 years, though, in the wake of dam building by government and utilities that created a large number of scenic artificial lakes, and highway building that broke down rural isolation, the long-term trend of out-migration has reversed. Increasing numbers of people are relocating for retirement to rural counties in the uplands and to several attractive small cities.

Oxford, Mississippi, and Fayetteville and Hot Springs, Arkansas, stand out as centers suitable for upscale retirement. Oxford and Fayetteville owe much of their success and character to the University of Mississippi and the University of Arkansas, respectively, while Hot Springs has long been famous for its "healing waters" and beautiful lake and mountain areas. The many amenities of these towns are available at a cost of living well below the national average.

Oxford, Mississippi

With its picturesque courthouse square, magnolia-studded University of Mississippi campus, and street and neighborhood scenes seemingly lifted from the novels of native son William Faulkner, Oxford is the quintessential southern college town. Founded in 1835 on land purchased from a Chickasaw Indian woman, the town was named Oxford after the English university town in hopes that its famous name would help the community attract its own university. The plan worked; state officials chose Oxford and the University of Mississippi opened its doors in 1848. Since that date the fate of Oxford has been inextricably linked to the fortunes of the university, affectionately known locally and throughout the state as Ole Miss. With a population of just over 12,000 in the city and 35,000 in Lafayette County, Oxford is a very small town. But thanks

Oxford, Mississippi

CLIMATE				
Month	Average Daily Temperature High Low		Daily Rel. Humidity Low	Average Monthly Precipitation
	°F		%	Inches
January	52	30	62	5.0
February	56	33	62	4.7
March	64	40	54	6.5
April	74	50	50	6.0
May	81	57	57	5.0
June	88	65	54	3.9
July	91	69	56	3.9
August	91	68	55	2.7
September	85	62	55	4.1
October	76	48	53	2.7
November	64	39	58	5.0
December	55	33	62	5.2

Annual Average

Total Days		Total Inches	
Clear	120	Precipitation	54.7
Partly Cloudy	97	Snowfall	3.0
Cloudy	148		

RATINGS

Rating Scale: 5 = excellent; 4 = very good; 3 = good; 2 = fair; 1 = poor

Rating:	1	2	3	4	5
Landscape				●	
Climate			●		
Quality of Life					●
Cost of Living				●	
Transportation			●		
Retail Services				●	
Health Care			●		
Community Services				●	
Cultural Activities				●	
Recreational Activities				●	
Work/Volunteer Activities				●	
Crime				●	

Total Points: 46

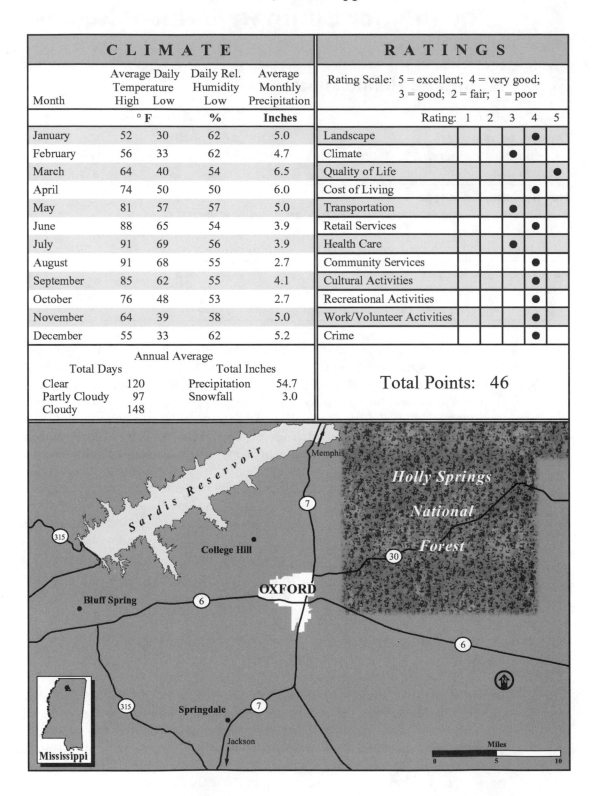

to the university, it is able to offer residents an upscale and fairly cosmopolitan existence. Amenities typically available in larger cities can be found in Memphis, Tennessee, 75 miles northwest, and Jackson, Mississippi, 165 miles south.

Landscape   Rating: 4

 Oxford is located in north central Mississippi about 50 miles south of the Tennessee state line. Nestled among rolling hills at an elevation of 450 feet, the town has an extraordinarily beautiful natural landscape. A luxuriant southern mixed forest of oak and pine envelops the community. In town, large magnolias are conspicuous on campus and along many residential streets. Flowering shrubs and vines such as redbud and wisteria add seasonal color, especially in spring.

Climate   Rating: 3

 Oxford experiences a temperate, four-season variant of the Southeast's humid subtropical climate. Summer afternoons are hot and tend to be uncomfortable because of high relative humidity; summer nights are warm. Spring and fall weather is generally very pleasant, with warm days and cool nights. Winters are mild with average daily highs in the 50s and lows in the 30s. The normal annual precipitation of 54 inches is well distributed throughout the year and only about three inches of snow accumulates on the ground in a typical winter. On average, the town enjoys a frost-free season of 210 days and is sunny about 63 percent of the time.

Quality of Life   Rating: 5

 Oxford is notable for its excellent quality of life. There is little noise from automobile traffic or airplanes, and air quality is excellent. The city and county comply fully with all federal air quality standards. Oxford is clean and uncrowded. There are no noxious industries, population densities are low, and traffic congestion is unknown. Parking is adequate downtown, at the mall, and on campus. The town is very well planned and its pleasant, wooded residential neighborhoods reflect the community's moderate affluence, good taste, and concern for historic preservation. The town is growing relatively slowly so it has been spared the rampant residential subdivision and commercial development characteristic of the periphery of many Sunbelt cities. Historic downtown Oxford is charming and economically thriving, thanks to the hard work of the Downtown Council and the loyalty of local shoppers. Residents are unusually friendly and congenial, even in comparison with those of other small college towns. They clearly appreciate the exceptional quality of life in their idyllic corner of the world and are determined to preserve it.

Cost of Living   Rating: 4

 The cost of living in Oxford is evaluated as follows:

- *Composite.* ACCRA data are currently unavailable for Oxford so statistics for Vicksburg, which were similar to those of Oxford in the recent past, are used here. On that basis, the composite cost of living in Oxford is estimated to be five percent below the national average.

- *Housing.* Housing costs are about ten percent below the national average. One local source recently gave $122,000 as the median price of a single-family residence and noted proudly that Oxford housing is the most expensive in the state. Be that as it may, this quaint garden town offers a variety of housing styles from grand pre-Civil War and smaller historic homes to modern bungalows. Most new construction occurs in the countryside around Oxford and is priced in the $150,000 to $200,000 range. Few resale houses are on the market at any one time, and the price of houses near the Ole Miss campus has risen rapidly in recent years.

- **Goods and Services.** ACCRA data suggest that goods and services in Oxford are priced at or slightly below their national averages. Costs of groceries, transportation and miscellaneous goods and services approximate their national averages, whereas health care and utilities are priced five to ten percent below national norms.

- **Taxes.** The overall tax burden is low in Oxford, especially for retirees. State income tax rates range from three to five percent of taxable income, but that is only the beginning of the good news. All income from federal, state, and private pensions and social security is totally exempt from state income tax. Those over 65 also receive a break on property taxes. The normal annual property tax of $1,078 on a $95,000 Oxford home is reduced to $482 for seniors. Only the seven percent state sales tax exceeds the national average.

Local and Regional Services

For a small town, Oxford provides a good array of services. The rich resources of Memphis, only 75 miles away, supplement these.

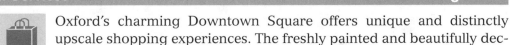

Transportation	Rating: 3

The private automobile dominates local transportation; the town is too small to support a fixed-route transit system. The needs of the transit dependent are not ignored, though. The State of Mississippi Elderly and Handicapped Transit Service provides dial-a-ride shuttle service to local facilities, and the city is planning to offer taxi service to the general population. Greyhound provides intercity bus service. Oxford/University Airport offers general aviation service but Memphis International Airport, 65 miles away, is the major regional airline hub. Memphis International is served by most major carriers and provides nonstop jet service to about 50 destinations. Amtrak service northbound to Chicago and southbound to New Orleans is available from Memphis.

Retail Services	Rating: 4

Oxford's charming Downtown Square offers unique and distinctly upscale shopping experiences. The freshly painted and beautifully decorated J. E. Neilson Company, the oldest department store in the South and the first business established in Oxford, is the pride of the community. Nearby is Square Books, an award-winning bookstore and a great place to browse. Additional specialty shops and several restaurants line the rest of the blocks facing the square.

Oxonians clearly love their little downtown; one local resident said that people prefer shopping there and that the mall is less successful. Even so, Oxford Mall is conveniently located just 1.5 miles west of downtown and does a good business. Anchored by JCPenney and Wal-Mart stores, it includes a number of small specialty shops and a movie theater complex. The Wal-Mart is moving in 2002.

Health Care — Rating: 3

Baptist Memorial Hospital/North Mississippi is Oxford's only general hospital and a major regional medical center. With over 200 beds and 90 physicians representing over 30 specialties on staff, Baptist Memorial meets the medical care needs of most residents. Much larger facilities and a wider range of medical services are only an hour away in Memphis.

Community Services — Rating: 4

Oxford, Lafayette County, the University of Mississippi, and religious and community organizations offer a fine variety of services to residents. The Oxford Public Library is unusually good for a small town facility, and its assets are easily supplemented by those of the University of Mississippi libraries. The Retired Senior Volunteer Program, AARP, and several fraternal associations of retirees provide social and recreational opportunities for seniors. Local churches sponsor, among other social services, a Meals-on-Wheels program and The Pantry, which provides food free of charge to those in need.

Leisure Activities

For a small town, Oxford offers an unusually rich assortment of leisure activities to its residents.

Cultural and Educational Activities — Rating: 4

Ole Miss is the main center of culture and education in northern Mississippi. The University Theatre operates year-round, hosting six or seven productions annually at Bryant Hall. The University Artist Series provides several major musical events each year. Recitals by top-flight faculty and graduate talent, and performances by visiting ensembles, are typically presented at Meek Hall Auditorium on campus. The Gertrude Ford Performing Arts Center will open in June 2002. The University Museum's permanent collections include classical Greek and Roman antiquities, scientific instruments of the 19th century, and the principal collection of the folk art of Theora Hamblett. In addition, eight to ten temporary and visiting exhibitions of the visual arts are shown annually. Blues lovers will appreciate the Ole Miss Blues Archive, the world's largest collection of blues recordings and related materials. Those 65 years and older are entitled to enroll in regular Ole Miss courses free of charge, and the university's Institute for Continuing Studies offers additional courses of interest to the general public for nominal fees. Free public lectures are frequent occurrences on campus, and each year the university hosts the Faulkner Conference, which attracts people from all over the world.

Recreational Activities — Rating: 4

Recreational opportunities appealing to most tastes are found in and around Oxford. Spectator sports are enjoyed by student and town folk alike. The Rebels of Ole Miss regularly host nationally ranked intercollegiate teams in football, basketball, baseball, tennis, track and golf. If your interests are participatory, the Oxford area also has much to offer. Golf is available at 3 challenging 18-hole public courses, while tennis can be played at over 40 outdoor courts. Swimming is popular at the 50-meter municipal pool and at the university's indoor and outdoor pools. The city maintains four local parks with picnic, playground and sporting facilities. Organized programs for football, baseball, softball, volleyball, soccer, and tennis exist for all age groups. Other recreational assets in Oxford include a skating rink, an 18-lane bowling center and six movie theaters. At nearby Sardis Lake, you can picnic, golf, hike, camp, swim, boat, and fish for bass and crappie. Within a 50-mile radius of town are Wall Doxey State Park, Holly Springs National Forest, and Lakes Enid, Grenada, and Arkabutla, each offering recreational opportunities similar to those of Sardis Lake. Back in Oxford, you can sample the fare at one of the city's fine restaurants, a number of which occupy very attractive sites on the Downtown Square. Quite a variety of menu styles, ranging from traditional southern fried chicken and fresh catfish to exotic ethnic cuisine, can be found locally.

Work and Volunteer Activities   Rating: 4

Oxford's economy has done well in recent years. Unemployment is insignificant and opportunities for work and volunteerism are available. Unfortunately, most part-time jobs are in the service sector and competition for work from the large college student population keeps wages low. Volunteer service is a way of life for many in the community and is coordinated effectively by the United Way, which publicizes the personnel needs of 29 agencies and recruits volunteers to fill them.

Crime Rates and Public Safety   Rating: 4

Oxford is one of the safer communities in the country even though its overall rate of property crime approximates the national average. Remarkably, in one recent year there were zero homicides and zero forcible rapes in Oxford, and an overall violent crime rate less than 50 percent of the national norm. The town has a very secure feel to it and residents do not hesitate to walk its streets at any time of day or night.

Conclusion

Overall Rating 46

Oxford is an idyllic little college town. In many ways it reminds me of Chapel Hill, North Carolina as it was 30 or 40 years ago: charming, friendly, safe, and uncrowded. Its physical and human environment is close to ideal. Its site on a rolling, wooded plain is pleasant, and its temperate subtropical climate provides four distinct seasons, with few severely cold or hot days. Oxford's quality of life is excellent. Environmental pollution, traffic congestion, and visual ugliness, the bane of many fast-growing Sunbelt cities, are almost entirely lacking here. The state's dial-a-ride shuttle service for the elderly and handicapped compensates for a lack of a fixed-route municipal transit system. The availability of retail and community services, culture and recreation, and work/volunteer activities is very good. Even health care, typically a weak point in smaller towns, is more than adequate locally. Remarkably, all the benefits of the good life in Oxford come at an overall cost of living five percent below the national average. All things considered, Oxford ranks as one of America's best places for sophisticated retirement in an exceptionally beautiful and unspoiled setting.

Hot Springs, Arkansas

CLIMATE				
Month	Average Daily Temperature High Low	Daily Rel. Humidity Low	Average Monthly Precipitation	
	°F	%	Inches	
January	52 31	60	3.8	
February	57 34	58	4.1	
March	65 42	55	5.3	
April	76 52	55	5.9	
May	82 59	57	6.4	
June	89 67	57	4.4	
July	93 71	54	5.2	
August	93 70	53	3.4	
September	87 63	55	4.4	
October	77 53	52	3.4	
November	63 42	57	4.8	
December	55 35	60	4.5	

Annual Average

Total Days		Total Inches	
Clear	119	Precipitation	55.4
Partly Cloudy	100	Snowfall	5.0
Cloudy	147		

RATINGS

Rating Scale: 5 = excellent; 4 = very good; 3 = good; 2 = fair; 1 = poor

Rating:	1	2	3	4	5
Landscape				●	
Climate			●		
Quality of Life				●	
Cost of Living					●
Transportation			●		
Retail Services			●		
Health Care			●		
Community Services			●		
Cultural Activities			●		
Recreational Activities				●	
Work/Volunteer Activities				●	
Crime		●			

Total Points: 41

Hot Springs, Arkansas

The famous thermal springs that issue from the lower slopes of Hot Springs Mountain have long attracted visitors and settlers to the area. First discovered by Native Americans perhaps 10,000 years ago, the springs were visited by Hernando de Soto and his Spanish troops in 1541 and by French trappers and traders during the 17th century. Shortly after the United States acquired the area from France in the 1803 Louisiana Purchase, American settlers attracted in part by the "healing waters" began to move into the area. In 1832 the federal government established the Hot Springs National Reservation, which became Hot Springs National Park in 1921. The City of Hot Springs has much to offer retirees. Surrounded by mountains and lakes, it offers abundant outdoor recreational opportunities in a beautiful environment where living costs are low. With a population near 36,000 in the city and 85,000 in surrounding Garland County, the urban area is large enough to offer the amenities most people want yet small enough to avoid congestion and environmental pollution.

Landscape   Rating: 4

 Hot Springs is nestled in several valleys amidst the gently rolling Ouachita Mountains in south central Arkansas. Elevations in the city range from 300 to 800 feet with summit levels in the adjacent national park rising several hundred feet higher. Dense forests of oak, hickory and short-leaf pine cover the mountains and much of the lowlands. Flowering trees are common and successive seasons feature changing displays of flowers and brightly colored foliage. Redbud and dogwood bloom in the woods in early spring while flowering southern magnolias lend a special beauty to historic Bathhouse Row in early summer. Most residential areas, whether in town next to the national park or on the periphery adjacent to Lake Hamilton, are well wooded with large shade trees that provide shelter from summer's sun.

Climate   Rating: 3

Hot Springs has a humid subtropical climate characterized by four distinct seasons, heavy precipitation, moderate amounts of sunshine, and pronounced day-to-day and seasonal weather changes. Rainfall is well distributed seasonally with 55 inches falling in an average year. Snowfall is insignificant with an average annual total of only five inches. Winter, spring and fall weather tends to be changeable from day to day, whereas summer weather is pretty consistently hot and humid. Winter days are mild, winter nights cold. Spring and fall weather is the most pleasant of the year, with generally warm days and cool nights. The city enjoys a frost-free period of 230 days so gardening is possible from late March through mid November. On average, Hot Springs is sunny 62 percent of the time, but winter is cloudier than the other seasons.

Quality of Life   Rating: 4

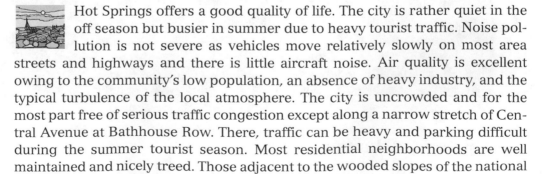 Hot Springs offers a good quality of life. The city is rather quiet in the off season but busier in summer due to heavy tourist traffic. Noise pollution is not severe as vehicles move relatively slowly on most area streets and highways and there is little aircraft noise. Air quality is excellent owing to the community's low population, an absence of heavy industry, and the typical turbulence of the local atmosphere. The city is uncrowded and for the most part free of serious traffic congestion except along a narrow stretch of Central Avenue at Bathhouse Row. There, traffic can be heavy and parking difficult during the summer tourist season. Most residential neighborhoods are well maintained and nicely treed. Those adjacent to the wooded slopes of the national

park in the northern part of town or alongside Lake Hamilton on the southern edge are especially scenic. Unfortunately, much of the landscape between these areas is uninspiring. The city sprawls outward along Central Avenue toward Lake Hamilton. Much of the strip and shopping center development along the road is distinctly unappealing and offers a startling contrast to the charming and historic Bathhouse Row commercial area.

Cost of Living — Rating: 5

 The cost of living in Hot Springs is evaluated as follows:

- **Composite.** Recent ACCRA data show the overall cost of living in Hot Springs to be about six percent below the national average.

- **Housing.** According to ACCRA, housing costs are fully 20 percent below the national average. Local sources and exploration of the Hot Springs area confirm an abundance of inexpensive housing, especially on the periphery toward Lake Hamilton. Relatively new and luxurious condominiums on the lake sell for less than $100,000. A good supply of single-family homes priced in the $50,000 to $200,000 range is found in several parts of the city.

- **Goods and Services.** Utilities are priced about 17 percent above the national average; groceries are about 5 percent above. Miscellaneous goods and services costs are about 4 percent below the national norm, while transportation and health care are bargains at prices 10 and 16 percent, respectively, below average.

- **Taxes.** The overall tax burden in Hot Springs approximates the national average. State income tax rates escalate rapidly with increasing income to a rate of seven percent on taxable income above $25,000. This means that most middle-income taxpayers pay higher-than-average state income taxes in Arkansas. The combined state/local sales tax rate of 6.92 percent in Hot Springs is also above the national average, whereas the property tax of $819 on a typical $100,000 home is very low by national norms.

Local and Regional Services

For a relatively small city, Hot Springs offers residents an unusually good supply of services. This reflects the city's dual status as a regional center and major tourist destination.

Transportation — Rating: 3

 Although most people who can drive do so in Hot Springs, Hot Springs Intracity Transit (IT) provides a useful alternative. Operated by the City of Hot Springs, IT provides local bus service from a downtown transit center to major destinations including Garland County Community College, St. Joseph's Regional Medical Center, National Park Medical Center, Hot Springs Mall and Lake Hamilton. Most suburban residential areas are not served. The basic fare is $1.00 per ride but use of discount coupon books or monthly passes can reduce travel costs considerably. A regular monthly pass costs $33 but seniors and the disabled pay only $22. Hot Springs Trolley Company provides excellent service in the downtown historic district including Bathhouse Row and to the observation tower on Hot Springs Mountain, for nominal fares. Limited commuter airline service is available out of Hot Springs Airport but Little Rock

International Airport is a better choice for commercial air travel. Located about 50 miles northeast and accessible from Hot Springs by shuttle bus, Little Rock International offers nonstop jet service to over 15 destinations including major hubs at Dallas and St. Louis. Amtrak provides limited service from Little Rock to points such as Chicago, San Antonio and Los Angeles via the Texas Eagle train. Currently this train makes three departures weekly northbound and three southbound.

Retail Services   Rating: 3

Retail services sufficient to meet the needs of most people are available locally. Hot Springs Mall, located on the southern edge of the city near Lake Hamilton, is the major regional shopping complex. Anchored by Dillard's, JCPenney, and Sears department stores, the mall houses many of the usual national and regional chain specialty stores and restaurants. A smaller shopping center, also on Central Avenue but closer to downtown, features Wal-Mart and Kroger stores. The city's historic downtown is no longer a major shopping area for local residents but remains commercially viable thanks to the popularity of its quaint shops among tourists frequenting Bathhouse Row on the other side of Central Avenue.

Health Care   Rating: 3

Two general hospitals provide adequate health care locally and the much greater medical resources of Little Rock are only an hour away. St. Joseph's Regional Health Center, a non-profit hospital operated by the St. Louis-based Sisters of Mercy Health Care System, has 317 private suites and offers a wide range of services. In addition to the usual clinical services like cardiac, cancer and diabetic care, the hospital reaches out to the community with its senior citizen centers and Meals-on-Wheels, home health, and mobile health programs. National Park Medical Center, a 166-bed for-profit hospital, also provides wide-ranging services including open-heart surgery and cardiac rehabilitation. The hospital's home health agency provides an array of in-home services including personal care.

Community Services   Rating: 3

Services of interest to seniors are well developed in this retirement-oriented city. The Senior Citizens Center, located just west of the city center, is a focus of social and recreational activities for retirees, while the Community Adult Center offers similar opportunities for the general adult population. Several retiree clubs and social organizations including the local AARP chapter provide additional support for active seniors.

Leisure Activities

The City of Hot Springs, Hot Springs National Park, and the surrounding lake and mountain countryside offer residents a remarkable variety of leisure activities.

Cultural and Educational Activities   Rating: 3

Although Hot Springs is too small to support classic resident ensembles like symphony orchestras and opera companies, its arts culture has broadened greatly during the past decade. Each year the Hot Springs Documentary Film Festival showcases over 50 classical and experimental American and foreign documentaries at the historic Malco Theatre, downtown. During the first two weeks in June, the city hosts the Hot Springs Music Festival. This musical extravaganza brings together over 200 musicians who perform in 300 orchestral and chamber music concerts and open rehearsals. The Hot Springs Jazz and Blues Festival, which features nationally known modern and traditional jazz artists, rounds out the summer season each September. The visual arts are also well represented. Artists and gallery owners have renovated many Victorian buildings in the historic district into attractive studios and galleries, while the Hot Springs Arts Center spotlights the work of resident artists in its monthly exhibits. Continuing education courses of interest to seniors are offered at the Shepherds Center and at the Senior Citizen Center of Hot Springs.

Recreational Activities   Rating: 4

 Surrounded by mountains and lakes, Hot Springs and its immediate surroundings offer excellent opportunities for recreation in a setting of great natural beauty. Nearby Lakes Catherine, Hamilton, and Ouachita are excellent sites for boating, fishing, water-skiing and swimming. Parks adjacent to the lakes feature picnicking, hiking, and camping, while Hot Springs National Park is especially notable for bathing, picnicking, walking and sightseeing along Bathhouse Row and hiking on the trails of its forested, mountainous areas. The city's nine neighborhood parks provide additional recreational facilities. Golf, tennis, and bowling facilities are more than adequate locally. Three area 18-hole public golf courses and one 9-hole public course are supplemented by eight additional courses at local country clubs and in nearby planned communities. Movie theaters and good, inexpensive restaurants featuring a surprising variety of cuisines are well represented in Hot Springs. Finally, fans of thoroughbred racing can try their luck at centrally located Oaklawn Park all year. Live racing extends from late January to mid-April and simulcast racing from other parks may be viewed there the rest of the year.

Work and Volunteer Activities   Rating: 4

 Wages are low in Hot Springs but so too are living costs. Many seniors find work in service industries and especially in tourist related activities. Offering volunteer services through over 150 volunteer organizations is a big part in the lives of many senior citizens not ready for total retirement. Volunteers in Parks (VIPs) lead guided tours, greet and assist visitors at the information desk, staff the bookstore, serve as campground aids, and maintain trails in Hot Springs National Park, while Friends of the Fordyce (Bathhouse) and Hot Springs National Park Inc. raise funds to upgrade park facilities.

Crime Rates and Public Safety   Rating: 2

 Potential exposure to crime varies drastically over relatively short distances in Hot Springs. Although rates of violent and property crime are well above national norms in the City of Hot Springs and approximate crime rates encountered in larger Sunbelt cities like Tucson, outlying suburban districts are much safer. Comparison of city and county data indicates that rates of violent and property crime are between 50 and 75 percent lower in county territory than in the city. This goes a long way toward explaining the seemingly reckless comment of a local woman who said that she doesn't lock her doors in daytime at Lake Hamilton. In fairness to the city and its residents, it should be noted that many lovely, older inner city neighborhoods bordering the national park appear very safe and peaceful. On the other hand, you can encounter sub-marginal living conditions in poor, inner city areas only a mile or two away.

Conclusion

Overall Rating 41

It is easy to understand why Hot Springs has become a favorite location for retirement. The city's physical site is very scenic with low mountains and a national park in town and three large lakes nearby. Its sunny, warm climate with four clearly defined seasons appeals to many, and its quality of life is good. The city is small and uncrowded and suffers from none of the problems of pollution and congestion characteristic of large cities. Its rankings in retail and community services and volunteer activities are good, and its health care and transportation assets are at least adequate. Together, the city, the national park, and the surrounding lake and mountain countryside offer residents a plethora of cultural and recreational options. The major drawbacks to retirement in Hot Springs are probably its hot, humid summers and an above-average incidence of crime. Not much can be done about the weather, but housing costs are so low in Hot Springs that one can more easily afford a very nice house in an upscale and relatively safe neighborhood here than in most other desirable communities. On that basis, Hot Springs is worthy of careful examination.

Fayetteville, Arkansas

Founded in 1828 when northwestern Arkansas was opened to American settlement and described 12 years later by a disgruntled resident as a lawless and uncivilized place, Fayetteville has matured since World War II into the region's most sophisticated and attractive city. To a large extent, the present success of Fayetteville has its roots in the efforts of local citizens in the immediate post-Civil War era to have their community chosen as the site for the Arkansas land grant college. Their efforts were rewarded with the 1872 opening of Arkansas Industrial College, which evolved ultimately into the University of Arkansas, the flagship institution of the state's higher education system. The university is justifiably the pride of Fayetteville, the center of its cultural and social life, and its principal employer. With a population approaching 55,000 in the city and 140,000 in Washington County, Fayetteville is large enough to offer the amenities most people seek, in a relaxed yet vibrant college town.

Landscape   Rating: 5

Fayetteville is situated at an elevation of 1,300 feet amidst the gently rolling hills of the Ozark Plateau in the northwestern corner of Arkansas. Although the city's setting is not as spectacular as that of Boulder, Colorado, the surrounding hills, mantled in a dense growth of broadleafed deciduous trees, provide a lovely backdrop to the community's well-treed and landscaped neighborhoods.

Climate   Rating: 4

Fayetteville experiences a temperate variant of the humid subtropical climate found throughout the southeastern United States. The town's moderate elevation causes the four distinct seasons to be a little cooler

Fayetteville, Arkansas

	CLIMATE				RATINGS						
Month	Average Daily Temperature High	Low	Daily Rel. Humidity Low	Average Monthly Precipitation	Rating Scale: 5 = excellent; 4 = very good; 3 = good; 2 = fair; 1 = poor						
	°F		%	Inches	Rating:	1	2	3	4	5
January	46	23	61	2.0	Landscape					●
February	51	28	60	2.7	Climate				●	
March	59	35	56	3.8	Quality of Life					●
April	70	46	55	4.6	Cost of Living					●
May	77	54	59	5.5	Transportation		●			
June	85	62	59	4.5	Retail Services				●	
July	90	67	56	3.7	Health Care				●	
August	89	64	54	3.5	Community Services		●			
September	82	57	58	4.2	Cultural Activities				●	
October	72	45	54	3.3	Recreational Activities				●	
November	59	35	59	3.4	Work/Volunteer Activities				●	
December	50	28	63	2.7	Crime		●			

Annual Average

Total Days		Total Inches	
Clear	116	Precipitation	44.0
Partly Cloudy	96	Snowfall	10.0
Cloudy	153		

Total Points: 48

than at lower elevations. Even so, summer afternoons can be uncomfortable because of high temperatures and humidity. Spring and fall weather is quite changeable from day to day but on average is the most pleasant of the year. Winters are not severe although occasional cold waves can temporarily drop temperatures well below seasonal norms. Annual precipitation averages 44 inches and is well distributed throughout the year; only 10 inches of snow accumulates on the ground in a typical winter and it melts within a few days. On average, the city enjoys a frost-free season of 180 days and is sunny about 60 percent of the time.

Quality of Life   Rating: 5

 The quality of life is excellent in Fayetteville. There is little noise pollution as the Interstate-540 freeway skirts the city's western side and there is minimal aicraft noise. The new regional airport will be miles away toward the northwest. Air quality is excellent; the city and county comply fully with all federal air quality standards. Some residents complain, though, that air-borne chicken dander causes allergic reactions. This would not be surprising since millions of broiler chickens are raised annually in northwest Arkansas. Traffic congestion is unknown and parking is more than adequate at the local mall and downtown, although it is tight adjacent to the old core of the university campus. Residential neighborhoods are quite varied but all are well treed, landscaped and maintained. Residents seem friendly, well educated, and proud of the peaceful ambiance of their community.

Cost of Living   Rating: 5

 The cost of living in Fayetteville is evaluated as follows:

- *Composite*. ACCRA data for Fayetteville reveal a composite cost of living about 10 percent below the national average.

- *Housing*. Housing is inexpensive. ACCRA data show housing costs to be about 20 percent below the national average. Exploration of the local area revealed a good variety of desirable housing. Attractive modern suburban houses on large wooded lots on the edge of town were priced between $100,000 and $150,000; those in slightly more remote locations were priced even lower. Several historic districts close to downtown and the University of Arkansas campus offer additional choices. The Washington/Willow historic district has some of Fayetteville's finest homes. Many large houses there, some newly renovated, are priced between $100,000 and $300,000. The nearby Wilson Park neighborhood has many mid-sized houses, built in the 1950s and 1960s, priced between $80,000 and $160,000.

- *Goods and Services*. Goods and services are all priced well below national norms. Miscellaneous goods and services are 5 percent; groceries, health care and transportation about 10 percent; and utilities 12 percent below their national averages.

- *Taxes*. The overall tax burden in Fayetteville approximates the national average. Arkansas state income tax rates escalate rapidly with increasing income to a rate of seven percent on taxable income above $25,000. As a result, most middle income residents pay higher than average income taxes. The combined state/local sales tax rate in Fayetteville is also above the national average but the property tax on a typical single-family home is low by national standards.

Local and Regional Services

Like many college towns, Fayetteville offers a very good array of services for a community of its size. Additional resources are available in nearby Springdale and Rogers.

Transportation — Rating: 3

 Although Fayetteville residents typically drive to most destinations, public transit alternatives are available. Ozark Regional Transit, the city-owned bus company, operates 39 buses and trolleys that offer service on fixed routes as well as door-to-door, dial-a-ride service. Razorback Transit, operated by the university, serves the campus community. Northwest Arkansas Regional Airport will soon provide the Fayetteville/Springdale/Rogers area with enhanced air transportation including jet passenger and cargo service. To date, Drake Field, the local Fayetteville airport, provides nonstop jet service to three hubs and commuter services to four others.

Retail Services — Rating: 4

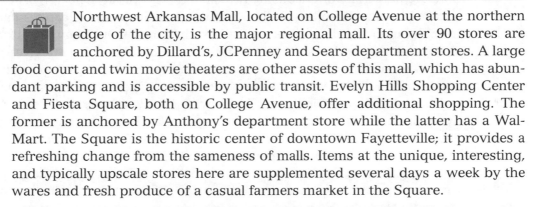 Northwest Arkansas Mall, located on College Avenue at the northern edge of the city, is the major regional mall. Its over 90 stores are anchored by Dillard's, JCPenney and Sears department stores. A large food court and twin movie theaters are other assets of this mall, which has abundant parking and is accessible by public transit. Evelyn Hills Shopping Center and Fiesta Square, both on College Avenue, offer additional shopping. The former is anchored by Anthony's department store while the latter has a Wal-Mart. The Square is the historic center of downtown Fayetteville; it provides a refreshing change from the sameness of malls. Items at the unique, interesting, and typically upscale stores here are supplemented several days a week by the wares and fresh produce of a casual farmers market in the Square.

Health Care — Rating: 4

 Washington Regional Medical Center, a not-for-profit facility with nearly 300 beds, is the city's major medical center. It offers a wide variety of medical services including, among others, emergency and intensive care, cardiac surgery and care, diabetic and pulmonary rehabilitation, and diagnostic radiology and special imaging. The local VA Medical Center, also located on College Avenue, provides specialty clinics for urology, orthopedics, diabetes, mental health, and substance abuse as well as dental, cardiopulmonary, and imaging services to veterans. Additional medical facilities and services are found in neighboring Springdale and Rogers.

Community Services — Rating: 3

Fayetteville, Washington County, and the University of Arkansas offer a fine array of services to the public. The Community Adult Center of Fayetteville organizes trips to nearby attractions, including musical performances in Branson, and hosts activities such as dances, cards, billiards, and pot-luck dinners. Classes in arts and crafts and exercise are also offered to seniors by the center.

Leisure Activities

Many and varied leisure activities are available in Fayetteville and in the country-side of the Ozark Plateau.

Cultural and Educational Activities	Rating: 4

 Thanks to the University of Arkansas and the philanthropy of the Walton family, Fayetteville is an oasis of higher education and culture. In addition to regular university courses, available for audit by seniors on a "space available" basis, the university's Continuing Education Center schedules a great variety of courses of interest to the general public and hosts an Elderhostel program of short courses, which attracts locals and visitors alike. Additionally, Fayetteville public schools offer a variety of personal enrichment and applied arts courses through their adult and community education program.

The performing arts are well represented on campus and off. A Fine Arts Concert Series, often featuring internationally acclaimed musicians, is hosted by the university Music Department at the Campus Fine Arts Concert Hall. In addition, the university offers quality drama at the University Theater, art exhibits at a gallery in the Fine Arts Building, and miscellaneous musical events ranging from open-air band concerts on the lawn in front of Old Main to rock concerts at Barnhill Arena. Just off campus in the heart of town is Fayetteville's magnificent Walton Arts Center with its three auditoriums, art gallery, and outdoor amphitheater. The Arts Center presents about 50 performances annually, varying from classical music by the North Arkansas Symphony and North Arkansas Symphonic Band to plays by Ozark Stageworks. Touring artist bookings at the Center have recently included the New York City Opera and professional productions of To Kill a Mockingbird and West Side Story.

Recreational Activities	Rating: 4

 Varied recreational opportunities are found in Fayetteville and the nearby Ozarks. The city's 23 parks, comprising over 3,100 acres in all, are mostly in a relatively natural state. Only three percent of their total acreage is devoted to sports facilities. Fishing and hiking are popular at Lake Fayetteville, Lake Sequoyah, and Lake Wilson parks. The latter facility also has an outdoor swimming pool. Walker Park has tennis, volleyball, racquetball, and handball courts, while the Fayetteville Youth Center has an indoor swimming pool plus youth and adult sports programs. The university has a variety of sports facilities including the Health, Physical Education, and Recreation (HPER) fitness complex available to the university community. It might be worth signing up for a course to gain access to them if you are not otherwise associated with the university. Alumnus or not, you are always welcome at Razorback Stadium and Bud Walton Arena for intercollegiate football and basketball. Golfers can choose among six local golf courses plus four more in the Greater Fayetteville/Springdale/Rogers area. A little farther afield, Ozark National Forest lakes, rivers, and mountains provide countless sites for fishing, swimming, boating, sightseeing, picnicking, camping, hiking and hunting. Back in town, the city is currently constructing a network of bike lanes along streets and off-road bike and hiking paths, some along abandoned railroad rights-of-way. These will make recreational bicycling even more attractive than it presently is. Finally, almost everyone can enjoy an occasional movie at one of the many cinema complexes or a meal at one of several excellent restaurants. Restaurant meals are a bargain in Fayetteville.

The economy of northwestern Arkansas has been booming in recent years, fueled especially by growth of the University of Arkansas and corporate giants Wal-Mart and Tyson. Jobs, especially part-time jobs, are plentiful although competition with students keeps wages low. Wal-Mart and other retailers are among the principal employers of seniors. The local RSVP can be helpful in placing you in a suitable niche in one of the community's many public facilities or service organizations.

Crime Rates and Public Safety   Rating: 3

The Fayetteville/Springdale/Rogers metropolitan area is one of the safer urban areas of its size. Unfortunately, the situation in Fayetteville itself is somewhat less positive. This anomaly is, in part, the result of Fayetteville having a large nonresident (student) population, which contributes somewhat to the incidence of crime but not to the population base on which crime rates are computed. Be that as it may, the property crime rate in Fayetteville is over 40 percent above the national average, largely because of a high incidence of larceny and theft, both petty crimes. Local burglary and auto theft rates are below national norms. The good news is that the violent crime rate is little more than half of the national average and the community feels safe. Indeed, many cars were observed with their windows left open, and several residents noted that Fayetteville is a safe college town with a good police department.

Conclusion

Overall Rating 48

Fayetteville is one of America's most pleasant and affordable college towns, and an excellent place for an active retirement. Its physical setting among the forested hills of the Ozark Plateau is very scenic and its urban character is quite attractive. Its four-season humid subtropical climate is tempered by elevation and is moderately sunny with little snow. Although some may deem its winters a little too cold or its summers a little too hot, few would criticize its excellent quality of life. There is little environmental pollution or traffic congestion. The city has good transportation facilities including satisfactory public transit, and is expanding its network of bike paths and lanes. Infrastructure development is keeping up with demand and residential neighborhoods are typically attractive. Retail, health care, cultural, community service and recreation assets are very substantial, as are opportunities for work and volunteerism. Fortunately, the many amenities of Fayetteville are available at a cost of living about 10 percent below the national average, making it a bargain among America's upscale retirement towns.

The Heart of Texas Retirement Region

Climate: Humid subtropical

Place Description	Overall Rating	Page
Austin, Texas	**49**	**131**
Economically thriving, Austin offers a wealth of resources for active retirement with excellent transportation, retail services, and work and volunteer opportunities.		
San Antonio, Texas	**49**	**137**
Despite some of the problems associated with recent growth, San Antonio has much to offer with its unique ambiance and affordable living.		
Kerrville, Texas	**not rated**	**143**
Kerrville offers small-town charm within reach of San Antonio's rich cultural and recreational resources.		
Fredericksburg, Texas	**not rated**	**143**
Fredericksburg offers a unique German village style feel and, like Kerrville, provides small-town living within easy reach of San Antonio.		

Texas is America's second largest state in land area (after Alaska) and in population (after California). Yet much of the state is not especially attractive for retirement. Its largest cities, Dallas/Fort Worth and Houston, suffer heavy air pollution and traffic congestion, high crime rates, and out-of-control urban sprawl. On the other hand, most small Texas cities suffer from inadequate public services and lack amenities important to seniors.

The Heart of Texas Retirement Region, located in south central Texas where the coastal plain meets the Texas Hill Country, is different. Its two major cities, Austin and San Antonio, are large enough to provide the services and amenities retirees demand but are not so large as to suffer the environmental degradation and declining quality of life characteristic of larger Texas cities. Austin, state capital of Texas and home of its flagship public university, is attracting retired alumni of the University of Texas from all over the country as well as retired Texas state employees and retirees from other states. San Antonio has long lured back Air Force and Army veterans once based at its five military bases, and in recent years has attracted many former visitors who came to the city as tourists or conferees and liked what they saw. On a smaller scale, people are moving into little Texas Hill Country towns like Fredericksburg and Kerrville, which offer a peaceful and high quality life in a lovely, clean environment only an hour or so from the many attractions of Austin and San Antonio.

Austin, Texas

Chosen as capital of the Republic of Texas in 1840 and named for Stephen F. Austin, pioneer American colonizer of Texas, Austin struggled along as a remote frontier capital until its physical and cultural isolation was broken after

Austin, Texas

CLIMATE

Month	Average Daily Temperature High (°F)	Average Daily Temperature Low (°F)	Daily Rel. Humidity Low (%)	Average Monthly Precipitation (Inches)
January	59	39	60	1.7
February	63	42	59	2.2
March	72	51	56	1.9
April	79	60	57	2.6
May	85	67	61	4.8
June	91	72	57	3.7
July	95	74	51	2.0
August	96	74	50	2.1
September	91	70	56	3.3
October	82	60	55	3.4
November	72	50	58	2.4
December	62	41	60	1.8

Annual Average

Total Days		Total Inches	
Clear	115	Precipitation	31.9
Partly Cloudy	114	Snowfall	0.9
Cloudy	136		

RATINGS

Rating Scale: 5 = excellent; 4 = very good; 3 = good; 2 = fair; 1 = poor

Rating:	1	2	3	4	5
Landscape				●	
Climate			●		
Quality of Life				●	
Cost of Living			●		
Transportation					●
Retail Services					●
Health Care				●	
Community Services				●	
Cultural Activities					●
Recreational Activities					●
Work/Volunteer Activities					●
Crime		●			

Total Points: 49

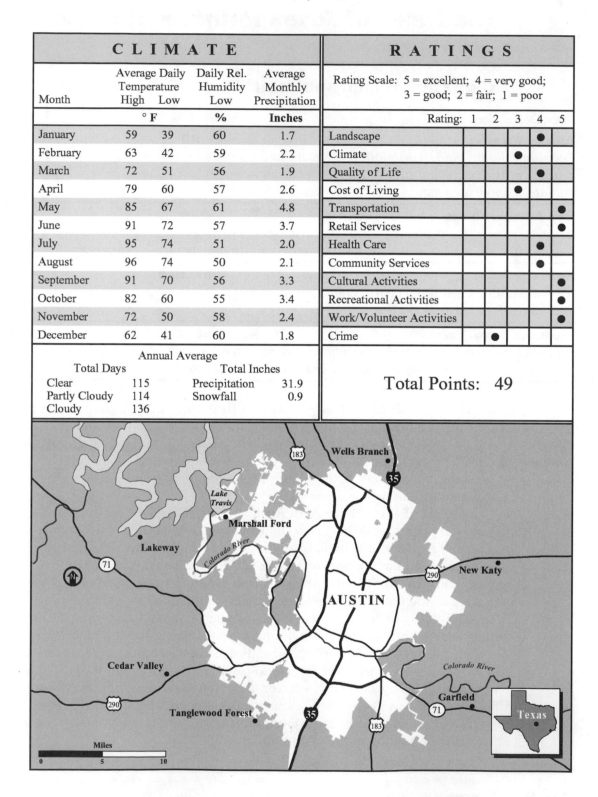

the Civil War by the arrival of the railroad and the establishment of the University of Texas. Now the flagship institution of the statewide University of Texas system, the University of Texas/Austin is the largest university in the South and a major center of scientific research. It has attracted remarkable academic talent to Austin, served as a catalyst for high-tech industrial development, and helped transform a formerly provincial and conservative city into a cosmopolitan, environmentally aware and progressive one.

For decades now, Austin has been rated as one of America's most pleasant mid-sized cities. Despite rapid population growth to over 550,000 in the city, 700,000 in Travis County, and 1,000,000 in the metropolitan area, Austin remains relatively unspoiled. Its beautiful site, warm sunny climate, good urban design, and abundant amenities should keep it for some time one of the nation's choice locales for an active retirement.

Landscape   Rating: 4

 Austin occupies a gently rolling plain in south central Texas. Toward the western edge of the city the land rises dramatically at the Balcones Escarpment, which marks the eastern edge of the Edwards Plateau (Texas Hill Country). The Colorado River, which traverses the city from northwest to southeast, has been impounded into a series of picturesque lakes including Lake Austin and Town Lake. A park-like landscape of oak and hickory groves separated by tall grass prairie is the predominant natural vegetation but a wide selection of broad-leafed and coniferous trees has been planted in the city. Most neighborhoods are well treed and landscaped.

Climate   Rating: 3

 Austin lies toward the western margin of the humid subtropical climatic region and is considerably drier than Houston or other Gulf Coast locations. Summers are consistently very hot and moderately humid, whereas winter weather is changeable with warm, humid and cool, dry conditions alternating. Spring and fall are nearly ideal with warm days and cool nights. Austin is sunny about 50 percent of the time in winter and more than 70 percent of the time in summer. Occasional winter frosts result in a frost-free season averaging 270 days, and snowfall averages less than one inch annually.

Quality of Life   Rating: 4

Overall, Austin provides a very good quality of life. Noise pollution is a problem chiefly near the airport and adjacent to Interstate-35, Loop-360, and several major boulevards. Lacking heavy industry and chronic traffic congestion, Austin meets all federal air quality standards. Parking is generally not a problem except on campus, near the capitol and downtown, but traffic is steadily increasing, especially downtown and on freeways and streets connecting it to the suburbs. Except for several large hotels just north of Town Lake, downtown Austin has not seen much construction in recent decades and is showing its age. On the other hand, residential neighborhoods, including several older ones north of the University of Texas, are nicely landscaped and very well maintained. The university is an enormous asset to the community, and the city's outstanding network of parks, recreation centers and natural areas adds greatly to its livability. Austin residents are strong environmentalists ensuring that planning and zoning are geared to preserve their high quality of life in the face of inevitable population growth.

The cost of living in Austin is evaluated as follows:

- **Composite.** ACCRA data indicate that the composite cost of living in Austin is about two percent above the national average.

- **Housing.** According to ACCRA, housing costs are just above the national average. Exploration of the area indicates that although Austin housing is not cheap it does offer good value. Attractive inner city neighborhoods a mile or two north of the university campus feature an eclectic variety of housing styles at prices between $100,000 and $200,000. Suburban areas offer new and near new tract homes at slightly higher prices.

- **Goods and Services.** Goods and services are priced near national norms. Groceries and transportation are bargains at prices about five percent below average, whereas miscellaneous goods and services and health care costs are four to nine percent above average. Utility costs are near the national norm.

- **Taxes.** The overall tax burden is relatively low in Austin because Texas does not tax income. Property taxes are above the national average, for example, about $3,600 annually on a $150,000 home. The combined state/local/transit sales tax of 8.25 percent is the highest in the state and well above the national average for sales taxes.

Local and Regional Services

Austin provides extensive and generally excellent services to its large and fairly affluent market.

Although not as elaborate as San Antonio's, Austin's street and freeway network is quite adequate and most people get around by car. Capital Metro's more than 250 clean and relatively new buses provide excellent transit service. Buses provide access to major malls and shopping centers, the central business district, the university, major parks and recreation areas, and the airport. The base fare is 65 cents but seniors 65 and older ride free. Bicycling is a popular transportation mode especially in central Austin in and around the University of Texas. Conveniently located only four miles northeast of the city center, Robert Mueller Municipal Airport provides nonstop jet service to over 30 destinations including major hubs at Dallas and Houston. Amtrak offers three trips weekly north to Chicago and west to Los Angeles. Greyhound and the Kerrville Bus Company provide frequent motor coach service to locations in Texas and neighboring states.

The central business district located between the capitol and Town Lake no longer dominates retailing and is looking a little shabby. Nonetheless, West Sixth Street downtown boasts an eclectic variety of unique stores, art galleries and restaurants. More conventional shopping is available in several major malls mostly located adjacent to loop highways. Highland Mall is the oldest of Austin's indoor shopping centers and perhaps the most attractive. Anchored by Dillard's, Foley's and JCPenney department stores, the mall has 130 specialty stores and restaurants. Barton Creek Square, with 180 stores and restaurants and a 14-screen cinema complex, is the largest Austin mall. Its department stores include Dillard's, Foley's, JCPenney and Sears. Lakeline Mall is anchored by Bell's, Dillard's, Foley's, JCPenney, Mervyns and Sears department stores and features 140 specialty retailers and restaurants and an eight-screen movie theater complex. On the northern periphery of the city is the well-named Arboretum with 46 upscale specialty shops in a greenbelt setting. Many small shopping centers and neighborhood shopping streets scattered about the city provide shopping experiences ranging from upscale boutiques to 1960s funky.

Health Care   Rating: 4

 Medical care is very good in Austin. Five major medical centers together furnish virtually every conceivable medical specialty and service. Largest of these, with nearly 500 beds, is Seton Medical Center, operated by the Daughters of Charity National Health System, which also runs Brackenridge Hospital. The latter facility is a teaching hospital and regional referral center especially notable for cancer and cardiac care. Other major facilities include Columbia St. David's Hospital, Columbia St. David's South Hospital, and Austin Diagnostic Medical Center. The latter specializes in cancer treatment and rehabilitation while the former two are typical general hospitals providing a broad repertoire of services.

Community Services   Rating: 4

 Basic public services as well as those catering to seniors are very good in Austin. Two senior centers host a variety of classes, social and recreational activities, and wellness programs; community centers offer additional social and recreation programs for all age groups. Austin's Capital Area Agency on Aging is an important source for information and counseling.

Leisure Activities

For a medium-size city, Austin provides a remarkable assortment of leisure activities.

Cultural and Educational Activities   Rating: 5

The University of Texas is an exceptional educational and cultural asset. Seniors may audit regular courses on a "space available" basis or participate for nominal fees in courses offered through the university's Learning Activities for Mature People Program. The Community Schools Program of Austin City Schools offers an enormous list of adult education courses and the Parks and Recreation Department targets seniors with arts and crafts and sports and fitness classes, among others. Austin Community College also fields courses in the liberal arts, communications, photography and other subjects of interest to seniors. Bass Concert Hall, Bates Recital Hall, and Hogg Auditorium on the University of Texas campus book everything from Broadway shows to classical and popular music performances by imported and local talent. Productions by the Austin Lyric Opera, Austin Symphony Orchestra and Ballet Austin are performed in the larger Bass Concert Hall; those by individual guest artists and smaller ensembles are typically staged in Bates Hall or Hogg Auditorium. Among Austin's other excellent musical groups are: the Austin Civic Orchestra, which performs classical and popular works, the Austin Vocal Arts Ensemble, which presents quality choral music both a cappella and with orchestra, and La Follia, Austin's baroque period instrumental ensemble. Some of Austin's best classical musicians may be heard for free at the Thursday Noon Concert Series at Central Presbyterian Church.

Popular music and theater are also vibrant in Austin. The city is famous for its country music and blues and rock, which can be seen live at over 100 nightspots. Free tickets are available for taping sessions at the KLRU studios of the PBS show Austin City Limits, which features performances of country and blues and rock by stars such as Willie Nelson, Lyle Lovett, and B. B. King. The city also boasts over 10 legitimate theaters that stage everything from comedy to tragedy and from classical to cutting-edge productions. In season, theater can be enjoyed under the stars at Zilker Hillside Theatre in Zilker Park. Among Austin's more than 20 museums are the Austin Museum of Art, the Huntington Gallery, the George Washington Carver Museum, and the Lyndon Baines Johnson (LBJ) Presidential Library and Museum. The Austin Museum of Art, housed in part in a 1916 Mediterranean villa overlooking Lake Austin, emphasizes twentieth century American art in its changing programs. The Huntington Gallery, housed in two locations on the University of Texas campus, includes over 12,000 works and is generally regarded as one of the top 10 university art museums in the country. The George Washington Carver Museum is the first African-American neighborhood history museum in Texas; it features artifacts, photographs, oral histories and archival materials. On a different scale is the monumental LBJ Presidential Library and Museum. Housing more than 36 million official and personal documents and exhibits, the complex depicts President Johnson's life from his boyhood to his retirement at his Texas Hill Country ranch.

Recreational Activities   Rating: 5

Austin and the adjacent Texas Hill Country are a mecca for the outdoors oriented. With 12,000 acres of undeveloped greenbelt around the city there is plenty of room for recreation and nature protection. Austin's excellent network of urban parks has nearly 30 swimming pools, 200 tennis courts, and all kinds of sports fields. Zilker Park, Austin's largest and most popular park, offers year-round swimming in the 68 degree water of Barton Springs pool, the most famous of several natural spring-fed swimming holes in and around Austin. The park also features a 10.1-mile hike and bike trail around Town Lake, playgrounds, picnicking facilities, a botanical garden and the Austin Nature Center. Upstream on the Colorado River are Lakes Austin and Travis where boating, fishing and swimming are popular. The nearby Texas Hill Country, with its many lakes and wild areas, provides plenty of opportunities for hiking, biking, horseback riding, swimming, fishing and hunting. Golfers can enjoy a round of golf on more than 20 municipal or daily fee courses in the metropolitan area.

Spectator sports are largely courtesy of the University of Texas. Its NCAA Longhorns basketball and football teams attract a loyal following. The city also boasts over 100 movie screens and a good selection of restaurants specializing in regional American, Southwest, Mexican and ethnic cuisines, and, of course, steak.

Work and Volunteer Activities   Rating: 5

The red hot Austin economy continues to generate new jobs at a phenomenal rate. Service industries, government, education and high-tech manufacturing are leading employers. Although thousands of college students compete for part-time service jobs with the general public and retirees, seniors can find work. The City of Austin's Experience Unlimited job referral system does a good job of putting them in touch with potential employers. Demand for volunteer help probably exceeds supply. Placements are readily available in Austin area schools, hospitals, libraries, social and recreational organizations, and places of worship.

Crime Rates and Public Safety   Rating: 2

Crime rates are fairly stable in Austin, although overall violent crime has declined modestly in the last several years. Overall crime in the city is currently about 60 percent and property crime about 65 percent above the national averages. In contrast, the violent crime rate is only marginally above the national average. As elsewhere, you must choose your neighborhood carefully in order to minimize potential exposure to crime.

Conclusion

Overall Rating 49 Economically thriving Austin, Texas offers a wealth of resources for active retirement. Often characterized as the live music capital of the world, Austin is one of only 14 American cities with its own ballet, opera and symphony. The University of Texas lends a cosmopolitan air to the community, hosts visiting performing artists, and fields competitive intercollegiate basketball and football teams. Environmentalists and the outdoors oriented will appreciate the city's abundance of greenbelt, parkland and recreation facilities. The city is also notable for the excellence of its transportation, retail services and work and volunteer opportunities. Health care and community services are very good, the urban landscape is well planned and attractive, and the quality of life is high. Long hot summers and rather high property crime rates are the principal drawbacks in Austin. Nonetheless, the city remains a premier choice for stimulating retirement at a reasonable cost.

San Antonio, Texas

With a population of 1,200,000 in the city and upwards of 1,600,000 in the metropolitan area, San Antonio is a unique place and one of very few large American cities that can be recommended for retirement. Despite rapid growth in recent decades, the city retains much of its old Spanish-Mexican flavor with its five missions, including the Alamo, numerous parks and plazas, and historic neighborhoods. About 50 percent of the population is Hispanic. The downtown, much of which dates from before 1930, has been revitalized in concert with construction of the 2.5-mile long Riverwalk, a tree-lined park and footpath beside the diminutive San Antonio River. Formerly a rundown residential area, the Riverwalk, with its lovely landscaping and adjacent shops and restaurants, has come to symbolize the beauty and romance of San Antonio and has served as a magnet drawing tourists, residents and investment back into the city center. Beyond downtown, countless residential neighborhoods and commercial areas sprawl outward, enveloping the five military bases that have long lent stability to the local economy. Although not without problems, San Antonio's unusual combination of urban character and amenities, climate and low cost of living make it a very appealing place for retirement.

San Antonio, Texas

CLIMATE				
Month	Average Daily Temperature High / Low	Daily Rel. Humidity Low	Average Monthly Precipitation	
	°F	%	Inches	
January	61 / 38	59	1.7	
February	66 / 41	57	1.8	
March	74 / 50	54	1.5	
April	80 / 58	56	2.5	
May	85 / 66	60	4.2	
June	92 / 73	57	3.8	
July	95 / 75	52	2.2	
August	95 / 75	51	2.5	
September	89 / 69	55	3.4	
October	82 / 59	54	3.2	
November	72 / 49	56	2.6	
December	64 / 41	58	1.5	

Annual Average

Total Days		Total Inches	
Clear	105	Precipitation	31.0
Partly Cloudy	119	Snowfall	0.7
Cloudy	141		

RATINGS

Rating Scale: 5 = excellent; 4 = very good; 3 = good; 2 = fair; 1 = poor

Rating:	1	2	3	4	5
Landscape				●	
Climate			●		
Quality of Life				●	
Cost of Living					●
Transportation					●
Retail Services					●
Health Care					●
Community Services				●	
Cultural Activities					●
Recreational Activities				●	
Work/Volunteer Activities			●		
Crime		●			

Total Points: 49

Landscape   Rating: 4

San Antonio is located in south central Texas just east of the Balcones Escarpment, which marks the eastern edge of the Texas Hill Country. The southern part of town is fairly flat at an elevation of about 600 feet.

Northward from downtown the land gradually rises to a rolling surface about 200 feet higher. The city is underlain by limestone so drainage is good. The San Antonio River flows southward through the downtown where it has been channeled and dammed to enhance the picturesque Riverwalk area. An oak and hickory woodland is the predominant natural vegetation but many exotic trees and shrubs add botanic variety.

Climate   Rating: 3

 San Antonio lies toward the western margin of the humid subtropical climatic region and is considerably drier than Houston or other Gulf Coast locations. Summers are consistently very hot and moderately humid, while winter weather is changeable with warm, humid and cool, dry conditions alternating. Spring and fall are nearly ideal with warm days and cool nights. San Antonio is sunny about 50 percent of the time in winter and more than 70 percent of the time in summer. Occasional winter frosts result in a frost-free period averaging 280 days and snowfall is insignificant.

Quality of Life   Rating: 4

 There are two very different San Antonios. The southern half of the city, on the flat plains near the military bases, is relatively poor, lacks amenities, experiences considerable crime, and is clearly unsuitable for retirement in style. In contrast, slightly hilly northern San Antonio, with most of the city's cultural attractions, parks, other amenities and better residential areas, is where most middle-class retirees prefer to live. The latter area is emphasized in the following discussion.

The quality of life is generally good. Noise pollution is principally a problem near the airport and adjacent to the freeways, of which there are many; the Texas Highway Department is an incorrigible builder of freeways! Despite the large number of vehicles on the roads, air quality is good and parking is more than adequate. Traffic congestion is worsening as the population grows but is not yet a serious problem except on the central part of the freeway network in and around downtown at rush hour. There are few heavy industries to foul air or water, and many excellent, well-treed and maintained neighborhoods, old and new, grace the landscape. The city's parks, recreation centers, museums and zoo add to its livability, and the lively central business district, embracing Hemisfair Plaza, Market Square, the Alamo, the Riverwalk and Rivercenter Mall, is among the best small downtowns in the nation. The city is tied together by an excellent road network and very good public transit. The people seem laid back and friendly, especially for residents of a large city.

Cost of Living   Rating: 5

 The cost of living in San Antonio is evaluated as follows:

- *Composite*. ACCRA data suggest that the composite cost of living in San Antonio is 10 percent below the national average.

- *Housing*. According to ACCRA, housing costs are about 16 percent below the national average. This makes San Antonio America's least expensive big city in which to own a home. Suburban areas to the north and east of the Interstate-410 Loop, 10 to 20 miles out from downtown, are growing rapidly. New and resale single-family residences there are priced in the $100,000 to $200,000 range. Housing in some excellent older San Antonio neighborhoods near Trinity University and Brackenridge and Basin Parks, and in Alamo Heights and Terrell Hills, is priced similarly.

- *Goods and Services.* All categories of goods and services are priced below national norms. Utilities and groceries are especially cheap, at 18 percent and 12 percent below their national averages. Transportation and health care costs are about 7 percent below average while miscellaneous goods and services are priced just under the national average.

- *Taxes.* The overall tax burden in San Antonio is among the lowest in the country because Texas does not tax income. Property taxes are close to the national average but the state/local sales tax of 7.75 percent is relatively high.

Local and Regional Services

As the largest city and regional capital of south central Texas, San Antonio supplies a large market with a wide range of services.

Transportation	Rating: 5

 San Antonio has excellent intracity and intercity transportation. The metropolitan area's outstanding street and freeway network encourages automobile use but VIA Trans, with 500 relatively new and clean buses, provides a handy alternative. You can easily access most destinations within the I-410 Loop and some beyond it by bus. Bus fare is 40 cents, 20 cents for seniors. A regular monthly pass costs $16, discounted to $8 for seniors. San Antonio International Airport, nine miles north of downtown, is a medium hub offering nonstop jet service to about 30 destinations including Dallas, Houston and Phoenix. Amtrak provides thrice-weekly service north to Chicago, east to Miami, and west to Los Angeles. Greyhound and Kerrville Bus Company provide frequent bus service to points in Texas and beyond.

Retail Services	Rating: 5

Rivercenter Mall is an elegant enclosed mall adjoining the San Antonio River and Riverwalk. Anchored by Dillard's and Foley's department stores, Rivercenter Mall has 135 shops and restaurants, many catering to tourists. Additional specialty shops and restaurants are clustered along downtown streets overlooking the Riverwalk. San Antonio's six suburban malls include five adjacent to the I-410 Loop, namely, Ingram Park Mall and Crossroads Mall in the northwest, North Star Mall in the north central sector, Windsor Park Mall in the east, and McCreless Mall in the southwest.

Rolling Oaks Mall, on the Highway 1604 Loop in extreme northeast San Antonio, is even more remote. All six malls are anchored by major department stores and boast many national chain specialty stores. Uniquely different is downtown's Market Square, since 1830 an open-air marketplace for fresh fruit, vegetables and eggs. In addition to produce, Indian and Mexican arts and crafts are sold.

Health Care	Rating: 5

 With 13 full-service general hospitals, several VA and military hospitals, and a state psychiatric hospital, San Antonio provides a comprehensive array of medical services consistent with its large population and regional centrality. South Texas Medical Center, located on a 700-acre site in northwest San Antonio, has an amazing assemblage of medical facilities. These include the University of Texas Health Science Center and Hospital, Southwest Texas Methodist Hospital, St. Luke's Lutheran Hospital, two Humana Hospitals, Santa Rosa Hospital, and several major clinics, laboratories, medical research, rehabilitation and nursing care units. Other major medical facilities, including several hospitals operated by Santa Rosa Health Care and Methodist Health Care Systems are scattered about the city.

Community Services   Rating: 4

 Basic public services such as fire and police protection, public transit, water supply, libraries, and parks and recreation facilities are excellent in San Antonio. Two major senior centers, several smaller ones, and more than 20 community centers provide social activities, information, arts and crafts classes, and field trips for seniors. The Bexar County Area Agency on Aging and the Senior Information Center are helpful in providing information and locating services for seniors. Branches of national organizations such as AARP are also active locally.

Leisure Activities

Whether your leisure preferences focus on high culture, education, outdoor activities or spectator sports, there is plenty to do in San Antonio.

Cultural and Educational Activities   Rating: 5

 The performing and visual arts are flourishing. Downtown's beautifully restored Majestic Theatre, formerly a vaudeville house, is now the home of the San Antonio Symphony and a venue for touring Broadway plays and guest artist concerts. In addition to formal classical performances, the symphony also performs chamber music, opera and pops series. Other resident ensembles include the Mid-Texas Symphony and the San Antonio Ballet. The Henry B. Gonzalez Convention Center Arena downtown is the scene of frequent jazz, pop and rock concerts, while the Theatre for the Performing Arts, next to the Majestic, hosts local and imported concerts, ballet, opera and theater. In nearby HemisFair Plaza, visiting dance and ballet troupes perform at Beethoven Hall and the Lila Cockerell Theatre. The respected San Antonio Little Theatre presents a varied program of comedies, drama, and musicals at San Pedro Playhouse and Trinity University's drama department stages upwards of 10 productions annually in its Ruth Taylor Theater on campus. The San Antonio Museum of Art, which occupies a splendid site in the old Lone Star Brewery along the San Antonio River, features southwestern and American art, Mexican folk art, Chinese art, and Greek and Roman antiquities. The McNay Art Museum is notable for French Post-Impressionist paintings, early twentieth century European art, modern American watercolors and Southwest folk art.

San Antonio has several fine universities and colleges. Largest of these is the University of Texas at San Antonio. Trinity University is much smaller yet ranks consistently as one of America's top liberal arts institutions. St. Mary's University and San Antonio (Community) College are also worth noting. Collectively these schools offer many courses of interest to seniors for enrollment or audit; additional choices are available through the city schools' adult education program. The San Antonio public library system, with over 2,000,000 books, is another important educational resource. The new downtown central library is spectacular.

Recreational Activities   Rating: 4

San Antonio's subtropical climate and varied landscape favor outdoor sports and recreation. The city owns over 6,800 acres of open space comprising 6 municipal golf courses, 135 parks and recreation centers, 22 swimming pools, and one of the best zoos in the nation. Over 20 additional golf courses, including 10 operating on a daily fee basis, dot the metropolitan area. Tennis is played on over 100 courts in the city, and bicycling and hiking are popular on many quiet roads and trails in northern residential areas and parks and in the nearby Texas Hill Country. The Hill Country is also popular for sightseeing, lake fishing, and deer and turkey hunting.

Spectator sports, especially San Antonio Spurs NBA basketball and University of Texas Roadrunners NCAA basketball, bring out the crowds, as do the Riverwalk's shops, restaurants and nightspots. San Antonio also boasts over 150 movie screens and countless excellent restaurants serving a good variety of American, Mexican, European and Asian cuisines in its regional malls and neighborhood shopping areas.

Work and Volunteer Activities   Rating: 3

San Antonio's economy has grown rapidly for a decade, generating an abundance of service jobs. Most, though, pay low wages and require fluency in English and Spanish. Demand for volunteers probably exceeds supply. Area hospitals, schools, libraries, places of worship and social organizations all depend heavily on volunteer help. United Way and the AARP help bring together volunteers and organizations needing them.

Crime Rates and Public Safety   Rating: 2

As in most other American cities, crime rates are declining in San Antonio. Even so, the overall crime rate is about 60 percent and property crime about 75 percent above the national averages. Fortunately, the city's violent crime rate is about 30 percent below the national average, reflecting an enviably low rate of aggravated assault. In general, areas of San Antonio south of downtown suffer disproportionately from crime, whereas the more affluent northern areas are much safer.

Conclusion

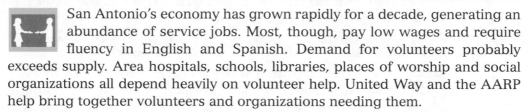

Overall Rating 49 San Antonio is not perfect but it has much to offer retirees. Rush hour traffic congestion getting in and out of downtown, high property crime rates, and very hot summers are all less than ideal. Yet despite recent growth, the city retains a unique ambiance and scores highly on most measures of desirability. You can live in San Antonio much more cheaply than in most large cities and still enjoy exceptional intracity and intercity transportation, retail services, cultural options and medical care. San Antonio's historic sites and its art deco downtown, revitalized by the charming Riverwalk and tourist oriented commercial development, help define San Antonio as a special place offering a high quality of life. Air and water are clean and residential areas in the wooded and gently rolling landscape of the northern half of the city are pleasant and peaceful.

Very good community services, a fine selection of outdoor recreation and spectator sports, and an easygoing way of life are other pluses. In summary, San Antonio should have special appeal to those seeking big city amenities without big city costs in a culturally stimulating, subtropical environment.

Kerrville, Texas and Fredericksburg, Texas

Kerrville and Fredericksburg, two delightful Texas Hill Country towns, are also worth considering for retirement. Situated in ruggedly beautiful terrain 65 miles northwest of San Antonio, both places are a world apart from the traffic, crime and urban sprawl of that fast-growing south Texas metropolis. Yet both are within an hour's drive of San Antonio's rich cultural and recreational resources and excellent health care and transportation facilities.

Kerrville, population 19,000 and Fredericksburg, population 8,000, are only 25 miles apart and have generally similar physical environments. Both town centers are at an elevation of 1,700 feet but nearby hills rise several hundred feet higher. The surrounding countryside is park-like, with scattered live oaks separated by tall grass prairie. Summer weather is consistently hot and moderately humid but in other seasons the weather can change drastically from day to day. Average high temperatures vary from the low sixties in winter to the low nineties in summer. There is abundant sunshine in all seasons and virtually no snow.

The quality of life is high in both towns although each has its own unique flavor. The oldest parts of Kerrville lie in the valley of the Guadalupe River, which meanders through the town center. Several riverside parks provide hiking, camping, fishing, swimming, boating and nature study. Outlying neighborhoods extend into the hills with some home sites offering splendid views of the lower town. Fredericksburg, on the other hand, occupies a gently rolling upland surface; a small creek runs through the town. Founded by German settlers in the 1840s, Fredericksburg still looks the part. Its wide main street is lined with buildings in German village style and most signage embodies Gothic script and German words. German is widely spoken here and the town is clean, orderly and well planned.

Kerrville and Fredericksburg will be most appreciated by those seeking a relatively tranquil retirement in a peaceful and friendly small town. The unspoiled natural environment, sunny subtropical climate, uncrowded streets and neighborhoods, low crime rates, lower than average living costs and taxes, and good health care are all highly desirable characteristics. On the other hand, both communities suffer from some of the limitations typical of small towns. Although you can get to and from San Antonio and Austin via intercity motor coach, there is no local bus service. Retail and community services are modest in both towns and especially so in Fredericksburg. Cultural and recreational resources are also limited. Nonetheless, golf, swimming, tennis, bicycling, hiking and gardening can be enjoyed year round in both communities so the outdoors oriented will find plenty to do.

The Southern Rockies Retirement Region

Climate: Semi-arid (steppe)

Place Description	Overall Rating	Page
Fort Collins, Colorado	**48**	**145**
Excellent cultural and recreational offerings, good services, and a cost of living only slightly above average make Fort Collins a good place to retire in a relaxed setting.		
Boulder, Colorado	**52**	**151**
Boulder offers an excellent quality of life and top-notch services in a beautiful, scenic setting.		
Colorado Springs, Colorado	**48**	**156**
For those who are able to withstand the high elevation of Colorado Springs, this medium-sized city offers a very good quality of life.		
Santa Fe, New Mexico	**46**	**162**
Although the cost of living is slightly higher than average in Santa Fe, it is a delightfully stimulating place in which to lead an active retirement, offering a physical and human environment that is close to ideal.		

The Southern Rockies Retirement Region extends for 400 miles from Fort Collins, Colorado to Santa Fe, New Mexico. Snug against the spectacular Front Range of the Rocky Mountains, the Colorado Piedmont cities of Fort Collins, Boulder, and Colorado Springs are becoming increasingly popular for retirement, as is Santa Fe, New Mexico, nestled at the foot of the scenic Sangre de Cristo Range.

The region is physically and culturally appealing. Catastrophic environmental problems are unlikely; hurricanes are unknown this far inland and earthquakes and tornadoes are extremely rare. All four cities provide an impressive list of amenities and services and offer easy access to the myriad recreational choices of the mountains. Although each community has its own unique character, all share a delightful, dry, sunny four-season climate and all rank among the best, if not the least expensive, upscale retirement towns.

Fort Collins, Colorado

Originally an army post on the western frontier and for a time merely a local market town for high plains farms and ranches, Fort Collins emerged in the late twentieth century as one of Colorado's principal educational, commercial, and industrial centers and a very pleasant residential community. Located only 60 miles north of Denver, 40 miles south of Cheyenne, Wyoming, and 3–4 miles from the foothills of the Rocky Mountains, Fort Collins lies at the northern extremity of a rapidly growing complex of Colorado Piedmont cities stretching 140 miles southward through Denver to Colorado Springs. It has easy access via Interstate-25 to the urban amenities of neighboring cities and via other routes to the limitless outdoor assets of Rocky Mountain National Park and other Front

Range parks and recreation areas. With a population nearing 100,000 plus over 20,000 Colorado State University students, Fort Collins has a relaxed atmosphere that reflects its residents' preference for a less frenetic lifestyle than is found in some other Colorado Piedmont cities.

Landscape   Rating: 4

Fort Collins is located in north central Colorado at an elevation of 5,000 feet. The city stretches across a gently sloping plain, which rises westward toward the foothills of the Rocky Mountains. Only 35 miles to the southwest the spectacular peaks of Rocky Mountain National Park grace the horizon. The natural landscape of the high plains is semi-arid with grassland grading into rather dry coniferous woodland in the foothills. In town, though, and in nearby agricultural areas, irrigation water obtained from streams emanating from the mountains creates a lush landscape more typical of humid, eastern U.S. locales than of the Great Plains.

Climate   Rating: 3

Fort Collins has a fairly severe four-season semi-arid climate characterized by light precipitation, ample sunshine, and dramatic seasonal and day-to-day changes in the weather. About 70 percent of the normal annual precipitation of 14.5 inches falls between April and September. Although an average of 51 inches of snow falls annually, snow seldom lasts more than two weeks on the ground because daytime temperatures typically rise well above freezing except during winter cold waves. Summer afternoons are warm but quite comfortable owing to low relative humidity; summer evenings are pleasantly cool. Spring and fall weather is changeable with average daytime highs ranging from the low 50s to the low 70s. Winters are cold with frequent and sometimes drastic departures from the average conditions documented on the climatic table. On average, Fort Collins is sunny about 66 percent of the time and enjoys a frost-free season of about 150 days.

Quality of Life   Rating: 5

The quality of life is excellent in Fort Collins. With no major airport and with Interstate-25 skirting the city on the east, noise pollution is minimal. Air quality is excellent. Low population density, satisfactory land use planning, and good transportation infrastructure combine to minimize crowding and traffic congestion. Even rush hour traffic moves fairly smoothly and parking is abundant and inexpensive or free. The city lacks major polluting industries and dilapidated neighborhoods; residential areas are typically well maintained and treed. The city appears well managed; the beautifully restored historic downtown is delightful. Unfortunately, urbanization pressures in the Fort Collins/Loveland corridor are so great that even the best efforts of the Larimer County Open Lands Program seem likely to preserve from development only a few of the remaining farms separating the two cities. On a happier note, the people of this major college town appear friendly, well educated, and appreciative of their community's high quality of life.

Cost of Living   Rating: 3

The cost of living in Fort Collins is evaluated as follows:

Fort Collins, Colorado

CLIMATE				
Month	Average Daily Temperature High Low		Daily Rel. Humidity Low	Average Monthly Precipitation
	°F		%	Inches
January	41	13	50	0.4
February	45	19	45	0.4
March	50	23	41	1.1
April	60	33	36	1.8
May	70	43	39	2.8
June	80	51	36	1.8
July	86	57	35	1.6
August	83	55	36	1.5
September	75	45	34	1.1
October	65	35	36	1.1
November	50	23	49	0.6
December	44	17	52	0.4

Annual Average

Total Days		Total Inches	
Clear	110	Precipitation	14.5
Partly Cloudy	128	Snowfall	51.0
Cloudy	127		

RATINGS

Rating Scale: 5 = excellent; 4 = very good; 3 = good; 2 = fair; 1 = poor

Rating:	1	2	3	4	5
Landscape				●	
Climate			●		
Quality of Life					●
Cost of Living			●		
Transportation				●	
Retail Services				●	
Health Care				●	
Community Services				●	
Cultural Activities					●
Recreational Activities					●
Work/Volunteer Activities				●	
Crime			●		

Total Points: 48

- *Composite*. ACCRA data for Fort Collins show that the composite cost of living is about five percent above the national average.

- *Housing*. Average housing costs are about 19 percent above the national average, according to ACCRA. This is consistent with a local realtor's estimate of an average sale price of $170,000 for a single-family residence. Quite a variety of housing is typically available in Fort Collins. Although prices seem a little high, the ambiance of most neighborhoods and the quality of the housing stock perhaps justify them.

- *Goods and Services.* ACCRA data show health care and groceries costs to be 10–15 percent above national norms, whereas transportation and miscellaneous goods and services costs are at the national average. Utilities are priced fully 25 percent below average.

- *Taxes.* The overall tax burden in Fort Collins is somewhat below the national average. Colorado income is taxed at a flat rate of 5 percent while the combined state, city and county sales tax rate is 6.65 percent. Local property taxes are perhaps 40 percent below the national average. At the current relatively low tax rate of $900 per $100,000 fair market value, the tax on an average $170,000 residence would be $1530.

Local and Regional Services

A good supply of services is available in Fort Collins and the substantially greater resources of Denver are only 60 miles away, a one-hour drive via I-25.

Transportation	Rating: 4

Local transportation is strongly oriented to the automobile; most families have one or two vehicles. The fairly good Transfort bus system is available to transit users. Its 11 bus routes take people and their bicycles to the mall, major work and educational sites, parks and downtown. Fares are very reasonable at 90 cents a ride for adults and 45 cents for seniors. Seniors 60 and older can buy an annual pass for only $17. The major problem of the system is that the orientation of its routes to three transit centers (major transfer points) means that many trips require the use of more than one bus, a time-wasting circumstance for riders. Intercity bus service is provided from Greyhound's downtown terminal. Fort Collins/Loveland Airport offers commuter flights to Denver International Airport but most people travel the 65 miles by car or use the Airport Express shuttle service. Denver International is served by 18 airlines and provides nonstop jet service to about 100 destinations, domestic and international. Amtrak rail passenger service and Greyhound motor coach service are also available in Denver.

Retail Services	Rating: 4

Foothills Fashion Mall, located on College Avenue three miles south of downtown, is the major enclosed mall. Foley's, Mervyn's, JCPenney, and Sears department stores anchor its 123 stores, restaurants and services. Nearby on College Avenue are Kmart, Target, and Wal-Mart discount stores. More interesting, perhaps, is Fort Collins' beautifully revitalized historic downtown along College Avenue and at Old Town Square just east of College. A great place to walk and people watch, the historic area features one-of-a-kind specialty shops, art galleries, restaurants and brewpubs.

Health Care	Rating: 4

Poudre Valley Hospital, a medium-sized facility with 222 beds, is the community's major medical center. It offers the usual wide variety of medical services provided by regional medical centers including

24-hour emergency and intensive care, cardiac care, stroke management, oncology and radiology, among others. Much larger facilities with a greater range of medical services are only an hour away in Denver.

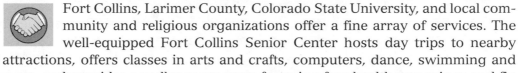

Community Services   Rating: 4

Fort Collins, Larimer County, Colorado State University, and local community and religious organizations offer a fine array of services. The well-equipped Fort Collins Senior Center hosts day trips to nearby attractions, offers classes in arts and crafts, computers, dance, swimming and yoga, and provides a wellness program featuring free health screenings and flu shots.

Leisure Activities

Leisure activities sufficient to satisfy most tastes are available in Fort Collins. Additional attractions are found nearby in Denver and the Rocky Mountains.

Cultural and Educational Activities   Rating: 5

Fort Collins has much to offer culturally and educationally. Colorado State University, with 22,000 students and 1,400 faculty, is the state's second-ranking public university. Its regular academic programs are open to all, whereas the Learning in Retirement Institute targets those 55 and older with programs of special interest to seniors. The university also hosts special lecture series, musical and theatrical events at the CSU Theatre, and art exhibits at its two galleries. Front Range Community College regularly offers credit and noncredit courses on academic and applied topics on weekday, evening, and weekend schedules. Lincoln Center, conveniently located downtown, is the city's principal center for the performing arts. This elegant facility includes a 1,180-seat auditorium, a 220-seat mini-theater, galleries, meeting rooms and a banquet hall. The excellent Fort Collins Symphony Orchestra, Canyon Concert Ballet, several resident chamber music, chorale, operatic, and theatrical companies, and over 100 touring artist bookings make Lincoln Center a busy place throughout the year. Of particular interest is the February Fort Collins Bluegrass Festival, a continuous three-day live band and food extravaganza. On summer evenings Old Town Square comes alive with weekly free concerts featuring rock and roll, bluegrass, country, jazz, and swing musical styles.

Recreational Activities   Rating: 5

Abundant recreational opportunities are found in and around Fort Collins. Golf enthusiasts can choose among six golf courses in town, all with greens fees in the very reasonable $12–$25 range for 18 holes. The city's complement of parks and playground facilities is exceptional. City Park has an outdoor pool, a lake with boat rentals, tennis courts, playing fields, playgrounds, trails and picnicking facilities. Indoor pools are found at the Senior Center, at the Mulberry Pool Recreation Center, and at Eldora Pool and Ice Center. Numerous other parks, large and small, dot the landscape; no neighborhood is far from one. Bicycling enthusiasts will appreciate Fort Collins' more than 75 miles of bikeways which enable people to bike, walk or roller blade through many scenic areas of the city without encountering motorized traffic. Horsetooth Reservoir and adjacent Lory State Park, just west of town in the Rocky Mountain foothills, offer boating, fishing, biking, horseback riding, hiking, rock climbing and camping. In winter, Lory State Park's trails, roads, and hills provide excellent surfaces for cross-country skiing. Downhill skiers need to travel a little farther; two resorts are within two hours by car with several others a little more distant. The Cache la Poudre River, which flows out of its canyon and into Fort Collins at the northwestern edge of town, is an exceptional trout-fishing stream, and well suited to whitewater rafting. A one-hour drive takes you to the Estes Park entrance to Rocky Mountain National Park. The park's Trail Ridge Road is one of the great alpine highways of the United States. Open from about Memorial Day through mid-October, this 50-mile scenic drive provides breath-taking views of the mountains on its way to a peak elevation of 12,183 feet above sea level. Back in Fort Collins, fitness buffs can join Colorado State University's adult fitness program, which provides fitness guidelines and assessment and access to the university's indoor track, pool and exercise equipment. Others might prefer to attend intercollegiate basketball or football games at the university, or movies at one of Fort Collins' six multiscreen cinema complexes. Everyone will enjoy an occasional meal at one of the city's gourmet or casual restaurants, many of which are clustered in the vibrant historic downtown.

Work and Volunteer Activities   Rating: 4

The local service and high-tech economy has flourished recently, so opportunities for work and volunteerism are plentiful. Most part-time jobs are in the service sector, while volunteer work is available in many public facilities and community service organizations.

Crime Rates and Public Safety   Rating: 3

The crime situation in Fort Collins is satisfactory. The overall property crime rate is about 10 percent above the national average. This total is largely a result of the city's high larceny-theft rate; rates of burglary and auto theft, the other property crime components, are below their respective national averages. The incidence of violent crime is fairly low in Fort Collins, at about 35 percent below the national average; the city feels quite safe as you walk its streets.

Conclusion

Overall Rating 48
Fort Collins is one of the most pleasant small towns in America and a very good place for an active retirement in a rather relaxed setting. Its physical and human environment is very good. Its site on an irrigated plain near the Rocky Mountain foothills and within view of the snow-capped peaks of Rocky Mountain National Park is scenic. Its sunny, semi-arid, four-season climate is a bit too cold in winter for some, but few would criticize the excellent quality of life of the community. The city has very good transportation facilities including good public transit and an excellent network of bike paths. Its retail, medical and community services are very good, as are opportunities for work and volunteerism. Its cultural and recreational offerings are notable for their excellence, and the cost of living is only a little above the national average. About the only drawback to life in Fort Collins is the city's moderate crime situation, with an above average property crime rate balanced by a below average rate of violent crime. All in all, Fort Collins ranks very highly as a place for a low-key but active retirement.

Boulder, Colorado

First settled in 1858, Boulder has matured from its early role as a center for cattle ranching on the plains and a base for gold prospecting in the Rocky Mountains to its present status as an exquisite small city offering virtually everything required to retire in style. With a population nearing 100,000 in the city and 290,000 in Boulder County, Boulder has carefully managed growth in order to preserve its very high quality of life.

Located only 30 miles from downtown Denver, it offers easy access to Denver's many amenities while remaining just far enough away to avoid many of the environmental and social problems of the metropolis. Those who want to live an active lifestyle in a rich cultural and gorgeous physical environment at the foot of the Rocky Mountains will find Boulder's many advantages compelling.

Landscape   Rating: 5

Boulder is situated at an elevation of 5,400 feet on a gently sloping plain at the foot of the Flatiron Range, a craggy extension of the Front Range of the Rocky Mountains. Most of the city is built on a relatively flat surface but some charming older neighborhoods west of the University of Colorado and the downtown area slope up to the very base of the mountains. Boulder's site is spectacular from almost any vantage point. From the eastern part of town out on the plains there is a great view of the snow-capped 14,000 foot peaks of Rocky Mountain National Park, whereas from points closer to the mountains you will be captivated by the forests and unique flatiron-shaped rock formations of the foothills.

Boulder is located in a semi-arid environment with steppe (grassland) natural vegetation. But nature has been improved upon in Boulder. With an excellent municipal water supply available from the city-owned Arapahoe Glacier, Boulder supplements natural precipitation with enough irrigation water to create an appealing landscape of lawns, flowers and trees.

Climate   Rating: 4

Boulder has an invigorating four-season semi-arid climate characterized by modest precipitation, abundant sunshine, and marked day-to-day and seasonal changes in weather. About two-thirds of the normal annual precipitation of 18 inches falls between April and September. Although an average of 82 inches of snow falls annually, snow seldom lasts more than a week or two on the ground as daytime temperatures generally rise well above freezing even in winter. Summer afternoons are generally in the 80s and low 90s yet are fairly comfortable thanks to low relative humidity, and summer evenings are pleasantly mild. Spring and fall weather is highly changeable from day to day but is normally pleasant. Winter is normally cool to cold with sunny weather interrupted by occasional winter storms. On average, Boulder is sunny about 70 percent of the time and enjoys an average frost-free period of 160 days.

Quality of Life   Rating: 5

Boulder offers it residents an excellent quality of life. There is little noise pollution except immediately adjacent to the busiest thoroughfares. The city complies fully with all federal air quality standards even though an

Boulder, Colorado

CLIMATE						RATINGS						
Month	Average Daily Temperature High	Low	Daily Rel. Humidity Low	Average Monthly Precipitation		Rating Scale: 5 = excellent; 4 = very good; 3 = good; 2 = fair; 1 = poor						
	°F		%	Inches		Rating:	1	2	3	4	5	
January	45	20	47	0.6		Landscape					●	
February	49	24	42	0.8		Climate				●		
March	53	27	39	1.5		Quality of Life					●	
April	62	36	35	2.3		Cost of Living		●				
May	72	45	38	3.3		Transportation					●	
June	82	54	35	2.0		Retail Services				●		
July	88	60	34	1.8		Health Care				●		
August	86	58	35	1.5		Community Services					●	
September	78	49	34	1.6		Cultural Activities					●	
October	68	40	34	1.2		Recreational Activities					●	
November	54	29	46	1.0		Work/Volunteer Activities					●	
December	48	24	49	0.7		Crime			●			

Annual Average

Total Days		Total Inches	
Clear	115	Precipitation	18.0
Partly Cloudy	130	Snowfall	82.0
Cloudy	120		

Total Points: 52

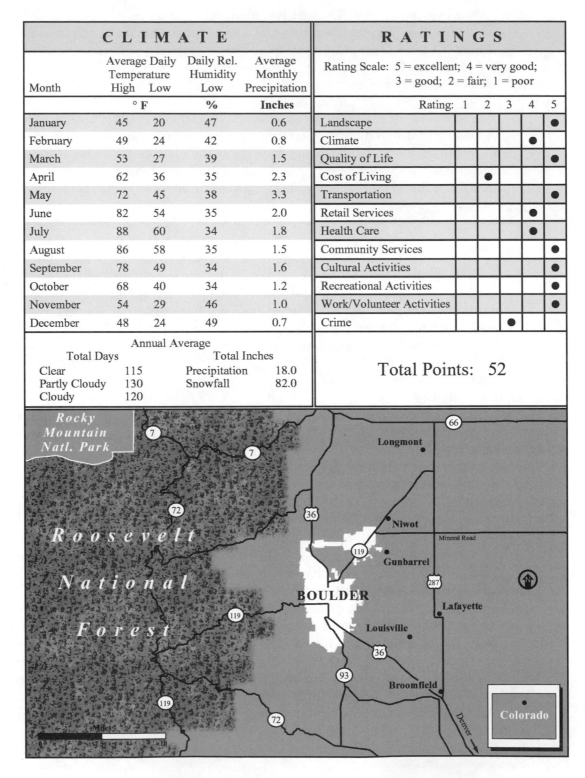

inflow of Denver smog occasionally reduces visibility in winter. Low population density, careful land use planning, and good road infrastructure combine to minimize crowding and traffic congestion, although parking is often scarce downtown and near the university. The community is affluent so there are many very pleasant neighborhoods, including older historic districts adjacent to downtown and the university and newer tract developments on the periphery. Despite strong growth pressures the city has not sprawled outward as the city and county of Boulder tightly control land use. Other niceties of Boulder's well-designed human landscape include: well-treed but not overgrown streets, beautiful parks and greenways, the vibrant Pearl Street Mall, and the exceptionally beautiful University of Colorado campus. Happily, Boulder's affluent and well-educated populace appreciates its exceptional quality of life and seems determined to preserve it by effectively managing inevitable economic and population growth.

Cost of Living   Rating: 2

 The cost of living in Boulder is evaluated as follows:

- *Composite*. ACCRA data for Boulder show a composite cost of living nearly 20 percent above the national average.

- *Housing.* According to ACCRA, housing costs are about 60 percent above the national average. Data from the Boulder County Assessor confirm the high cost of Boulder housing. The average single-family residence now sells for about $300,000 in the city and slightly over $200,000 in the county. Condominiums are about half as expensive in both city and county. Housing prices can be expected to remain high in Boulder because of anti-growth policies that restrict the rate of new construction.

- *Goods and Services*. Costs of health care and groceries are about 20 percent and 13 percent, respectively, above national norms whereas transportation and miscellaneous goods and services are priced near the national average. Utilities are a bargain at a cost about 15 percent below average.

- *Taxes*. The overall tax burden in Boulder is little different than the national average. The state income tax rate of 5 percent is at the national average but the combined state/local sales tax rate of 7.26 percent significantly exceeds the national norm. In contrast, the property tax rate is relatively low. Expect to pay about $2300 annually on an average single family residence, and much less on a typical condominium.

Local and Regional Services

An unusually rich array of services is available in Boulder. These are easily supplemented by the even greater resources of Denver, which is only 30 miles away.

Transportation   Rating: 5

 As is true in most affluent communities, the private automobile dominates local transportation. However, unlike the situation in most small cities, public transit is a reasonable alternative here. The Regional Transportation District (RTD) operates 13 local (Boulder) routes, and 11 regional routes connecting Boulder with other parts of the Denver/Boulder Consolidated Metropolitan Area. In addition, HOP and SKIP shuttle buses operated by RTD provide frequent service on several routes in central Boulder. Buses are clean, efficient and inexpensive to ride. Substantial discounts are available to seniors. Boulder Municipal Airport offers general aviation service but Denver International Airport, 42 miles away, is the major commercial aviation facility. Denver

International is served by 18 airlines and provides nonstop jet service to about 100 domestic and international destinations. Amtrak service eastbound to Chicago and westbound to Oakland, and Greyhound service to many points, is also available in Denver.

Retail Services   Rating: 4

 Boulder offers an impressive variety of retail services and venues. The Pearl Street Mall, Boulder's revitalized historic downtown, is the heart and soul of the community. Easily reached by automobile, bicycle or public transit, this beautifully landscaped brick-surfaced pedestrian mall is a great place to shop, eat, or just stroll and people watch. More typical shopping experiences are available at Crossroads Mall, Boulder's major enclosed shopping mall, and at six smaller shopping centers. Crossroads Mall is anchored by Sears, Foley's and JCPenney department stores and a Target store is adjacent. The local Kmart is a mile north on 28th Street.

Health Care   Rating: 4

 Boulder Community Hospital, a medium-sized facility with 197 beds, is the city's major medical center. It offers a wide variety of medical services including 24-hour emergency care, intensive and cardiac care, and 30 other full-care services. Much larger facilities with a greater range of medical services are only 30 minutes away in Denver.

Community Services   Rating: 5

The city and county of Boulder, the University of Colorado, and local religious and community organizations offer an amazing array of services. For example, Boulder Senior Services, run by the City of Boulder Department of Housing and Human Services, operates two senior centers, one in the western part of town, one in the eastern. Senior Services provides day and overnight travel programs, hikes, sports and social activities, a variety of classes from fitness to computers, and a wellness program.

Leisure Activities

Boulder offers an enormous variety of leisure activities; additional attractions are found nearby in Denver and the Rocky Mountains.

Cultural and Educational Activities   Rating: 5

The culturally and educationally inclined will never want for things to do in Boulder. The schedule of musical, theatrical, and visual arts events and educational opportunities is so full that only a hint of its richness can be conveyed here. Historic Chatauqua Auditorium is the venue for a summer season of concerts and talks from early June through mid September. The auditorium also hosts the Colorado Music Festival, which features a chamber music series and an orchestral series in July and August. Another summer highlight is the Colorado Shakespeare Festival, staged at the outdoor Mary Rippon Theatre and the indoor University Theatre on the University of Colorado campus. The university's Imig Music Building is the site for operas and musicals courtesy of the College of Music. The Boulder Philharmonic Orchestra is also worthy of note as are several museums including the Boulder Museum of Contemporary Art and the University of Colorado Museum. With 25,000 students and 150 fields of study, the University of Colorado is a first-rate academic institution with one of the most beautiful campuses in the country. The university's continuing education division offers a bonanza of credit and noncredit classes and workshops of interest to all age groups.

Recreational Activities   Rating: 5

An amazing assortment of recreational opportunities exists in and around Boulder. The city has nearly 7,000 acres of parkland, 25,000 acres of open space, and 150 miles of trails. The city's parks and three recreation centers are very well equipped and staffed. Whether your interests are walking, running, hiking, biking, fishing, swimming, inline skating, tennis, volleyball, rock climbing or golfing, Boulder can accommodate you. You can even water-ski at Boulder Reservoir on the northern edge of town or whitewater canoe or kayak on Boulder Creek. Boulder has one private and three public golf courses with six more in neighboring communities. Alpine and Nordic skiing are locally available at Eldora Mountain Resort, 20 miles west of Boulder, and at nine other ski areas within a radius of 110 miles. If spectator sports are your preference, you can enjoy varsity basketball and football locally at the University of Colorado and Denver Broncos and Colorado Rockies professional football and baseball in Denver. Also nearby are the spectacular scenic and recreational resources of Eldorado and Golden Gate Canyon State Parks and Rocky Mountain National Park. Whatever your taste in food or preference in restaurant style, your needs are apt to be met in Boulder. The city's 300 restaurants run the gamut from informal sidewalk cafes downtown, specializing in sandwiches and desserts, to five-star dining at Flagstaff House, which overlooks the city from its perch high in the Flatiron Range.

Work and Volunteer Activities   Rating: 5

Boulder's economy has boomed in recent years and unemployment rates are very low so opportunities for work and volunteerism are plentiful. Most part-time jobs are in the service sector, while volunteer work is found at parks and recreation centers, the hospital and public library, the chamber of commerce, and in many community service organizations. Boulder Senior Services can give good advice on where to look.

Crime Rates and Public Safety   Rating: 3

Boulder's crime situation is somewhat mixed. The property crime rate, which is 40 percent above the national average, largely reflects the high larceny-theft rate. The latter indicator is somewhat inflated by the large population of university students, which is not counted in the population base on which crime rates are calculated. That said, the property crime rate is somewhat disquieting. On the other hand, Boulder's violent crime rate is 30 percent below the national average, and most residents do not hesitate to walk its streets day or night.

Conclusion

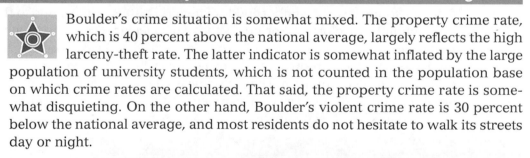

Overall Rating 52

Boulder is one of the most sophisticated small cities in America and a wonderful place in which to lead an active retirement. Its physical and human environment is nearly ideal. Its site on an irrigated plain at the foot of the Flatiron Range, within view of the 14,000-foot peaks of Rocky Mountain National Park, is spectacular. Its sunny, semi-arid climate provides four genuine seasons yet few days in the year are severely cold or hot. The quality of life is excellent, a tribute to sound land use and transportation planning by the municipality and to the environmental awareness of Boulder residents. The city has excellent transportation facilities including an excellent bus system and one of the best bike path networks in the nation. Retail and medical services are very good and community services, cultural and recreational offerings, and work and volunteer activities are excellent. The principal drawbacks to retirement in Boulder are an above average incidence of crime against property and a cost of living about 20 percent above the national average. That said, Boulder ranks as one of America's very best places for an active and sophisticated retirement.

Colorado Springs, Colorado

William J. Palmer founded Colorado Springs at the foot of Pikes Peak in 1871. Palmer planned to develop a resort city linked by road to the supposedly curative waters at Manitou Springs six miles to the west. Within a few years a well-planned small settlement with wide streets, irrigated cottonwood trees, parks, and buildings existed on the formerly barren site. As predicted, lured by spectacular mountain scenery, Manitou Springs waters, the tourist facilities being built, and the hope of getting rich by speculating in gold mining in the Colorado Rockies, newcomers began to pour into the city. In later years, huge military bases including the Air Force Academy, high-tech industries, and the growing service economy have combined to further spur economic and population growth. With a population nearing 360,000 in the city and 500,000 in El Paso County (the metropolitan area), Colorado Springs is and seems likely to remain Colorado's second largest city. It is only 70 miles south of Denver via Interstate-25, and is highly accessible to the mountains via Highway-24. Its beautiful setting at the foot of the Front Range and its many amenities make it a very attractive place for retirement.

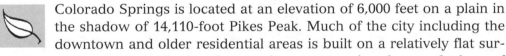

Landscape   **Rating: 5**

Colorado Springs is located at an elevation of 6,000 feet on a plain in the shadow of 14,110-foot Pikes Peak. Much of the city including the downtown and older residential areas is built on a relatively flat surface but some newer neighborhoods extend up a steepening slope to the base of the mountains. Colorado Springs' site is spectacular. From the eastern part of town one gets a superb view of snow-capped Pikes Peak, whereas from most points west of downtown the forested foothills, quite beautiful themselves, eclipse the larger mountain. The cityscape is well wooded, especially in the older neighborhoods, despite the rather dry environment. Plenty of irrigation water is available to keep the city green.

Climate   **Rating: 3**

Colorado Springs is cool for its latitude because of its high elevation. Its moderately severe four-season climate features light precipitation, plenty of sunshine, and dramatic day-to-day and seasonal changes in weather. About 80 percent of the normal annual precipitation of 15.4 inches falls between April and September. Although an average of 43 inches of snow falls annually, snow seldom lasts more than a week or two on the ground because

Colorado Springs, Colorado

CLIMATE					RATINGS					

Month	Average Daily Temperature High	Low	Daily Rel. Humidity Low	Average Monthly Precipitation
	°F		%	Inches
January	41	16	46	0.3
February	45	20	40	0.3
March	49	24	38	0.8
April	60	33	34	1.4
May	69	43	36	2.3
June	80	52	34	2.0
July	85	57	39	2.9
August	82	56	42	2.6
September	75	47	37	1.3
October	65	37	35	0.8
November	50	25	45	0.5
December	44	19	51	0.3

Annual Average

Total Days		Total Inches	
Clear	127	Precipitation	15.4
Partly Cloudy	120	Snowfall	43.4
Cloudy	118		

Rating Scale: 5 = excellent; 4 = very good; 3 = good; 2 = fair; 1 = poor

Rating:	1	2	3	4	5
Landscape					●
Climate			●		
Quality of Life				●	
Cost of Living			●		
Transportation				●	
Retail Services				●	
Health Care				●	
Community Services				●	
Cultural Activities					●
Recreational Activities					●
Work/Volunteer Activities				●	
Crime			●		

Total Points: 48

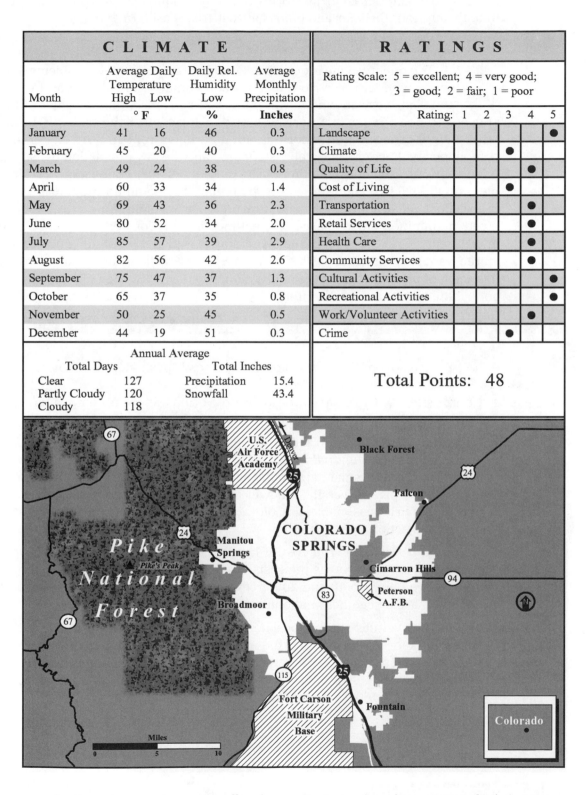

daytime temperatures usually rise well above freezing except during severe winter cold waves. Summer days are pleasantly warm and summer evenings comfortably cool, with low relative humidity. Spring and fall weather is quite changeable but is dominantly sunny with cool to warm temperatures. Winters are cold, dry and occasionally stormy. The city is sunny about 70 percent of the time throughout the year and enjoys a frost-free season of 150 days.

Quality of Life   Rating: 4

 The quality of life is generally good but there are a few problems. There is some jet noise from military and commercial aviation and the city seems very automobile oriented. I-25 runs through the center of town and traffic noise impacts a narrow corridor adjacent to the freeway. In most other neighborhoods traffic noise is not a serious problem. The city is in full compliance with federal air quality standards and the low population density and good road infrastructure minimize crowding and traffic congestion. Parking is plentiful in the city center and at the main mall. The community's housing stock is excellent. Neighborhoods near downtown are remarkably attractive with nicely maintained older houses of great individuality located along shady tree-lined streets. Great pride of home ownership is evident there and in newer manicured suburban areas as well. Colorado Springs' striking physical setting and its excellent parks including the internationally known "Garden of the Gods" also contribute to its high quality of life.

Cost of Living   Rating: 3

 The cost of living in Colorado Springs is evaluated as follows:

- *Composite.* ACCRA data for Colorado Springs show a composite cost of living near the national average.

- *Housing.* According to ACCRA, housing costs are about 15 percent above the national average. Hundreds of charming Victorian and early twentieth century homes, large and small, are found just north of downtown, and suburban areas offer a great diversity of newer houses. Housing prices can be expected to remain fairly reasonable, as Colorado Springs is quite growth oriented and new construction is rampant.

- *Goods and Services.* The cost of health care is about 25 percent above the national average, whereas the costs of miscellaneous goods and services and utilities are between 10 and 20 percent below average. Groceries and transportation are priced near national norms.

- *Taxes.* The overall state and local tax burden is significantly below the national average. Colorado income is taxed at a flat rate of 5 percent and the combined state/local sales tax rate is 6.1 percent in Colorado Springs. Both rates are near the national average. Property taxes, though, are well below average; the tax on an average $160,000 home is about $1200 annually.

Local and Regional Services

Colorado Springs offers residents a very good assortment of services. The larger resources of Denver, which is only 68 miles north via I-25, easily supplement these.

Transportation   Rating: 4

 Local transportation is strongly dominated by the private automobile. With its excellent road infrastructure and ample parking the city is distinctly automobile friendly. Public transit is used mostly by the transit dependent. The City of Colorado Springs operates Springs Transit whose 19 routes provide access to most parts of town except on Sundays and major holidays. Fares are reasonable at 75 cents a ride for adults and 35 cents for seniors. A monthly pass costs $25 with no provision for a senior discount. Additional local transportation is provided by Springs Mobility, a door-to-door service for the handicapped. Intercity bus service is provided by TNM&O, a regional carrier that connects with Greyhound Lines national routes. Colorado Springs Airport Shuttle provides convenient access to Colorado Springs Airport and to Denver International Airport, 100 miles north. Colorado Springs Airport is served by nine airlines and provides nonstop jet service to 20 cities including Dallas, Denver and Phoenix. Denver International is served by 18 airlines and provides nonstop jet service to about 100 domestic and international destinations. Amtrak rail passenger service and Greyhound bus service are available in downtown Denver, 70 miles north.

Retail Services   Rating: 4

Colorado Springs offers very good shopping even though retailing is very weak downtown. The Citadel in the east central part of the city and Chapel Hills Mall in the north are the major enclosed malls. The Citadel is anchored by Dillard's, Foley's, JCPenney, and Mervyn's department stores and includes over 170 specialty retailers. Its tropically foliated, sky-lighted Food Court is unusually attractive with restaurants on two levels and seating on three. A Wal-Mart Supercenter is located just south of the mall across Platte Avenue. Chapel Hills Mall, with 140 stores and restaurants, is only slightly smaller than the Citadel. It is anchored by JCPenney, Joslin's, Mervyn's and Sears department stores.

Health Care   Rating: 4

Medical services are a bit thin relative to population in rapidly growing Colorado Springs. Although the city has five hospitals with a total of over 1,000 beds, only two of them qualify as major general hospitals. Memorial Hospital, with 340 beds, offers a wide variety of medical services including 24-hour emergency care, critical and cardiac care, oncology and surgery. Penrose Hospital, part of Penrose/St. Francis Health Services, specializes in cardiac care, oncology, and internal medicine, but also offers the usual array of primary care medical services. Larger facilities with a wider range of medical specialties are only an hour away in Denver.

Community Services   Rating: 4

The city, El Paso County, Pikes Peak Community College, and local religious and community organizations offer a great variety of services to seniors and the general public. The Colorado Springs Senior Center organizes social activities, screens seniors for medical problems, and offers numerous academic and applied classes in concert with the community college. The Pikes Peak Area Agency on Aging provides information and referral services for seniors.

Leisure Activities

Plenty of leisure activities are found in Colorado Springs, in the nearby Rocky Mountains, and in Denver.

Cultural and Educational Activities	Rating: 5

 Colorado Springs is one of America's best small cities for cultural and educational activities. Downtown's Pikes Peak Center is the principal venue for major musical events. The Colorado Springs Symphony Orchestra performs its winter season there from September through May. The orchestra also performs a summer season of free concerts in area parks. In late July the Colorado Opera Festival is held at the Center and during the winter season the Colorado Dance Theatre hosts the Colorado Ballet and internationally acclaimed touring companies such as the Balletto di Toscana and the Bolshoi Ballet. The U.S. Air Force Academy Band presents free concerts at the Center in spring and at the Air Force Academy in summer.

The Colorado Springs Fine Arts Center, the Broadmoor International Center, the Iron Springs Chateau and Playhouse, and Colorado College are also important centers for the arts. The Fine Arts Center houses collections of Native American and Hispanic art, an art school, and a 450-seat theater. The theater hosts performances by the Civic Music Theater, as well as legitimate theater, concerts, dance productions, and a classical film series. The Broadmoor International Center features touring nationally known performers in concerts and theatrical productions. Dinner theater is popular at the Iron Springs Chateau and Playhouse and plays may also be seen at Colorado College. Colorado College, the Continuing Education Department of the University of Colorado at Colorado Springs, and Pikes Peak Community College, offer courses on academic and applied subjects of interest to seniors. Some courses are offered for nominal fees at the Senior Center.

Recreational Activities	Rating: 5

 Outdoor recreation is plentiful in and around Colorado Springs. Within the city limits golfers can choose among three 18-hole public courses and three 18-hole resort courses at the Broadmoor Hotel. Several additional 18-hole courses are found in county territory. The city's supply of parks and playgrounds is exceptional. The Parks and Recreation Department manages 156 public areas totaling 10,762 acres. Most city parks have tennis courts, sports fields, playgrounds, biking and hiking trails, and picnicking facilities. Swimming is possible at three indoor pools.

Palmer Park and the justifiably famous Garden of the Gods Park at the foot of Pikes Peak are special gems of the park system. Towering red sandstone formations intricately carved by forces of erosion are the trademark of the 1,300-acre Garden of the Gods, but the park also offers foot and horse trails and picnicking areas. Palmer Park is a 740-acre site located in the newer northeastern part of town. Much of the park is a rocky, wooded and relatively wild area providing a spectacular view westward to the mountains from its sandstone bluffs. Other attractions of the park include hiking trails, picnicking areas and ball diamonds. Other city parks, large and small, dot the urban landscape so no location is far from one.

County parks add an additional 2,800 acres of metropolitan area parkland. El Paso County operates seven regional and neighborhood parks, one recreation area, and trailheads accessing 48 miles of regional and park trails. Just west of town is Pikes Peak (elevation 14,110 feet) and the 1,100,000-acre Pike National Forest. The summit can be reached by highway, cog railway, or via the 12-mile long Barr National Recreation Trail. Pike National Forest is known for its scenic drives, camping, fishing, hunting and cross-country skiing. There are no major downhill ski resorts near Colorado Springs but the great ski resorts of central Colorado, including Aspen, are only about 150 miles away. Fans of spectator sports can enjoy intercollegiate basketball, football, baseball and hockey at the Air Force Academy, and professional baseball and football games can be attended in Denver. Movies are shown at 10 multiscreen cinema complexes in Colorado Springs, and area restaurants offer a remarkable variety of cuisines in casual to formal settings.

Work and Volunteer Activities   Rating: 4

 The Colorado Springs economy, based heavily on the military, high-tech industries, service activities, tourism and construction, has boomed in recent years so jobs and volunteer positions are available. Most part-time jobs are in the service and tourism industries, while volunteer work is found in public facilities, community service and not-for-profit organizations.

Crime Rates and Public Safety   Rating: 3

 The Colorado Springs crime situation is somewhat mixed. The city's overall crime rate is 20 percent above the national average, a figure directly attributable to its high (30 percent above the national average) property crime rate. Significantly, the rate of violent crime in Colorado Springs is about 25 percent below the national norm. Local police officers report that much of the crime occurs in the poor southern part of town near the Fort Carson military base, and that central and northern neighborhoods of the city are comparatively safe.

Conclusion

 Colorado Springs is one of the most attractive medium-sized cities for retirement. Its physical site at the foot of Pikes Peak is very scenic and its sunny, semi-arid climate with four distinct seasons appeals to many. The air is clean and there are no serious environmental threats. The city has an excellent road infrastructure and residents rely largely on the private automobile for transportation. Even so, public transit is adequate and the quality of life is very good. Just north of downtown along Nevada Avenue and in the blocks between it and the freeway are historic districts containing hundreds of beautiful Victorian homes. Mixed among them and concentrated just east of Nevada Avenue are hundreds of smaller 1,000–1,500 square foot frame craftsman-style houses, most of which, whether modernized or not, seem in excellent condition and reflect considerable pride of ownership. The city's retail, health care, and community services and work/volunteer opportunities are very good, and its cultural and recreational offerings are excellent. About the only drawbacks to retirement in Colorado Springs are the above average incidence of property crime, a winter season that might not appeal to all, and for those with heart, circulatory or respiratory problems, the 6,000 foot elevation and resultant thin air.

CLIMATE					RATINGS						

Month	Average Daily Temperature High	Low	Daily Rel. Humidity Low	Average Monthly Precipitation
	°F		%	Inches
January	42	19	51	0.3
February	48	24	46	0.3
March	55	28	40	0.5
April	64	33	30	0.7
May	72	42	27	1.6
June	83	51	20	1.4
July	86	56	38	3.2
August	83	54	42	3.5
September	78	48	37	1.5
October	67	37	36	1.1
November	52	26	43	0.6
December	44	19	51	0.4

Annual Average

Total Days		Total Inches	
Clear	167	Precipitation	14.9
Partly Cloudy	111	Snowfall	35.3
Cloudy	87		

Rating Scale: 5 = excellent; 4 = very good; 3 = good; 2 = fair; 1 = poor

Rating:	1	2	3	4	5
Landscape				●	
Climate				●	
Quality of Life					●
Cost of Living		●			
Transportation				●	
Retail Services				●	
Health Care				●	
Community Services				●	
Cultural Activities					●
Recreational Activities					●
Work/Volunteer Activities		●			
Crime			●		

Total Points: 46

Santa Fe, New Mexico

First settled by the Spanish in 1607, 13 years before the Pilgrims set foot in America, Santa Fe was designated capital of the province of New Mexico by the newly appointed governor Don Pedro de Peralta only three years later. It has remained a vital center of New Mexican political and cultural life ever since, whether the flag atop the Palace of the Governors on the north side of the Plaza was Spanish, Mexican, Confederate or American. Today the self-styled City Different revels in the diversity of its Native American, Spanish, and Anglo cultures and in its historical, architectural, cultural and environmental amenities. With a population of nearly 70,000 in the city and 110,000 in Santa Fe County, Santa Fe is large enough to meet the needs of most residents yet small enough to manage growth and resources effectively and preserve its unique character and high quality of life. Located only 60 miles from Albuquerque, Santa Fe has convenient access to that city's transportation facilities and attractions yet is far enough away to avoid many of its social and environmental problems. Those desiring an active lifestyle in a rich cultural and beautiful high plateau and mountain environment may find Santa Fe attractive indeed.

Landscape   Rating: 4

Santa Fe is located at an elevation of 7,000 feet in a transition zone between northern New Mexico's high plateaus and the foothills of the Sangre de Cristo Mountains, the southernmost range of the Rocky Mountains. The western part of town is quite flat, the eastern part hilly. Nearby peaks reach elevations of 12,000 feet, providing a spectacular backdrop to the city. Local natural vegetation varies from stunted pinyon pine/juniper woodland in lower, drier areas to a more luxuriant coniferous forest in the wetter foothills. The city is well treed as precipitation is supplemented by irrigation.

Climate   Rating: 4

Santa Fe enjoys an invigorating semi-arid, four-season climate characterized by modest precipitation, abundant sunshine, and marked day-to-day and seasonal changes in weather. About three-quarters of the normal annual precipitation of 15 inches occurs during the six months May through October. Although an average of 35 inches of snow falls annually, snowfalls seldom persist more than a week or so on the ground as daytime temperatures typically rise well above freezing even in winter. Summer afternoons are generally warm to hot yet are fairly comfortable thanks to low relative humidity. Summer evenings are pleasantly cool. Spring and fall weather is changeable but usually dry, with temperatures in the cool to warm range. Winter weather tends to be cool and generally sunny and dry. Occasionally, though, a winter storm brings a blanket of snow followed by severely cold temperatures for a few days. Even so, the city enjoys a frost-free period of about 170 days and, with sunny days about 75 percent of the time throughout the year, is one of America's sunniest locations.

Quality of Life   Rating: 5

Santa Fe offers its residents an excellent quality of life. There is little noise except along busy Cerrillos Road, the major commercial thoroughfare. The city meets all federal air quality standards and noxious industries are distinctly lacking in a local economy dominated by government and tourism. Although the automobile dominates intracity transportation, the small size of the city prevents serious traffic congestion. Even so, the narrow streets around the Plaza are busy during the summer tourist season and Cerrillos Road and streets leading into the city center are crowded at rush hour.

Parking is adequate in most areas but tight near the Plaza. The community is affluent overall but not uniformly so. Residential areas are typically pleasant. The historic neighborhoods northeast and southeast of the Plaza are especially attractive but newer developments on the periphery of the city and in county territory are also built in Santa Fe (pueblo or territorial) style. The city has very strong zoning and architectural standards, a good network of parks and recreational facilities, and appears well planned and run. The cozy narrow streets that wind through much of the city are a pleasant contrast to the unappealing commercial-strip development along Cerrillos Road.

Cost of Living   Rating: 2

 The cost of living in Santa Fe is evaluated as follows:

- **Composite.** ACCRA data for Santa Fe show a composite cost of living about 15 percent above the national average.

- **Housing.** According to ACCRA, housing costs are perhaps 40 percent above the national average and local sources suggest that the median price of a house is around $190,000. In reality, prices vary substantially from neighborhood to neighborhood. On average the most expensive housing is found in the southeastern quadrant of the City of Santa Fe, and to the northwest, northeast and southeast of town in unincorporated county territory. Median prices for single-family residences range upward from $300,000 in all these areas. In contrast, in blue-collar southwestern Santa Fe prices average around $140,000.

- **Goods and Services.** ACCRA data show transportation and health care to be fairly expensive at about 10 percent above national norms. Groceries and miscellaneous goods and services are only slightly above the national average, while utilities are a bargain at a cost about 10 percent below average.

- **Taxes.** The overall tax burden in Santa Fe is significantly below the national average. State income tax rates on taxable income vary from 1.7 to 8.5 percent, with the marginal rate of 8.5 percent applying only to family income above $100,000. For those of moderate means this translates into a tax liability 10–20 percent below the national average. The combined state/local sales tax rate of 6.25 percent in the City of Santa Fe is just above the national average whereas the property tax of $1203 on an average $200,000 house is low by national norms.

Local and Regional Services

Santa Fe offers residents a rich array of services not commonly found in small cities. Those of Albuquerque, which is only 60 miles away via Interstate-25, easily supplement these.

Transportation   Rating: 4

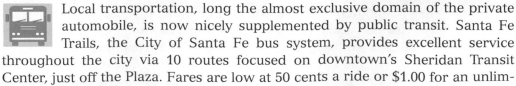 Local transportation, long the almost exclusive domain of the private automobile, is now nicely supplemented by public transit. Santa Fe Trails, the City of Santa Fe bus system, provides excellent service throughout the city via 10 routes focused on downtown's Sheridan Transit Center, just off the Plaza. Fares are low at 50 cents a ride or $1.00 for an unlimited-ride day pass. The city also provides van and taxi service for the elderly and

disabled. Intercity rail service is provided by Amtrak's Southwest Chief whose westbound (to Los Angeles) and eastbound (to Chicago) trains stop daily in Lamy, 18 miles south. The Lamy Shuttle connects the city center with the train station. Greyhound and TNM&O intercity buses stop at the Santa Fe bus station on St. Michael's Drive. Commercial airline service is available at Albuquerque International Airport, 60 miles south. Albuquerque International is served by 10 airlines and provides nonstop jet service to over 30 destinations including major hubs at Dallas, Denver and Phoenix.

Retail Services   Rating: 4

 Thanks in part to its status as a major tourist destination, Santa Fe has a much stronger retailing base than do most cities of its size. Streets fronting the Plaza and just off it are lined with distinctly upscale shops and restaurants. These charming and rather expensive facilities attract tourists and affluent locals alike. Villa Linda Mall, in a suburban location just off Cerrillos Road, is a fairly typical but not unattractive enclosed mall. Anchored by Dillard's, JCPenney, Mervyn's and Sears department stores, Villa Linda Mall houses over 80 shops and restaurants. Many of the usual national chain stores and a few locally owned businesses are present here.

Health Care   Rating: 4

 Santa Fe offers very good medical care. St. Vincent Hospital, with nearly 300 beds, is the city's only general hospital. St. Vincent possesses state-of-the-art diagnostic services including CT scanning, magnetic resonance imaging, radiology and ultrasound. Cardiac and intensive care units, a trauma center, and a comprehensive cancer unit, among other specialized facilities, are available at St. Vincent. Additional and quite exceptional health care services are available in Albuquerque, only an hour's drive away.

Community Services   Rating: 4

The city, Santa Fe County, local colleges, and area religious and community organizations offer an excellent variety of services. Particularly notable is the Santa Fe Senior Citizens Program, which oversees more than 20 programs for seniors. Senior centers offering recreational activities such as dancing, games, sports, and arts and crafts are found in Santa Fe itself and in some outlying communities. The centers also provide health screenings free or at minimal cost, meals, and transportation for seniors.

Leisure Activities

You will find an enormous variety of leisure activities in Santa Fe, in its rural surroundings, and in nearby Albuquerque.

Cultural and Educational Activities   Rating: 5

Those inclined toward culture and education will find plenty to do in Santa Fe. Santa Fe is the arts capital of the Southwest with over 150 art galleries, marvelous museums, and a world-class performing arts scene. Santa Fe's galleries claim to specialize in 16 different categories of art and to house 1,000,000 pieces in a square mile. Downtown museums include the Georgia O'Keefe Museum, which possesses the world's largest permanent collection of her works, the Museum of Fine Arts, and the Palace of the Governors. Within a few miles south of the city center are the excellent Museum of Indian

Arts and Culture, the Wheelwright Museum of the American Indian, and the Museum of International Folk Art.

The city's schedule of the performing arts is also impressive. The world renowned Santa Fe Opera now performs its two-month season in July and August in its newly remodeled outdoor theater a few miles north of town. Major orchestral works are performed by the Santa Fe Symphony Orchestra and Chorus at the Sweeney Convention Center downtown. Chamber music and chorale works are offered by the Santa Fe Chamber Music Festival, which hosts a mini-festival in spring and a Festival of Chamber Music and Jazz in summer, at the St. Francis Auditorium. The Santa Fe Pro Musica alternates chamber music performances at the James A. Little Theatre, the Loreto Chapel, and the St. Francis Auditorium. New Mexico's only professional vocal ensemble, the Desert Chorale, presents a six-week summer season as well as Christmas concerts. In addition to the resident ensembles, the Santa Fe Concert Association presents an impressive number of nationally and internationally known guest artists each year.

Theater, dance, and formal education are well represented in Santa Fe. Santa Fe Stages now offers summer and winter seasons at the College of Santa Fe's Greer Garson Theatre. Shakespeare in Santa Fe, a troupe of professional equity actors and local amateur talent, performs outdoors at St. John's College in summer. Other professional theater groups include Theater Grottesco and Theaterwork, while amateur theater is represented by the popular Santa Fe Playhouse. Professional dance productions are staged in summer by the Maria Benitez Teatro Flamenco and the Santa Fe Festival Ballet. Santa Fe Community College offers several hundred continuing education courses each semester, many of interest to seniors. St. John's College, in addition to its regular course offerings, schedules special readings/discussions for the wider community, while the local campus of the University of New Mexico offers a special peer learning program for seniors.

Recreational Activities   Rating: 5

Outdoor recreation galore exists in and near Santa Fe. The city recreation department's many assets include a new Municipal Recreation Complex with a 27-hole golf course, 4 heated pools, 44 tennis courts, and numerous small parks and playgrounds. The 18-hole public golf course at Cochiti Lake and the private fairways of the Santa Fe Country Club are also open much of the year. For its size the city boasts an adequate complement of movie theaters, with upwards of 16 screens in all, and an excellent array of restaurants that offer good food in all price ranges with an emphasis on quality cuisine of the Southwest. The Santa Fe National Forest, the Pecos Wilderness, Bandelier National Monument, and several New Mexico state parks include over 3,000,000 acres of forested public lands. Here are wonderful places for sightseeing, hiking, backpacking, horseback riding, hunting, fishing, rafting, rock climbing, and cross-country and downhill skiing. Only half an hour from town, the Santa Fe Ski Area boasts terrain between 10,350 and 12,000 feet elevation, over 200 inches of snow in a typical winter, 7 lifts and 39 downhill trails. Although not a large ski area, it offers some of the best skiing in America.

Work and Volunteer Activities   Rating: 2

 Part-time work opportunities for seniors are severely limited. The local economy is heavily dependent on tourism and state government for jobs, and wages for part-time work are low relative to the cost of living. Acute competition for jobs exists with those of normal working age, many of whom commute into the city from rural areas where living costs are low and work scarce. Prospects for volunteer work are more favorable. A host of social clubs and service organizations offer openings ranging from trail maintenance in Santa Fe National Forest to providing assistance to teachers, the sick, elderly or visitors.

Crime Rates and Public Safety   Rating: 3

 Santa Fe's crime situation is complex but not particularly threatening. In recent years the city has experienced a property crime rate well below the average for U.S. urban places and a violent crime rate about 50 percent above average. Closer examination of the violent crime data suggests that the city is not especially dangerous. Rates for homicide, rape, and robbery are all below national norms; only the assault rate, at twice the national average, is problematic. Significantly, most assaults occur among a small, economically disadvantaged segment of the population; few happen in areas lived in or frequented by middle-class retirees. Among the property crimes, only burglary rates approach the national average. Theft and automobile theft rates are very low.

Conclusion

Overall Rating 46 Santa Fe is a very sophisticated small city and a delightfully stimulating place in which to lead an active retirement. Its physical and human environment is close to ideal. Its physical site, where the high plateaus of northern New Mexico run up against the foothills of the Sangre de Cristo Range, is beautiful. Its sunny, semi-arid climate with four distinct seasons and relatively few severely cold or hot days is delightful. Its quality of life is excellent thanks to its manageable size and to sound planning by the city. Santa Fe greatly improved its transportation facilities recently by complementing its adequate road network with an excellent bus system. Retail and medical services are very good, and community services, cultural and recreational offerings, and volunteer opportunities are good to excellent. The principal drawbacks to retirement in Santa Fe are an above average rate of violent crime, minimal opportunities for part-time employment, and a cost of living perhaps 15 percent above the national average. The city's elevation of 7,000 feet may also be of concern to those with cardiovascular, lung or asthma problems. That said, for many people Santa Fe ranks as one of America's premier locales for an active and stimulating retirement.

The Desert Southwest Retirement Region

Climate:
Semi-arid (steppe)–Prescott, Carson City, Reno
Desert–Las Cruces, Tucson, Boulder City, Las Vegas, St. George

Place Description	Overall Rating	Page
Las Cruces, New Mexico	**39**	**170**
Las Cruces offers a good quality of life, thanks to the town's modest size, low population density, and the presence of New Mexico State University.		
Tucson, Arizona	**47**	**176**
With a desert climate and landscape, coupled with the vibrancy of a major city, Tucson offers good to excellent services and a good quality of life.		
Prescott, Arizona	**38**	**182**
Prescott is a pleasant small town in a scenic and unspoiled part of the Desert Southwest, with a peaceful ambiance and an excellent quality of life.		
Boulder City, Nevada	**47**	**187**
An oasis in many ways, Boulder City is a quiet place that offers high-quality services and easy access to the amenities provided by nearby Las Vegas.		
Las Vegas, Nevada	**46**	**192**
Las Vegas is a dynamic, new, and exciting city whose greatest strengths are in cultural and recreational activities, retail services and health care.		
Carson City, Nevada	**42**	**198**
Carson City provides a safe, laid-back lifestyle in an unspoiled, beautiful mountain and high desert environment.		
St. George, Utah	**43**	**203**
In a beautiful setting amidst the mountains, canyons, and mesas of southwestern Utah, St. George offers easy access to some of America's greatest national parks.		
Reno, Nevada	**not rated**	**208**
Although it suffers from a high cost of living and occasional air pollution, Reno offers exceptional recreation, very good transportation and health care, and a good quality of life.		

The Desert Southwest Retirement Region is large in area and varied in its physical geography. Stretching 900 miles from Carson City and Reno in northwestern Nevada to Las Cruces in southern New Mexico, the Desert Southwest is walled off from the moisture and moderating influence of the Pacific Ocean by California's Sierra Nevada and Coast Ranges. As a result, the entire region is sunny and dry although not uniformly so. Precipitation and temperatures vary from place to place owing to differences in elevation and latitude. Rugged mountains, plateaus and canyons not only provide gorgeous vistas but also influence local weather. High desert locales in the north like Carson City and Reno and high plateau cities like Prescott are distinctly more pleasant in summer but colder in winter than low desert cities like Las Vegas and Tucson. And, contrary to conventional wisdom, summer nights are not pleasantly cool in summer in low desert cities; they are very warm.

Rapidly growing Tucson and Las Vegas are stereotypical Sunbelt cities. A flood of retirees has been attracted to them for their superior services, health care and mild winters. Unfortunately, these mid-sized cities suffer from fairly high crime rates as does Las Cruces. The smaller cities and towns of the region, though, most notably Carson City, Boulder City, Prescott and St. George, boast low crime rates, a very high quality of life and gorgeous physical environments. The tradeoff for these benefits is a more modest availability of services and health care here than in larger places.

Las Cruces, New Mexico

Although Spanish settlement in the Mesilla Valley pre-dates the landing of the Pilgrims at Plymouth Rock, the Las Cruces area remained a rather sleepy agricultural and trade-based community well into the twentieth century. Its present status as the second largest city of New Mexico and a location possessing many of the attributes necessary for successful retirement symbolizes a remarkable and continuing transformation of this dynamic corner of the state. With a population nearing 80,000 in the city and 190,000 in the metropolitan area (Dona Ana County), Las Cruces remains a small town but one with suburban development spilling outward in all directions. Located only 50 miles from El Paso, Texas, it has easy access to that city via Interstate-25 (I-25) which also connects it with Albuquerque and Santa Fe, 225 and 285 miles north, respectively. Those seeking an active lifestyle in an attractive valley and mountain setting with a sunny climate may find Las Cruces quite appealing.

Landscape	Rating: 4

Las Cruces is centered at an elevation of 3,900 feet on the flood plain of the Rio Grande in southernmost New Mexico. Immediately east the jagged peaks of the Organ Mountains tower several thousand feet above the city, providing a scenic backdrop to the downtown area. High bluffs west of the river mark the edge of the Mesilla Valley's irrigated farmland and the beginning of the arid Chihuahuan Desert. Newer residential areas extend westward up the slope and atop the bluffs and eastward into the foothills of the Organ Mountains. Sites in these locations offer superb views of mountains, desert, and, in some cases, the river valley and lower town. Although Las Cruces has a desert climate that naturally supports only scanty desert vegetation, nature has been improved upon through intensive irrigation. As a result, many residential areas, especially the older ones, are now dotted with large shade trees providing relief from summer's scorching sun.

Climate	Rating: 4

Las Cruces has a warm four-season climate characterized by scanty precipitation, abundant sunshine, and marked day-to-day and seasonal weather changes. About two-thirds of the normal annual precipitation of 10 inches falls between July and October. Less than four inches of snow accumulates in an average year and snow seldom persists on the ground for more

Las Cruces, New Mexico

CLIMATE				
Month	Average Daily Temperature High / Low		Daily Rel. Humidity Low	Average Monthly Precipitation
	°F		%	Inches
January	58	23	35	0.4
February	63	26	27	0.4
March	69	33	21	0.3
April	77	41	16	0.2
May	86	48	17	0.3
June	95	57	18	0.5
July	95	63	29	1.9
August	92	61	33	2.2
September	87	53	34	1.4
October	79	41	29	1.1
November	67	30	32	0.4
December	58	23	38	0.5

Annual Average

Total Days		Total Inches	
Clear	193	Precipitation	9.6
Partly Cloudy	100	Snowfall	3.4
Cloudy	72		

RATINGS

Rating Scale: 5 = excellent; 4 = very good; 3 = good; 2 = fair; 1 = poor

Rating:	1	2	3	4	5
Landscape				●	
Climate				●	
Quality of Life			●		
Cost of Living			●		
Transportation			●		
Retail Services				●	
Health Care			●		
Community Services				●	
Cultural Activities				●	
Recreational Activities		●			
Work/Volunteer Activities	●				
Crime	●				

Total Points: 39

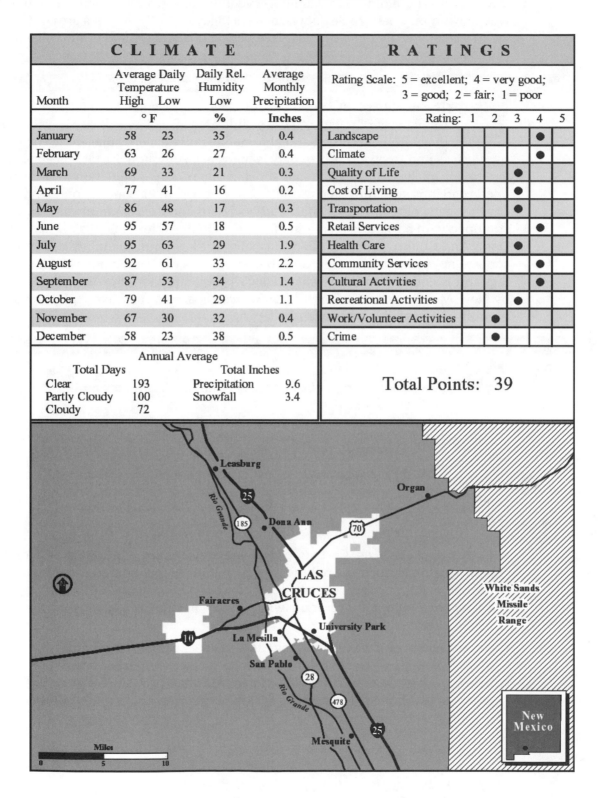

than a day. Winter days are fairly mild, winter nights cold. Summer is hot in Las Cruces, but thanks to the city's moderate elevation, not quite so hot as in lower desert locations like Phoenix and Las Vegas. Summer afternoon highs are typically around 95 degrees, which is not too uncomfortable owing to very low relative humidity, and summer evenings are pleasant. Spring and fall weather is quite changeable but warm days followed by cool nights are common. On average, the city enjoys a frost-free period of 208 days and is sunny 84 percent of the time.

Quality of Life   Rating: 3

 The quality of life is good in Las Cruces. The small local airport is well to the west of town so there is little aircraft noise. The city is also relatively free of railroad and automobile noise except adjacent to the railroad tracks and freeways. Air quality is marginal. Although the city meets some federal air quality standards, it falls short in others. Low population density and good road infrastructure keep traffic moving freely and parking is abundant. The city has many pleasant residential neighborhoods and the community is very well equipped with parks and recreation facilities. On the other hand, Las Cruces and Dona Ana County probably need to tighten their present planning and zoning codes. Rapid expansion of the suburban fringe has decimated downtown retailing, and is eating into the Mesilla Valley's prime farmland. Fortunately, backed by New Mexico State University, Las Cruces is a culturally lively place with a friendly and peaceful ambiance.

Cost of Living   Rating: 3

 The cost of living in Las Cruces is evaluated as follows:

- **Composite.** ACCRA data show that the overall cost of living approximates the national average.

- **Housing.** According to ACCRA, housing costs are eight percent above the national average. Local sources and exploration of the local housing market confirm the essential correctness of these data. A good supply of mid-sized single-family residences is available in the $90,000 to $160,000 price range but many large, luxury homes in prime locations sell at higher prices.

- **Goods and Services.** Costs of goods and services are typically at or slightly below national norms. Groceries are priced at the national average; utilities, health care and miscellaneous goods and services are two to four percent below their national averages, while transportation is about eight percent below average.

- **Taxes.** The overall tax burden in Las Cruces is below the national average. State income taxes for those of moderate means are perhaps 10–20 percent below the national norm, and the property tax of $1,500 on a typical $150,000 home is low indeed. The combined state/local sales tax rate of 6.375 percent is slightly above average.

Local and Regional Services

Las Cruces provides a satisfactory range of services, especially for a small city. These may be supplemented in nearby El Paso, Texas or, better still, in Albuquerque, New Mexico or Tucson, Arizona. The latter two are a half-day drive by freeway.

Transportation   Rating: 3

Local transportation is strongly dominated by the private automobile but alternatives to the car do exist. City-owned Roadrunner Transit provides fixed route bus service to the central part of the city and as far east as Mesilla Valley Mall, but its buses run infrequently and do not penetrate newer suburban areas. Targeted at the transit dependent, Roadrunner's basic fare is only 50 cents, with a 25-cent discount offered to seniors. The city also provides door-to-door dial-a-ride service to seniors and the disabled; advanced reservations for this service are required. Greyhound provides intercity bus service to El Paso, Albuquerque, and Tucson and to points beyond these cities from its terminal on North Valley Drive. Commercial air service is available at El Paso International Airport, 52 miles south. El Paso International offers nonstop service to 20 destinations including major hubs at Dallas and Phoenix. Las Cruces Shuttle Service provides door-to-door ground transportation from Las Cruces to the airport. Amtrak offers limited service from El Paso to points east and west like New Orleans, Chicago and Los Angeles via the Sunset Limited/Texas Eagle train. Currently the combined train makes three weekly departures in each direction.

Retail Services   Rating: 4

Las Cruces has developed a strong retail sector thanks to its status as New Mexico's second largest city. Mesilla Valley Mall, located in an affluent suburban area of east Las Cruces just off Interstate-25, is southern New Mexico's preeminent retailing complex. Anchored by Bealls, Dillard's, JCPenney, Sears, and Service Merchandise department stores, Mesilla Valley Mall also houses 100 specialty stores, services and restaurants. Competition from this mall has virtually wiped out retailing in Las Cruces' downtown mall, itself created as an impressive urban renewal project in the early 1970s. No major stores survive downtown; abundant parking is available but there are few takers. The fate of Mesilla, a historic New Mexican town only four miles south of Las Cruces, is a much happier one. The plaza and surrounding buildings, now included in La Mesilla State Monument, have been beautifully restored to their nineteenth century condition and house a charming assemblage of emporiums, restaurants and bars. Old Mesilla is a great place to stroll, people watch, shop, and enjoy authentic New Mexican food and drink.

Health Care   Rating: 3

Medical care options are somewhat limited in Las Cruces. Memorial Medical Center, with nearly 300 beds, is the city's only general hospital but additional facilities are available in nearby El Paso. Memorial Medical Center is one of the largest hospitals in New Mexico as it serves much of the southern part of the state. It offers a fairly wide range of services including magnetic resonance imaging, cardiovascular care, critical care, orthopedics, emergency care, oncology services and neurology, among other specialties. About 220 physicians are on staff.

Community Services   Rating: 4

 Las Cruces and neighboring communities in Dona Ana County offer an excellent range of services of interest to seniors. Munson Senior Citizen Center provides recreational activities such as card playing, dancing, arts and crafts, writing and computer classes, and social activities, as well as lunch for minimum donations. Recreational and social activities and meals for seniors are also available at the Benavidez Community Center and at Hospitality House in Las Cruces, and at a number of other senior and community centers in nearby communities including La Mesilla. Las Cruces discounts utility rates for qualified seniors, provides books-on-wheels for shut-ins, and subsidizes transit services for those over 60.

Leisure Activities

Thanks in part to the presence of New Mexico State University, Las Cruces and its adjacent areas offer residents a rich variety of leisure activities.

Cultural and Educational Activities   Rating: 4

 The culturally inclined have many choices in Las Cruces including quality symphonic, operatic, ballet, theatrical and dance performances. Principal venues include the Pan American Center and the University Recital Hall, both located on the campus of New Mexico State University. The Las Cruces Symphony Orchestra performs six concerts annually. Several traditional light operatic works are performed each year by the Dona Ana Lyric Opera and ballet performances at Christmas and in spring are produced by the Las Cruces Chamber Ballet. Professional and amateur theater is offered by the Southwest Theater Company and the Las Cruces Community Theater, and dance recitals occur regularly on campus. In addition to the resident ensembles, nationally known guest artists and shows are regularly scheduled at the Pan American Center.

New Mexico State University and Dona Ana Branch Community College provide many learning opportunities for young and old alike. Seniors can take regular courses at the university, attend Weekend College classes there, and participate in public lectures and field trips. Dona Ana Branch Community College's Community Education Program schedules more than 100 courses annually for very nominal tuition and offers Elderhostel programs on southwestern topics at Holy Cross Retreat. Other options for seniors include the series of scholarly mini-courses on topics like exploring local history and appreciating opera, offered by the Academy for Learning in Retirement. The reading resources of New Mexico State University Library, Branigan Public Library, and Munson Senior Center Library are also of interest.

Recreational Activities   Rating: 3

 Recreational opportunities of great variety exist in Las Cruces and vicinity. City parks are numerous and well distributed but most are just relatively small playgrounds with grills and picnic tables. A few larger parks and recreation centers have a wider range of sports facilities including two outdoor swimming pools, a lake with swimming facilities, one indoor pool, numerous ball fields, and tennis, volleyball, racquetball and basketball courts.

Additionally, the city has responded to rising interest in bicycling by designating bike lanes on several streets. Plans are also afoot to build off-street bike paths alongside the many irrigation ditches coursing through the lower part of the city. The three local 18-hole golf courses are open all year as are two additional courses located in St. Anthony, 20 miles south. Spectator sports include intercollegiate football and basketball played by the New Mexico State University Aggies. For a city of its size, Las Cruces is somewhat short of movie theaters with over half of the community's screens being located at Cinema 8 in Mesilla Valley Mall. Good restaurants, though, especially those specializing in New Mexican fare, are abundant and their menus are reasonably priced.

Nearby areas offer additional attractions. Hiking, mountain biking, picnicking, camping and sightseeing are popular at sites such as Aguirre Springs National Recreation Area in the Organ Mountains, a few miles east of town. About a hundred miles to the northeast one can ski downhill in winter at Ski Apache, which boasts ski runs at elevations between 9,600 and 11,500 feet. Boaters and fishermen can enjoy the Caballo and Elephant Butte Reservoirs, about an hour's drive north of town, while desert and mountain areas provide opportunities for hunters and rock hounds alike.

Work and Volunteer Activities   Rating: 2

Employment prospects for seniors are not good in Las Cruces. Negatives include low wages, high unemployment, and strong competition for jobs from college and university students. Even so, Wal-Mart and Mesilla Valley Mall, among other service sector employers, recruit retirees. Prospects for volunteer work are distinctly better. The City of Las Cruces Retired and Senior Volunteer Program (RSVP) typically places about 1,000 volunteers annually in over 100 programs. Other placements are arranged through the Munson Senior Center, Memorial Medical Center, and local places of worship and service organizations.

Crime Rates and Public Safety   Rating: 2

Crime rates are soberingly high in Las Cruces itself and moderately high in the metropolitan area (Dona Ana County). The overall rate of violent crime in Las Cruces is about 30 percent above the national average, whereas the city's overall rate of property crime is 87 percent above the national norm. Closer examination of the data shows rape and assault rates to be relatively high, and homicide and robbery rates to be relatively low, among the violent crime categories. All categories of property crime rank above national norms, with burglary and larceny-theft rates being especially high.

According to the Las Cruces Police Department, most violent crime in the city is attributable to drugs and gang activity, with most violent crimes being committed against gang members. This suggests that most citizens, especially those who do not frequent areas where gang activity is present, are quite safe. Regarding property crime, the local police are also somewhat reassuring in noting that most property crimes can be avoided through common sense and awareness. Be that as it may, most middle-class neighborhoods in Las Cruces look attractive and feel safe. Here, as elsewhere, you can minimize your exposure to crime by picking your retirement site carefully. Luckily, homes in very nice neighborhoods are quite affordable in Las Cruces.

Overall Rating 39

Las Cruces has a lot to offer, especially for a small city. Its physical setting in the Rio Grande Valley at the foot of the jagged peaks of the Organ Mountains is striking. Its sunny, warm, dry climate with four distinct seasons is appealing. The local quality of life is good thanks to the town's modest size, low population density, and the presence of New Mexico State University. Environmental problems are few, although air pollution occasionally exceeds federal standards and dust storms sometimes reduce visibility in the Mesilla Valley. Las Cruces' rankings in retail and community services, volunteer opportunities, and cultural and recreational offerings are good and health care is at least adequate. And all this is available at an average cost of living. The principal drawbacks to retirement in Las Cruces are above average crime rates and minimal opportunities for part-time employment. Even so, those seeking retirement in a southwestern college town in a sunny, warm and scenic environment may find Las Cruces very attractive indeed.

Tucson, Arizona

With a population exceeding 450,000 within its city limits and around 800,000 in the metropolitan area, Tucson is one of few cities of its size that can be recommended for retirement. So far, its explosive growth of recent decades has not seriously damaged its environment or quality of life. Although increasingly varied ethnically, its Mexican heritage is strongly felt in typical pueblo and territorial style adobe buildings with their flat-tiled roofs, and in living cultural monuments like Mission San Xavier del Bac. For those seeking a stimulating, amenity-rich lifestyle in a warm, sunny, and very scenic desert and mountain environment, Tucson has much to offer.

Landscape   Rating: 5

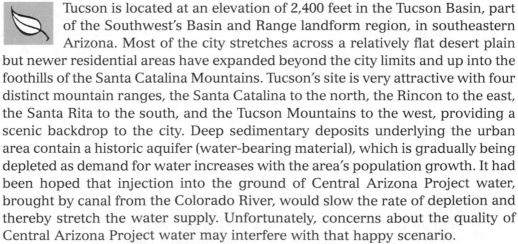

Tucson is located at an elevation of 2,400 feet in the Tucson Basin, part of the Southwest's Basin and Range landform region, in southeastern Arizona. Most of the city stretches across a relatively flat desert plain but newer residential areas have expanded beyond the city limits and up into the foothills of the Santa Catalina Mountains. Tucson's site is very attractive with four distinct mountain ranges, the Santa Catalina to the north, the Rincon to the east, the Santa Rita to the south, and the Tucson Mountains to the west, providing a scenic backdrop to the city. Deep sedimentary deposits underlying the urban area contain a historic aquifer (water-bearing material), which is gradually being depleted as demand for water increases with the area's population growth. It had been hoped that injection into the ground of Central Arizona Project water, brought by canal from the Colorado River, would slow the rate of depletion and thereby stretch the water supply. Unfortunately, concerns about the quality of Central Arizona Project water may interfere with that happy scenario.

Although located in a true desert, the natural vegetation of the area is unusually lush, certainly much more so than in the Colorado Desert of southeastern California and southwestern Arizona. Indeed, higher parts of the city border Saguaro National Park, where a luxuriant growth of giant saguaro cacti and other exotic Sonoran Desert plants dominate the landscape. In the city itself, drought resistant trees, shrubs and cacti, mostly of local origin, are characteristic plantings along streets, in parks, and on private properties. Because of local

Tucson, Arizona

CLIMATE									RATINGS					

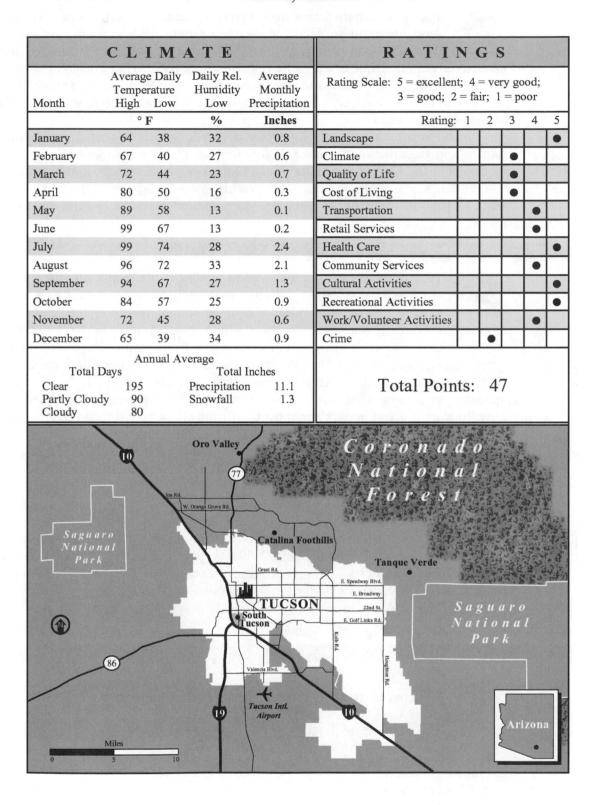

Month	Average Daily Temperature High	Low	Daily Rel. Humidity Low	Average Monthly Precipitation
	°F		%	Inches
January	64	38	32	0.8
February	67	40	27	0.6
March	72	44	23	0.7
April	80	50	16	0.3
May	89	58	13	0.1
June	99	67	13	0.2
July	99	74	28	2.4
August	96	72	33	2.1
September	94	67	27	1.3
October	84	57	25	0.9
November	72	45	28	0.6
December	65	39	34	0.9

Annual Average

Total Days		Total Inches	
Clear	195	Precipitation	11.1
Partly Cloudy	90	Snowfall	1.3
Cloudy	80		

Rating Scale: 5 = excellent; 4 = very good; 3 = good; 2 = fair; 1 = poor

Rating:	1	2	3	4	5
Landscape					●
Climate			●		
Quality of Life			●		
Cost of Living			●		
Transportation				●	
Retail Services				●	
Health Care					●
Community Services				●	
Cultural Activities					●
Recreational Activities					●
Work/Volunteer Activities				●	
Crime		●			

Total Points: 47

constraints on water use and a preference for natural-looking southwestern landscapes, green lawns are much less a feature of the scene in Tucson than in Phoenix or Palm Springs.

Climate

 Tucson's climate is true desert characterized by long, hot, sunny summers and mild, sunny winters. Average daily high temperatures exceed 90 degrees on most days from May through September, but are generally bearable because of very low relative humidity. Spring and fall temperatures are nearly ideal with warm days and cool nights. Winter high temperatures average in the 60s but vary considerably from day to day, with frosts occurring occasionally at night.

Tucson is unusual among American desert locations in that it experiences winter and summer rainy seasons. Nonetheless, the city is one of the sunniest locations in the United States and has a high skin cancer rate to match. Clearly, the outdoors oriented need to cover up with loose-fitting clothing and use protective sunscreen in order to minimize skin damage in this very sunny environment.

Quality of Life

 Tucson measures up quite well in quality of life, especially for a moderate-sized city. Noise pollution from military aircraft and to a lesser degree from commercial aviation is somewhat annoying, but noise from automobiles is not severe as the major freeway, Interstate-10 (I-10) skirts the city and does not run through its center. The freeway and major streets are getting busier year by year but still remain relatively free of congestion compared with larger cities. With a rather low population density and with development spread over a large area, parking tends to be plentiful where needed. Remarkably, Tucson, unlike Phoenix and most California cities, is in full compliance with all federal air quality standards.

Tucson is not rich; there are more modest neighborhoods than upscale ones in the city proper. Still, there are few really shabby areas, and the suburbs in the Catalina Foothills are lovely. The planted desert vegetation of the city blends nicely into the remaining natural vegetation of the area, while many beautifully landscaped parks and playgrounds dot the landscape. Overall, the urban area seems fairly well planned, although the enormous strip development along Oracle Road is visually unappealing. With its great diversity of population and income levels, it is not surprising that Tucson is not uniformly peaceful or upscale in character. However, its better neighborhoods, especially those in the northern half of the urban area and just east of the University of Arizona, are very nice indeed.

Cost of Living

 The cost of living in Tucson is evaluated as follows:

- *Composite.* According to ACCRA, the composite cost of living in Tucson is at the national average.

- *Housing.* ACCRA data show housing costs to be about nine percent below the national average. Housing costs in Tucson tend to be kept down by the low to moderate incomes of much of the population and by the rapid construction of new housing. Growth controls are unknown in Tucson. Most of the political city is characterized by unpretentious housing priced between $90,000 and $130,000 but several outstanding neighborhoods, where typical prices exceed

$300,000 also exist. The suburban Catalina Foothills area tends to offer newer, nicer, and pricier housing than is typical for Tucson.

- **Goods and Services**. Utilities costs, reflecting high electricity consumption for air conditioning, are about 30 percent above the national average. Grocery prices are about 7 percent above average, whereas transportation and health care costs approximate national norms. Miscellaneous goods and services are priced about 6 percent below average.

- **Taxes**. The exact tax burden on a typical household in Tucson is difficult to estimate because of the complexities of state income tax and local property tax rates and structures. At a combined state and city rate of seven percent, Tucsonians pay above average sales taxes, whereas their state income taxes and local property taxes are somewhat below average.

Local and Regional Services

Tucson offers its residents an abundance of services not always available in smaller places.

Transportation	Rating: 4

For a medium-sized city, Tucson has remarkably good public transportation. Sun Tran, the municipal transit agency, provides excellent bus service along major streets throughout the city, especially on weekdays. Unfortunately, except for a few express lines that extend into the suburbs, bus service is confined to the City of Tucson. Suburbanites in neighboring cities and in unincorporated areas like Catalina Foothills are heavily automobile dependent. At 75 cents, basic bus fares are very reasonable, but monthly passes, priced at around $10 for seniors, are an even better deal. Tucson International Airport, located only six miles from the city center, offers very good commercial airline service. Nineteen destinations including Dallas, Los Angeles, and Phoenix are reached by nonstop jet service. Amtrak provides limited service to points east and west like New Orleans and Los Angeles via the Sunset Limited/Texas Eagle train. The combined train currently makes six weekly departures from Tucson, three in each direction. Intercity bus service to most major cities is available from the downtown Greyhound Bus station.

Tucson has endeavored successfully to keep freeways out of much of the city. Since the I-10 freeway skirts the city on the south, most local travel is along major north-south and east-west boulevards. These tend to become moderately congested at rush hour but traffic delays are not yet severe.

Retail Services	Rating: 4

Tucson provides an excellent range of retail services. Three major enclosed shopping malls dominate the metropolitan area retailing structure. The central business district (downtown) is very weak. Tucson Mall, located on Oracle Road in the northwestern part of town, is Tucson's newest and largest major retail complex. Anchored by Dillard's, JCPenney, Macy's, Mervyn's, Robinsons-May, and Sears department stores, the mall has 200 smaller stores, restaurants and service establishments. In east central Tucson, two major malls are found along Broadway. El Con Mall features about 100 specialty shops and restaurants, and is anchored by Dillard's, JCPenney and Robinsons-May department stores. Park Mall, located a little to the east, is anchored by Dillard's, Macy's, and Sears and has about 90 smaller businesses. Retailers are also found in smaller shopping centers and in freestanding locations along major Tucson boulevards. Larger stores and warehouse operations widely scattered around the urban area include Costco, Kmart, Sams Warehouse, three Wal-Marts and four Targets. Like the latter stores, movie theaters tend to be stand-alone complexes along major boulevards. Finally, all major malls and retail complexes have abundant parking, and all those within the city limits are served by Sun Tran buses on a frequent basis.

Health Care   Rating: 5

 Tucson offers exceptional health care. The University of Arizona Medical Center, located on the university campus near downtown, is a major teaching hospital offering the widest possible range of medical services and specialties. Tucson Medical Center, Carondelet St. Joseph's Hospital, and Carondelet St. Mary's Hospital are among the community's other large and excellent medical facilities. Several smaller general hospitals, numerous clinics, and a VA medical center are also present.

Community Services   Rating: 4

 A great variety of services of interest to retirees is widely available in Tucson. The Senior Resource Network provides information about programs for seniors and four senior centers offer a plethora of recreational and social activities including games, sports, classes and field trips.

Leisure Activities

Leisure activities appealing to every taste are plentiful in Tucson and vicinity.

Cultural and Educational Activities   Rating: 5

Many cultural and educational resources including the University of Arizona Theatre, the Arizona Theatre Company, and the University Museum of Art, are found on campus. The nearby Civic Center boasts an arena, convention center and two concert halls. Among the city's excellent resident ensembles are the Arizona Opera, Tucson Light Opera, Tucson Ballet and Tucson Symphony Orchestra. Frequent visits by well-known touring groups are hosted in Tucson's excellent facilities and nicely round out the theatrical and musical scene. The Tucson Museum of Art, located downtown, and the DeGrazia Gallery in the Sun, in Catalina Foothills, are among the city's leading art museums and galleries. Only 14 miles west of downtown, in Tucson Mountain Park, is the Arizona-Sonora Desert Museum where more than 300 animal species and 1,300 plant species indigenous to the Sonoran Desert are displayed in their natural settings. You will want to visit this jewel of a museum again and again.

Recreational Activities   Rating: 5

 The Tucson area abounds in recreational opportunities. Renowned for golf, Tucson has more than 30 courses including 7 relatively inexpensive public facilities. Spectator sports include Pacific Coast Conference football and basketball games hosted by the University of Arizona Wildcats and Greyhound racing at Tucson Greyhound Park. Tucson's many municipal parks offer endless choices for recreation. Centrally located Reid Park is the city's largest and most varied in its attractions. With its tall trees, grassy areas, picnicking and sports facilities and zoo, it is the park of choice for many Tucsonans. Residents remote from Reid Park have a wide choice among smaller playground-type parks, which typically offer tennis, swimming, ball playing and picnicking.

Camping, hiking, and sightseeing choices are almost endless in nearby foothill and mountain areas. Sabino Canyon, in the Santa Catalina Mountains 17 miles northeast of downtown, is easily accessed by shuttle bus or on foot. Swimming and picnicking are permitted there, but for most visitors walking along the road or trails in a gorgeous mountain and canyon environment is the basic attraction. Tucson Mountain Park and Saguaro National Park, just west of the city, and the Catalina Mountains, just to the north, also offer camping, hiking and sightseeing. High up in the Catalina Mountains at Mount Lemmon, one can even ski downhill or cross country for at least a few weeks each winter at America's southernmost ski area. In town, you can bicycle until your heart's content on Tucson's excellent bike path and bike lane network.

If all this exercise makes you hungry, you might consider lunch or dinner at one of Tucson's fine restaurants. Reflecting the area's varied ethnic mix, the city's eateries feature a wonderful variety of cuisine at reasonable prices. Mexican restaurants are everywhere, serving unique Tucson-style dishes in addition to standard Mexican fare found elsewhere in the Southwest. You might also like to try some of the sandwich shops adjacent to the university. Their specialties are excellent and inexpensive.

Work and Volunteer Activities   Rating: 4

 Opportunities for paid and volunteer work are numerous. The booming local economy has generated many jobs in recent years including a good number of part-time service openings of interest to seniors. Unfortunately, in many economic sectors wages are low because of acute competition for jobs among long-time residents, newcomers and students. For those preferring to contribute to the community through volunteerism, the local Volunteer Bureau is helpful in placing seniors in interesting positions as docents, for example, at the Arizona-Sonora Desert Museum or the Tucson Botanical Gardens, or in countless other activities.

Crime Rates and Public Safety   Rating: 2

 Anyone contemplating relocating to Tucson should review the city's crime rates. In Tucson proper, crime rates are well above the national average; indeed Tucson ranks among the most crime-ridden of American retirement towns. Closer examination of crime data on a geographical basis, though, reveals marked spatial variations in potential exposure to crime across the urban area. Crime rates are worse in the City of Tucson than in more affluent suburbs outside the city limits. Thus Catalina Foothills in unincorporated Pima County territory north of town is a comparatively safe area. Furthermore, many violent crimes are gang related and tend to occur primarily in the poorer southern part of the city. That said, and although much of Tucson doesn't feel like a high crime area, the statistics are probably not lying. So choose your retirement site carefully. If you can afford it, you would probably feel more secure in the suburbs or in one of the better urban neighborhoods near the university than in one of the ordinary neighborhoods south or east of downtown.

Conclusion

Overall Rating 47 Tucson is not utopia but it does have a lot going for it. Although the urban area is growing very rapidly, it is still quite livable and should remain so for some time. Careful land use and transportation planning are probably vital, though, if Tucson is to avoid urban ills such as air pollution and traffic congestion that generally accompany long-term population growth. Fortunately, the city is generally spared serious environmental hazards. Tornadoes, hurricanes, and serious earthquakes are unknown here, and the Tucson region is blessed by a beautiful landscape, a warm sunny climate, and a generally good quality of life. The city has very good transportation and very good to excellent ratings for medical, retail and community services. Cultural, educational and recreational offerings are plentiful and of excellent quality. And all these amenities are available in the context of an average cost of living. If you like a desert climate and landscape and the vibrancy of a major city, give Tucson a careful look.

Prescott, Arizona

First settled by gold prospectors in 1864 and capital of the Arizona Territory from 1863 to 1867 and again between 1877 and 1889, Prescott has gradually evolved to its present status as a very pleasant resort and retirement community. With a population of around 32,000, Prescott suffers none of the serious environmental and quality of life problems that plague Phoenix 96 miles to the southeast. Thanks to the concern of its citizens for the town's historic legacy, much of its past has been preserved in its architecture. The downtown Courthouse Square, adjacent Whiskey Row, the first territorial governor's residence and hundreds of Victorian homes in the historic district, all lend a note of authenticity to its western frontier image. For those desiring a high quality of life in a historic town in a mild, sunny, and scenic plateau and mountain area, Prescott has much to offer.

Landscape	Rating: 4

Prescott is situated at an elevation of 5,500 feet on the gently rolling surface of the Colorado Plateau in central Arizona. Several hills including Thumb Butte rise above the general level adding interest to the landscape and providing good vantage points from which to view the city and its surrounding areas. As a result of its moderate elevation, Prescott receives more precipitation than do low-desert cities like Phoenix and Tucson.

Natural moisture levels are just adequate to support a drought resistant ponderosa pine forest that almost completely surrounds the populated area. Watson Lake and the towering, strangely shaped rock formations of the Granite Dells are just north of town along U.S.-89. A little farther afield but still within day-trip range are better known wonders of the Colorado Plateau such as Sedona's red rock monoliths and Oak Creek Canyon, Flagstaff's snow-capped San Francisco Mountains and the incomparable Grand Canyon.

Climate	Rating: 4

Prescott has a moderate four-season climate as a result of its mile-high elevation and southerly location. Indeed, at 34 degrees north latitude, it is about the same distance from the equator as subtropical Los Angeles. Prescott is considerably cooler in all seasons than Phoenix, and is a favorite refuge of southern Arizonans from the scorching temperatures of low-desert locales. Afternoon temperatures are warm to hot in summer but marked overnight cooling makes for temperatures pleasant for sleeping. Winters are brisk, with mild days and cold nights. Spring and fall are delightful seasons with

Prescott, Arizona

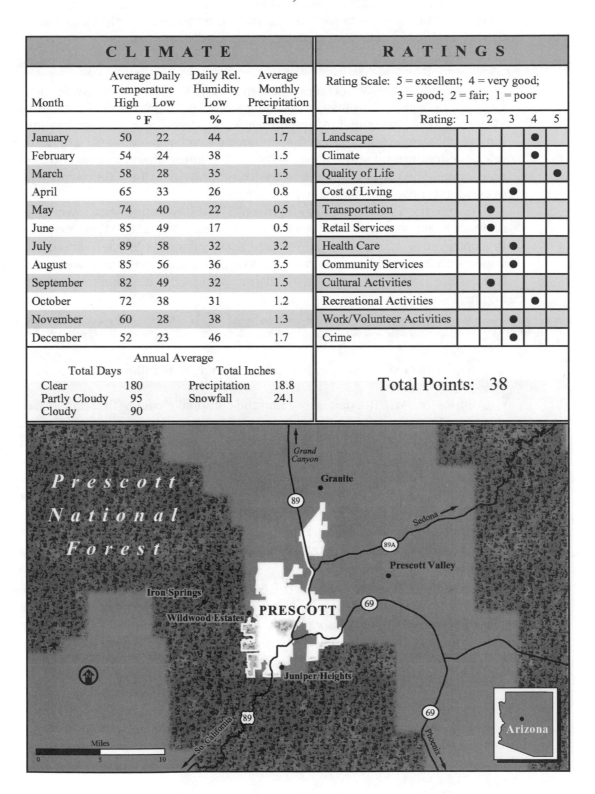

CLIMATE					RATINGS						
Month	Average Daily Temperature High Low		Daily Rel. Humidity Low	Average Monthly Precipitation	Rating Scale: 5 = excellent; 4 = very good; 3 = good; 2 = fair; 1 = poor						
	°F		%	Inches	Rating:	1	2	3	4	5	
January	50	22	44	1.7	Landscape				●		
February	54	24	38	1.5	Climate				●		
March	58	28	35	1.5	Quality of Life					●	
April	65	33	26	0.8	Cost of Living			●			
May	74	40	22	0.5	Transportation		●				
June	85	49	17	0.5	Retail Services		●				
July	89	58	32	3.2	Health Care			●			
August	85	56	36	3.5	Community Services			●			
September	82	49	32	1.5	Cultural Activities		●				
October	72	38	31	1.2	Recreational Activities				●		
November	60	28	38	1.3	Work/Volunteer Activities			●			
December	52	23	46	1.7	Crime			●			

Annual Average

Total Days		Total Inches	
Clear	180	Precipitation	18.8
Partly Cloudy	95	Snowfall	24.1
Cloudy	90		

Total Points: 38

generally mild days and cool nights. Although the city receives an annual average of 17 inches of rain and 24 inches of snow, Prescott is mostly sunny and dry with relative humidity readings in the low to moderate range. The frost-free period is about 150 days, extending from early May through early October, so gardening is mostly a summertime endeavor. Gardeners and others enjoying the outdoors need to protect exposed skin against the area's strong and persistent sunshine. The combination of low latitude and moderately high elevation leads to very high ultraviolet index values, especially in summer.

Quality of Life   Rating: 5

 Prescott provides an excellent quality of life. With no freeways, no heavily traveled highways, and no major airports in the local area, intrusive noise is minimal. Although traffic on streets and highways is increasing steadily, especially during the summer tourist season, traffic congestion is seldom encountered and parking is more than adequate on streets and at shopping malls. The air is pristine and the community is in full compliance with all present and proposed air quality standards.

Despite the fact that per capita income levels are somewhat lower than the national average, the city has an aura of modest prosperity. While neighboring Prescott Valley has somewhat of an urban sprawl character, Prescott itself appears well planned. Its generally pleasant neighborhoods are so well treed that from some points it is difficult to discern where the city ends and the forest begins.

Cost of Living   Rating: 3

 The cost of living in Prescott is evaluated as follows:

- *Composite.* ACCRA data show that the composite cost of living in Prescott is about eight percent above the national average.

- *Housing.* Housing costs are about 14 percent above the national average according to ACCRA. Chamber of Commerce figures indicate that an average home in the Prescott/Prescott Valley area costs about $180,000 but many smaller single-family residences are available for less. Housing of varied styles from California ranches to Santa Fe adobes to traditional frame Victorians is on the market much of the time. Most new developments are found outside the city limits whereas attractive, older resale homes are found in Prescott itself.

- *Goods and Services.* Grocery prices are about 13 percent above the national average, whereas health care, transportation, and miscellaneous goods and services costs are about six percent above national norms. Utilities are priced four percent below the national average.

- *Taxes.* Prescott residents pay above-average sales taxes. The combined state, county and city rate is 7.5 percent. In contrast, the local property tax burden approximates the national average and state income taxes are somewhat below average.

Local and Regional Services

Prescott offers residents a modest array of services typical of smaller communities.

A small private bus company provides daytime service to shopping centers and medical complexes, while local shuttles connect the city with Sky Harbor International Airport in Phoenix, about 100 miles distant. Sky Harbor offers excellent commercial airline service including nonstop jet service to about 80 destinations including Chicago, Las Vegas and Los Angeles. Taxi and dial-a-ride service, the latter for seniors and the disabled, are available in Prescott but as is typical in many small towns nearly everyone but the transit dependent prefers to drive.

Retail Services   Rating: 2

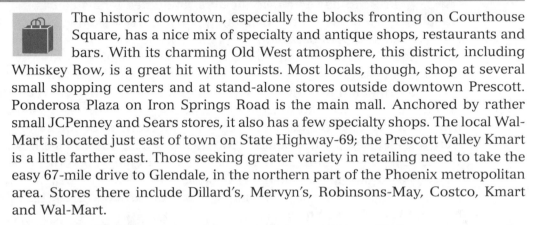 The historic downtown, especially the blocks fronting on Courthouse Square, has a nice mix of specialty and antique shops, restaurants and bars. With its charming Old West atmosphere, this district, including Whiskey Row, is a great hit with tourists. Most locals, though, shop at several small shopping centers and at stand-alone stores outside downtown Prescott. Ponderosa Plaza on Iron Springs Road is the main mall. Anchored by rather small JCPenney and Sears stores, it also has a few specialty shops. The local Wal-Mart is located just east of town on State Highway-69; the Prescott Valley Kmart is a little farther east. Those seeking greater variety in retailing need to take the easy 67-mile drive to Glendale, in the northern part of the Phoenix metropolitan area. Stores there include Dillard's, Mervyn's, Robinsons-May, Costco, Kmart and Wal-Mart.

Health Care   Rating: 3

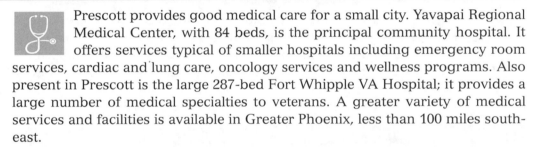 Prescott provides good medical care for a small city. Yavapai Regional Medical Center, with 84 beds, is the principal community hospital. It offers services typical of smaller hospitals including emergency room services, cardiac and lung care, oncology services and wellness programs. Also present in Prescott is the large 287-bed Fort Whipple VA Hospital; it provides a large number of medical specialties to veterans. A greater variety of medical services and facilities is available in Greater Phoenix, less than 100 miles southeast.

Community Services   Rating: 3

 The Adult Center of Prescott makes available classes in Spanish, computers, and various crafts and organizes field excursions, dances, and card games, among other activities. It also runs a popular wellness clinic.

Leisure Activities

Leisure activities of considerable variety are available in Prescott and nearby areas. Not surprisingly, as it is a rather small place, its principal strengths are in recreational activities in the surrounding area rather than in cultural and educational opportunities in the town.

Cultural and Educational Activities   Rating: 2

 Prescott's modest endowment of cultural and educational activities is sufficient for most residents and the immense assets of the Phoenix area are only an hour or so away by car. The Prescott Fine Arts

Association presents locally produced plays and the Yavapai Symphony Association schedules chamber music and symphonic concerts, some featuring imported soloists. The June Bluegrass Festival and most other major cultural events are hosted at a 1,200-seat performing arts center at Yavapai Community College. The college, with over 6,000 students, makes available to seniors a wide range of academic and applied arts courses at reduced fees. The community's several art museums and galleries, many featuring western art, and the downtown public library are also of interest.

Recreational Activities   Rating: 4

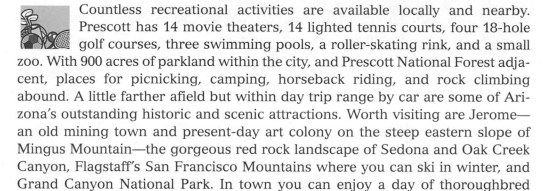

Countless recreational activities are available locally and nearby. Prescott has 14 movie theaters, 14 lighted tennis courts, four 18-hole golf courses, three swimming pools, a roller-skating rink, and a small zoo. With 900 acres of parkland within the city, and Prescott National Forest adjacent, places for picnicking, camping, horseback riding, and rock climbing abound. A little farther afield but within day trip range by car are some of Arizona's outstanding historic and scenic attractions. Worth visiting are Jerome—an old mining town and present-day art colony on the steep eastern slope of Mingus Mountain—the gorgeous red rock landscape of Sedona and Oak Creek Canyon, Flagstaff's San Francisco Mountains where you can ski in winter, and Grand Canyon National Park. In town you can enjoy a day of thoroughbred horse racing during the summer racing season, Memorial Day through Labor Day, and round out the day savoring food and drink at one of the historic restaurants on Courthouse Square.

Work and Volunteer Activities   Rating: 3

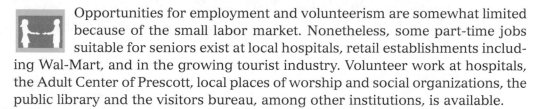

Opportunities for employment and volunteerism are somewhat limited because of the small labor market. Nonetheless, some part-time jobs suitable for seniors exist at local hospitals, retail establishments including Wal-Mart, and in the growing tourist industry. Volunteer work at hospitals, the Adult Center of Prescott, local places of worship and social organizations, the public library and the visitors bureau, among other institutions, is available.

Crime Rates and Public Safety   Rating: 3

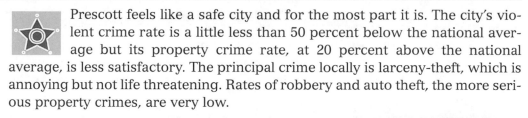

Prescott feels like a safe city and for the most part it is. The city's violent crime rate is a little less than 50 percent below the national average but its property crime rate, at 20 percent above the national average, is less satisfactory. The principal crime locally is larceny-theft, which is annoying but not life threatening. Rates of robbery and auto theft, the more serious property crimes, are very low.

Conclusion

Overall Rating 38

Prescott is not perfect but it is a very pleasant small town in a scenic and unspoiled part of the Desert Southwest. Because of its location, moderate elevation, and underlying geology, the city enjoys a mild sunny, four-season climate and a general absence of environmental hazards. Many people from large cities appreciate the peaceful ambiance and excellent quality of life of Prescott. Those attracted to the great outdoors will doubtless enjoy the natural beauty of the city's wooded hilly site and the ease of visiting some of the geologic and historic wonders of the American West via relatively short automobile trips. Although a little above the national average, the cost of living remains affordable and health care, community services, and work and volunteer opportunities are at least satisfactory. Prescott's principal weaknesses are those typical of small towns. Public transit is inadequate so a car is a virtual necessity. Cultural offerings are obviously very limited as are retail choices. All in all, though, Prescott measures up quite well among smaller places as a retirement haven. It is worth a careful look.

Boulder City, Nevada

Founded in 1931 by the federal government to house workers constructing Hoover Dam, Boulder City is today a beautiful little oasis in the desert of southern Nevada. Only 8 miles from Hoover Dam and 24 miles from downtown Las Vegas and technically part of the Las Vegas metropolitan area, Boulder City has little but its desert setting and climate in common with Las Vegas. With a population of 16,000 in 1999, a well-planned urban structure and a controlled growth ordinance that limits the number of building permits issued each year to about 3.5 percent of existing development, this well-run city is determined to do whatever is necessary to preserve its high quality of life. To that end Boulder City has never allowed gambling within its city limits and has recently increased its size from 34.5 square miles to 200 square miles. The annexation of 165.5 square miles of desert stretching south of town is intended to protect the natural environment and prevent Las Vegas suburbs from eventually engulfing the community.

Landscape   Rating: 4

Boulder City is located on a gently sloping upland surface at an elevation of 2,500 feet. A low range of hills separates it from the urban sprawl and frenzied pace of Las Vegas and adds scenic interest to its setting. High mountains in the distance frame dramatic views of Lake Mead from the hilltop park and civic center complex in the heart of the historic district. The natural vegetation of the area is low desert scrub but the heavily irrigated urban landscape is lush indeed. As in Las Vegas, green lawns, flowers, and exotic tree species including palms, rather than drought-resistant desert plants, are favored locally. Fortunately, Boulder City, unlike Las Vegas, has a large enough allocation of water from Lake Mead to meet its needs for the foreseeable future.

Climate   Rating: 3

Boulder City's climate is true desert with long, very hot, sunny summers and cool, sunny winters. Among American desert locations, Boulder City, like Las Vegas, is unusually dry. It receives an average of only 5.7 inches of precipitation annually. Measurable precipitation falls on an average of only 13 days per year. Average daily high temperatures exceed 95 degrees during summer months and overnight temperatures are rather warm. Spring and fall are the most pleasant seasons with generally warm days and cool nights. Winters are fairly cool with normal highs in the upper 50s. Snowfall is insignificant and the frost-free season is nearly 300 days long on average, with light frost occurring frequently at night from December through February. The city is sunny about 85 percent of the time and is one of America's sunniest locations; use of a good sunscreen is essential.

Boulder City, Nevada

CLIMATE				
Month	Average Daily Temperature High Low		Daily Rel. Humidity Low	Average Monthly Precipitation
	°F		%	Inches
January	54	38	33	0.6
February	61	43	27	0.5
March	67	46	23	0.7
April	76	53	17	0.4
May	85	61	15	0.3
June	96	70	14	0.1
July	102	76	18	0.5
August	99	74	20	0.8
September	93	68	19	0.5
October	80	58	21	0.4
November	65	46	28	0.5
December	56	39	33	0.4

Annual Average			
Total Days		Total Inches	
Clear	212	Precipitation	5.8
Partly Cloudy	82	Snowfall	0.6
Cloudy	71		

RATINGS

Rating Scale: 5 = excellent; 4 = very good; 3 = good; 2 = fair; 1 = poor

	Rating: 1	2	3	4	5
Landscape				●	
Climate			●		
Quality of Life					●
Cost of Living	●				
Transportation				●	
Retail Services				●	
Health Care				●	
Community Services				●	
Cultural Activities				●	
Recreational Activities					●
Work/Volunteer Activities			●		
Crime					●

Total Points: 47

Quality of Life — Rating: 5

The overall quality of life is excellent. McCarren International Airport is 20 miles away in Las Vegas, no freeway approaches the city limits, and the U.S.-93 truck route bypasses the center of town. As a result

there is little noise from road traffic or commercial aircraft. Boulder City meets all federal air quality standards and, according to the city manager, lies in a different air basin and has distinctly cleaner air than neighboring Las Vegas. The city's small size, low population density, lack of major commercial development, and location on the fringe of the Las Vegas urban region prevent crowding and traffic congestion. Parking is plentiful and free, even in the downtown area, and no heavy industries or garish gambling casinos blight the landscape. Residential neighborhoods, whether in the historic district around the civic center or in new areas on the periphery, are well maintained with green lawns or desert gardens fronting on clean tree-shaded streets. The city's beautifully landscaped small parks, plazas, and playgrounds add additional notes of peaceful ambiance to the community.

Cost of Living   Rating: 2

 The cost of living in Boulder City is evaluated as follows:

- **Composite.** ACCRA data are unavailable for Boulder City but costs there, except for housing, are likely little different from those of Las Vegas. The overall cost of living is probably 10–15 percent above the national average.

- **Housing.** Housing costs are well above the national average in part because the housing supply in Boulder City has been limited since the late 1970s by a controlled growth ordinance. Other factors driving up house prices include the well-known ambiance of the community and the influx of equity-rich Californians who tend to bid up prices in the most desirable parts of the Las Vegas region. According to Boulder City's city manager, housing costs there are about 30 percent higher than in Las Vegas. Small construction era homes in the historic district are priced in the $125,000 to $160,000 range, while at the other extreme, new large homes near Lake Mead are priced over $300,000. Typical single-family residences in average neighborhoods are available for prices between $140,000 and $220,000.

- **Goods and Services.** Extrapolating from ACCRA data for Las Vegas, one would expect local costs of health care and transportation to be about 24 percent above national norms, whereas miscellaneous goods and services and groceries would be 5 percent and 15 percent above their national averages. Utilities, priced about 10 percent below average by the municipality, are a comparative bargain.

- **Taxes.** The overall tax burden is low. As noted in the Las Vegas discussion, Nevada does not tax income and municipal property taxes are well below the national average. At current rates you would pay about $1,400 annually on a home in Boulder City worth $170,000. The seven percent state sales tax is well above the national average.

Local and Regional Services

Services available locally in Boulder City are adequate for day-to-day needs and the virtually unlimited attractions of Las Vegas are within a 30-minute drive.

Transportation   Rating: 4

Citizen's Area Transit (CAT) provides local bus service and connects Boulder City with Las Vegas. Fares are very reasonable; seniors pay 50 cents per ride or $10 for a monthly pass. Bus service is also provided for seniors by the senior center. McCarran Airport, only 24 miles away in Las Vegas, can be reached via the Boulder City Shuttle Service or by car. As noted more fully in the Las Vegas discussion, McCarran provides excellent jet service to numerous U.S. locations.

Retail Services   Rating: 4

The historic downtown shopping district is quaint but oriented mainly to tourists. Residents shop locally at a small shopping center on Nevada Highway on the south side of town. A supermarket and several specialty stores are found there. The nearest major shopping mall is the Galleria at Sunset in Henderson, 18 miles away. There you will find Dillard's, JCPenney, Mervyn's California, and Robinsons-May department stores, and a host of specialty shops, restaurants and service establishments. The immense retailing resources of Las Vegas' three other major enclosed malls are only a few miles farther.

Health Care   Rating: 4

Boulder City Hospital and its staff of 100 doctors provide adequate routine medical care. Facilities and services at the 72-bed hospital include a 24-hour emergency unit, clinical laboratory, intensive care unit, radiology department, CT and MRI scanners, and nuclear medicine. Larger facilities with a greater range of medical specialties and services are only half an hour away in Las Vegas (see Las Vegas Health Care discussion for details).

Community Services   Rating: 4

The municipality, places of worship, and more than 50 community organizations offer an exceptional range of services to residents. Of special interest to retirees are the many activities and services provided by "Seniors Helping Seniors" at the Senior Center of Boulder City. Social activities include playing pool in the center's fully equipped poolroom, card games, bingo, chess, horseshoes and croquet. Arts and crafts, movies, travel to casinos, and other attractions are also popular. The center provides assistance with legal problems, income tax preparation, and social security applications and offers a number of onsite health services including complete physicals, blood pressure and vision screenings, and nutrition education. The center also serves weekday lunches, provides transportation to and from the center and to points within Boulder City on weekdays, and delivers Meals-on-Wheels on request.

Leisure Activities

Boulder City provides a good variety of leisure activities and an enormous diversity is found only a few miles away in Las Vegas and the Lake Mead National Recreation Area.

Cultural and Educational Activities   Rating: 4

 Boulder City is a little too small, too protective of its residential ambiance, and too close to Las Vegas to develop a strong cultural identity of its own. However, it has on its eastern side a branch campus of the Community College of Southern Nevada and several art galleries downtown. It even hosts numerous art shows including the annual "Art in the Park Festival," and its Boulder City "First Nighters" is the oldest amateur theater group in southern Nevada. The town library, located in the civic center complex, boasts 33,000 books and 150 magazine and newspaper subscriptions.

Those seeking more advanced education or more sophisticated popular or classical culture need only travel the 24 miles to Las Vegas to have their needs met (see Las Vegas Cultural and Educational Activities discussion for details). There is never a shortage of cultural events in Las Vegas.

Recreational Activities   Rating: 5

 Recreational assets abound locally and nearby. The city's 34 acres of landscaped park and plaza areas offer facilities for picnicking, community events, shuffleboard, tennis, basketball and baseball. The downtown Boulder City Recreation Center features year-round indoor swimming and racquetball. An 18-hole municipal golf course, an oasis of green on the edge of the desert, is open all year. Other recreational facilities in town include a movie theater, bowling alley, and a BMX bicycle track. Just outside of town is Lake Mead, created by impounding the Colorado River at Hoover Dam. The Lake Mead National Recreation Area, an element of the National Parks System, has 500 miles of shoreline and is a mecca for water sports enthusiasts and fishermen, as well as for campers, bikers, hikers and sightseers. Those seeking an even greater variety of recreation need only travel to Las Vegas where there are golf courses, parks, participant and spectator sports, and restaurants galore (see Las Vegas Recreational Activities discussion for details).

Work and Volunteer Activities   Rating: 3

 Opportunities for employment and volunteerism are somewhat limited by the small size of Boulder City. Even so, some part-time jobs exist in the service sector, and volunteer work at the hospital, the senior center, the public library, the chamber of commerce, the National Parks Service, and local service organizations is available. Individuals willing to travel to Las Vegas will find additional employment and volunteer opportunities.

Crime Rates and Public Safety   Rating: 5

 Boulder City is one of America's safest communities. Recent FBI data show that the city's violent crime rate is about 70 percent below the national average, while its property crime rate is about 60 percent below the national norm. Clearly, the town's geographic isolation from Las Vegas, its relatively stable, affluent, and alert population, excellent city government and police, and the absence of casinos and large-scale commercial development all help make Boulder City an enviably peaceful and safe place.

Overall Rating 47 Boulder City ranks very highly as a retirement town. Although officially part of the Las Vegas metropolitan area, it is quite unlike the city and its sprawling suburbs. It is an oasis according to both meanings of the term. It is an area of the desert made fertile by the presence of water and, more importantly, it is a quiet, peaceful place in the midst of turbulent surroundings. At the same time it is close enough to Las Vegas for its residents to enjoy easy access to the many amenities of that lively city.

Boulder City is fortunate in its physical and human environment. Its site overlooking Lake Mead and the surrounding desert and mountains is striking and its climate is varied enough to offer four distinct seasons. Those seeking to escape from big city stresses will find Boulder City's excellent quality of life attributes and very low crime rates attractive. The city is well planned and run and offers its residents high-quality public services including, among others, excellent parks and recreation facilities and a fine police department. Taking into account the fact that Boulder City residents can easily supplement local resources with those of nearby Las Vegas and Henderson, the community's ratings in transportation, retail services, health care, community services, and cultural and recreational activities are very good indeed. Admittedly, all these benefits come at the price of a cost of living perhaps 10–15 percent above the national average. But that premium is a small price to pay for the privilege of living in Boulder City.

Las Vegas, Nevada

Las Vegas, with a population exceeding 400,000 in the city and 1,200,000 in the metropolitan area, is fast becoming one of America's most popular retirement locales. Explosive economic and population growth is so much the norm that people scarcely notice when hotels along the Strip, only 20 or 30 years old, are replaced in record time by larger and more luxurious ones. But Las Vegas is far more than the famous hotels and gambling casinos of the Strip and downtown. Outside these dynamic and intensely developed areas, you will find a relatively low population density city, not unlike the newer suburban areas of many other mid-sized American cities. A suburban lifestyle in a sunny, warm, desert environment within a few miles of exciting Las Vegas attractions appeals to many people, young and old. Every month about 6,000 people move here.

Las Vegas sprawls across a flat desert basin in southern Nevada at an elevation of 2,500 feet. The physical site is uninteresting but some isolated mountains, including Mt. Charleston, which is high enough to be snow-capped in winter, add relief to the terrain. The natural vegetation of the area consists of low desert scrub but this is not apparent amidst the greenery of the heavily irrigated city. The Las Vegas approach to water use is the antithesis of that of Tucson. Instead of Tucson's plantings of drought-resistant desert trees, shrubs and cacti, Las Vegas grows green lawns, flowers, humid land tree species and palms. As a result, per capita water use is twice that of Tucson and will soon exceed Nevada's allocation of Colorado River water. Where additional supplies can be obtained is uncertain.

Las Vegas, Nevada

CLIMATE				
Month	Average Daily Temperature High Low	Daily Rel. Humidity Low	Average Monthly Precipitation	
	°F	%	Inches	
January	56 33	31	0.5	
February	62 38	26	0.5	
March	68 42	22	0.4	
April	77 50	16	0.2	
May	87 59	13	0.2	
June	99 69	11	0.1	
July	105 76	15	0.5	
August	102 74	17	0.5	
September	95 66	17	0.3	
October	82 54	19	0.3	
November	66 41	27	0.4	
December	57 34	32	0.3	

Annual Average

Total Days		Total Inches	
Clear	212	Precipitation	4.2
Partly Cloudy	82	Snowfall	1.3
Cloudy	71		

RATINGS

Rating Scale: 5 = excellent; 4 = very good;
3 = good; 2 = fair; 1 = poor

	Rating: 1	2	3	4	5
Landscape			●		
Climate			●		
Quality of Life			●		
Cost of Living			●		
Transportation				●	
Retail Services					●
Health Care					●
Community Services				●	
Cultural Activities					●
Recreational Activities					●
Work/Volunteer Activities				●	
Crime		●			

Total Points: 46

Climate   **Rating: 3**

The Las Vegas climate is true desert characterized by long, very hot, sunny summers and cool, sunny winters. Even among desert cities Las Vegas is unusually dry; it receives on average only four inches of precipitation annually as a result of its location in the rain shadow of high mountains to the west. Average daily high temperatures exceed 98 degrees during the summer and are typically pleasantly warm in spring and fall. Winter is much cooler with normal highs in the upper 50s. Snowfall is insignificant but frosts occur on an average of 32 nights per year, mostly in December, January and February. In contrast, summer nights are very warm as a result of the "thermal heat island effect" typical of large cities. Overnight lows average 76 degrees in July. On average, the city is sunny 85 percent of the time and ranks with Tucson as one of America's sunniest cities. Careful use of sunscreen is essential to minimize skin damage.

Quality of Life   Rating: 3

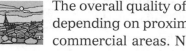 The overall quality of life is good but significant variation occurs locally depending on proximity to the airport and to busy streets, freeways and commercial areas. Neighborhoods away from tourist attractions tend to be relatively quiet, except for occasional noise from automobile traffic and commercial or military aircraft. Las Vegas meets all federal air quality standards. Nonetheless, the atmosphere is not entirely clear; some reduction in visibility occurs as a result of mixing together of dust and locally generated photochemical smog from the region's large automobile fleet. The city and the state of Nevada have aggressively built a high-capacity street and freeway network to accommodate the burgeoning car population. Two major freeways, Interstate-15 and Interstate-515, crisscross the metropolitan area and connect with most major east-west and north-south boulevards. Regrettably, as elsewhere, improvements in road infrastructure in Las Vegas appear to contribute to additional low-density urban sprawl, longer average motor trips, greater total travel, and ultimately to increased traffic congestion. To date, though, heavy traffic congestion remains largely a rush hour phenomenon, except on Las Vegas Boulevard (the Strip), which is nearly always busy. Plenty of parking is available where needed.

Ideally, urban growth on the massive scale that is occurring in Las Vegas would seem to mandate careful physical planning and zoning in order to preserve the present good quality of life. Unfortunately, the political will to constrain or guide development seems to be lacking with the result that Las Vegas is rather quickly developing into a smaller version of Los Angeles. Its older, pleasant inner city neighborhoods are becoming lost in a sea of quite decent but all-too-similar, newer tract homes.

Cost of Living   Rating: 3

 The cost of living in Las Vegas is evaluated as follows:

- *Composite.* ACCRA data show that the composite cost of living in Las Vegas is six percent above the national average.

- *Housing.* Average housing costs approximate the national average. Since growth controls are unknown and housing is being built at a rapid pace, housing costs should remain reasonable despite the massive influx of new residents. At present, a typical single-family home sells for around $150,000 but many larger, upscale homes on the suburban fringe sell at considerably higher prices.

- *Goods and Services*. ACCRA data show health care and transportation to be priced about 25 percent above national norms, while groceries are 15 percent above average. Costs of miscellaneous goods and services approximate the national average and utilities are a bargain at a price 10 percent below average.

- *Taxes*. The absence of a state income tax in Nevada is a big attraction to the state, especially now that federal law forbids states taxing the pension benefits of former residents, as California and several other states did until recently. Another advantage of Nevada is that its property taxes are well below the national average. But Nevada has been unable to shift the entire tax burden to visitors. Residents too must pay sales taxes and the sales tax burden of seven percent is well above the national norm.

Local and Regional Services

Las Vegas provides residents and visitors a great number of services typically unavailable in smaller places.

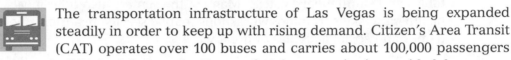

Transportation	Rating: 4

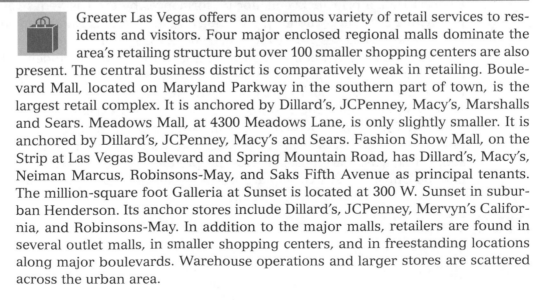

The transportation infrastructure of Las Vegas is being expanded steadily in order to keep up with rising demand. Citizen's Area Transit (CAT) operates over 100 buses and carries about 100,000 passengers daily on its 39 scheduled routes. Twenty-four hour service is provided downtown and along the Strip but hours of service and frequency of service are less elsewhere. Seniors pay 50 cents per ride or $10 for a monthly pass. Not surprisingly in such a sprawling city, most people are wedded to their cars and leave the buses to the transit dependent. McCarran Airport, located just southeast of the Strip and only six miles from the city center, is currently the nation's tenth busiest airport. A major hub, McCarran offers nonstop jet service to numerous domestic locations. New terminals, gates, and a 9,700-foot runway have recently been added and no end is in sight for the airport's expansion. Those preferring to stay on the ground can reach many destinations from the downtown Greyhound bus station.

Retail Services	Rating: 5

Greater Las Vegas offers an enormous variety of retail services to residents and visitors. Four major enclosed regional malls dominate the area's retailing structure but over 100 smaller shopping centers are also present. The central business district is comparatively weak in retailing. Boulevard Mall, located on Maryland Parkway in the southern part of town, is the largest retail complex. It is anchored by Dillard's, JCPenney, Macy's, Marshalls and Sears. Meadows Mall, at 4300 Meadows Lane, is only slightly smaller. It is anchored by Dillard's, JCPenney, Macy's and Sears. Fashion Show Mall, on the Strip at Las Vegas Boulevard and Spring Mountain Road, has Dillard's, Macy's, Neiman Marcus, Robinsons-May, and Saks Fifth Avenue as principal tenants. The million-square foot Galleria at Sunset is located at 300 W. Sunset in suburban Henderson. Its anchor stores include Dillard's, JCPenney, Mervyn's California, and Robinsons-May. In addition to the major malls, retailers are found in several outlet malls, in smaller shopping centers, and in freestanding locations along major boulevards. Warehouse operations and larger stores are scattered across the urban area.

Health Care   Rating: 5

 Las Vegas offers comprehensive medical care although at prices well above the national average. University Medical Center, affiliated with the University of Nevada School of Medicine, is a county-operated complex that provides a wide range of medical services. It was the first hospital in Nevada to develop an organ transplant program, and offers special health programs for Nevada's senior population. Other large general hospitals include: Columbia Sunrise Hospital and Medical Center, Columbia Sunrise Mountain View Hospital, Desert Springs Hospital, Lake Mead Hospital, St. Rose Dominican Hospital, Summerlin Medical Center, and Valley Hospital Medical Center. Several smaller specialty hospitals and numerous clinics are also present. A new military and veteran's hospital opened in 1994.

Community Services   Rating: 4

The metropolitan area's more than 15 neighborhood senior centers are a major resource. These offer a variety of recreational facilities including gymnasiums, swimming pools, libraries, exercise rooms, billiard tables and shuffleboard courts. Many of the centers also offer meals, preventive health care, skills training, workshops, public service programs, field trips, and games and social activities of great variety.

Leisure Activities

Leisure activities of enormous diversity are found in Las Vegas and surrounding areas in southern Nevada.

Cultural and Educational Activities   Rating: 5

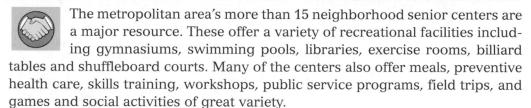 Significant cultural and educational resources are available to all age groups at the University of Nevada, Las Vegas (UNLV) and the Community College of Southern Nevada (CCSN). Now 40 years old, the university currently enrolls 20,000 students on its 335-acre campus. UNLV's excellent theatre arts department stages modern plays and the classics on campus at the Judy Bayley Theatre on Maryland Parkway. The Nevada Dance Theater also performs here regularly. Also on campus is the Artemus W. Ham Concert Hall, a principal venue for performances by the Las Vegas Civic Symphony, the Nevada Symphony, and the Nevada Opera Theatre. Popular music and jazz performances are also scheduled here. CCSN, with three main campuses and 50 extension centers, is highly accessible to its 26,000 students. Its 2,500 courses in the academic and applied arts, scheduled seven days a week in daytime and evening, should appeal to nearly every taste.

Las Vegas hotels and casinos host an enormous variety of popular entertainment. Big-room shows typically feature a star performer and orchestra, supported by a vocalist or comedian; lounge shows feature a main performer and supporting acts. If art museums are your preference, the Las Vegas Art Museum and the University Art Gallery are worth visiting. The Las Vegas Public Library, with over 1,500,000 books in its eight branches, is also a useful resource.

Recreational Activities   Rating: 5

 Recreational opportunities are abundant locally. Over 40 golf courses, most open to the public on a daily fee basis, dot the landscape. Over 30 municipal parks offer some combination of ball fields, courts for basketball, tennis and volleyball, as well as playgrounds and picnic areas. Snow-skiing facilities on Mount Charleston, water sports sites on Lake Mead, and the spectacularly eroded red sandstone cliffs of Valley of Fire State Park are within an hour's drive. A little farther afield but still reachable by one- or two-day car trips are Death Valley, Grand Canyon, and Zion National Parks. In town, spectator sports enthusiasts can enjoy Las Vegas Thunder professional ice hockey, and varsity basketball and football played by UNLV's Runnin Rebels. Las Vegas has many fine restaurants to enjoy after the game. Whether your preference is fine French or continental dining in a semi-formal setting or the more casual ambiance of American, Italian, or ethnic restaurants, the choices are almost infinite.

Work and Volunteer Activities   Rating: 4

 Many opportunities exist for post-retirement work and volunteerism. Rapid growth of tourism and the gaming industry creates countless full-time and part-time jobs, some of which might be of interest to retirees. Those preferring to contribute through volunteerism may take advantage of the AARP community service employment program to find their niche in one of the city's numerous service organizations.

Crime Rates and Public Safety   Rating: 2

Crime rates and public safety issues should be carefully examined by those considering a move to Las Vegas. The metropolitan area suffers from crime rates well above the national average and not too different from those of San Antonio and Tucson. Significant variations in potential exposure to crime exist across the metropolis. North Las Vegas, economically one of the poorest parts of the urban area, has a violent crime rate nearly twice that of the City of Las Vegas and more than twice that of the metropolitan area. You would be well advised to avoid the metropolitan area's poorer neighborhoods where gang activity and crime go hand in hand. On a more positive note, property crime rates, although 10–15 percent above the national average in the city and metropolitan region, are not inordinately high. Indeed, taking into account the 30,000,000 visitors who come to Las Vegas annually, the threat of crime to a particular individual, resident or nonresident, is less than FBI data imply. Even so, it would be wise to choose your retirement site carefully in one of the better neighborhoods. There are many to choose from.

Conclusion

Overall Rating 46 Las Vegas ranks highly on most standard measures of suitability for retirement but it is not without problems. Its greatest strengths are in cultural and and recreational activities, retail services and health care. It is also very strong in transportation, community services, and work and volunteer activities. Despite tremendous recent population growth, much of the urban area still rates fairly highly in quality of life factors. However, if such growth persists for another 20 years as seems almost certain, air quality and traffic congestion could worsen and water use might need to be curtailed. Luckily, major environmental hazards are virtually unknown in southern Nevada. Unfortunately, serious crime is not. It is a potential threat that can be minimized but not entirely avoided by choosing an upscale neighborhood. Finally, it must be admitted that the newness and relative uniformity of much of the urban landscape may be unsatisfying to some. There are no charming historic neighborhoods and the various malls cannot entirely make up for the lack of a vibrant downtown. Nonetheless, for those well suited to a suburban lifestyle in a dynamic, new, exciting city full of cultural and recreational attractions, Las Vegas might be a good and fairly economical choice.

Carson City, Nevada

From its humble origins as a commercial and industrial center serving the silver miners of nearby Virginia City in the late 1850s, Carson City has blossomed into one of the country's most beautiful state capitals. Located only 14 miles east of Lake Tahoe, 30 miles south of Reno, and 130 miles east of Sacramento, California, it offers easy access to countless outdoor recreational pursuits in the Lake Tahoe region and the Sierra Nevada. The shopping, cultural and educational attractions, and gaming establishments of Reno are also nearby. Carson City, with a population just over 50,000 in 1999, is only one-third the size of Reno and retains a laid-back atmosphere that reflects a preference for tranquility and a high quality of life over rapid growth. The local economy, owing to the city's role as capital of Nevada, is strongly service oriented and relatively stable.

Landscape	Rating: 5

Carson City is situated in northwestern Nevada at an elevation of 4,700 feet on a gently sloping plain at the foot of the Sierra Nevada, a massive mountain range separating the Central Valley of California from the desert and semi-arid areas of Nevada. Lying just east of the Sierra Nevada and in its rain shadow, Carson City occupies a pleasant and scenic site. Its low profile, irrigated, well-treed urban landscape is framed by the forested Sierra Nevada to the west and by desert to the north, east and south. Although the natural vegetation of the area is semi-arid grass and shrub, the city and bordering farmland are well watered and spectacularly green in summer. Local water supplies are not unlimited, however, and the municipality mandates water conservation. Water use may need to be restricted further if population growth continues.

Climate	Rating: 4

Carson City experiences an invigorating four-season semi-arid climate characterized by modest precipitation, abundant sunshine and marked day-to-day and seasonal changes in weather. As in neighboring California, the precipitation regime is Mediterranean with about two-thirds of the normal annual precipitation of 11 inches occurring during the November through March rainy season. About 26 inches of snow fall in a normal winter but snow seldom persists on the ground for more than a week or so because daytime temperatures usually rise well above freezing even in mid winter. Summer afternoons are warm to hot but are fairly comfortable owing to very low relative humidity. Marked cooling occurs soon after sunset as a result of the high elevation and clear dry air so a sweater or jacket is required for summer evening walks. Spring and fall weather is pleasant with cool to warm days and cold nights. Winters are cool with average high temperatures around 50 degrees and average low temperatures around 20 degrees. The frost-free period averages only 120 days. The city is sunny about 90 percent of the time in summer and 65 percent in winter.

Carson City, Nevada

CLIMATE				
Month	Average Daily Temperature High Low		Daily Rel. Humidity Low	Average Monthly Precipitation
	°F		%	Inches
January	46	21	50	2.1
February	52	24	39	1.5
March	56	27	33	1.0
April	62	32	28	0.5
May	71	39	25	0.6
June	80	45	22	0.4
July	89	50	18	0.3
August	87	48	20	0.3
September	81	41	22	0.4
October	70	32	27	0.5
November	56	25	42	1.0
December	48	20	51	2.1

Annual Average

Total Days		Total Inches	
Clear	159	Precipitation	10.8
Partly Cloudy	93	Snowfall	26.2
Cloudy	113		

RATINGS

Rating Scale: 5 = excellent; 4 = very good; 3 = good; 2 = fair; 1 = poor

Rating:	1	2	3	4	5
Landscape					●
Climate				●	
Quality of Life					●
Cost of Living			●		
Transportation		●			
Retail Services			●		
Health Care			●		
Community Services			●		
Cultural Activities		●			
Recreational Activities				●	
Work/Volunteer Activities			●		
Crime					●

Total Points: 42

Quality of Life   Rating: 5

The overall quality of life is excellent. With no freeway or major airport and only moderate street traffic, noise levels are minimal. The city easily meets all federal air quality standards. The city's small size, low population density and modest commercial and industrial development gives the community an uncrowded, almost rural feeling. Plenty of parking is available at local malls and in the small central business district. Most residential neighborhoods, whether in the old core just west of Nevada Highway (U.S.-395) or in newer areas, are very pleasant. Several newer subdivisions on the edge of town feature large homes, many of which look westward across a pastoral landscape toward the mountains. The city seems decently planned and inhabited by an educated, moderately affluent population appreciative of its high quality of life.

Cost of Living — Rating: 3

 The cost of living in Carson City is evaluated as follows:

- *Composite.* ACCRA data show that the composite cost of living in Carson City is about nine percent above the national average.

- *Housing.* According to ACCRA, housing costs are about seven percent above the national average. Recently the average price of a new single-family residence was $170,000 while the average resale house sold for $130,000. Although relatively few houses are for sale at any particular time in the small Carson City market, the city offers quite a variety of housing types, from apartments and manufactured homes at the low end of the market to large custom-built single-family homes at high end.

- *Goods and Services.* Costs of goods and services are moderately high. Health care and transportation are priced about 20 percent above national norms, whereas groceries and miscellaneous goods and services are 16 percent and 4 percent above their national averages. Utility costs approximate the national average.

- *Taxes.* The overall tax burden is relatively low because Nevada does not tax income. Municipal property taxes are significantly below the national average. Annual property taxes on a $150,000 home in Carson City would be about $1350. At seven percent, the state sales tax is well above the national average.

Local and Regional Services

Local services are quite adequate for day-to-day needs. The considerably larger resources of Reno are only 30 miles away.

Transportation — Rating: 2

 The city is automobile oriented. Taxi service is available, as are rental cars, but there is no bus service. Carson City has a general aviation airport but the nearest commercial aviation facility is Reno/Tahoe International Airport in Reno. Reno/Tahoe is served by 10 airlines and provides nonstop jet service to numerous destinations including Los Angeles, Las Vegas, Phoenix and San Francisco. Amtrak service eastbound to Chicago and westbound to Oakland is available daily from Reno.

Retail Services — Rating: 3

 Most shopping is done at eight shopping centers, two of which, Carson Mall and Southgate Mall, are typical enclosed malls. Carson Mall is anchored by Gottschalks whereas Southgate Mall is anchored by

JCPenney and Mervyn's department stores. Freestanding Wal-Mart, Kmart and Sears stores are found on Carson Street, the city's major commercial thoroughfare.

Health Care   Rating: 3

 Carson/Tahoe Hospital, a public non-profit community facility, is the principal medical center. With 124 beds and a medical staff of over 120 physicians representing over 20 specialties, the hospital provides good medical care to Carson City and vicinity. Major services offered include 24-hour emergency care, geriatric and psychiatric care, nutrition counseling, CPR and wellness programs, home health and hospice care, rehabilitative and physical therapy, and cardiac care and catheterization. Larger facilities with a wider range of medical services are only 30 minutes away in Reno.

Community Services   Rating: 3

 The city and county, churches and community organizations offer the usual array of services to residents. A senior citizens center hosts sports, games, social and educational activities, and a wellness program. A seniors volunteer program helps retirees find their niche in community service.

Leisure Activities

Leisure activities of great variety are available in Carson City and an even greater diversity is found in nearby places including the Lake Tahoe region, Virginia City and Reno.

Cultural and Educational Activities   Rating: 2

Western Nevada Community College, the Brewery Arts Center, and the Community Center are Carson City's principal artistic venues. The college, a two-year public institution enrolling about 5,000 students, offers several Associate of Arts programs and a variety of community service classes. The Brewery Arts Center schedules numerous arts and crafts classes and hosts a variety of visual and performing arts displays and programs. The Nevada Artists Association's gallery resides in the center, and the Procenium Players Community Theatre Company, Carson City Chamber Orchestra, Carson Chamber Singers, and the Community Band perform there as well as at the Community College and Community Center. Several museums including the State Railroad Museum, the Stewart Indian Cultural Center, the Capitol Museum, and the State Museum (housed in the old U.S. Mint of silver coinage days) are well worth visiting.

Individuals desiring additional educational and cultural opportunities can find them in Reno, only 30 miles north. The University of Nevada, Reno, in addition to offering a wide range of undergraduate and graduate academic courses and programs, is a center for the arts. Theatrical productions are staged in the university's Church Fine Arts Theatre, whereas concerts are performed in the Nightingale Music Hall.

Recreational Activities   Rating: 4

 Recreational opportunities are plentiful in and around Carson City. Five challenging public golf courses are found locally with several others nearby. Golf is played in all seasons even though winter mornings can be freezing. The city has three major parks and several neighborhood parks with a total area of 600 acres. Park facilities include an aquatic center with indoor and outdoor pools, a community center with a gymnasium and theater, an equestrian center, exercise courses, lighted sports fields and tennis courts, and a nature area. The parks department provides recreation programs for all age groups throughout the year. Other recreational facilities in town include casinos, bowling alleys, movie theaters and restaurants. Within an hour's drive are world-class ski resorts at Lake Tahoe, the Lake Tahoe fishery, hiking trails galore in the Sierra Nevada, and excellent trout fly-fishing in the Carson and Walker rivers. Virginia City, a very lively ghost town, is less than 15 miles away via scenic route (SR-341). Its downtown has been lovingly restored to the way it looked in 1870 at the height of the Comstock Lode silver boom. Another 20 miles travel north along highways 341 and 395 brings you to Reno, the self-styled "Biggest Little City in the World." Although its downtown hotel and casino district has lost some of its luster as a consequence of increased competition from legalized gambling throughout the country, Casino Row on Virginia Street is still a fun place to be 24 hours a day. Alternatives to gambling include visiting the Fleishmann Planetarium, the National Automobile and Nevada Historical Society museums, or one of the city's parks or riverside walks. Shopping is also quite good in Reno, offering a broader selection of goods and services than is available in the smaller Carson City market.

Work and Volunteer Activities   Rating: 3

 Carson City provides significant opportunities for employment and volunteerism. Many seniors find part-time jobs in the retail trade or in the hotel, gaming and recreational services. The Retired Senior Volunteer Program assists retirees in finding volunteer work at, among other places, the hospital, the senior center, the public library, and at several local museums and historic homes. Annual events such as the Carson Rendezvous in June, the Fourth of July celebration, and the Nevada Day celebration in October offer additional ways of contributing to community life.

Crime Rates and Public Safety   Rating: 5

 Carson City is one of the safest communities in America. According to recent FBI data, its rates of violent crime, property crime and total crime are all about 65 percent below national norms. Even more remarkably, Carson City's rate in every category of violent and property crime is well below average. In a recent year there were zero homicides in the city. Clearly, a favorable combination of factors including geographic isolation from large, high-crime cities, a relatively stable middle class population, and an excellent police force, make Carson City enviably peaceful and safe.

Conclusion

 Carson City ranks highly as a place for retirement, especially for those seeking a laid-back lifestyle in an unspoiled, beautiful mountain and high desert environment. Located on a flat plain in the shadow of the Sierra Nevada only 14 miles east of Lake Tahoe and 30 miles south of Reno, Carson City offers residents a high quality of life in a stimulating climate with four clearly defined dry and sunny seasons. Air pollution, tornadoes and hurricanes are unknown locally, although there is a significant long-term threat of earthquakes. The community is virtually free of serious crime and offers excellent parks and recreation facilities, as well as at least adequate retailing, health care, and work and volunteer opportunities. Only in transportation and culture is Carson City, like many small cities, below par. Luckily, the greater assets of nearby Reno are readily available. Finally, although somewhat above the national average, the cost of living in Carson City is distinctly affordable, especially taking into account the excellent quality of life in one of America's most beautiful natural settings.

St. George, Utah

Founded in 1861 by Mormon settlers sent south by Brigham Young, St. George was still only a quiet village of 7,000 residents in 1970. Thereafter, its isolation in the southwestern corner of Utah broken by completion of Interstate-15 (I-15), St. George has grown at an accelerating pace to become the attractive city of 50,000 people that it is today. Located only 40 miles west of Zion National Park and within a few hours' driving time of Bryce Canyon and Grand Canyon National Parks, St. George has long been a gateway to these parks and a winter resort for retirees. Increasingly, attracted by the city's red rock setting, leisure activities, peaceful ambiance, and mild sunny climate, visitors are returning in droves to St. George for permanent residence. In so doing they are emulating a choice made by Brigham Young in the 1870s when he bought a second home there in order to spend his winters in comfort.

Landscape   Rating: 5

St. George is located in the Virgin River Valley of southwestern Utah at an elevation of 2,800 feet. The city occupies a small basin near the western edge of the Colorado Plateau, in a gorgeous red rock canyon and mesa landscape. Lying east of and in the rain shadow of California's high mountains, the area has an arid to semi-arid natural vegetation complex with desert shrub dominating the lower areas, and steppe grasses higher up. Along the river, though, and in the well-irrigated city, native riverbank trees like cottonwood and exotic deciduous trees lend a pleasing green contrast to the reds and browns of the surrounding desert. Local water supplies, mostly derived from the diminutive Virgin River, are adequate for now, but continued growth may require strict water conservation measures in the future.

Climate   Rating: 4

 St. George enjoys a four-season, high-desert climate characterized by low precipitation and humidity, abundant sunshine, and marked seasonal weather changes. The normal annual precipitation of eight inches falls mainly as rain. Three inches of snow falls in an average winter but it seldom lies on the ground for more than a day. On average, the city is sunny about 80 percent of the time, with winter being nearly as sunny as summer. Summer afternoons are very hot but the heat is not oppressive as the relative humidity is very low. Because of the clear air and moderate elevation, overnight low temperatures in summer average in the mid-60s, providing a pleasant contrast from the daytime heat. In spring and fall, weather is more variable but most days are warm and nights are cool. Winters are pleasant with generally sunny, cool days and clear, cold nights. The average frost-free season of 217 days allows outdoor gardening from early April through early November.

St. George, Utah

CLIMATE				
Month	Average Daily Temperature High Low	Daily Rel. Humidity Low	Average Monthly Precipitation	
	°F	%	Inches	
January	54 27	33	1.0	
February	61 32	27	0.9	
March	67 37	23	1.0	
April	76 44	17	0.5	
May	85 52	14	0.5	
June	96 61	12	0.2	
July	102 68	16	0.6	
August	99 66	18	0.7	
September	93 57	18	0.5	
October	80 45	20	0.6	
November	65 34	28	0.8	
December	56 27	33	0.7	

Annual Average

Total Days		Total Inches	
Clear	200	Precipitation	7.9
Partly Cloudy	88	Snowfall	3.0
Cloudy	77		

RATINGS

Rating Scale: 5 = excellent; 4 = very good; 3 = good; 2 = fair; 1 = poor

Rating:	1	2	3	4	5
Landscape					●
Climate				●	
Quality of Life					●
Cost of Living			●		
Transportation		●			
Retail Services			●		
Health Care			●		
Community Services					●
Cultural Activities		●			
Recreational Activities				●	
Work/Volunteer Activities				●	
Crime			●		

Total Points: 43

Quality of Life   Rating: 5

St. George offers residents an excellent quality of life. Noise pollution is minimal except adjacent to I-15. There is no air pollution; the city easily meets all federal air quality standards. Owing to its small size and low population density, the community has an uncrowded and nearly rural character. Plenty of parking is available at local malls and along St. George Boulevard downtown; traffic congestion is unknown. Residential neighborhoods, whether in the old central core or in newer sections like Bloomington and Bloomington Hills, are very pleasant in an understated way. Thanks to intensive tree planting and irrigation, long Mormon traditions in this desert environment, older neighborhoods particularly are well shaded, a blessing in the heat of summer. Mormon values are also reflected in the careful physical planning of the city, in its attractive and varied parks and recreation facilities, and in its peaceful ambiance. Its prosperous and well-educated population seems determined to preserve its high quality of life while accommodating inevitable growth.

Cost of Living   Rating: 3

 The cost of living in St. George is evaluated as follows:

- **Composite.** ACCRA data for St. George reveal a composite cost of living two percent above the national average.

- **Housing.** According to ACCRA, housing costs are about two percent below the national average. This is consistent with data from the Washington County Board of Realtors, which reports that an average 1,500-square foot home with three bedrooms and two bathrooms sells for $130,000 in the St. George area. In fact, a good supply of housing of varied sizes, styles, and prices is generally available. Construction of new housing appears to be keeping up with demand so prices should remain reasonable for some time.

- **Goods and Services.** Goods and services are priced near national norms. Miscellaneous goods and services, transportation, and groceries are all priced between three and nine percent above their national averages, whereas health care costs and utility costs are four percent and ten percent below national norms.

- **Taxes.** Utah depends heavily on the income tax for revenue; consequently, the average income tax burden in St. George is 30–40 percent above average. The six percent state sales tax is slightly above the national average for sales taxes, whereas property taxes are considerably below the national norm. The annual property tax on an average $130,000 home in St. George is about $1,100.

Local and Regional Services

St. George has emerged as southwestern Utah's principal service center. Local services, which were meager 20 years ago, are now quite adequate for everyday needs.

Transportation   Rating: 2

 Like most small cities in the west, St. George depends heavily on the automobile. Taxis and rental cars are available but there is no fixed-route bus service. However, the St. George Shuttle provides dial-a-ride service for seniors, the autobus connects with Las Vegas International Airport, and Greyhound offers intercity motor coach service along I-15 to Salt Lake City, Las Vegas and to points beyond these cities. Commuter air service connects St. George with major air transport hubs in Salt Lake City and Las Vegas.

Retail Services   Rating: 3

The downtown shopping district, which stretches along St. George Boulevard and Bluff Street, has a number of quite varied specialty shops and restaurants. Red Cliffs Mall, located just off I-15, features about 70 national chain stores and restaurants, and is the largest shopping center in southwestern Utah. It is anchored by JCPenney and Wal-Mart stores and Red Cliffs Cinemas. The adjacent Promenade Mall features a Sears. Also along I-15 is Zion Factory Stores, a complex of 39 corporation-owned stores. A freestanding Kmart is located on Bluff Street.

Health Care   Rating: 3

Dixie Regional Medical Center (DRMC)—part of Intermountain Health Care (IHC), a private nonprofit hospital system based in Salt Lake City—is the principal medical complex in southwestern Utah. Like the other 24 IHC hospitals, it provides quality care to those with medical needs regardless of their ability to pay. Reflecting its regional referral role for nearly 100,000 people in southern Utah and neighboring areas of Nevada and Arizona, the 137-bed, 96-physician hospital provides many specialized services including 24-hour emergency care, intensive and critical care, oncology, cardiology, radiology and medical imaging, and weight management, nutrition and wellness programs, among others.

Community Services   Rating: 5

City, county, religious, and civic organizations offer a rich assortment of services. The St. George Leisure Services Department provides dozens of activities for residents and visitors. Senior citizen centers are operated throughout Washington County. They provide a great variety of programs including Meals-on-Wheels, bus service, free health screening, games such as pool, bingo, and horseshoes, ballroom dancing and educational classes. More than 60 civic organizations give almost unlimited opportunities for community and charitable involvement.

Leisure Activities

Quite an array of leisure activities is available in St. George and adjacent rural areas in Utah and Arizona.

Cultural and Educational Activities   Rating: 2

Dixie College, a junior college enrolling 5,000 students, is St. George's premier educational and cultural center. In addition to normal two-year college emphases like general education, liberal arts and humanities, science, and business and technology, Dixie College hosts on-site bachelors and masters programs from universities within Utah. Its Institute for Continued Learning is run by and for retirees and its popular Elderhostel program offers week-long noncredit classes featuring special events, field trips, and other group activities for those 60 and older. The college's musical and theatrical programs are popular with all age groups. Dixie Center on campus is the principal venue for the Dixie College Celebrity Concert Series and the Southwest Symphony Orchestra. The summer concert series at the Tanner Amphitheater attracts residents and visitors alike, as do locally produced plays.

Recreational Activities   Rating: 4

 Recreational activities to suit many tastes are available locally. Relative to population, St. George probably offers more golf than all but a few Sunbelt locations. Of the area's eight golf courses, four are city owned and operated by St. George Leisure Services, which also runs the 19 city parks. Greens fees at St. George Public golf courses are very reasonable, especially for residents. Leisure Services also provides activities such as arts and crafts, photography and framing, computing, cooking, bridge and dance. Free day hikes are sponsored Saturdays throughout the year and historical lectures are provided Saturday evenings in winter. Each year a marathon race and arts festival are hosted. Other recreational facilities in town include bowling alleys, movie theaters, and restaurants of varied culinary styles.

Some of America's greatest natural wonders are within a few hours drive. The incomparable Zion National Park lies only 42 miles east of town. Cedar Breaks National Monument, a smaller version of Bryce Canyon, is 75 miles away, while Bryce Canyon National Park itself is only 126 miles away. The North Rim of Grand Canyon National Park, which is higher, cooler, and much less overrun with tourists than the South Rim, is only 140 miles from St. George. There is excellent downhill skiing at Brian Head, 80 miles northeast. Add to these national treasures two ghost towns, Snow Canyon State Park and Quail Creek Reservoir, all of which are within 20 miles of town, and it is obvious that there is no better base in the country than St. George from which to set off on day trips to sightseeing and hiking paradise.

Work and Volunteer Activities   Rating: 4

 St. George provides good opportunities for employment and volunteerism. Service industries are predominant locally with medical care, retailing, and tourism creating the largest number of jobs. Volunteer work is available at, among other places, the several county senior citizen centers, the hospital, the public library, schools and at approximately 60 civic and charitable organizations.

Crime Rates and Public Safety   Rating: 3

 Despite its geographic remoteness and small size, St. George is not remarkably free of crime. Its overall crime rate approximates the national average and its property crime rate is about 10 percent above the national norm. These totals largely reflect the fairly high incidence of larceny-theft in St. George; rates of burglary and auto theft are relatively low. Significantly, the violent crime rate in St. George is 60 percent below the national average, making the city of one the safest retirement towns in terms of freedom from violent crime.

Conclusion

 St. George is one of the better small retirement towns in the Desert Southwest. Because of its location, moderate elevation and geology, the city experiences a warm, sunny four-season climate and is spared serious environmental hazards. The air is clean, urban stress is largely lacking, and the quality of life is excellent. Devotees of the great outdoors will undoubtedly enjoy St. George's beautiful setting amidst the mountains, canyons, and mesas of southwestern Utah and appreciate the fact that some of America's greatest national parks are nearby. With a cost of living barely above the national average and good to very good ratings in retail services, health care, public safety, recreation, and work and volunteer activities, St. George has great appeal. Its major weaknesses are transportation and a lack of major cultural attractions. That said, St. George measures up very well for retirement and merits careful consideration.

Reno, Nevada

Reno, Nevada is also worth considering for retirement. Situated on a high desert plain just east of the Sierra Nevada, Reno enjoys a spectacular setting and an invigorating, four-season semi-arid climate similar to that of nearby Carson City. Self-styled "The Biggest Little City in the World," Reno has long been known as the gambling and entertainment capital of northern Nevada and as a gateway to the Lake Tahoe region. With a population of 160,000 in Reno and 320,000 in Washoe County, the metropolitan area is large enough to offer many of the services and amenities sought by retirees.

Only a high cost of living—especially for housing—and occasional air pollution episodes that cause the city to exceed some federal air quality standards for particulates detract from Reno's desirability for retirement. The city offers exceptional recreation, very good transportation and health care, and a good quality of life. Golf, tennis, horseback riding and hiking are popular summer pursuits; cross-country and downhill skiing and ice-skating are popular in winter. Nearby Lake Tahoe and the Sierra Nevada offer excellent camping, hiking, boating and fishing in summer and some of America's best downhill skiing in winter. Reno has good public transit and excellent intercity air, motor coach and rail passenger service. The city's four hospitals provide very good medical care and retail and community services are more than adequate. Reno is alive with the performing and visual arts. It has its own ballet, opera and philharmonic orchestra, and numerous theaters and galleries. The University of Nevada, Reno (UNVR) is a major educational, cultural and recreational asset. Reno residents love to watch UNVR Wolfpack basketball and football. Last, but not least, the city has low rates of crime and unemployment and provides many opportunities for paid and volunteer work.

10 The California Retirement Region

Climate:
Desert–Palm Springs/Palm Desert
Mediterranean–San Luis Obispo, Chico

Place Description	Overall Rating	Page
San Luis Obispo, California	**45**	**209**
San Luis Obispo is a perfect little college town offering a fairly quiet yet amenity-rich lifestyle.		
Chico, California	**39**	**215**
With beautiful landscapes and an excellent quality of life, Chico offers a pleasant, laid-back and affordable lifestyle.		
Palm Springs/Palm Desert, California	**not rated**	**221**
Lying 120 miles east of Los Angeles, these low desert communities have enjoyed an economic boom in recent years that has restored their distinction as a world-class resort and retirement area.		

The California Retirement Region occupies the greater part of America's most physically appealing and culturally diverse state. Long a favorite region for retiree relocation thanks to its mild, sunny climate; lovely coastal, mountain and desert landscapes; abundant services; and cultural and recreational opportunities, the Golden State has lost some of its luster as a retirement haven in recent decades. Rampant population growth and urban sprawl have stressed the natural environment, pushed public services to the limit and overwhelmed the urban transportation infrastructure. Even though California has the toughest smog controls in the nation, smog persists as a health and aesthetic problem not only in Los Angeles and the San Francisco Bay Area but also throughout much of the state. Meanwhile, traffic congestion has reached epic proportions and the cost of housing has risen so high in Los Angeles and the Bay Area that home ownership is out of the question for people of moderate means.

As a result of these problems, few California cities now provide a high quality of life and an amenity-rich lifestyle at affordable prices. That said, San Luis Obispo and Chico, two delightful cities along the central California coast and in the Sacramento Valley, respectively, remain very attractive for retirement. Both offer a gentle pace of life, sunny weather, clean air and amenities and services typical of small college towns. Also worth considering is Palm Springs/Palm Desert, a resort and retirement area in southern California. None of these places is inexpensive but each offers better value than the large coastal metropolitan areas of the state.

San Luis Obispo, California

Blessed by a year-round water supply, fertile soil and a mild, sunny climate, the beautiful valley of San Luis Obispo seemed an ideal site for settlement

San Luis Obispo, California

CLIMATE				
Month	Average Daily Temperature High Low	Daily Rel. Humidity Low	Average Monthly Precipitation	
	°F	%	Inches	
January	62 42	60	5.5	
February	65 43	60	4.4	
March	65 44	63	3.2	
April	67 45	60	2.0	
May	69 47	60	0.4	
June	74 50	60	0.0	
July	77 52	62	0.0	
August	78 53	57	0.1	
September	79 52	56	0.3	
October	76 50	58	0.8	
November	70 46	59	2.5	
December	64 42	59	3.9	

RATINGS

Rating Scale: 5 = excellent; 4 = very good; 3 = good; 2 = fair; 1 = poor

Rating:	1	2	3	4	5
Landscape					●
Climate					●
Quality of Life					●
Cost of Living	●				
Transportation		●			
Retail Services		●			
Health Care		●			
Community Services				●	
Cultural Activities				●	
Recreational Activities				●	
Work/Volunteer Activities		●			
Crime				●	

Annual Average

Total Days		Total Inches	
Clear	176	Precipitation	23.0
Partly Cloudy	110	Snowfall	0.0
Cloudy	80		

Total Points: 45

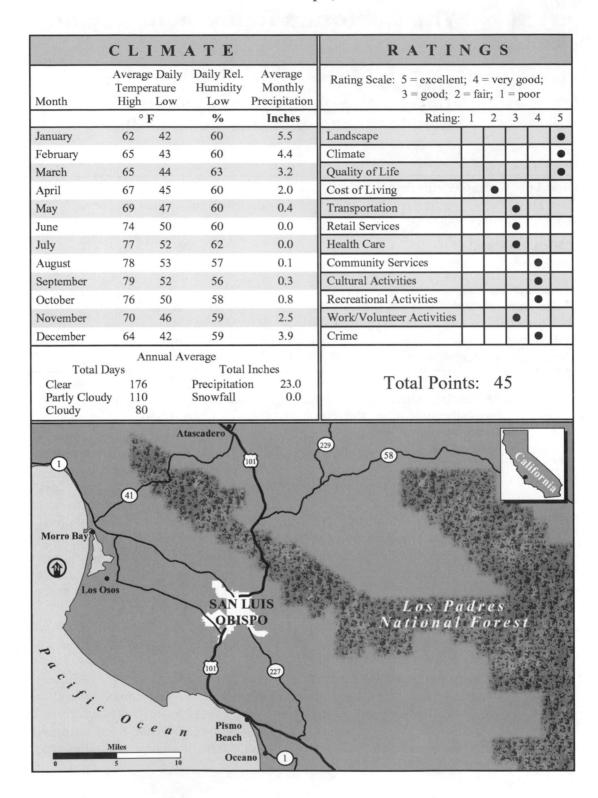

when Father Junipero Serra established Mission San Luis Obispo de Tolera on the banks of San Luis Creek in 1772. Even so, the settlement surrounding the mission grew rather slowly until the isolation of the community was broken by the arrival of the Southern Pacific Railroad in 1894. Subsequent growth, owing in part to the city's location halfway between and over 200 miles from San Francisco and Los Angeles, has proceeded at a modest pace. This has allowed San Luis Obispo to retain a nostalgic early California ambiance unique in a state characterized by frenzied growth. Over 20 percent of the local labor force is employed by government, with others working mostly in retail, tourist and miscellaneous services. California Polytechnic State University, San Luis Obispo (Cal Poly), with over 17,000 students and 2,700 faculty and staff, is a vital economic and cultural force making the community younger and livelier than most cities with populations of around 40,000. Along with Mission San Luis Obispo and Mission Plaza, adjacent San Luis Creek, the charming downtown shopping district and the city's attractive and varied residential neighborhoods, the university makes San Luis Obispo a special place well worth considering for upscale retirement.

Landscape   Rating: 5

The town occupies a splendid site at an elevation of 315 feet in a gently rolling lowland between a string of extinct volcanic foothills and the Santa Lucia Mountains. The Pacific Coast is only five to ten miles away at Port San Luis and Morro Bay. Oak parkland, a mix of drought-resistant grasses and trees, is the dominant natural vegetation but a greater variety of local and exotic trees, shrubs and flowering plants is grown in the city with the help of irrigation. The hill and valley setting of the town and the Cal Poly campus, buttressed by the towering Santa Lucia Range on the east, is strikingly beautiful whether colored in winter's green or summer's collage of green, gold and brown.

Climate   Rating: 5

San Luis Obispo enjoys a cool-summer variant of the Mediterranean climate. Proximity to the cool waters of the Pacific Ocean and relatively low latitude and elevation make for a very mild climate with few storms or drastic changes in weather. There are really only two seasons here. A mild, fairly wet winter is balanced by a warm, dry summer. Over 90 percent of annual precipitation falls from November through April. Because it is several miles inland, San Luis Obispo is somewhat warmer in summer and sunnier in all seasons than places right on the coast. The town is sunny over 70 percent of the time, with only modest variations from month to month. The frost-free period averages 320 days and frosts are rarely severe enough to damage gardens or citrus.

Quality of Life   Rating: 5

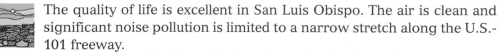

The quality of life is excellent in San Luis Obispo. The air is clean and significant noise pollution is limited to a narrow stretch along the U.S.-101 freeway.

The small size and low population density of the city translate into little crowding or traffic congestion. Parking is adequate downtown, at suburban malls and on campus. Heavy industries and neglected neighborhoods are unknown and the urban landscape is well planned and maintained, with parks and playgrounds well distributed across the city. Municipal authorities and downtown business interests have carefully preserved and enhanced the charming and historic central business district, which in many ways is the heart and soul of San Luis Obispo. Residents are typically well educated and friendly and their town exhibits the peaceful ambiance of a former and almost forgotten California era.

The cost of living in San Luis Obispo is evaluated as follows:

- **Composite.** ACCRA data are unavailable for San Luis Obispo so their statistics for Santa Barbara, the nearest comparable California city, are used. On that basis, the composite cost of living is about 20 percent above the national average.

- **Housing.** Higher-than-average family incomes and growth controls cause housing to be relatively expensive. ACCRA data suggest that housing in San Luis Obispo is priced about 50 percent above the national average, while local chamber of commerce data suggest a median price of $250,000 for a single-family home. Field research indicates that homes priced between $200,000 and $300,000 are modest by national standards. Condominiums offer better value if present cost rather than potential appreciation is the buyer's primary concern.

- **Goods and Services.** Groceries, utilities, transportation and health care are all priced between 10 and 20 percent above national norms. Miscellaneous goods and services costs approximate the national average.

- **Taxes.** The overall tax burden is near the national average. California state income taxes are slightly below average for those with moderate incomes but exceed the national average for incomes above $90,000. The combined state/county/city sales tax rate of 7.25 percent is well above the average rate but property taxes, rolled back to little more than 1 percent of assessed (fair market) value by Proposition 13, two decades ago, remain comparatively low. The property tax on an average $250,000 home in San Luis Obispo is about $2,800 annually.

Local and Regional Services

Because San Luis Obispo serves a large and fairly affluent market area along the Central California coast, it is able to provide a better range of services than most small cities.

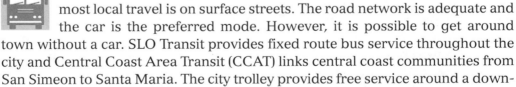 The U.S.-101 freeway traverses the city from southwest to northeast but most local travel is on surface streets. The road network is adequate and the car is the preferred mode. However, it is possible to get around town without a car. SLO Transit provides fixed route bus service throughout the city and Central Coast Area Transit (CCAT) links central coast communities from San Simeon to Santa Maria. The city trolley provides free service around a downtown loop. Ride-On Transportation offers door-to-door travel seven days a week on a reservation basis. Intercity travel is possible by air, bus and rail. San Luis Obispo Airport, three miles south, provides nonstop commuter service to Los Angeles, Sacramento and San Francisco. Greyhound offers frequent scheduled service north to San Francisco and south to Los Angeles. Amtrak provides one train northbound and two trains southbound daily, plus several additional southbound trains via connecting motor coach service to Santa Barbara.

Retail Services Rating: 3

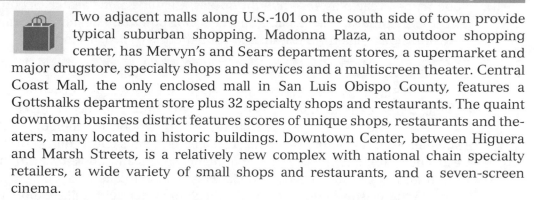

Two adjacent malls along U.S.-101 on the south side of town provide typical suburban shopping. Madonna Plaza, an outdoor shopping center, has Mervyn's and Sears department stores, a supermarket and major drugstore, specialty shops and services and a multiscreen theater. Central Coast Mall, the only enclosed mall in San Luis Obispo County, features a Gottshalks department store plus 32 specialty shops and restaurants. The quaint downtown business district features scores of unique shops, restaurants and theaters, many located in historic buildings. Downtown Center, between Higuera and Marsh Streets, is a relatively new complex with national chain specialty retailers, a wide variety of small shops and restaurants, and a seven-screen cinema.

Health Care Rating: 3

For a city of its size, San Luis Obispo offers unusually good health care. Three rather small acute-care hospitals, Sierra Vista Regional Medical Center, San Luis Obispo General Hospital and French Hospital Medical Center, with a total of about 300 beds and 150 physicians on staff, meet the everyday medical needs of local residents. A greater variety of sophisticated medical care is available 200 miles away in Los Angeles and San Francisco.

Community Services Rating: 4

Very good public services including some of special interest to seniors are available. The San Luis Obispo Senior Center, located downtown in Mitchell Park, is open five days a week. Popular activities there include an exercise class, bridge and other card games, arts and crafts, reading in the small library and socializing. Each month the center hosts a luncheon and a free legal advice session with a local lawyer. Meeting rooms are available for special events including meetings of the local chapter of AARP.

Leisure Activities

On the quiet side compared to major metropolitan areas, San Luis Obispo nonetheless provides residents and visitors a good range of recreational choices.

Cultural and Educational Activities Rating: 4

Cal Poly is a major community asset in terms of its course and program offerings and as the site of the spectacular new Performing Arts Center of San Luis Obispo. Cal Poly and Cuesta Community College field courses of interest to seniors. Fees for California residents are low at the university and nominal at the college. The brand-new 1,350-seat Harman Concert Hall at the Performing Arts Center is reputed to be acoustically outstanding. It is the principal venue for major artistic performances including classical and pop concerts by the San Luis Obispo Symphony and modern dance, theater, opera and ballet by resident and visiting companies. The 500-seat Cal Poly Theater also schedules musical, dance and theatrical events. Performances by the university's Chamber Orchestra, Choir, and Jazz and Wind Orchestras and recitals by faculty and students are frequent occurrences throughout the academic year. The San Luis Obispo Mozart Festival is held annually in July and August at several venues on campus and around town.

Resident ensembles perform professional ballet, opera and theater, as well as amateur theater. The Civic Ballet of San Luis Obispo is known especially for its December staging of The Nutcracker. The Pacific Repertory Opera stages two operas per year plus several light operas. Center Point Theater Group emphasizes contemporary works and San Luis Obispo Little Theater performs a variety of productions from classical to contemporary all year long.

Recreational Activities   Rating: 4

San Luis Obispo's near perfect climate favors year-round outdoor recreation. Sixteen city parks, playgrounds and recreation centers scattered around town collectively provide a good selection of facilities. Sinsheimer Sports Complex, with its swim center, tennis courts and sports fields, is especially well equipped. Additional tennis courts and pools open to the public are found at Cuesta College and Cal Poly. Laguna Lake Park and Open Space, toward the western edge of town, is ideal for water sports like canoeing, windsurfing and fishing. Hiking is also popular there. The considerably larger Lopez, Nacimiento and Santa Margarita Lakes, known for their bass, catfish and bluegill fishing, are within 45 miles of the city. At Lopez and Nacimiento Lakes you can also camp, picnic, boat, water-ski and swim. Boating and ocean fishing are available at nearby Port San Luis and Morro Bay but Central California beaches and waters are a little chilly for sunbathing and swimming.

Golf is played in comfort all year at six 18-hole courses and two 9-hole courses open to the public in and around San Luis Obispo. Bicycle routes lead to coastal communities and hiking trails to vantage points offering stunning views of the Pacific Ocean and valley and mountain terrain. Quiet country roads provide access to some of America's most beautiful agricultural landscapes, which produce everything from organic fruits and vegetables to milk, grapes and fine wines.

Cal Poly individuals and teams compete in many varsity sports. The university's NCAA Division 1 football and women's basketball teams are local favorites. College students, city residents and visitors support a very good selection of movie theaters and restaurants. Clustered downtown are multiplex movie theaters and an eclectic mix of eateries serving everything from American sandwiches to exotic Asian dishes. Several restaurants offer outdoor dining on terraces overlooking San Luis Creek. The San Luis Obispo Farmers Market, located on a blocked off section of Higuera Street, downtown, is a special highlight every Thursday evening. Now a revered local tradition, the market offers everything from fresh produce to barbecued ribs and plenty of live entertainment and community fellowship.

Work and Volunteer Activities   Rating: 3

Growth controls that resulted in part from drought-caused water rationing in the early 1990s and a shortage of building lots in the city have slowed economic growth. The population was about the same in 2000 as in 1990. Although there is little unemployment, there is acute competition among college students, seniors and the general public for jobs in the strongly service oriented economy. Many opportunities exist, though, for volunteers in senior and community organizations, schools, hospitals, libraries and museums. An active chapter of RSVP helps place volunteers where they are most needed.

San Luis Obispo continues to be one of America's safer small college towns. Rates of total crime, violent crime and property crime have all declined in recent years and are now 10–20 percent below national norms. Homicides are almost unknown locally and all parts of town from the Cal Poly campus to the busy downtown have a safe and secure feel about them.

Conclusion

 Overall Rating 45 Just far enough inland to escape coastal fog and far enough from Los Angeles and San Francisco to avoid metropolitan pressures, San Luis Obispo is a near perfect little college town offering a fairly quiet yet amenity-rich lifestyle. Its lovely physical setting between California's spectacular central coast and the Santa Lucia Mountains, its mild sunny climate, and its excellent quality of life, absent the smog and traffic characteristic of many California cities, are perhaps its greatest assets. But San Luis Obispo has other strengths as well. Thanks to Cal Poly, civic musical, theatrical and arts associations, and numerous parks and recreation facilities located in town, along the nearby coast and in the Santa Lucia Mountains, the community boasts a very good selection of cultural, educational and recreational activities and community services. Despite a daily influx of students, workers and visitors, the city is relatively free of serious crime. Transportation, retail services, health care and opportunities for volunteer work are quite good for a small town. Except for a moderately high cost of living, there is little to criticize about life in San Luis Obispo. Those already living there obviously think it is worth the price; perhaps you will too.

Chico, California

Chico was founded in 1860 by John Bidwell who had made a fortune in the California Gold Rush. Attracted to the area by cheap land, a warm, sunny climate and a year-round water supply from streams flowing into the Sacramento Valley from the mountains to the east, Bidwell became Chico's largest land owner and its principal booster. In 1887, the fortunes of the small, agriculturally based town took a significant turn when a state teachers college was established in downtown Chico on land donated by Bidwell. In 1905, Annie Bidwell, wife of the town's founder, donated an additional 2,300 acres of the Bidwell ranch to the City of Chico in order to establish Bidwell Park. The park has since grown to 3,600 acres, making it the third largest municipal park in the United States. Meanwhile, the original teachers college had evolved into California State University, Chico (Chico State) with over 16,000 students and 1,000 faculty members. The university makes Chico younger and livelier than most cities of 50,000 people (there are about 90,000 in the urban area and 200,000 in Butte County). The park, the university, the traditional downtown with its shops, restaurants, and delightful City Plaza, and the city's varied and attractive residential neighborhoods define Chico as a unique place well worth considering for quality retirement.

Landscape   **Rating: 4**

 Chico is located toward the eastern edge of the Sacramento Valley in northern California. The oak-studded foothills of the Sierra Nevada and Cascade Range lie immediately east and northeast and provide a scenic

Chico, California

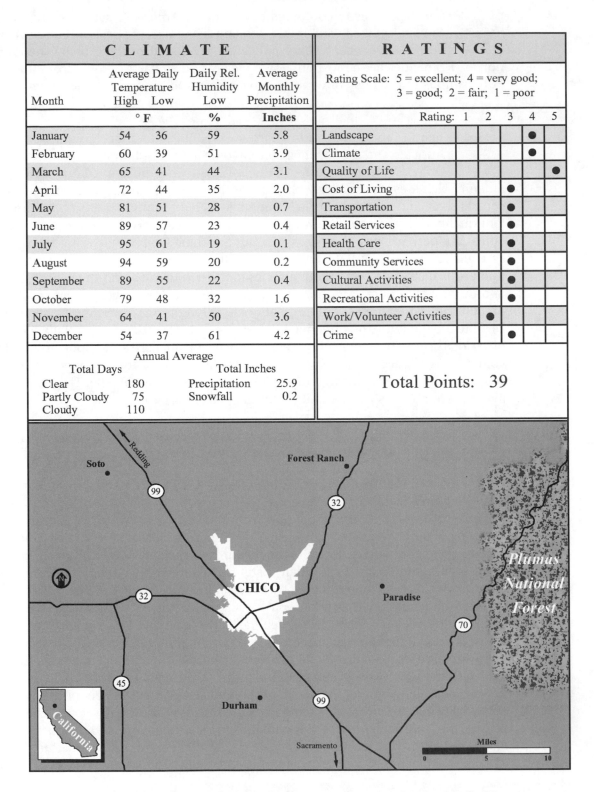

CLIMATE				
Month	Average Daily Temperature High Low		Daily Rel. Humidity Low	Average Monthly Precipitation
	°F		%	Inches
January	54	36	59	5.8
February	60	39	51	3.9
March	65	41	44	3.1
April	72	44	35	2.0
May	81	51	28	0.7
June	89	57	23	0.4
July	95	61	19	0.1
August	94	59	20	0.2
September	89	55	22	0.4
October	79	48	32	1.6
November	64	41	50	3.6
December	54	37	61	4.2

Annual Average

Total Days		Total Inches	
Clear	180	Precipitation	25.9
Partly Cloudy	75	Snowfall	0.2
Cloudy	110		

RATINGS

Rating Scale: 5 = excellent; 4 = very good; 3 = good; 2 = fair; 1 = poor

Rating:	1	2	3	4	5
Landscape				●	
Climate				●	
Quality of Life					●
Cost of Living			●		
Transportation			●		
Retail Services			●		
Health Care			●		
Community Services			●		
Cultural Activities			●		
Recreational Activities			●		
Work/Volunteer Activities		●			
Crime			●		

Total Points: 39

backdrop to the city. Located far inland from the cool, foggy California coast, Chico lies in a hot Mediterranean environment typical of interior, northern California. However, its riparian site along Chico Creek only a few miles east of the Sacramento River allows growth of luxuriant natural vegetation including large valley oaks. Some of these survive in town and especially in Bidwell Park but many exotic trees and shrubs have been planted throughout the city. Shade provided by the leafy canopy is much appreciated on scorching summer afternoons.

Climate   Rating: 4

 Chico experiences the hot-summer variant of the Mediterranean climate with four distinct seasons. Because it is so far inland, Chico is much warmer in summer and somewhat cooler in winter than coastal California locations at the same latitude. Summer days are hot, sunny and extremely dry. Less than an inch of rain falls during each of the five months, May through September. Fortunately, marked cooling typically drops overnight temperatures into the 50s or low 60s in mid summer. Winter weather is mild and moderately rainy with many cloudy or foggy days. Spring and fall are delightful intermediate seasons with typically warm days, cool nights and a good deal of sunshine. Chico is sunny over 90 percent of the time in summer, 70 percent in spring and fall, and a little less than 50 percent in winter.

Quality of Life   Rating: 5

 The quality of life is excellent in Chico. All federal air quality standards are currently met and traffic noise is mostly confined to the busiest commercial streets. Downtown streets and those adjacent to the university are busy at rush hour but congestion levels are modest compared to those in larger cities. The road infrastructure appears satisfactory for present demand and parking is generally adequate although it can be tight at Chico State. The university campus is park-like. Its lovely, tree-shaded grounds and collegiate architecture enhance the downtown. Chico's varied neighborhoods are typically well treed and nicely kept. Several small neighborhood parks add to the general ambiance and Bidwell Park, a jewel among American urban parks, is an enormous asset to the entire community.

Cost of Living   Rating: 3

 The cost of living in Chico is evaluated as follows:

- *Composite.* ACCRA data are unavailable for Chico so their statistics for Visalia, another pleasant interior California city, are used. On that basis, the composite cost of living in Chico is about seven percent above the national average.

- *Housing.* ACCRA data suggest that Chico housing is priced at or a little below the national average. A good supply of single-family residences and condominiums is usually available. The average price of a single-family residence is around $150,000 and condominiums are considerably cheaper. Many small houses cost little more than $100,000 but these are modest places by national standards.

- *Goods and Services.* Miscellaneous goods and services, groceries, health care, transportation and utilities are all priced between 10 and 17 percent above their national norms.

- *Taxes.* The overall tax burden in Chico is somewhat below the national average. California state income taxes are slightly below average for those with moderate incomes but exceed the national average for those with family incomes above $90,000. The combined state/county/city sales tax rate is well above the average rate of five percent, but property taxes, rolled back to little more than one percent of assessed (fair market) value by Proposition 13, remain low. The property tax on an average $150,000 Chico home is roughly $1,700 annually.

Local and Regional Services

Chico serves a fairly large market area in the Sacramento Valley and thus is able to supply a broader range of services than most small cities.

Transportation — Rating: 3

The California-99 (CA-99) freeway traverses the eastern fringe of Chico but most travel within the city is on surface streets that are generally adequate for present traffic flows. The car is the preferred mode of travel but many students bike around the campus community. Chico Area Transit (CAT) provides minimal transit service with 12 buses that serve the Chico urban area during daytime hours, Monday through Saturday. Chico Clipper Service furnishes dial-a-ride transportation for the elderly and disabled, seven days a week. Intercity travel is possible by air, bus and rail. Chico Airport offers limited commuter air service to hub airports at San Francisco and Sacramento. Greyhound provides daily service to San Francisco and Sacramento, among other California locations, and Butte Transit serves communities within the county. Amtrak's Coast Starlight train provides daily service north to Portland and Seattle and south to Oakland and Los Angeles.

Retail Services — Rating: 3

Chico Mall, located just south of downtown and east of CA-99, is the largest regional mall in Butte County. It is anchored by Gottschalk's, JCPenney, Sears and Troutman's department stores and features about 80 specialty stores, restaurants and services, mostly branches of regional or national chains. Scattered about Chico in smaller shopping centers and along commercial streets are other retailers including Costco, Home Depot, Kmart, Mervyn's and Wal-Mart. Chico's traditional downtown is home to numerous quaint galleries, cafes and specialty shops and is an interesting place to walk about. Farmers markets boasting an excellent selection of local produce are open on Wednesday mornings, June through October, at North Valley Plaza Mall and Saturday mornings, year-round, downtown.

Health Care — Rating: 3

For its size, Chico offers good medical care. Two general hospitals serve Chico proper; two others are located in other Butte County communities. Countywide there are 610 hospital beds, 109 general practitioners, 85 medical specialists and 92 surgical specialists. Enloe Memorial Medical Center and Chico Memorial Hospital are the principal hospitals in town. Enloe Memorial is designated a Level II Trauma Center for a six-county area. Its specialties include cancer and cardiac care, home and hospice care, neuro-trauma care, occupational therapy and orthopedic services. Chico Community Hospital is noted for its emergency and acute care facilities and specialized respiratory center.

Passages Adult Resource Center, a program of the California State University's Chico Research Foundation, serves as a source of information on community resources, government benefits, and volunteer opportunities and as an advocate for seniors' health care and consumer rights. Persons age 50 and over may participate in Chico Area Recreational Park District (CARD) Senior Programs. The CARD Recreation Center, located just east of downtown adjacent to Bidwell Park, provides health screenings, tax assistance and recreational activities including pool, card games, dances, yoga and fitness programs.

Leisure Activities

Despite its small size, Chico provides a good choice of leisure pursuits. Additional resources are found nearby in the Cascade Range and Sierra Nevada and the boundless cultural and recreational resources of San Francisco are only 190 miles away.

Cultural and Educational Activities   Rating: 3

California State University, Chico is a major educational and cultural asset. Its beautiful campus, which occupies 119 acres next to downtown Chico, is a lively activity center. The university's diverse offerings include 128 majors and 51 graduate and professional programs. Known for its commitment to the liberal arts and sciences, the university also fields strong programs in agriculture, business administration, computer science, nursing and teacher training. Classes of particular interest to seniors are provided by the continuing education program at the university and by Butte Community College, located 12 miles south of town. Fees for California residents are low at the university and nominal at the college.

Numerous cultural events are held in the two theaters and the recital hall of Chico State's Performing Arts Center and at several other venues in town. Live performances of classical music, dance, jazz and musical theater ensembles, including those by the Chico City Light Opera and Chico Symphony Orchestra, are well supported. Downtown Chico's City Plaza is a perfect place for lunch and relaxation. Free concerts are performed at its gazebo every Friday evening, May through September. Amateur theater is produced by Chico Children's Theater and Chico Community Theater. Popular music and dance programs are provided by the Chico Community Band, the Chico International Folkdancers and the Bidwell Generals Chorus.

The visual arts are showcased at the Janet Turner Print Gallery, the Third Floor Gallery and the University Art Gallery at Chico State. The works of local area artists can be seen at several commercial studios and galleries, downtown. The Chico Art Center, an art school and gallery operated by local artists, is especially noteworthy.

Recreational Activities   Rating: 3

Chico's warm, sunny climate, excellent municipal parks and the town's proximity to the mountains all favor year-round outdoor recreation. Bidwell Park, which occupies over 5.5 square miles and extends from the valley floor into the foothills of the Sierra Nevada, is the crown jewel of the

Chico park system. Each of its three major sections has its own unique character. Lower Park is a vehicle-free area—its roads and paths, winding among oak groves, are reserved for walkers, runners, cyclists and roller-bladers. Children's playgrounds, picnic areas and natural swimming areas are the principal attractions. Middle Park is open to motorized traffic and provides a perfect venue for outdoor cultural events such as Shakespeare in the Park and the Chico World Music Festival. Middle Park also features ball fields, picnic areas, the World of Trees Walk (which is accessible to the physically challenged) and the Chico Creek Nature Center. Upper Park remains largely undeveloped with much of its hill and canyon terrain approaching wilderness status. A mecca for mountain bikers, equestrians and hikers, Upper Park has 35 trails, 25 of which are open to cyclists. Swimming holes along Chico Creek offer some of the best swimming in northern California.

Golf is played all year at four 18-hole and two 9-hole courses in and around Chico. Two of the 18-hole courses are private; the rest are open to the public. The warm, sunny climate and bicycle-friendly transportation planning encourage bicycle use. Bike lanes on city streets, quiet country roads leading to scenic orchard and ranch landscapes and the trails of Bidwell Park provide safe and interesting places to cycle. Farther afield but within a 100-mile radius are several scenic wonders and recreation sites in the Sierra Nevada and Cascade Range. Plumas National Forest is directly east of Chico; Lassen National Forest and Lassen Volcanic National Park lie to the northeast. Plumas National Forest comprises more than 1,000,000 acres of forest and wilderness including the 93-mile-long Middle Fork of the Feather River, a federally-designated wild and scenic river. Spectacular canyons, rapids and waterfalls are scenic highlights here. Camping, hiking, fishing, and canoeing and tubing in designated areas are popular activities. Lassen National Forest's 1,400,000 acres of rugged terrain includes several lakes. Summer visitors enjoy camping, hiking, fishing, sailing, swimming and water-skiing; cross-country skiing is popular in winter. Lassen Volcanic National Park is a 106,000-acre mini-Yellowstone. The park is a bizarre wonderland of volcanic features including Lassen Peak (10,457 feet), lava flows, boiling springs and mudpots. Camping, hiking, fishing, nature walks and sightseeing are popular activities in summer while cross-country skiing is a winter highlight. Watersports of all kinds are enjoyed at Lake Oroville State Recreation Area, 30 miles south of Chico. You can camp, bike, hike and picnic here but most people come for boating, fishing, swimming, water-skiing and windsurfing.

Perhaps because outdoor recreation is so compelling in and near Chico, indoor recreational assets are modest. For its size, Chico is underendowed with movie theaters, bowling alleys and good restaurants. Steak and seafood and traditional American cuisine are local favorites.

Work and Volunteer Activities   Rating: 2

 Like many other interior California cities, Chico has not shared in the economic boom of coastal metropolitan areas. Unemployment remains stubbornly high at about seven percent of the labor force. Competition for jobs in the service sector among college students, seniors and the general population is acute and wages are correspondingly low. Volunteer opportunities, though, are plentiful in senior and community organizations, children's services, hospitals, libraries, parks and recreation, schools and visitor services.

Crime rates are declining in Chico but the overall crime rate in the city is still slightly above the national average. The property crime rate is about 20 percent above the national norm but violent crime is well below average. Crime rates for the city are skewed upward by the large student population because most students do not count as residents of Chico yet can be victims and perpetrators of crime. Crime rates for Butte County, which has an older demographic profile than the City of Chico, are lower than the rates for Chico and the nation.

Conclusion

 Chico is a world apart from the sprawling metropolitan areas of central and southern California. For the most part it has escaped the serious social and environmental problems that limit their appeal as retirement places. In many ways, Chico is a throwback to a more innocent age when small, neighborly communities, built at a human scale, offered a pleasant, laid-back and affordable lifestyle. Chico's ratings for cost of living, transportation, retail services, health care, community services, culture, recreation and crime are all good. Only in opportunities for paid work is the community below average. Its greatest strengths are the beautiful landscapes of the town and adjacent areas, the Mediterranean climate with four distinct yet fairly mild, sunny seasons, and an excellent quality of life. Chico neighborhoods, the Chico State campus, Bidwell Park and the nearby Sierra Nevada and Cascade Range each offers a unique, tree-shaded ambiance that is especially appreciated on hot summer afternoons. There is little air pollution, traffic noise or congestion, the earthquake risk is relatively low and housing is affordable. Few California retirement places offer so much at such modest cost.

Palm Springs/Palm Desert, California

Palm Springs/Palm Desert, California is also worth considering for retirement. Lying 120 miles east of Los Angeles at the base of 10,804-foot Mount San Jacinto, these low desert cities and neighboring Coachella Valley communities have enjoyed an economic boom in recent years that has restored their distinction as a world-class resort and retirement area. Only high living costs, moderately high crime rates, scorching summer heat and serious air pollution (from Los Angeles) keep these cities off the list of Top 40 Retirement Places.

Palm Springs (population 41,000) and Palm Desert (population 24,000) are anchor cities of a rapidly growing urban complex with a population exceeding 200,000 residents. When visitors are added, the area houses over 400,000 people at the height of the winter tourist season. This affluent population supports a wide range of services and amenities that make the Desert Cities desirable. Medical care is excellent. Eisenhower Medical Center is nationally known for the variety and quality of its services. Recreation and culture abound in this desert playground. There are more golf courses here than anywhere else in the world. You can play golf or tennis on a winter morning, then take the Palm Springs Aerial Tram to the 8500-foot level of Mount San Jacinto and cross-country ski in the afternoon. The upper part of the mountain offers limitless hiking, picnicking and sightseeing in summer amidst spectacular mountain scenery. Musical and theatrical events take place at the McCallum Theater for the Performing Arts and shopping is good in downtown Palm Springs and at the Palm Desert Town Center Mall. Palm Springs/Palm Desert also boasts good public transit and inter-city transportation and lively senior centers. It is among California's best and most affordable retirement places.

The Pacific Northwest Retirement Region

Climate:
Mediterranean–Medford/Ashland
Semi-arid (steppe)–Bend
Marine–Eugene, Salem, Portland, Olympia, Bellingham

Place Description	Overall Rating	Page
Medford/Ashland, Oregon	48	224
Medford–Ashland offers an outstanding quality of life in an unhurried, yet stimulating environment.		
Eugene, Oregon	48	229
An attractive college town, environmental quality is evident in Eugene's excellent city parks and pleasant residential areas.		
Salem, Oregon	39	235
With very good to exceptional services and quality of life, Salem offers an opportunity for a relaxed retirement in a region of great natural beauty.		
Portland, Oregon	50	241
Portland offers a physical and human environment that is close to ideal, with sound land use, excellent transportation, and a revitalized downtown.		
Olympia, Washington	42	247
Olympia is conveniently close to Seattle's amenities yet far enough away to avoid its rapid urbanization, high housing prices and increasing traffic congestion.		
Bellingham, Washington	45	253
With a splendid physical setting on Bellingham Bay, Bellingham offers a pristine environment with good to excellent services.		
Bend, Oregon	not rated	258
Bend, with a climate that is sunnier and drier than most Pacific Northwest locations, is appealing to those who enjoy outdoor activities in all seasons.		

The Pacific Northwest Retirement Region is a Garden of Eden jealously guarded by environmentalists bent on preserving its nearly pristine environment. In the 1970s, Oregon Governor Tom McCall went so far as to urge tourists to enjoy their visits to his state and then "please go home." Similar sentiments persist to this day among many residents of the region. Nonetheless, attracted by gorgeous coastal, valley and mountain scenery, clean air and water, mild but rainy weather and livable cities boasting plentiful services, low crime rates and outstanding cultural and recreational amenities, Californians and residents of other states continue to migrate to the Pacific Northwest to live, work and retire in style.

The best retirement towns are found in a 500-mile corridor along Interstate-5 (I-5). Just inside Oregon you will encounter Medford/Ashland amidst the orchards and ranches of the beautiful Rogue River Valley. An additional 150 miles brings you to Oregon's Willamette Valley, a fertile agricultural area bounded by the Cascade Range on the east and the Coast Range on the west, and site of the cities of Eugene, Salem and Portland. Each of these cities has a unique style but all are very attractive for retirement. About 125 miles after crossing the Columbia River you will enter Olympia, the lovely little Washington State capital at the southern end of Puget Sound. Traveling another 150 miles north, skirting the shores of Puget Sound and within view of the Cascade and Olympic Mountains, you will reach Bellingham, a charming seaside college town. Also worth considering in the Pacific Northwest is Bend, Oregon, an all-season resort and retirement town on the sunny, eastern slope of the Cascade Range. Californians are flocking there.

Medford/Ashland, Oregon

The Rogue River Valley of southern Oregon, site of present-day Medford and Ashland, was the preserve of the Rogue Indian tribe until the middle of the nineteenth century. The discovery of gold in 1852 brought in the first wave of white settlers followed soon by farmers attracted by the valley's productive soils and mild climate. Today a new wave of migrants, especially retirees from California, is flooding into the Medford/Ashland area in search of the good life. Medford, with a population nearing 60,000, is the business, commercial and professional center of Jackson County. Just 12 miles south is Ashland, a quaint community of 20,000 that is home to Southern Oregon University and the Oregon Shakespeare Festival and the site of numerous excellent shops and restaurants. Medford/Ashland is sheltered by distance from the hustle and bustle of city life. Eugene, the nearest major city, is 170 miles north via Interstate-5 (I-5) and Portland is 115 miles farther.

Landscape	Rating: 5

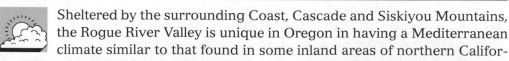

Medford/Ashland is located just north of the California state line in southern Oregon's beautiful Rogue River Valley. Fruit and vegetable farms and the oak-studded grasslands of large livestock ranches surround both cities and several neighboring small towns. Medford occupies a gently rolling surface with gorgeous views of nearby hills and mountains. Ashland extends from the valley floor into the foothills of the Siskiyou Mountains, offering a bird's-eye view of the valley's park-like landscape, a scene reminiscent of oak parkland areas in California.

Climate	Rating: 4

Sheltered by the surrounding Coast, Cascade and Siskiyou Mountains, the Rogue River Valley is unique in Oregon in having a Mediterranean climate similar to that found in some inland areas of northern California. Winters are cloudy and mild with many showery days; summers are sunny, hot and dry. Valley locations average only 19 inches of precipitation annually but mountain slopes a few thousand feet higher receive considerably more. About 75 percent of annual precipitation falls in the rainy season between October and March and only 4.5 inches falls during the dry season between April and September. Snow accumulation totals an average of 7.2 inches annually and seldom lasts on the ground for more than a few days at a time. Winter days are cloudy and mild, spring and fall weather is quite variable from day to day, and summer

Medford-Ashland, Oregon

CLIMATE				
Month	Average Daily Temperature High Low		Daily Rel. Humidity Low	Average Monthly Precipitation
	° F		%	Inches
January	46	30	71	2.7
February	53	32	57	1.9
March	59	35	50	1.8
April	65	38	45	1.2
May	73	43	39	1.0
June	82	51	33	0.6
July	91	55	26	0.3
August	90	55	26	0.5
September	83	48	29	0.9
October	69	40	43	1.5
November	53	36	68	3.2
December	44	31	76	3.3

Annual Average

Total Days		Total Inches	
Clear	117	Precipitation	18.9
Partly Cloudy	79	Snowfall	7.2
Cloudy	169		

RATINGS

Rating Scale: 5 = excellent; 4 = very good; 3 = good; 2 = fair; 1 = poor

	Rating: 1	2	3	4	5
Landscape					●
Climate				●	
Quality of Life					●
Cost of Living			●		
Transportation			●		
Retail Services			●		
Health Care				●	
Community Services				●	
Cultural Activities					●
Recreational Activities					●
Work/Volunteer Activities				●	
Crime			●		

Total Points: 48

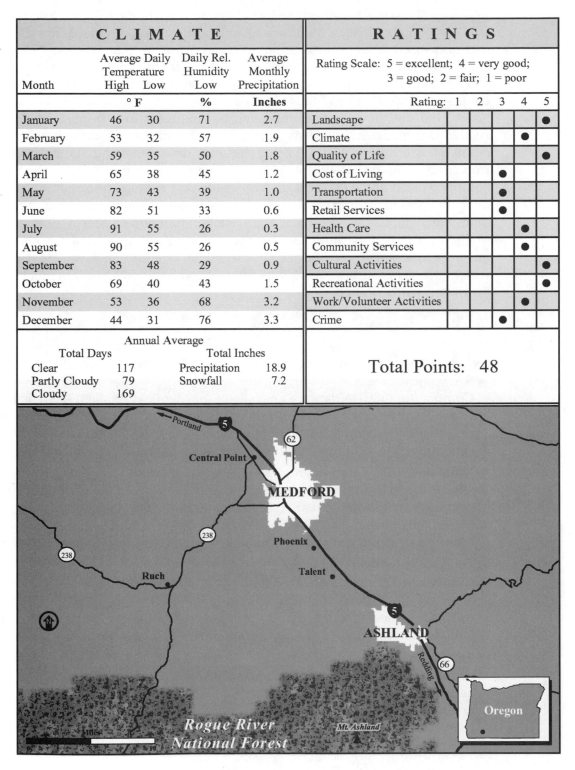

weather is relatively steady with warm to hot days, cool nights, very low relative humidity and ample sunshine. On average, Medford/Ashland is sunny about 60 percent of the time, varying seasonally from about 35 percent in winter to over 80 percent in summer. The frost-free period averages about 160 days with outdoor gardening possible from early May through mid October.

Medford/Ashland provides a very good to excellent quality of life. There is little serious noise pollution except along I-5, which skirts Ashland but bisects Medford. All federal air quality standards are currently met and smog testing of automobiles to keep the air clean is mandatory. The small population of the urban area (60,000 in Medford, 20,000 in Ashland and 180,000 in Jackson County) makes for minimal traffic congestion and no difficulties parking. Noxious industries are lacking and most residential neighborhoods, old and new, feature appealing but unpretentious frame dwellings. In Ashland, particularly, hundreds of beautifully maintained Victorian homes, many painted pastel colors, occupy choice sites near downtown and Southern Oregon University. Both cities are graced with numerous aesthetically appealing, well-equipped parks and woodland landscapes thanks to careful tree planting and frequent irrigation. Unfortunately, Medford's historic downtown area, although marginally viable, has lost much of its retailing function to nearby Rogue Valley Mall. In contrast, downtown Ashland is a thriving and architecturally charming business district. The enormously successful Oregon Shakespeare Festival, which attracts thousands of visitors into central Ashland, deserves much credit for downtown's vitality.

The cost of living in Medford/Ashland is evaluated as follows:

- *Composite.* ACCRA data are unavailable for Medford/Ashland so statistics for Corvallis, the closest economically comparable Oregon city, are used here. On that basis, the composite cost of living in Medford/Ashland is about 10 percent above the national average.

- *Housing.* Housing costs are perhaps 25 percent above the national average. According to local realtors, prices for comparable dwellings are about 20 percent higher in Ashland than in Medford. In mid 1999, an average house with three bedrooms and two baths sold for $187,000 in Ashland and $157,000 in Medford. Despite the moderately high prices, area housing appears to offer good value considering its style and good quality.

- *Goods and Services.* ACCRA data suggest that transportation and health care costs are 15 to 25 percent above their national averages. Groceries and miscellaneous goods and services are priced near their national averages whereas utilities are priced about 12 percent below the national norm.

- *Taxes.* The overall tax burden in Medford/Ashland is slightly above the national average. There is no sales tax in Oregon but the state's steeply graduated income tax rates more than compensate for this advantage. Property taxes approximate the national average having declined sharply in recent years owing to property tax reform by the state.

Local and Regional Services

Medford/Ashland's distance from major cities, combined with its moderate affluence, has allowed it to become the regional capital of a large trade area in southern Oregon and northern California. Consequently, residents and visitors have access to a fine array of services.

Transportation   Rating: 3

 Most local travel is by automobile on a very good street and highway network. Public transit is furnished by Rogue Valley Transit District (RVTD). With a small bus fleet, transit service is marginal at best. Buses run only during daytime hours on weekdays and at intervals of 30, 60 or 90 minutes, depending on the route. There is no weekend service. Fares are low throughout the transit district and especially so within Ashland city limits. There, anyone can buy 25 tokens or a basic monthly pass for $10; seniors (62 and over) and the disabled pay only $5 for a monthly pass. Special service is available for people whose disabilities prevent travel by conventional bus.

Intercity travel is possible by several modes. Greyhound provides bus service along I-5 and daily Amtrak service north to Portland and Seattle and south to Los Angeles is available in Klamath Falls, 80 miles east. Rogue Valley International Airport in Medford provides nonstop jet service to Portland, San Francisco and Seattle. Locals complain, though, that fares are high because of a lack of competition.

Retail Services   Rating: 3

The downtown areas of Ashland and Medford provide an interesting contrast. Downtown Ashland's quaint galleries, shops and restaurants are prospering as a result of their proximity to Southern Oregon University and the Oregon Shakespeare Festival, a big tourist draw. Downtown Medford, although significantly revitalized in recent years, is more ordinary having lost much of the retail market to nearby Rogue Valley Mall. Anchored by JCPenney, Meier and Frank, and Mervyn's, the mall includes over 120 specialty stores, services, and restaurants and a five-screen movie theater complex. Medford also has stand-alone Wal-Mart and Sears stores.

Health Care   Rating: 4

Medford/Ashland has three hospitals with a total capacity of 575 beds and over 320 resident physicians. Rogue Valley Medical Center in Medford, with approximately 250 beds and 150 doctors on staff, is the largest hospital in southern Oregon. It boasts cardiac and cancer treatment centers as well as the usual array of diagnostic and treatment services found in a major regional medical referral facility. Providence Medford Medical Center, a 140-bed hospital, is known particularly for its heart care and rehabilitation, and low cost health screening program for seniors. Ashland Community Hospital, with 37 beds, is affiliated with Rogue Valley Medical Center in Medford.

Community Services   Rating: 4

 Public and community services are very good in Ashland and Medford. Five senior centers and several additional senior clubs and community centers offer varied programs of interest to seniors. Medford Senior Center, the largest in the Rogue Valley Region, provides classes in crafts, Spanish, writing and painting as well as daily card games and pool. The center's travel club offers day trips to Oregon attractions and long distance bus or air travel to destinations such as Reno, Branson and Puerto Vallarta. Various support services including daily luncheons, tax help, and monthly hearing and blood pressure checks are popular with Medford seniors. Similar social and recreational programs are available at senior and community centers in Ashland and in smaller towns including Central Point, Eagle Point and Rogue River.

Leisure Activities

Many leisure activities are available in Ashland, Medford, Jacksonville and nearby valley and mountain areas.

Cultural and Educational Activities	Rating: 5

 Medford/Ashland's cultural and educational assets far exceed those normally found in small metropolitan areas. The nationally respected Oregon Shakespeare Festival, whose season runs from late February through October, stages 11 plays annually in its three Ashland theaters. Its theatrical calendar includes Shakespearean and other classic and contemporary plays. From mid-June through August, internationally known musicians present open-air concerts three or four evenings a week at Jacksonville's Peter Britt Festival. Jacksonville, a National Historic Landmark Town famous for a gold rush era downtown and historic homes, is only 5 miles west of Medford and 19 miles northwest of Ashland. The newly renovated, historic Craterian Ginger Rogers Theater in downtown Medford is the area's third major performing arts venue. It is home to the Rogue Valley Chorale and Rogue Opera and the site for performances of touring professional dance, operatic, orchestral and theatrical companies.

Southern Oregon University has much to offer seniors and the general public. Its Music Recital Hall is the Ashland home of the Rogue Valley Symphony, which also performs in Medford. University programs especially tailored to seniors include a Lectures and Lunches program, Southern Oregon Learning in Retirement (SOLIR) and Senior Ventures. The Lectures and Lunches program combines lunches and lectures on the Oregon Shakespeare Festival. SOLIR actively involves seniors in developing courses and selecting teachers. For an annual fee of less than $100 seniors can participate in a great variety of noncredit courses. Senior Ventures provides educational travel opportunities in the United States and abroad for reasonable fees.

Recreational Activities	Rating: 5

 The lovely landscape and mild climate of southern Oregon favor all kinds of outdoor recreation. Golfers of all skill levels can find suitable courses on which to play year round. Four 18-hole and six 9-hole layouts are found locally with several others within 30 miles of Medford. Ashland, Medford and Jackson County all boast excellent park systems. Medford alone has over 30 municipal parks ranging from small neighborhood picnic areas and playgrounds to large community parks featuring tennis courts, outdoor swimming pools and hiking trails. Lithia Park, which occupies 100 acres in downtown Ashland, is a magnificent resource for residents and visitors. Its walking trails, wooded areas, gardens, and sports and playground facilities are intensively used. Every Monday evening, June through August, the State Ballet of Oregon provides free performances at the outdoor amphitheater in the park. Among the more popular county facilities is Emigrant Lake Park, five miles southeast of Ashland. Regular activities there include swimming, boating, canoeing, fishing, camping, hiking and bird watching. A little farther afield in the Cascade, Siskiyou and Coast Mountains are several wonderful natural areas for exploration and recreation. The incomparable Crater Lake National Park, 80 miles north of Medford/Ashland, offers a unique volcanic landscape, summer camping, hiking and picnicking, and cross-country skiing much of the year. One can ski downhill at Mount Ashland, 20 miles south of Ashland, Thanksgiving through April, and whitewater raft the Rogue River or bicycle the Bear Creek Greenway much of the year. Indoor sports facilities in Medford include the YMCA swimming pool and racquetball courts, two bowling establishments, and roller-skating and ice-skating rinks.

For a small metropolitan area, Medford/Ashland has a good selection of movie theaters and many excellent restaurants. Menus available range from standard American and Italian to French, Japanese, Mexican, Russian and Middle Eastern.

Work and Volunteer Activities   Rating: 4

Although the Jackson County unemployment rate remains stubbornly above the national average, the local economy has boomed in recent years. Part-time employment opportunities are plentiful in retailing and in other service industries. All kinds of volunteer work can be found especially in tourist-oriented activities like the Shakespearean Festival, visitor centers, and local, state and federal parks. Oregon Shakespeare Festival alone has 850 volunteers in Ashland. Senior centers, hospitals, public libraries, the Salvation Army and the Red Cross also depend heavily on volunteers.

Crime Rates and Public Safety   Rating: 3

The metropolitan area (Jackson County) has low to moderate crime rates. Considering the massive influx of visitors this is not bad. The overall property crime rate approximates the national average, whereas the violent crime rate is about 40 percent below the national norm. Crime rates are somewhat higher in Medford than in smaller communities like Ashland and Jacksonville.

Conclusion

Overall Rating 48 Medford/Ashland is one of America's best places for an unhurried yet stimulating retirement. Its lovely oak-studded hill and valley landscape and mild Mediterranean climate make the area very appealing. The quality of life is outstanding. Air and water are clean and noise pollution is minimal except along I-5. Residential areas and parks are very attractive and downtown Ashland is delightful. Cultural and educational opportunities are outstanding in Medford, Ashland and the surrounding area, while health care, community services and work and volunteer activities are unusually good. Only the area's moderate cost of living, average property crime rate, and somewhat limited transportation choices detract from its overall excellence for retirement. That said, Medford/Ashland ranks as a wonderful place to live if one is seeking small town ambiance along with educational and cultural amenities characteristic of much larger cities.

Eugene, Oregon

Long primarily a place for wood processing and a market town for Willamette Valley farmers, Eugene has blossomed in recent decades into one of Oregon's principal educational, commercial and manufacturing centers and a

Eugene, Oregon

CLIMATE							
Month	Average Daily Temperature High	Low	Daily Rel. Humidity Low	Average Monthly Precipitation			
	°F		%	Inches			
January	46	35	80	7.9			
February	51	37	73	5.6			
March	56	39	64	5.5			
April	61	41	58	3.1			
May	67	45	54	2.2			
June	74	50	49	1.4			
July	82	53	38	0.5			
August	82	53	39	1.1			
September	76	49	43	1.7			
October	65	44	62	3.4			
November	52	40	79	8.3			
December	46	36	84	8.6			

Annual Average

Total Days		Total Inches	
Clear	75	Precipitation	49.4
Partly Cloudy	82	Snowfall	6.4
Cloudy	209		

RATINGS

Rating Scale: 5 = excellent; 4 = very good; 3 = good; 2 = fair; 1 = poor

Rating:	1	2	3	4	5
Landscape				●	
Climate			●		
Quality of Life				●	
Cost of Living			●		
Transportation					●
Retail Services				●	
Health Care				●	
Community Services					●
Cultural Activities					●
Recreational Activities					●
Work/Volunteer Activities			●		
Crime			●		

Total Points: 48

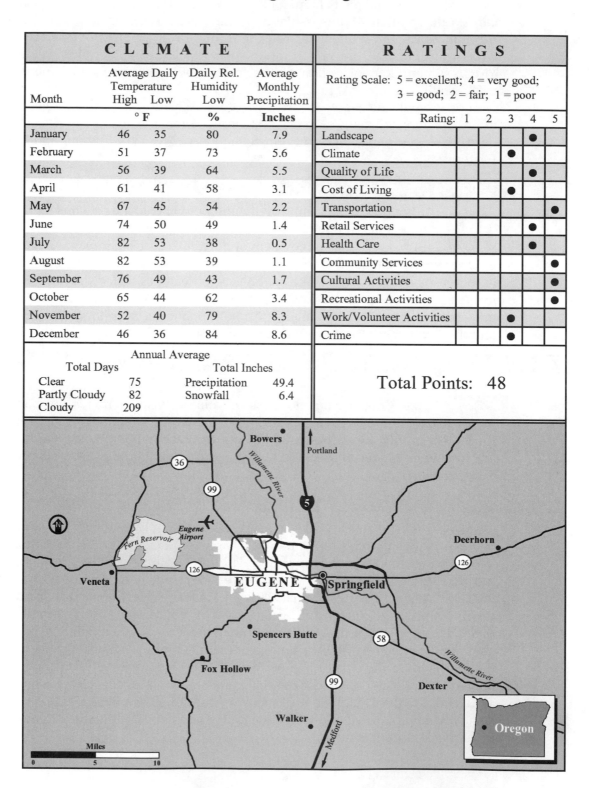

very attractive residential community. Home of the University of Oregon and Lane Community College, Eugene offers an unusually rich mix of services to residents as well as easy access to the outstanding urban amenities of Portland and to the varied recreational assets of the Oregon shoreline and Coast and Cascade Mountains. With a population nearing 150,000 in Eugene proper and 350,000 in

Lane County, Eugene retains much that is good in America's best small towns. It is a progressive, tolerant and welcoming community, supportive of the arts, education, and environmental protection and determined to keep Eugene relaxed and livable despite inevitable pressures of growth.

Landscape   Rating: 4

Eugene is situated on a gently rolling to hilly surface along the Willamette River near the southern end of the scenic and fertile Willamette Valley. The city site is very attractive with high wooded hills like Spencer Butte overlooking the downtown area. Residential neighborhoods extend from flat terrain near the river up into the hills to the south where some home sites offer splendid views of the city, valley and distant mountains. The Oregon Coast Range lies 40 miles west with Pacific beaches 20 miles farther; the crest of the Cascade Range is 60 miles east. Thanks to its sheltered inland valley location, Eugene receives only two-thirds as much rain as coastal towns west of the Coast Range. Even so, Eugene is wet enough to support a luxuriant forest of coniferous and deciduous trees including Douglas fir, oak and maple. The city is nicely landscaped although not as heavily treed as one might expect. Eugenians prefer a mix of wooded and open terrain so that they can enjoy the sun whenever it shines.

Climate   Rating: 3

Eugene's climate is generally similar to that of Portland and Salem. Mild, cloudy, wet winters, and warm, sunny, relatively dry summers are characteristic. Eugene receives an annual average of 49 inches of precipitation with nearly 80 percent of the total falling during the rainy season between October and March. The drier half of the year, April through September, gets only 10 inches on average. Annual snowfall totals less than seven inches and seldom lasts more than a few days on the ground. Winters are very mild for the latitude. Spring and fall weather is quite variable with cool to warm days followed by cool nights. Summers are typically delightful with warm, sunny days and cool nights. The frost-free season averages 190 days and skies are generally cloudy or partly cloudy, except in summer. On average, Eugene is sunny about 50 percent of the time, varying seasonally from about 25 percent in winter to 70 percent in summer.

Quality of Life   Rating: 4

Eugene provides a very good quality of life. There is some noise pollution alongside the Interstate-5 and 105 freeways and several major streets, and on a few days per year federal air quality standards are not met. Most industries, except for several wood-processing mills, are innocuous, and traffic usually flows well, although it is worsening year by year. Parking is plentiful and the city's popular bike routes and public transit reduce demand for additional automotive infrastructure. Most neighborhoods, modest or affluent, central or suburban, are nicely treed, landscaped and well maintained. Eugene has an excellent inventory of parks and playgrounds, and the University of Oregon adds to the ambiance of the city. Downtown has been renewed in the last 20 years and boasts the Hult Center, the focus of community cultural life, and a few interesting stores and restaurants. Unfortunately, major department stores, discount outlets and most national chain stores have fled from central Eugene to nearby regional malls.

The cost of living in Eugene is evaluated as follows:

- *Composite.* According to ACCRA, the composite cost of living in Eugene is 10 percent above the national average.

- *Housing.* Housing costs are 25 percent above the national average yet offer good value. Eugene housing is plentiful, varied in style and well built. Attractive 1,600 square-foot homes with three bedrooms and two bathrooms are typically priced in the $150,000 to $190,000 range according to local sources. Larger suburban homes are generally priced higher, condominiums and small central city homes somewhat lower.

- *Goods and Services.* ACCRA data suggest that transportation and health care costs are 10–20 percent above the national average. Groceries and miscellaneous goods and services are priced just above national norms, whereas utilities are priced about 30 percent below average.

- *Taxes.* The overall tax burden in Eugene is somewhat above the national average. Although there is no state sales tax, Oregon's steeply graduated income tax rates more than compensate for this advantage. Property taxes are moderate and have declined in recent years due to property tax reform by the state.

Local and Regional Services

Eugene provides a fine array of services. Additional resources of great variety are available in Portland, 115 miles north.

Transportation   Rating: 5

 Most intracity travel is by car but buses and bicycles provide alternatives for many residents. Lane Transit District (LTD) furnishes excellent transportation throughout Eugene and neighboring Springfield and to several destinations outside the urban area. LTD's 50-route system is focused on the new full-service downtown Eugene station, with routes radiating to 10 smaller transit stations strategically located in or near major destinations in the metropolitan area. Schools, colleges, hospitals, parks, shopping malls and downtown, among other locations, are all easily reached via LTD. Fares are reasonable. The general public pays $1.00 per ride, $26 for a monthly pass, or $60 for a three-month pass. Seniors pay half these rates. Bicycling is also a rational transportation choice for many people owing to Eugene's excellent network of bicycle paths and lanes. Over 25 miles of off-street bike trails are available, some along the scenic Willamette River, and more than 300 miles of stripped bike lanes on city streets.

Amtrak, Greyhound and several airlines provide intercity transportation. Amtrak runs four daily trains north to Portland and Seattle and one train south to Los Angeles. Greyhound service to these locations and other points is possible from the downtown Greyhound bus station. Eugene Airport, eight miles northwest of the city center, provides nonstop jet service to Denver, Portland and San Francisco and commuter service to several other western cities. Portland International Airport, 125 miles north via I-5, furnishes nonstop jet service to over 45 destinations.

Retail Services — Rating: 4

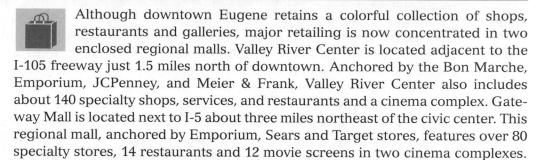

Although downtown Eugene retains a colorful collection of shops, restaurants and galleries, major retailing is now concentrated in two enclosed regional malls. Valley River Center is located adjacent to the I-105 freeway just 1.5 miles north of downtown. Anchored by the Bon Marche, Emporium, JCPenney, and Meier & Frank, Valley River Center also includes about 140 specialty shops, services, and restaurants and a cinema complex. Gateway Mall is located next to I-5 about three miles northeast of the civic center. This regional mall, anchored by Emporium, Sears and Target stores, features over 80 specialty stores, 14 restaurants and 12 movie screens in two cinema complexes.

Health Care — Rating: 4

Two major hospitals in Eugene and neighboring Springfield provide comprehensive medical care. Sacred Heart Medical Center, a 433-bed facility in Eugene, is the regional center for several specialties including the Oregon Heart Center, the Cancer Care Center and the Oregon Rehabilitation Center. McKenzie-Willamette Hospital in Springfield is a 114-bed acute care, surgical and outpatient facility providing a wide range of medical services. Area hospitals have state-of-the-art technology such as magnetic resonance imaging, CT scanning, nuclear medicine and ultrasound. With nearly 500 physicians in all, Eugene/Springfield has an excellent supply of general/family practitioners as well as medical and surgical specialists.

Community Services — Rating: 5

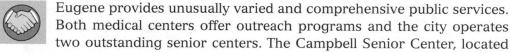

Eugene provides unusually varied and comprehensive public services. Both medical centers offer outreach programs and the city operates two outstanding senior centers. The Campbell Senior Center, located in a lovely riverfront park just north of downtown Eugene, provides an extensive list of excursions, outdoor activities, classes, drop-in activities and special services for seniors. Vans and buses take seniors to destinations such as coastal Oregon towns, Crater Lake, Salem museums, and to jump-off points for rural hiking, bicycling and canoeing and rafting trips. Classes at the center are taught primarily by volunteers and fees are reasonable. Classes in several arts and crafts, computers, fitness and languages are offered regularly. Drop-in activities include card and table games, dancing, pool and woodworking. Special services include outreach programs to improve seniors' access to community resources, health and foot-care clinics and Wednesday luncheons. Broadly similar activities and programs are available at the Trudy Kauffman Senior Center, a few blocks west of the civic center.

Leisure Activities

Eugene and nearby coastal and mountain areas offer a great variety of leisure activities. The substantial additional cultural and recreational resources of Portland are only two hours away.

Cultural and Educational Activities — Rating: 5

Eugene is very well endowed culturally and educationally, especially for a small city. Downtown's architecturally stunning Hult Center for the Performing Arts is Eugene's cultural focus. Its 500-seat Soreng Theatre is ideal for small-scale opera, dance, chamber music and film, while the magnificent 2,500-seat Silva Concert Hall hosts large-scale musical and theatrical productions. Major companies calling Hult Center home include the Eugene Symphony Orchestra, Eugene Ballet Company, Eugene Opera, Oregon Bach Festival, Oregon Mozart Players, Eugene Festival of Musical Theatre, and Actor's Cabaret/Mainstage Theatre. In addition to the offerings of the Hult Center's excellent resident companies, the Center presents six or seven multi-disciplinary performing arts series annually. Ranging from early music to jazz, from modern dance to musical theater, from international music and dance to one-person portrayals of historical figures, Hult Center programs offer something for everyone. In summer, Eugene's cultural scene expands into the great outdoors. Following the Fourth of July performance by the Eugene Symphonic Band, the Washburn Park Classical Series provides 10 free Sunday evening light classics concerts from early July through mid September. Free mid-week concerts offering varied musical fare are performed at other Eugene parks and recreation centers in July.

The University of Oregon and Lane Community College are strong assets for seniors as well as the community at large. The university has an excellent Elderhostel program each summer as well as continuing education programs for seniors 65 and older. Lane Community College, recognized since 1985 as one of the top community colleges in the United States, helps local residents develop talents, hobbies and leisure pursuits to better enjoy all that Oregon has to offer. Seniors may audit courses at the University of Oregon and at Lane Community College for nominal fees.

Recreational Activities   Rating: 5

Eugene and its surrounding areas offer an abundance of recreational amenities. The city's 49-unit park and recreation system, covering nearly 2,000 acres, is among the best in the country. Whatever your preference, be it viewing the roses, rhododendrons and azaleas of Owen Rose Garden or Hendricks Park; walking, jogging or biking the trails of Spencer Butte Park or those in the series of parks fronting the Willamette River; or playing tennis or golf at numerous locations, Eugene city parks have the facilities you need. Within a 15-mile radius of Eugene there are over 10 golf courses, and area rivers and reservoirs afford ample opportunities for rafting, canoeing and fishing. Fern Ridge Reservoir, just west of town, is especially popular for sailing. Several ski resorts in the Cascades including Mount Bachelor, the incomparable Crater Lake National Park, and endless opportunities for sightseeing and fishing along the Oregon coast are also within easy driving distance.

For a small city Eugene is well endowed with good restaurants and movie theaters. One can enjoy NCAA Division 1 basketball and football games played by the University of Oregon Ducks, and travel to Portland to enjoy NBA basketball and other cultural and recreational attractions.

Work and Volunteer Activities   Rating: 3

Despite recent growth in high technology industry, the Eugene and Lane County economy remains heavily dependent on service industries. Unemployment is now at about five percent, the lowest level in decades, and part-time jobs are readily available, although college students compete aggressively for many of them. Many organizations provide volunteer opportunities through Eugene senior centers. Examples include hospitals, schools, the library, Hult Center, Meals-on-Wheels and Eugene Senior Services.

The overall incidence of crime in Eugene is near the national average. Although the city's overall property crime rate is slightly above the average for U.S. metropolitan areas, with larceny-theft being a particular problem, the violent crime rate is low at about 50 percent of the national norm. Despite concerns expressed locally about a tiny, militant anarchist group, described as urban terrorists by the mayor, Eugene is enviably safe and comfortable.

Conclusion

Overall Rating 48

Eugene is a particularly attractive college town. Its physical site on hilly terrain astride Oregon's Willamette River is beautiful and its mild, marine climate quite agreeable. The local quality of life is very good even though there is some noise alongside busy streets and freeways and light air pollution a few days per year.

Environmental quality is a high priority here as manifested in the excellent city parks and very pleasant residential areas. Transportation, community services, and cultural and recreational activities are excellent, and retail services and health care are very good. Only the city's moderate cost of living, moderate crime statistics, and limited openings for paid part-time work detract from its excellence for retirement. Even so, Eugene ranks as one of America's very best places for a relaxed yet sophisticated retirement.

Salem, Oregon

Salem was founded in 1841 by a Methodist missionary intent on converting local American Indians to a settled life of farming and Christianity. Failure in this venture led to the laying out of a town and the selling of lots to finance the Oregon Institute, which developed into Willamette University, one of the oldest universities west of the Mississippi and a central pillar of culture and education in present-day Salem. Capital of Oregon and an important commercial center for the Willamette Valley, Salem depends heavily on service employment for its economic vitality. With a population approaching 130,000 in the city and 350,000 in the metropolitan area, Salem is an increasingly busy small city. Despite substantial suburbanization of residents and services, its downtown business district, buttressed by Salem Center and abundant free parking, is thriving as is evidenced by heavy pedestrian and vehicular traffic downtown. In contrast, the tree-lined streets of Salem's older middle class neighborhoods project a welcome tranquility.

Landscape | Rating: 3

Salem is located on the banks of the Willamette River in the heart of the agriculturally fertile Willamette Valley. The city is laid out on a mostly flat surface with a few neighborhoods occupying low hills a hundred feet or so above downtown's official elevation of 171 feet. Such favored and high-priced sites offer distant views of Mount Hood and other Cascade Range volcanoes on clear days. Several small streams including Pringle and Mill Creeks drain into the Willamette River from the east, adding variety to the otherwise flat landscape just south of downtown. Salem is only 50 miles south of

Salem, Oregon

CLIMATE				
Month	Average Daily Temperature High Low	Daily Rel. Humidity Low	Average Monthly Precipitation	
	°F	%	Inches	
January	46	33	75	5.9
February	52	34	68	4.5
March	56	36	60	4.2
April	60	38	57	2.4
May	67	42	53	1.9
June	75	48	49	1.3
July	82	51	40	0.6
August	82	51	40	0.8
September	76	47	45	1.6
October	64	41	60	3.0
November	52	38	77	6.3
December	46	34	80	6.8

Annual Average

Total Days		Total Inches	
Clear	77	Precipitation	39.2
Partly Cloudy	80	Snowfall	6.6
Cloudy	208		

RATINGS

Rating Scale: 5 = excellent; 4 = very good; 3 = good; 2 = fair; 1 = poor

Rating:	1	2	3	4	5
Landscape			●		
Climate			●		
Quality of Life				●	
Cost of Living			●		
Transportation			●		
Retail Services			●		
Health Care			●		
Community Services				●	
Cultural Activities		●			
Recreational Activities				●	
Work/Volunteer Activities				●	
Crime			●		

Total Points: 39

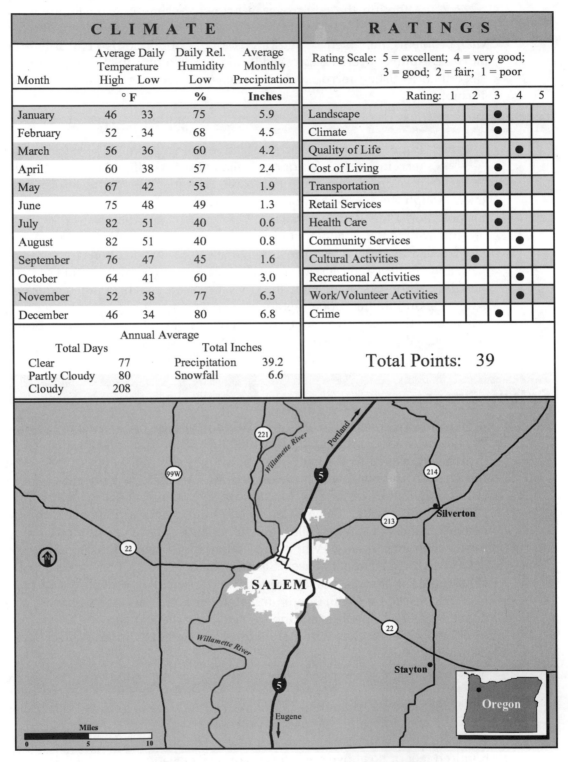

Portland and 64 miles north of Eugene; the Pacific coast is 50 miles west, the Cascade Range about 70 miles east. In its natural state the area was nicely wooded with oak and fir; today the surrounding area is intensively farmed while the city is well treed and landscaped. Residential gardens typically include lawns, flowering shrubs such as rhododendron and seasonal plantings of flowers.

Like Portland, Salem has a marine climate featuring mild, cloudy, wet winters and warm, sunny and relatively dry summers. The Coast Range has a significant rain-shadow effect on Salem and other Willamette Valley cities. The city gets only 39 inches of precipitation annually whereas locations west of the Coast Range receive upwards of 80 inches. Over 75 percent of Salem's annual precipitation falls in the rainy season between October and March; between April and September, only 8.5 inches fall on average. Snowfall totals an average of less than seven inches annually and seldom persists on the ground for more than a few days. Winters are mild for the latitude and spring and fall weather is variable with mild to warm days and cool nights. Summers are near perfect with generally warm days, cool nights, low relative humidity and plenty of sunshine. The frost-free season averages 180 days and skies are generally cloudy or partly cloudy except in summer. On average, Salem is sunny about 50 percent of the time, varying seasonally from about 27 percent in winter to 70 percent in summer.

Quality of Life   **Rating: 4**

Salem offers a very good quality of life. There is some noise pollution adjacent to Interstate-5 (I-5) and alongside major streets but the city meets all federal air quality standards. Heavy industry is lacking and although major streets are busy, traffic flows well. Bicycling is encouraged by the city's many bike trails and lanes. Parking is adequate in commercial areas including downtown Salem and Lancaster Mall. Most neighborhoods are quite attractive and peaceful. Some older ones, like Gaiety Hill near Bush's Pasture Park and Willamette University, are aging gracefully as gentrification takes place. Streets generally are well treed and the city is dotted with large and small parks. Thanks to downtown renewal including the development of Salem Center, a large enclosed mall in the heart of the city, and the recent creation of Riverfront Park along the Willamette, Salem's central core remains a vital center of community life.

Cost of Living   **Rating: 3**

The cost of living in Salem is evaluated as follows:

- *Composite.* ACCRA data for Salem show that the composite cost of living is seven percent above the national average.

- *Housing.* According to ACCRA, housing costs are about 12 percent above the national average. Nonetheless, Salem real estate offers good value. Attractive single-family residences in good areas are typically priced in the $100,000 to $200,000 range. Even the very desirable South Salem neighborhood, a peaceful refuge where many homes offer panoramic views of the Willamette Valley and its bordering mountains, has excellent housing valued at an average of $170,000.

- *Goods and Services.* Health care is priced about 20 percent above, miscellaneous goods and services about 9 percent above and transportation about 7 percent above their respective national averages. The cost of groceries is at the national average whereas utilities are a bargain at a price 15 percent below the national norm.

- *Taxes.* The overall tax burden in Salem is somewhat above the national average. Although there is no state sales tax, Oregon's steeply graduated income tax rates and Salem's moderate property taxes more than compensate for this advantage.

Local and Regional Services

Salem provides a good array of services commensurate with its rankings as Oregon's second largest metropolitan area and third largest city. Many additional resources are available in Portland, 50 miles north.

Transportation — Rating: 3

The street and highway network is currently adequate but traffic is getting heavier year by year as the area's population grows. Most local travel is by car but Salem Charriots, with upwards of 50 buses, provides adequate public transit in much of the city. Greyhound furnishes intercity bus service via I-5 and Amtrak runs four trains a day north to Portland and Seattle and south to Eugene with one train continuing on to Los Angeles. Portland International Airport, 60 miles north, provides nonstop jet service to over 45 destinations.

Retail Services — Rating: 3

The decline of downtown Salem has been reversed by an aggressive community revitalization effort and downtown remains the economic heart of the city. Salem Center, a modern enclosed mall on Liberty Street and astride Center Street downtown, competes effectively with Lancaster Mall and stand-alone super stores on the east side of town. Adequate parking is provided in four major downtown parking structures, three with ground floor retail space. Salem Center is anchored by JCPenney, Meier and Frank, Mervyn's and Nordstrom. It also boasts about 80 stores, services and restaurants and a cinema complex. Enclosed sky-bridges above city streets link various elements of the retail complex and two of the parking structures. Dozens of additional specialty shops, restaurants and service establishments line nearby streets.

Lancaster Mall, off I-5 in the eastern part of town, is Salem's principal suburban shopping center. The Bon Marche, Emporium and Sears anchor this large enclosed facility. It also features approximately 100 stores, restaurants and services plus Lancaster Quad Cinema. Large stand-alone stores including Costco, Home Base, Home Depot, Kmart, Shopko, Target and two Wal-Marts are also found in suburban Salem.

Health Care — Rating: 3

Salem Hospital is the metropolitan area's major medical facility. Licensed for 454 beds, the hospital has satellite clinics for rehabilitation and psychiatric services, among others. The usual wide range of diagnostic services and medical treatments offered by major medical centers is available at Salem Hospital. Excellent HMO services are provided in Salem by Kaiser Permanente, which operates three medical offices there and contracts with Salem Hospital for routine medical services including surgery. Kaiser Permanente members may also obtain services at Kaiser hospitals and clinics in Portland, 50 miles away.

Community Services Rating: 4

 Like other Oregon cities, Salem provides comprehensive public services. The Salem Senior Center, which offers an excellent program of services to those 55 and older, is of particular interest. Well equipped hobby areas and instruction in arts and crafts such as jewelry making, lapidary, photography, pottery and woodworking are available in house, as are various games including cards, chess and pool, movies and dancing. The Senior Center also provides various support services, volunteer opportunities, health screenings and weekday hot luncheons for seniors. Local and regional excursions and hiking trips depart from the Senior Center and local branches of the AARP and RSVP are based there.

Leisure Activities

Salem and adjacent coastal, mountain and valley areas provide a good selection of leisure activities. Nearby metropolitan Portland offers many additional cultural and recreational choices.

Cultural and Educational Activities Rating: 2

 Salem has cultural and educational attributes typical of a small city. Willamette University Theatre and the Pentacle Theatre are principal venues for theatrical performances. Plays are also staged at downtown's Historic Elsinore Theatre, a Tudor Gothic movie palace, which also hosts visiting ballet companies, symphony orchestras and other musical ensembles. Portland's Oregon Symphony performs several concerts each year in Salem. Special events including jazz concerts and book and poetry readings are frequently scheduled at the Salem Central Library. The city also boasts several art galleries and museums. The Bush Barn Art Center in Bush's Pasture Park and the Hallie Ford Museum of Art at Willamette University are especially notable.

Willamette University, which occupies a 57-acre campus just south of downtown, is nationally known for the high quality of its academic programs. The oldest college in the west, Willamette includes colleges of liberal arts and law, and the Atkinson Graduate School of Management. Chemeketa Community College, located in suburban northeast Salem, offers a comprehensive program of academic and applied courses in regular and extension formats. Each term the college fields 15 to 20 classes at the Salem Senior Center; fees are reduced for seniors 62 and over.

Recreational Activities Rating: 4

 Salem and nearby areas offer a plethora of outdoor recreation. The city has an excellent park system featuring four large multi-purpose parks near downtown and dozens of smaller neighborhood parks and recreation centers elsewhere. Bush's Pasture Park, with its rose garden and plantings of exotic trees and shrubs, is a gorgeous place in which to walk, picnic, and play tennis or baseball. Riverfront Park, a beautiful new 22-acre park alongside the Willamette River in downtown Salem, features a promenade, paved paths for biking, running and skating, picnic facilities, a playground and amphitheater. Just across the river is Wallace Marine Park, which boasts an indoor sports complex and boat launching, among other facilities. Minto/Brown Island City Park is Salem's largest park. Partly farmland, partly wildlife refuge, this two-square mile area offers endless opportunities for biking, hiking, nature study and fishing. More than 10 golf courses grace the Salem landscape, with 10 more within a half-hour drive.

A little farther afield in the Cascade Range, the Coast Range and along the Pacific coast are wondrous natural areas for touring and recreation. One can ski Mount Bachelor or Mount Hood in the Cascades and camp, hike, hunt or fish at dozens of sites in the Cascade and Coast Mountains. Silver Falls State Park, 25 miles east of Salem in the Cascade foothills, is especially delightful in summer. Oregon's largest state park, Silver Falls, has 10 waterfalls reachable by hiking trails, 6 of which are more than 100 feet high. The park also offers natural pool swimming, camping, picnicking and fishing. Fishing, boating and sightseeing are also popular along the magnificent Oregon coast 60 miles west of Salem.

Salem is modestly endowed with good restaurants and movie theaters. Luckily, much larger numbers of both are found only 50 miles away in Portland.

Work and Volunteer Activities   Rating: 4

 Trade, services and government are the leading industries in Salem and the work force is heavily concentrated in administrative and clerical occupations. Part-time jobs of interest to seniors are concentrated largely in the retail and service sectors. Volunteer opportunities are plentiful. The Senior Center and Senior Townhouse Inc., the organization for Meals-on-Wheels in Salem, both rely heavily on volunteers. Senior Townhouse alone involves 450 volunteers in its food preparation and distribution program. Salem Hospital, Salem Public Library, schools, governmental facilities, and service clubs also employ large numbers of volunteers.

Crime Rates and Public Safety   Rating: 3

 Salem's overall incidence of crime approximates the national rate, with the overall property crime rate being about 20 percent above the national average. This result largely reflects the city's high larceny-theft rate; other property crime rates are below national norms. The incidence of violent crime in Salem is enviably low with an overall rate only 50 percent of the national average. Despite concerns expressed locally about growing gang activity (politicians and police are promising a crackdown), Salem, including the downtown area, feels well policed and safe.

Conclusion

Overall Rating 39 Located along I-5 only 50 miles south of Portland, Salem is close enough to the Oregon metropolis to enjoy its many amenities yet far enough away to avoid its relatively high cost of living and moderately high crime rates. Salem's physical setting on the banks of the Willamette River in a rich agricultural region is pleasant and its mild, four-season climate with little snow will appeal to many, despite the preponderance of cloudy, rainy weather during half of the year. Salem offers residents a very good quality of life, with very good availability of community services, recreational activities, and paid and volunteer work. There is little air, water or noise pollution, and catastrophic environmental events are unlikely. Salem housing offers excellent value and most residential neighborhoods are attractive and convenient to community parks and recreation areas. Transportation facilities and retail and health care services are exceptional, and the overall cost of living is only slightly above the national average. Only Salem's moderately high property crime rate and modest cultural assets detract from its ranking as one of the country's better places for relaxed retirement in a region of great natural beauty.

Portland, Oregon

Thirty years ago no one would have forecast that Portland would be a wonderful place to live at the beginning of the 21st century. In the late 1960s the city was beset by several devastating trends that were most pronounced downtown and in the central city. Historic structures and housing were being lost to parking lots and new freeways, retail activity was dwindling and the Willamette River waterfront was blighted by industrial decline. Capital, jobs and families were fleeing to the suburbs, traffic congestion was developing, and regional air quality was deteriorating. Today, thanks to 25 years of careful planning and the cooperative efforts of state and local government, businesses and citizens, downtown Portland has been reborn as an attractive, dynamic, exciting and pedestrian-friendly center of the metropolitan area. There, and in the outlying areas, development is now better planned, the environment better protected, and pollution controlled than in previous decades. As a result, Portland, with a population of 450,000 within its city limits and around 1,300,000 in the metropolitan area, is one of the few cities of its size that can be recommended for retirement.

Landscape   Rating: 5

Portland possesses an enviable site astride the Willamette River and within sight of Mount Hood and the Cascade Range. Much of the terrain west of the river is hilly and forested, with lower areas and gentler slopes occupied by upscale neighborhoods scattered among several of Portland's excellent parks. Some of these, most notably Washington Park, reach down from the hills almost into downtown. It is an easy walk or a short drive from the city center to Washington Park's zoo, gardens or picnic areas. East of the river the land is fairly flat with several high hills adding interest to the landscape. Oak and Douglas fir are the principal trees native to Portland, but many exotic broad-leafed tree varieties including magnolia are widely planted in the city and suburbs. Residential gardens often include rhododendrons and other flowering shrubs, flowers and lush green lawns.

Climate   Rating: 3

Portland's variant of the marine climate is characterized by mild, cloudy, wet winters and warm, sunny and relatively dry summers. Portland is a little warmer in summer than Seattle as a result of its Willamette Valley location and its 60-mile distance from the cold waters of the Pacific Ocean. Portland averages 36 inches of annual precipitation with fully 27 inches falling during the rainy season between October and March. The six-month period between April and September gets less than 10 inches and is much sunnier. Nearly all precipitation occurs as rain; snow totals an average of less than seven inches annually and seldom persists more than a day or two on the ground because winter days are typically mild. Spring and fall weather is variable with cool to warm days and cool nights. Summer is nearly ideal with warm

Portland, Oregon

	CLIMATE			
Month	Average Daily Temperature High Low	Daily Rel. Humidity Low	Average Monthly Precipitation	
	°F	%	Inches	
January	45 34	75	5.4	
February	51 36	67	3.9	
March	56 39	60	3.6	
April	61 41	55	2.4	
May	67 47	53	2.1	
June	74 53	49	1.5	
July	80 57	45	0.6	
August	80 57	45	1.1	
September	75 52	48	1.8	
October	64 45	62	2.7	
November	53 40	74	5.3	
December	46 35	78	6.1	

Annual Average

Total Days		Total Inches	
Clear	68	Precipitation	36.3
Partly Cloudy	74	Snowfall	6.5
Cloudy	222		

RATINGS

Rating Scale: 5 = excellent; 4 = very good; 3 = good; 2 = fair; 1 = poor

Rating:	1	2	3	4	5
Landscape					●
Climate			●		
Quality of Life					●
Cost of Living		●			
Transportation					●
Retail Services					●
Health Care				●	
Community Services					●
Cultural Activities					●
Recreational Activities					●
Work/Volunteer Activities				●	
Crime		●			

Total Points: 50

days, cool nights, low relative humidity and abundant sunshine. The frost-free period is long for the latitude, averaging about 200 days annually. Cloudy to partly cloudy skies are more typical than clear skies except in summer. On average, Portland is sunny about 48 percent of the time, varying seasonally from about 26 percent in winter to 66 percent in summer.

Portland offers residents an excellent quality of life, an unusually high rating for a medium-sized American city. There is some noise pollution adjacent to the freeways and near the airport but the city meets all federal air quality standards. Noxious industries are lacking and although area freeways are busy at rush hour, traffic generally flows freely. Metropolitan Portland's excellent public transit system helps by diverting some travel from the private automobile. Parking is plentiful in suburban areas but is tight downtown because Portland uses traffic calming measures including low speed limits, wide sidewalks, and reductions in street capacity and parking to favor walking and transit use. There are some rather uninspiring 1960s era neighborhoods in the eastern suburbs, but much of the metropolitan area is attractive, well treed, well planned and dotted with community and regional parks. The residents are strongly environmentalist and devoted to Portland. They are now enjoying the fruits of downtown renewal, improved public transit, the transformation of the west bank of the Willamette from a freeway corridor into Tom McCall Waterfront Park and the cleaning up of the river, which is now fit for boating, fishing and water-skiing.

Cost of Living   Rating: 2

 The cost of living in Portland is evaluated as follows:

- **Composite.** ACCRA data for Portland reveal a composite cost of living about 12 percent above the national average.

- **Housing.** According to ACCRA, housing costs are 23 percent above the national average. As elsewhere, housing costs vary drastically across the city and metropolitan region. Prime properties near Washington and Mountain Parks sell for upwards of $500,000 while nicely renovated older homes in excellent Portland neighborhoods east of the Willamette River cost upwards of $200,000. Suburban communities like Beaverton, Hillsboro and Gresham offer good values with many attractive homes selling in the $100,000 to $200,000 price range.

- **Goods and Services.** ACCRA data show health care to be priced about 23 percent above, transportation 20 percent above, and groceries and miscellaneous goods and services 5–10 percent above their national averages. Utilities are a bargain at a price 20 percent below average.

- **Taxes.** The overall tax burden in Portland is modestly above the national average. Although there is no state sales tax, Oregon's steeply graduated income tax rates and the city's moderately high property taxes that reflect high property values more than compensate for this advantage.

Local and Regional Services

Consistent with its rank as Oregon's largest city, Portland provides a fine array of services. Additional resources are available in Seattle, 180 miles north.

Transportation   Rating: 5

 Portland has an excellent street and freeway network and most intracity travel is by car. That said, the bus and light rail services provided by Tri-Met, the metropolitan area public transit agency, provide alternative transportation to a broad cross section of residents, not just the transit dependent. Tri-Met's 101-route bus system, focused on the downtown transit mall and strategically located transit centers in Portland and suburban communities, links residential areas with schools, colleges, hospitals, malls and shopping centers, parks, the airport and the Amtrak station, among other destinations. Tri-Met's MAX (Metropolitan Area Express), a 33-mile light rail line, now links the eastern and western suburbs of Gresham and Hillsboro via downtown Portland. Once intended specifically to reduce auto use and improve air quality, Tri-Met and especially MAX is now so popular with riders that plans are afoot to build a branch MAX line to Portland Airport and a completely new north-south MAX line linking suburban Kenton and Clackamas via the city center.

Tri-Met is unusually user friendly for a big-city transit agency. All buses and trains are equipped with racks for bicycles and bike lockers are available at many transit centers, MAX stations and park & ride lots. All rides are free downtown and fares are reasonable elsewhere. For all-zone travel the general public pays $1.40 per ride, $49.00 for a monthly pass, or $540.00 for an annual pass. Seniors pay only 55 cents per ride, $12 for a monthly pass, or $130 for an annual pass.

Amtrak, Greyhound and numerous airlines provide intercity transportation. Amtrak runs four trains a day north to Seattle and south to Eugene; one southbound train daily continues on to Los Angeles. Greyhound service to these locations and other points is possible from Greyhound's downtown terminal, adjacent to the Amtrak station.

Portland International Airport, nine miles northeast of the city center, provides nonstop jet service to over 45 locations.

Retail Services   Rating: 5

Downtown Portland has been revitalized in recent decades and is once again the physical, cultural and economic heart of the city. Pioneer Place, an upscale enclosed shopping center in the heart of downtown, is the major retailing complex. It hosts 80 specialty shops and upwards of 15 informal eateries. Saks Fifth Avenue and Tiffany & Co. are among its many elite stores. A Nordstrom store is only two short blocks away, and dozens of specialty shops and restaurants line the streets of the downtown core.

Three large enclosed regional malls dominate retail trade outside downtown. Lloyd Center, located east of the Willamette River in Portland, is anchored by Meier and Frank, Marshals, Nordstrom and Sears department stores. It also features over 150 specialty shops and services, dozens of casual restaurants, a cinema complex and an ice-skating rink. Clackamas Town Center, in suburban Clackamas, is anchored by JCPenney, Meier and Frank, Nordstrom and Sears department stores. It also boasts over 150 specialty stores, a 22-unit food court, a cinema complex and an ice-skating rink. JCPenney, Meier and Frank, Mervyn's, Nordstrom and Sears department stores anchor Washington Square, in suburban Tigard. It features over 120 specialty stores, 20 casual eating places and a movie theater complex.

Health Care   Rating: 4

Portland provides very good state-of-the-art medical care. Site of the Oregon Health Sciences University, with its medical school and teaching hospitals, Portland has a total of 20 acute care hospitals that collectively offer virtually all medical specialties.

Community Services   Rating: 5

 Portland offers excellent public services. The metropolitan area's more than 30 senior/community centers are of particular interest to retirees. These offer an enormous variety of recreational facilities and programs including tai chi and yoga; instruction in computers, arts and crafts, dancing, piano and golf; swimming, hiking and fitness programs; and local and regional field excursions. Some centers also provide outreach services, information and referrals, health screenings, and group and/or home-delivered meals.

Leisure Activities

Leisure activities of high quality and great variety are found in Portland and in nearby coastal, valley and mountain areas.

Cultural and Educational Activities   Rating: 5

 Portland is very strong culturally and educationally. The magnificent Portland Center for the Performing Arts in downtown's cultural district includes the Portland Civic Auditorium, Arlene Schnitzer Concert Hall, and the New Theatre Building containing the Newmark and Dolores Winningstad Theatres. Performances by Portland's excellent Oregon Symphony, the Portland Opera and Oregon Ballet Theatre and local theater groups, jazz, baroque and chamber ensembles help make downtown a lively place. Several top-drawer touring artist series featuring some of the world's best musical, dance, theatrical and comedic performances and ensembles round out the Performing Arts calendar of events. In summer, Portland performing arts offerings spill out of downtown into city parks. Free concerts are scheduled a minimum of three evenings a week at various locations in July and August.

Portland State University, located downtown, is the city's largest university. Its nearly 20,000 students can choose from a wide range of courses and programs at undergraduate and graduate levels. Ten other colleges and universities in the metropolitan area, including the prestigious Reed College, offer undergraduate and/or graduate programs; the multi-campus Portland Community College offers a large number of academic and applied courses in Associate of Arts and continuing education programs at bargain prices. Also of general cultural and educational interest are downtown's Oregon History Center and Portland Art Museum; the Oregon Museum of Science and Industry is just across the Willamette River.

Recreational Activities   Rating: 5

 The Portland area is truly a paradise for outdoor recreation enthusiasts. Lush forests, sparkling waterways, awesome mountains, and an abundance of well-designed and maintained parks offer something for everyone. Portland has 9,400 acres of parkland, including Washington Park, nestled in the beautiful West Hills overlooking downtown. Washington Park is home to such attractions as the Oregon Zoo, International Rose Test Garden, Japanese Garden and the Hoyt Arboretum with its 10-mile network of hiking rails. Nearby Forest Park, with miles of hiking trails, is the largest urban wilderness park in the United States. All in all, the City of Portland has 247 parks of varying size and function. Collectively they offer a profusion of picnicking facilities, gardens and natural areas, playgrounds, sports fields, tennis courts, swimming pools, walking and jogging routes, and golf courses.

Additional opportunities for the adventurous are found within a one- or two-hour drive of town. Camping, fishing, hunting, mountain hiking and climbing, boating, windsurfing, whitewater rafting, water- and snow-skiing, and bike touring are widely available. During much of the year you can ski at Timberline Lodge on Mount Hood and play golf in the Willamette Valley on the same day. There are over 30 golf courses, mostly 18-hole public or semi-public facilities, within 20 miles of downtown Portland.

Portland is less notable for popular indoor activities than for outdoor recreation. For its size it is somewhat underendowed with movie theaters, although the downtown Guild Theater, with its program of art and foreign films, does provide a welcome alternative to the mainstream movies screened in cinema complexes in the regional malls. The city is known for the tremendous variety and excellence of its restaurants, many of which are clustered downtown or in interesting upscale neighborhoods like the Belmont, Hawthorne and Nob Hill districts. Pro sports fans can enjoy Portland Trail Blazers NBA basketball locally, or travel 180 miles to Seattle for big league baseball, basketball and football.

Work and Volunteer Activities   Rating: 4

The Portland economy has been booming in recent years and unemployment is low. Consequently, retirees desiring to return to work should be able to do so. As elsewhere, the service sector generates the majority of full-time and part-time jobs. Senior citizens are in high demand for volunteer work in schools, hospitals, senior and community centers, and for providing transportation to the elderly and disabled. Several volunteer referral services including the Volunteer Center/RSVP can help you get involved.

Crime Rates and Public Safety   Rating: 2

Portland's crime situation is slightly worse than average for American metropolitan areas. The property crime rate for the metropolitan area is approximately 10 percent above the national average and the violent crime rate exceeds the national norm by about 17 percent. On a more positive note, Portland's crime statistics have been improving in recent years and most parts of the city including downtown feel safe enough. In a city as large as Portland there are obviously considerable variations from place to place in potential exposure to crime, and here (as elsewhere), it would be wise to avoid high-crime areas.

Conclusion

Overall Rating 50

Portland is a very special place. Its physical and human environment is close to ideal. Its location astride the Willamette River in the shadow of the Cascade Range is beautiful and its mild, marine climate is seldom severely hot or cold. Tornadoes and hurricanes are unknown and serious earthquakes are unlikely. Even the Cascades' famous volcanoes are too far away to pose a major threat. Portland's quality of life is excellent thanks to sound land use and transportation planning and heavy private and public sector investment that has revitalized and humanized downtown and greatly strengthened the metropolitan area public transit system. Environmental protection is high on the list of Portland priorities as reflected in the area's clean air and water, excellent parks and well maintained neighborhoods. The city provides very good health care and work and volunteer opportunities. Its transportation, retail and community services are excellent indeed, as are its vast array of cultural and recreational activities. The principal drawbacks to retirement in Portland are crime rates and a cost of living somewhat above national norms. That said, Portland ranks as one of America's very best places for a lively and sophisticated retirement.

Olympia, Washington

European settlers first arrived at the southern end of Puget Sound in the 1840s. Their little community of Smithfield became the site of the first United States customhouse in the Pacific Northwest. Soon renamed Olympia for its spectacular view of the Olympic Mountains, Olympia became capital of the Washington Territory in 1853, and has managed to retain its status as capital of the State of Washington despite occasional challenges from Seattle, Tacoma and other cities. With a population of 40,000 in the city and 200,000 in Thurston County, Olympia retains a small town atmosphere yet offers amenities typical of larger places. The city is rich in history and natural beauty and prized for its high quality of life. Elegant old homes, tree-lined streets, and a popular farmers market add to its charm.

Landscape   Rating: 4

Olympia is located on the shores of Budd Inlet, the southernmost arm of Puget Sound, and Capitol Lake. Elevations rise from sea level to about 200 feet within the city limits but are slightly higher in neighboring Tumwater. Olympia is built on a gently rolling surface with many vantage points offering outstanding views of the snow-capped ridges of the Olympic Mountains on clear days. The city is only 60 miles from Seattle and 120 miles from Portland, Oregon. The natural vegetation of luxuriant coniferous forest is associated with the area's mild, wet climate, but broad-leafed tree varieties, including magnolia, have been planted widely in town to add aesthetic variety. Residential gardens typically include rhododendrons, other flowering shrubs, seasonal flowers and vibrant green lawns.

Climate   Rating: 3

Olympia has a very mild marine climate broadly similar to but somewhat rainier than that of Seattle. Olympia averages 51 inches of annual precipitation with fully 40 inches falling between October and March. The summer half of the year is much drier and sunnier. Most precipitation occurs as rain; snow totals an average of 17 inches annually and seldom lasts long on the ground because winter days are typically mild. Spring and fall weather varies considerably from day to day with daytime highs in the cool to warm range and cool to cold nights. Summer weather is generally pleasant with average highs around 75 degrees and lows around 50 degrees. The frost-free season averages 150 days. Overcast conditions are more typical than clear skies, especially in winter. On average, Olympia is sunny about 40 percent of the time, varying seasonally from about 25 percent in winter to 60 percent in summer.

Quality of Life   Rating: 4

Olympia offers residents a very good quality of life. Noise pollution is confined to a narrow corridor along Interstate-5 (I-5) and Highway 101 and local air quality is excellent. The city is uncrowded and there is adequate parking downtown, at the mall, at the university and at other activity cen-

Olympia, Washington

<table>
<tr><th colspan="5">C L I M A T E</th></tr>
<tr>
<th rowspan="2">Month</th>
<th colspan="2">Average Daily Temperature
High   Low</th>
<th>Daily Rel. Humidity
Low</th>
<th>Average Monthly Precipitation</th>
</tr>
<tr><th>° F</th><th></th><th>%</th><th>Inches</th></tr>
<tr><td>January</td><td>44</td><td>32</td><td>80</td><td>8.0</td></tr>
<tr><td>February</td><td>50</td><td>33</td><td>71</td><td>5.8</td></tr>
<tr><td>March</td><td>54</td><td>34</td><td>62</td><td>5.0</td></tr>
<tr><td>April</td><td>59</td><td>36</td><td>57</td><td>3.3</td></tr>
<tr><td>May</td><td>65</td><td>41</td><td>55</td><td>2.1</td></tr>
<tr><td>June</td><td>71</td><td>46</td><td>54</td><td>1.6</td></tr>
<tr><td>July</td><td>77</td><td>49</td><td>50</td><td>0.8</td></tr>
<tr><td>August</td><td>77</td><td>50</td><td>50</td><td>1.3</td></tr>
<tr><td>September</td><td>71</td><td>45</td><td>54</td><td>2.3</td></tr>
<tr><td>October</td><td>61</td><td>39</td><td>67</td><td>4.3</td></tr>
<tr><td>November</td><td>50</td><td>35</td><td>80</td><td>8.1</td></tr>
<tr><td>December</td><td>44</td><td>32</td><td>84</td><td>8.1</td></tr>
</table>

Annual Average

Total Days		Total Inches	
Clear	52	Precipitation	50.6
Partly Cloudy	84	Snowfall	16.7
Cloudy	228		

RATINGS

Rating Scale: 5 = excellent; 4 = very good; 3 = good; 2 = fair; 1 = poor

Rating:	1	2	3	4	5
Landscape				●	
Climate			●		
Quality of Life				●	
Cost of Living			●		
Transportation				●	
Retail Services			●		
Health Care				●	
Community Services				●	
Cultural Activities			●		
Recreational Activities				●	
Work/Volunteer Activities			●		
Crime			●		

Total Points: 42

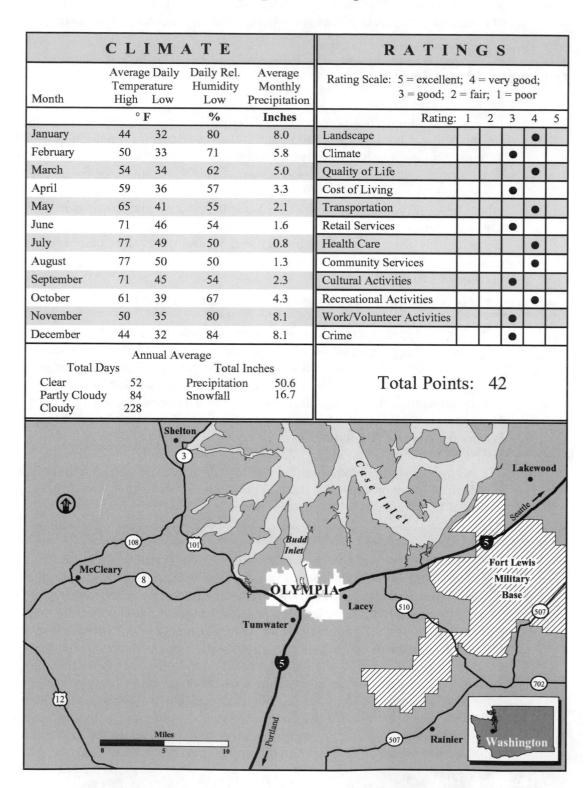

ters. Traffic is generally light and free flowing even at rush hour. With its economy dominated by state government, retail services, and education, Olympia lacks noxious industry and seems decently managed. The residents are generally liberal and progressive with a laissez-faire attitude that allows them to tolerate an odd mix of housing styles in some neighborhoods and the presence of a seemingly transient population in a downtown park in summer. Upscale neighborhoods, though, whether central like the South Capitol Historic District or on the several peninsulas stretching beyond the city limits far out into Puget Sound, are attractively designed, well treed and landscaped and moderately priced. A number of municipal and county parks, some largely undeveloped woodlands, others more activity oriented, add much to the general ambiance.

Cost of Living   Rating: 3

 The cost of living in Olympia is evaluated as follows:

- **Composite.** ACCRA data show that the composite cost of living in Olympia is seven percent above the national average.

- **Housing.** According to ACCRA, housing costs are about 18 percent above the national average. This estimate is higher than the average price of $160,000 for a single-family residence recently quoted for Olympia by the Thurston County Multiple Listing Service. Condominiums are about $20,000 cheaper than comparable single-family homes.

- **Goods and Services.** Health care is priced about 30 percent above, transportation 10 percent above, and groceries 7 percent above their national averages. Miscellaneous goods and services are priced near the national average while utilities are a bargain at a price 25 percent below the national norm.

- **Taxes.** The overall tax burden in Olympia is below the national average. There is no state income tax but the state/local sales tax rate in Thurston County is well above the national average, as are property taxes.

Local and Regional Services

In line with its position as the largest place in Thurston County, Olympia provides a high level of services to residents. Additional resources are available in Seattle, 60 miles north.

Transportation   Rating: 4

 Although most residents drive, the comprehensive transit services offered by Intercity Transit (IT) provide a useful alternative. Intercity Transit's excellent fixed route bus system, focused on a new downtown transit center, provides service to destinations throughout the city and county including schools, Evergreen State College, major area hospitals, Capital Mall and smaller shopping centers, the Amtrak station and most residential areas. Specialized transportation services are provided to those requiring door-to-door service. Fares are low. The general public pays 60 cents per ride or $20 for a monthly pass; seniors and the disabled pay only 30 cents per ride or $10 for a monthly pass. Amtrak runs four trains daily north to Seattle and south to Portland and Greyhound service to these and other points is possible from the Greyhound bus station downtown. Seattle/Tacoma International Airport, 45 miles northeast, provides flights to a large number of points including nonstop jet service to over 60 destinations.

Retail Services   Rating: 3

Capital Mall, located two miles west of downtown, is the major enclosed regional mall. Anchored by JCPenney, Lamonts, Mervyn's and The Bon Marche, the mall also features nearly 100 specialty shops, restaurants, services and a cinema complex. A large Target store is located adjacent to Capital Mall while Sears and an additional Mervyn's are found in South Sound Shopping Center in Lacey, a few miles east of Olympia. Historic Downtown Olympia has revived nicely in recent years and now boasts an interesting mix of specialty shops, galleries, restaurants and theaters. Just north of the city center and next to the harbor is an exceptionally good farmers market that operates on Saturday and Sunday, April through December.

Health Care   Rating: 4

Providence St. Peter Hospital and Columbia Capital Medical Center provide very good health care. Providence St. Peter, a 390-bed hospital with a medical staff of 450 primary care and specialist physicians, is the largest medical center in the southern Puget Sound Region. It offers a full range of acute care, specialty and outpatient services including 24-hour emergency care, outpatient surgery, and cardiac surgery and rehabilitation. A teaching hospital, Providence St. Peter is affiliated with the University of Washington Medical School and trains physicians in primary care. Columbia Capital Medical Center is a 119-bed unit of the nationwide Columbia network of health care facilities. Columbia furnishes 24-hour emergency care, a diabetes wellness program, and community health lectures, among other services, and operates several family-practice clinics in Thurston County.

Community Services   Rating: 4

Senior citizens can give and get help, and stay active socially, in a variety of programs in Olympia and Thurston County. Olympia, Lacey, Tumwater and several other towns have senior centers. The Olympia Senior Activity Center offers classes in arts and crafts, history and politics, and languages and exercise, among others, and organizes day trips and longer tours. The center's wellness program provides medical tests, referrals and subsidized meals. Tumwater's senior program in Old Town Center provides another outlet for senior activities. During morning and early afternoon hours, much of the community center is given over to seniors for cards, classes, exercise programs, other social activities and meals. Senior Information and Assistance Services and the Retired Senior Volunteer Program (RSVP) provide additional resources for seniors.

Leisure Activities

The modest assemblage of leisure activities available in Olympia is augmented greatly by the recreational resources of its rural areas and by the cosmopolitan attractions of nearby Seattle.

Cultural and Educational Activities   Rating: 3

For a small city, Olympia is well endowed culturally and educationally. Downtown's Washington Center for the Performing Arts is the principal venue for resident and touring music, dance and theater groups. Its season runs from early October through early May and recently included

diverse fare from the Chicago Jazz Band, Seattle Symphony, Trinity Irish Dance Company and the Royal Winnipeg Ballet, among other visiting ensembles. Tickets are reasonably priced and discounts are available to seniors and those attending eight or more events. The Center is also home to the Olympia Chamber and Symphony Orchestras, and hosts the Washington Shakespeare Festival in August. On Fridays in July and August, free outdoor concerts are scheduled in Sylvester Park, downtown. Cultural events at area colleges are also open to the public.

The Evergreen State College, ranked by Thomas Gaines in his seminal monograph *The Campus as a Work of Art* as one of the most beautiful college campuses in the country, is also notable for its experimental curriculum and its hospitality to seniors. Senior residents of the State of Washington may audit a maximum of two courses (eight quarter units) per term for a $20 fee. Courses at any level may be taken and range from culture, language, and the expressive arts to environmental studies, social science and scientific inquiry. Lifelong learning classes are available at nominal cost at South Puget Sound Community College and through the Olympia Parks and Recreation Department. Their offerings include computers, languages, yoga, karate and sailing, among others.

Recreational Activities	Rating: 4

 Outdoor recreation is abundant in Olympia and its gorgeous surroundings but rainy-day alternatives are also available locally. Major league sports and other big city attractions are only 60 miles away in Seattle. Percival Landing's 1.5-mile boardwalk skirting Budd Inlet at the downtown Olympia waterfront is a great place for a stroll. In addition to offering access to restaurants and the marina, it provides fine views of the capitol building and Olympic Mountains. You can watch for migrating salmon, in season, and might see an occasional lost whale from the nearby Fourth Street bridge. Another nice place to walk is Tumwater Falls Park where one can watch salmon climb the fish ladder beside the falls during spawning season, and also see the now abandoned early incarnation of the famed Olympia brewery. Olympia's other parks, there are 14 within the city limits, vary from small neighborhood playgrounds to the large and complex Priest Point Park along Budd Inlet. Collectively they provide a comprehensive list of recreational facilities including nature trails, picnicking facilities, playgrounds and sports fields, tennis courts and boating. There are three 9-hole and six 18-hole golf courses within 20 miles of Olympia. Two ski areas, Crystal Mountain and White Pass, are less than 100 miles away in the Cascade Range. Three unique and spectacular national parks are within two or three hours of Olympia by car. Mount Rainier National Park, which includes the towering ice-clad volcano for which it is named, lies 100 miles east of Olympia. Olympic National Park, with its luxuriant temperate rain forest and countless snow-capped peaks, is about 100 miles northwest; Mount St. Helens, which was reshaped by a 1980 explosion that blew the top 1,313 feet off the volcano, lies 100 miles south. Each park offers remarkable opportunities for hiking and sightseeing. Closer to town, one can sail and fish on Puget Sound or hike its shoreline. Should the weather turn bad, one can always retreat to the Olympia Family Sport Center, which features an indoor soccer field, basketball courts, batting cages, miniature golf and video games.

Olympia's modest endowment of movie theaters, restaurants, and other foul-weather attractions are easily supplemented by the much greater resources of

Seattle. Seattle boasts a plethora of excellent restaurants, shopping facilities and recreational attractions of all kinds. For many, the city's big league baseball, basketball and football teams are of particular interest.

Work and Volunteer Activities   Rating: 3

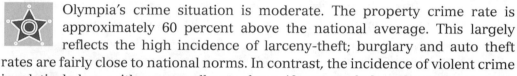 The local economy is dominated by government, education, and service activities and has not shared in the high-tech boom of metropolitan Seattle. This fact, combined with competition for jobs with the large college student population, limits part-time work opportunities for seniors. Volunteer jobs, though, are plentiful. Senior citizens help in schools, hospitals, soup kitchens, senior centers, government facilities and in animal shelters. In Lacey, the Lacey Senior Patrol assists the Police Department's crime prevention unit by performing non-hazardous duties such as fingerprinting, patrolling shopping areas and checking on empty houses.

Crime Rates and Public Safety   Rating: 3

Olympia's crime situation is moderate. The property crime rate is approximately 60 percent above the national average. This largely reflects the high incidence of larceny-theft; burglary and auto theft rates are fairly close to national norms. In contrast, the incidence of violent crime is relatively low, with an overall rate about 40 percent below the national average. Outlying suburban areas of the county are somewhat more crime free than Olympia itself.

Conclusion

Overall Rating 42 Located just 60 miles southwest of Seattle, Olympia is conveniently close to its amenities yet far enough away to avoid its rapid urbanization, high housing prices and increasing traffic congestion. Olympia's physical setting overlooking Budd Inlet and within sight of the Olympic Mountains is very attractive. Its mild, four-season marine climate is seldom too hot or cold but the persistence of cloudy and showery weather during much of the year can wear thin. Olympia's quality of life is very good. Noxious industries are lacking, air and water are clean, there is little traffic noise or congestion, and catastrophic environmental events are unlikely. Tornadoes and hurricanes are absent in this mild climatic zone but a moderate threat of earthquakes does exist in the Puget Sound region. The city has good transportation including excellent public transit, good intercity bus and rail service, and reasonably convenient access to Seattle/Tacoma Airport. The housing stock is quite varied and—although priced about 18 percent above the national average—offers good value, especially when compared to that of Seattle. The city's health care, community services and recreational facilities are very good, and its retail services, cultural life, opportunities for work and volunteer activities, and public safety situation are good. If you are seeking a small laid back town with better than average amenities and with easy access to one of America's most desirable large cities, Olympia might prove an excellent and economical choice.

Bellingham, Washington

C L I M A T E					R A T I N G S					

	Average Daily Temperature		Daily Rel. Humidity	Average Monthly Precipitation	Rating Scale: 5 = excellent; 4 = very good; 3 = good; 2 = fair; 1 = poor					
Month	High	Low	Low							
	°F		%	Inches	Rating:	1	2	3	4	5
January	42	31	74	4.8	Landscape					●
February	48	34	67	3.5	Climate			●		●
March	50	35	61	3.0	Quality of Life					●
April	56	39	58	2.4	Cost of Living			●		
May	62	45	54	2.0	Transportation				●	
June	67	50	53	1.7	Retail Services			●		
July	72	53	49	1.1	Health Care			●		
August	71	53	50	1.4	Community Services				●	
September	67	48	57	2.0	Cultural Activities				●	
October	59	42	67	3.5	Recreational Activities					●
November	50	36	75	4.6	Work/Volunteer Activities			●		
December	45	34	78	5.1	Crime			●		

Annual Average

Total Days			Total Inches	
Clear	71	Precipitation	35.3	
Partly Cloudy	93	Snowfall	14.3	
Cloudy	201			

Total Points: 45

Bellingham, Washington

Long the hunting and fishing grounds of the Lummi Indians, who flourished in the area for thousands of years before the arrival of Europeans,

Bellingham is largely a creation of the twentieth century. Incorporated in 1902, the City of Bellingham became the county seat of Whatcom County and an important center of coal mining, salmon canning and saw milling. In recent decades these frontier industries have been largely replaced by a service economy based on retailing, government, education, tourism and retirement. With a population of 60,000 in Bellingham itself and 150,000 in the metropolitan area (Whatcom County), Bellingham is surrounded by the natural beauty of the Cascade Mountains, Bellingham Bay and the San Juan Islands. The city is small enough to offer the intimacy and friendliness of a small town while providing a good array of urban services and amenities. Additional attractions are nearby in Vancouver and Victoria, British Columbia and in Seattle.

Landscape   Rating: 5

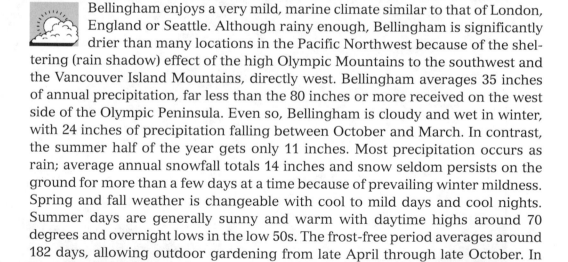

Bellingham occupies a splendid site on the eastern shore of Bellingham Bay, an arm of the Strait of Georgia, in the northwestern corner of Washington state. Elevations in the city proper vary from sea level to around 500 feet but only 30 miles to the east, Mount Baker—a spectacular snow-capped volcano—towers to 10,778 feet. Bellingham is within sight of Washington's famous San Juan Islands, which, like nearby Victoria, are reached easily by inter-island ferries. The city is only 90 miles from Seattle and 60 miles from Vancouver, B. C. Bellingham is rather hilly with many home sites offering superb views of the ocean, the islands or the Cascades. In the surrounding area the natural vegetation consists of oak and Douglas fir forests, with the same species as well as many other mild-climate trees and shrubs including magnolia and rhododendron gracing the town.

Climate   Rating: 3

Bellingham enjoys a very mild, marine climate similar to that of London, England or Seattle. Although rainy enough, Bellingham is significantly drier than many locations in the Pacific Northwest because of the sheltering (rain shadow) effect of the high Olympic Mountains to the southwest and the Vancouver Island Mountains, directly west. Bellingham averages 35 inches of annual precipitation, far less than the 80 inches or more received on the west side of the Olympic Peninsula. Even so, Bellingham is cloudy and wet in winter, with 24 inches of precipitation falling between October and March. In contrast, the summer half of the year gets only 11 inches. Most precipitation occurs as rain; average annual snowfall totals 14 inches and snow seldom persists on the ground for more than a few days at a time because of prevailing winter mildness. Spring and fall weather is changeable with cool to mild days and cool nights. Summer days are generally sunny and warm with daytime highs around 70 degrees and overnight lows in the low 50s. The frost-free period averages around 182 days, allowing outdoor gardening from late April through late October. In summary, Bellingham's climate has four distinct seasons, with few severely cold or excessively warm days and ample precipitation. Its principal negative is the cloudy and drizzly weather characteristic of all seasons except summer.

Quality of Life   Rating: 5

Bellingham provides an excellent quality of life. Noise pollution is insignificant except along a narrow strip paralleling Interstate-5 (I-5). Local air quality is excellent and the city appears clean and uncrowded

with plenty of parking available downtown, at the mall, at the university and at other activity centers. Traffic is light and flows freely even at rush hour. The city seems well planned and managed; its traditional downtown is attractive and viable, as is the smaller historic Fairhaven business district toward the southern edge of town. Residential neighborhoods are typically well maintained and pleasantly landscaped as are the numerous city and county parks and natural areas.

Cost of Living   Rating: 3

 The cost of living in Bellingham is evaluated as follows:

- **Composite.** ACCRA data shows that the composite cost of living in Bellingham is eight percent above the national average.

- **Housing.** According to ACCRA, housing costs are about 20 percent above the national average. This estimate is consistent with the advertised prices of mid-priced homes seen in the area. A good variety of excellent housing is generally available.

- **Goods and Services.** Health care is priced about 20 percent above the national average. In contrast, groceries, miscellaneous goods and services, and transportation are all priced about 5 percent above national norms, while utilities are available at a cost fully 25 percent below the national average.

- **Taxes.** The overall tax burden is less than the national average. Although there is no state income tax, other tax rates are fairly high. The state/local sales tax rate of 7.8 percent in Whatcom County is well above average as are property taxes.

Local and Regional Services

Bellingham offers a wide range of goods and services consistent with its role as the regional capital of northwestern Washington. Additional resources are available in Seattle and Vancouver, B. C.

Transportation   Rating: 4

 Although travel by car is easy in Bellingham, the varied transit services provided by the Whatcom Transportation Authority (WTA) offer convenient alternatives. WTA's excellent fixed-route bus system, focused on a new transit center downtown, provides service to destinations throughout the city including schools, Western Washington University, the hospital, malls and shopping centers, the senior center and residential areas. Dial-a-ride and specialized transportation services are also available to those needing door-to-door service. Fares are low. The general public pays 50 cents per ride, $15 for a monthly pass, or $150 for an annual pass. Seniors and the disabled pay considerably less: 25 cents per ride, $7 per month, or $80 per year. At the Fairhaven Transportation Center in southwest Bellingham, one may choose among Amtrak and Greyhound service to Seattle and Vancouver, inter-island ferry service to the San Juan Islands and Victoria, or the Alaska Marine Highway service to coastal Alaska. Bellingham International Airport offers a modest level of commuter service, primarily to Seattle, but Seattle/Tacoma International

Airport, 100 miles south, provides a much greater variety of flights including nonstop jet service to over 60 destinations. Vancouver International Airport, 50 miles north, with over 32 nonstop jet destinations including Los Angeles, is another convenient option.

Retail Services   Rating: 3

Bellis Fair, located at I-5 and Guide Meridian Road in the northern part of town, is the city's main retail center. Built in part to attract customers from the Greater Vancouver area, Bellis Fair is a very large mall for a small city. Anchored by The Bon Marche, Mervyn's, JCPenney, Sears and Target stores, the enclosed mall also features over 100 specialty shops, restaurants, services, and a cinema complex. An unusually pleasant east-facing food court offers customers a gorgeous view of Mount Baker on clear days. Sunset Square, at I-5 and Sunset Drive in northern Bellingham, is anchored by a Kmart and includes a collage of unique shops and restaurants and Sunset Cinemas. Downtown Bellingham and the Fairhaven Historic District provide the traditional ambiance of old fashioned central business districts. Both feature an interesting assortment of arts and crafts galleries, specialty stores and restaurants. Downtown also boasts the historic Mount Baker Theatre and a farmers market on weekends, April through October.

Health Care   Rating: 3

St. Joseph Hospital is Bellingham's only full-service general hospital. With 206 beds and 270 physicians covering a fairly wide range of specialties, St. Joseph Hospital provides good health care to the community. Outstanding comprehensive medical care is less than 100 miles away in Seattle and Vancouver.

Community Services   Rating: 4

Local government and the private sector make available a fine assortment of services to seniors and the general public. The Bellingham Senior Activity Center, which may be reached via its own WTA bus line, is a centrally located, well-equipped and well-run facility. Bustling with activity, the center offers daily classes, a music and dance program, walking and hiking, day trips and multi-day tours, games and exercise programs. The center's wellness program provides a battery of medical tests, foot care and massage therapy, and information on health goals free or at nominal cost. Hot lunches are available at nominal cost for those 60 and over.

Leisure Activities

Leisure activities of great variety are available in Bellingham, in the San Juan Islands and surrounding waters, in the Cascade Mountains and in nearby Seattle, Vancouver and Victoria.

Cultural and Educational Activities   Rating: 4

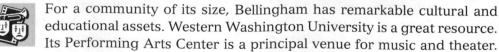

For a community of its size, Bellingham has remarkable cultural and educational assets. Western Washington University is a great resource. Its Performing Arts Center is a principal venue for music and theater. A summer highlight there is the Bellingham Festival of Music held from late July through mid August. This series presents world-class music making by the American Sinfonietta, the festival's 40-member ensemble, at bargain prices.

Season tickets for the entire 14-concert package cost only $199 for orchestra seats. During the winter season (October through May), a Performing Arts Center Series featuring musical and dance performances by distinguished guest artists, and a theater arts series of drama and comedy, occupy much of the calendar. Downtown's historic Mount Baker Theatre provides another venue for classical and children's theater, ballet and musical entertainment. It is the home of the Whatcom Symphony Orchestra and nationally known entertainers perform there regularly. In summer, free outdoor evening concerts are scheduled in Boulevard, Big Rock Garden and Marine Heritage Parks.

Western Washington University is notable for high academic standards and generous treatment of seniors. Permanent residents of the State of Washington who are 60 years of age or older may register at no cost for a maximum of two courses per quarter on a space-available basis. Alternately, anyone may audit courses at nominal cost. Auditors, unlike regular students, do not write papers, take tests, complete class projects or receive credits.

Recreational Activities   Rating: 5

Outdoor recreation reigns supreme in Bellingham and Whatcom County but major league spectator sports and other big city attractions are only an hour or two away in Vancouver and Seattle. Bellingham and Whatcom County operate superb park systems that are well designed, equipped and maintained. Bellingham's award-winning parks system occupies 2,200 acres with 70 miles of trails. Hiking, biking and horseback riding are popular in many city and county parks, including the city's very scenic 1,000-acre Lake Padden Park, which also offers fishing, swimming, wind surfing, tennis, playgrounds, ball fields and an 18-hole public golf course. Thirteen other golf courses, many providing spectacular views of Mount Baker, Georgia Strait and the San Juan Islands, are found within the county. The Civic Field Complex, near downtown, features facilities for football, soccer, track, softball, ice-skating, year-round swimming and professional baseball.

Water sports enthusiasts will appreciate the Bellingham area for its numerous lakes, rivers and miles of shoreline. Opportunities for canoeing, river rafting, kayaking, scuba diving and whale watching are virtually endless. Snow-skiing is available at Mount Baker Ski Area, 50 miles east of town. Also nearby are the cosmopolitan pleasures of Seattle and Vancouver and the quainter delights of Victoria. Seattle and Vancouver are especially notable for the excellence of their shopping facilities and restaurants. Both also field major league sports teams. Seattle boasts teams playing baseball, basketball and football while Vancouver has teams playing basketball, Canadian football and hockey. Varsity basketball and football are played in Seattle by the University of Washington Huskies.

Work and Volunteer Activities   Rating: 3

Bellingham's economy has not shared in the high-tech boom of the Seattle area and local unemployment rates remain above the state average. This fact, along with competition for jobs with college students, limits opportunities for the retired to work part-time. Volunteer work, though, is plentiful and many placements are arranged through RSVP. The Bellingham/Whatcom County Convention and Visitors Center, city hall, the hospital and public library, public parks and recreation facilities, the senior center, and the Women's Care Shelter, all depend heavily on volunteer staff.

The crime situation is somewhat mixed. The overall property crime rate is approximately 75 percent above the national average. This result largely reflects the city's high larceny-theft rate. Other property crime rates are close to or below national norms. The really good news is that the incidence of violent crime in Bellingham is enviably low with an overall rate 40 percent below the national average. Outlying parts of the metropolitan area are even safer.

Conclusion

Overall Rating 45

Situated between Seattle and Vancouver, British Columbia, Bellingham is close enough to each for residents to enjoy their amenities yet far enough away to avoid runaway urbanization, high prices and environmental deterioration. Its physical setting on Bellingham Bay, with the San Juan Islands and the Cascade Range within view, is splendid. Its mild, four-season marine climate with little snow appeals to many, although some may find its cloudy, rainy winters less than ideal. Its quality of life is excellent. Air and water are clean, there is little traffic noise or congestion and catastrophic environmental events are unlikely. The city has good transportation facilities including excellent public transit, a good network of bike lanes and trails, and good intercity bus, rail and ferry service. Although housing is priced above the national average, it offers good value. Residential neighborhoods are typically very attractive with well-maintained homes and lovely gardens, many offering views of Bellingham Bay, Whatcom Lake or the Cascade Range. Retail services and health care are good, community services, cultural life, and parks and recreation assets are excellent, and the overall cost of living is only slightly above the national average. All in all, Bellingham clearly ranks among America's best locales for quality retirement. It will appeal especially to those who would enjoy an active lifestyle in a charming seaside town.

Bend, Oregon

Bend, Oregon is also worth considering for retirement, especially by those who enjoy outdoor activities in all seasons. Bend is located in central Oregon just east of the Cascade Range. Lying in the rain shadow of the Cascades, Bend has a drier and sunnier climate than most Pacific Northwest locations. To the west the land slopes gradually upward to Mount Bachelor and The Three Sisters, which provide a spectacular backdrop to the town on clear days. Small and isolated from major cities, Bend offers residents a very good quality of life free of pollution and most urban ills. Residential neighborhoods are typically attractive and the old-fashioned downtown has been nicely refurbished and is an attractive place to walk, shop and dine.

With a population of 21,000 in the city and about 100,000 in Deschutes County, Bend is too small to rank highly in transportation, cultural amenities and part-time and volunteer work. There is no local public transit but CAC Transportation offers shuttle service to Portland (160 miles away) and Greyhound connects Bend with other cities. Surprisingly, Bend suffers from a property crime rate twice the national average. Fortunately, the violent crime rate is low.

Bend's greatest assets are its gorgeous high desert and mountain landscape, high quality of life and wonderful outdoor recreation. The city has excellent parks and recreation facilities. In spring and fall one can ski in the morning on Mount

Bachelor and golf in the afternoon in town. Trout fishing is excellent on several streams emanating from the Cascades and hiking and horseback riding are popular on desert and mountain trails. Retail, health care and community services are more than adequate and the cost of living is only slightly above average. All in all, Bend is a quite desirable retirement place.

Epilogue:
Choosing Your Place to Retire in Style

People often ask, "Where is the best place to retire?" There is obviously no simple answer to this question. Indeed, there is no single best place in which to retire because individuals vary in their wants and needs. Only you can determine what you want, need and can afford. And only you can choose among the unique and special communities described in this book.

Remember that the point totals (overall ratings) are not meant to rank the retirement towns from best to worst. Rather, the ratings charts help you assess a community's overall resources for retirement and its relative strength in each of 12 criteria important to retirees. In this book, each criterion is weighted equally. You might want to weight them differently depending on your priorities.

But numbers cannot tell the whole story about a place. Each town and city has a unique character and ambiance, which I have tried to capture in the place descriptions. But to fully appreciate the nuances that differentiate an irresistible place from a merely likable one, you must visit in person.

This book can help you narrow your choices to a few outstanding locales worthy of additional consideration. You can learn more about each by requesting information, mostly provided free of charge, from local chambers of commerce and visitors bureaus. Their postal addresses, telephone numbers, and Internet addresses are listed following the epilogue. If you are seriously contemplating relocating, you should visit your favorite cities and towns as I have done in the course of researching and writing this book. Ideally, you should visit the selected places for extended periods in summer and winter in order to get to know the places, people and their way of life. With a little luck, you will discover that special place where you can retire in style at an affordable price.

Sources of Relocation Information

Free or inexpensive information useful to those contemplating relocation is available in printed and/or digital form from a variety of sources. Chambers of commerce and visitors bureaus typically respond to inquiries from potential new residents with miscellaneous promotional brochures, cost of living data, economic statistics, maps and real estate information. A list of chambers of commerce and visitors bureaus contacted for this book's 50 top-rated retirement places follows.

Chambers of Commerce and Visitors Bureaus List

Northeast Region

Burlington, Vermont

Lake Champlain Regional Chamber of Commerce
60 Main Street, Suite 100
Burlington, VT 05401
Attn: Kerry Chernin, Communications Director
(802) 863-3489
vermont@vermont.org

Ithaca, New York

Tompkins County Chamber of Commerce
Ithaca/Thompkins County Convention and Visitors Bureau
904 East Shore Drive
Ithaca, NY 14850
(607) 272-1313

Hanover/Lebanon, New Hampshire

Hanover Area Chamber of Commerce
37 S. Main St.
Hanover, NH 03755
(603) 643-3115
han.area.chamber@valley.net

Greater Lebanon Chamber of Commerce
2 Whipple Place
Lebanon, NH
(603) 448-1203

Midwest Region

Madison, Wisconsin

Greater Madison Chamber of Commerce
P O Box 71
Madison, WI 53701
(608) 256-8348
grtmadcc@midplains.net

Bloomington, Indiana

Greater Bloomington Chamber of Commerce
400 W. 7th St. #102
Bloomington, IN 47404
(812) 336-6381

Upper South Region

Annapolis, Maryland

Greater Annapolis Chamber of Commerce
1 Annapolis St.
Annapolis, MD 21401
(410) 268-7676

Annapolis & Anne Arundel County Conference and Visitors Bureau
26 West St.
Annapolis, MD 21401
(410) 280-0445
info@visit-annapolis.org

Charlottesville, Virginia

Charlottesville/Albemarle Chamber of Commerce
P O Box 1564, Fifth and Market Streets
Charlottesville, VA 22902
Attn: Michele Sprouse, Director of Communications and Information
(804) 295-3141
cacoc@cfw.com

Charlottesville/Albemarle Convention and Visitors Bureau
P O Box 178, Dept. CE
Charlottesville, VA 22902
(804) 977-1783
caccbb@comet.net

Lexington, Virginia

Lexington/Rockbridge County Chamber of Commerce
100 E. Washington St.
Lexington, VA 24450
(703) 463-5375

Historic Lexington Visitor Center
106 E. Washington St.
Lexington, VA 24450
(703) 463-3777

Chapel Hill, North Carolina

Chapel Hill/Carrboro Chamber of Commerce
P O Box 2897
Chapel Hill, NC 27514
Attn: Stacey Orcutt
(919) 967-7075
chamber@mindspring.com

Chapel Hill/Orange County Visitors Bureau
105 N. Columbia St., Suite 600
Chapel Hill, NC 27516
(919) 968-2060

Pinehurst/Southern Pines, North Carolina

Sandhills Area Chamber of Commerce
P O Box 458
Southern Pines, NC 28387
(919) 692-3926

Pinehurst/Southern Pines Convention and Visitors Bureau
P O Box 2270
Southern Pines, NC 28388
(800) 346-5362
cvb4golf@mindspring.com

Asheville, North Carolina

Asheville Area Chamber of Commerce
Asheville Convention and Visitors Bureau
P O Box 1010
Asheville, NC 28802
Attn: Steven Tanner, Director of Research
(704) 278-6101
chamber@interpath.com

Brevard, North Carolina

Brevard Chamber of Commerce and Visitor Center
P O Box 589
Brevard, NC 28712
(704) 883-3700
brevchamber@citcom.net

Hendersonville, North Carolina

Greater Hendersonville Chamber of Commerce
330 North King St.
Hendersonville, NC 28792
(704) 692-1413

Henderson County Travel and Tourism
201 South Main St.
Hendersonville, NC 28792
(800) 828-4244 (704) 693-9708

New Bern, North Carolina

New Bern Area Chamber of Commerce
233 Middle St.
New Bern, NC 28563
(919) 637-3111
nbchamber@coastalnet.com

New Bern/Craven County Convention and Visitors Bureau
P O Box 1413
New Bern, NC 28563
(800) 437-5767

Southeast Coast Region

Naples, Florida

Naples Area Chamber of Commerce
3620 Tamiami Trail North
Naples, FL 34103
Attn: Robert Cahners
(813) 262-6141
chamber@naples-online.com

Naples Visitor Center
895 5th Avenue South
Naples, FL 34102
(813) 262-6141

Sarasota, Florida

Greater Sarasota Chamber of Commerce
1819 Main Street, Suite 240
Sarasota, FL 34236
(813) 955-8187

Gainesville, Florida

Gainesville Area Chamber of Commerce
P O Box 1187
Gainesville, FL 32602-1187
(904) 336-7100

Alachua County Visitors and Convention Bureau
30 East University Avenue
Gainesville, FL 32601
(904) 374-5231

Thomasville, Georgia

Thomasville/Thomas County Chamber of Commerce and Visitor Center
P O Box 1652
Thomasville, GA 31799
Attn: Lynn Gwaltney, City Clerk
(912) 226-9600
palmer@rose.net

Savannah, Georgia

Savannah Area Chamber of Commerce and Visitors Bureau
222 W. Oglethorpe Ave.
Savannah, GA 31499
(912) 944-0444

Covington, Louisiana

St. Tammany-West Chamber of Commerce
832 E. Boston St., #15
Covington, LA 70434
(504) 892-3216
info@sttammanychamber.org

Fairhope, Alabama

Eastern Shore Chamber of Commerce
324 Fairhope Ave.
Fairhope, AL 36532
(205) 928-6387

Interior South Region

Oxford, Mississippi

Oxford-Lafayette County Chamber of Commerce and
Economic Development Foundation, Inc.
P O Box 147
Oxford, MS 38655
Attn: Elaine Abadiy, Director, Retiree Attraction Program
(601) 234-46451

Fayetteville, Arkansas

Fayetteville Chamber of Commerce
123 West Mountain
Fayetteville, AR 72702
(501) 521-1710

Hot Springs, Arkansas

Greater Hot Springs Chamber of Commerce
Grand and Ouachita
Hot Springs, AR 71902
Attn: Millie Patrick, Vice President, Retirement/Relocation
(501) 321-1700

Heart of Texas Region

Austin, Texas

Austin Chamber of Commerce
111 Congress Ave.
Austin, TX 78701
(512) 478-9383

Greater Austin Chamber of Commerce
P O Box 1967
Austin, TX 78767
(512) 478-9383

Austin Convention and Visitors Bureau
305 S. Congress Ave.
Austin, TX 78704
(800) 926-2282

San Antonio, Texas

Greater San Antonio Chamber of Commerce
602 E. Commerce
San Antonio, TX 78205
Attn: Julie Ottersdorf, VP Information Systems
(210) 229-2100
julio@chamber.org

San Antonio Chamber of Commerce
P O Box 460706
San Antonio, TX 78246
Attn: John Meek, President

Fredericksburg, Texas

Fredericksburg Chamber of Commerce and Convention and Visitors
Bureau
Gillespie County Economic Development Commission
106 N. Adams
Fredericksburg, TX
(830) 997-6523

Kerrville, Texas

Kerrville Area Chamber of Commerce
1700 Sidney Baker, Suite 100
Kerrville, TX 78028
(830) 896-1175
kerrcc@ktc.com

Convention and Visitors Bureau
1700 Sidney Baker, Suite 200
Kerrville, TX 78028
(830) 792-3535
kerrcvb@ktc.com

Southern Rockies Region

Fort Collins, Colorado

Fort Collins Area Chamber of Commerce
225 South Meldrum
Fort Collins, CO 80521
Attn: Kelly Coble, Program Coordinator
(970) 482-3746
general@fcchamber.org

Fort Collins Chamber of Commerce
225 South Meldrum
Fort Collins, Co 80521
Attn. Breez Daniels, President

Fort Collins Convention and Visitors Bureau
P O Box 1998
Fort Collins, CO 80522
(303) 482-5821   (800) 274-3678

Boulder, Colorado

Boulder Chamber of Commerce
P O Box 73
Boulder, Co 80302
Attn: Tom Clark, President
(303) 442-1044

Boulder Convention & Visitors Bureau
2440 Pearl St.
Boulder, CO 80302
(303) 442-2911   (800) 444-0447
visitorsbureau@chamberboulder.co.us

Colorado Springs, Colorado

Colorado Springs Chamber of Commerce
2 North Cascade Ave., Suite 110
Colorado Springs, CO 80903
(719) 635-1551
chamber@cscc.org

Colorado Springs Convention & Visitors Bureau
104 S. Cascade, Suite 104
Colorado Springs, CO 80903
(800) 368-4748

Santa Fe, New Mexico

Santa Fe Chamber of Commerce
P O Box 1928
Santa Fe, NM 87504
(505) 983-7317

City of Santa Fe Convention & Visitors Bureau
P O Box 909
Santa Fe, NM 87504-0909
(800) 777-2489

Desert Southwest Region

Las Cruces, New Mexico

Greater Las Cruces Chamber of Commerce
P O Box 519
Las Cruces, NM 88004
Attn: Joe Biedron, President
(505) 534-1968
chamber@lascruces.org

Tucson, Arizona

Tucson Metropolitan Chamber of Commerce
465 W. St. Mary's Road
Tucson, AZ 85702
Attn: Dan Anderson, Assistant Vice President
(520) 792-1212
center@azstarnet.com

Prescott, Arizona

Prescott Chamber of Commerce
P O Box 1147
Prescott, AZ 86302
(602) 445-2000
chamber@prescott.org

Boulder City, Nevada

Boulder City Chamber of Commerce
1305 Arizona St.
Boulder City, Nevada 89005
Attn: Bob Crow, President
(702) 293-2034
freetime@accessnv.com

Las Vegas, Nevada

Las Vegas Chamber of Commerce
711 E. Desert Inn Rd.
Las Vegas, NV 89109-2712
(702) 735-2450

Carson City, Nevada

Carson City Chamber of Commerce
1900 South Carson St., Suite 100
Carson City, NV 89701
Attn: Larry Osborne, Executive Vice President
(702) 882-1565
ccchamber@semp.net

Reno, Nevada

Reno/Sparks Chamber of Commerce
P O Box 3499
Reno, NV 89505
Attn: Harry York, CEO
(775) 337-3030
info@reno-sparkschamber.org

St. George, Utah

St. George Area Chamber of Commerce
97 East St. George Blvd.
St. George, Utah 84770
(801) 628-1658
hotspot@infowest.com

California Region

San Luis Obispo, California

San Luis Obispo Chamber of Commerce
1039 Chorro St.
San Luis Obispo, CA 93401
(805) 543-1323
slochamber@slonet.org

Chico, California

Chico Chamber of Commerce
500 Main St.
Chico, CA 95927
(916) 891-5556

Palm Spring/Palm Desert, California

Palm Springs Chamber of Commerce
190 West Amado Rd.
Palm Springs, CA 92262
(760) 325-1577
pschamber@worldnet.att.net

Palm Desert Chamber of Commerce
72-990 Highway 111
Palm Desert, CA 92260
(760) 346-6111

Pacific Northwest Region

Medford/Ashland, Oregon

Ashland Chamber of Commerce
110 E. Main St.
Ashland, OR 97520
(503) 482-3486

The Chamber of Medford/Jackson County and
Medford Visitors and Convention Bureau
101 East 8th Street
Medford, Or 97501
Attn: Brad Hicks, Marketing Director
(541) 779-4847
business@medfordchamber.com

Eugene, Oregon

Eugene Area Chamber of Commerce
1401 Willamette
Eugene, OR 97440
Attn: David Hauser, Executive VP
(541) 484-1314
admin@eugene-commerce.com

Salem, Oregon

The Salem Area Chamber of Commerce
1110 Commercial St. N.E.
Salem, OR 97301
Attn: Mike McLaren, Executive Director
(503) 581-1466
salemchamber@viser.net

Salem Convention and Visitors Bureau
1313 Mill St. S.E.
Salem, OR 97301
(503) 581-4325

Portland, Oregon

Portland Metropolitan Chamber of Commerce
221 N.W. Second Avenue
Portland, OR 97209-3999
Attn: Deanna Palm, Vice President
(503) 228-9411
dpalm@pdxchamber.org

Bend, Oregon

Bend Area Chamber of Commerce/Visitor & Convention Center
63085 North Hwy 97
Bend, OR 97701
Attn: Gary Capps, Executive Director
(503) 382-3221
bend@empnet.com

Olympia, Washington

Olympia/Thurston County Chamber of Commerce
521 Legion Way S.E.
Olympia, WA 98501
(360) 357-3362

Bellingham, Washington

Bellingham/Whatcom Chamber of Commerce & Industry
1425 Railroad Ave.
Bellingham, WA 98225
Attn: Michael Brennan, President
(360) 734-1330
chamber@bellingham.com

The Bellingham/Whatcom County Convention and Visitor Bureau
904 Potter St.
Bellingham, WA 98226
(360) 671-3990

Resources for Climatic Information

Climatic data are often included in chamber of commerce and visitors bureau mailings but can be misleading. The best source for comparative climatic data of the highest quality is the National Climatic Data Center (NCDC) in Asheville, North Carolina. The center's best-selling Comparative Climatic Data for the United States, published annually, was the primary source of climatic data for the larger places described in this book. It provides a wealth of information in 17 climatic tables for over 250 American cities. It is free online and costs five dollars in printed form. Climatography of the United States, Series 20, is a good source of climatic information for smaller towns. It costs two dollars for each location and is not available online. Check the NCDC Website (www.ncdc.noaa.gov) for complete information about ordering their data and products. You can telephone the NCDC at (828) 271-4800 between 8:00 a.m. and 6:00 p.m. EST.

Resources for Cost of Living Information

Cost of living data for more than 300 American cities, including most of those covered in *Retire in Style,* are published by ACCRA (formerly called the American Chamber of Commerce Researchers Association). The ACCRA Cost of Living Index, published quarterly, provides a useful and relatively accurate measure of living cost differences among urban areas. Single copies of current or back issues cost $65 each or $130 for four consecutive issues. Order forms are available from the ACCRA Subscription Office at (703) 522-4980, or at www.accra.org.

Resources for Crime Rate Information

Crime rates for cities and all but the smallest towns can be calculated from data in the FBI's annual publication, Crime in the United States: Uniform Crime Reports. Be sure to utilize city/town data whenever possible, as we did for *Retire in Style.* Countywide crime rates, reported in some retirement places books, are too generalized to give a clear picture of the crime threat in particular cities and towns within county boundaries. Crime in the United States: Uniform Crime Reports is available in many libraries and may be ordered from:

> The U.S. Government Printing Office
> Mail Stop: SSOP
> Washington, DC 20402-9328

If the town you are interested in is not listed in this source, feel free to contact the municipal police chief or county sheriff. They are generally very helpful and willing to provide crime data for their communities.

Resources for Health Care Information

Health care information is available in a number of guidebooks, the best of which is probably the American Hospital Association's annual Guide to the Health-Care Field. Organized by state and city, this guide provides data on every hospital in the United States. Most importantly, it specifies which of over 80 specialized facilities and services are available in each hospital. This is important information as small-town hospitals may lack one or more services potentially important to you. Check the reference department of your local public or college library to see if they have a copy.

Resources on the Web

A variety of retirement resources are available on the worldwide web. Here are a few, in alphabetical order, that are filled with useful information.

aarp.com
aoa.gov
elderhostel.org
retirementliving.com
seniornet.org
seniorsource.com
seniors-site.com

Index

Notes

BOOK ORDER FORM

(please check at your local bookstore before using this form)

Two easy ordering methods:

1. Credit Card Orders—call Independent Publishers Group (IPG)
   Telephone: 800-888-4741.

2. Check or Money Order—complete this form, attach your payment,
   and mail to:

Next Decade, Inc.
39 Old Farmstead Road
Chester, NJ 07930

If you have any questions, call us:
Telephone: 908-879-6625
Email: info@nextdecade.com

YOUR NAME AND TITLE:_____

NAME OF ORGANIZATION (if applicable):_____

STREET ADDRESS:_____

CITY:_____STATE:_____ZIP: _____

TELEPHONE:_____FAX:_____

E-MAIL:_____

Please ship_____copy/copies of **Retire in Style.**

I've enclosed $22.95 per copy for_____copies. $_____

NJ orders ONLY add 6% sales tax if required ($1.38 per copy) $_____

Shipping: Add $5.00 for the first copy and $1.00 for each additional copy $_____

TOTAL $_____

A check/money order made payable to Next Decade, Inc. for $_____ is enclosed.